THE CAMBRIDGE COMPANION TO
THE FRENCH ENLIGHTENME~

The Enlightenment has long been seen as synor
modern Western intellectual and political c~·'
movement, this historical moment, the ´
eighteenth century, is marked by attemp   ⌐ns.
The Cambridge Companion to the Frenc   ⌐r essays
by leading scholars representing disciplin   ⌐phy, religion
and literature, to art, medicine, anthropolo⌐   ⌐e, to analyse the
French Enlightenment. Each essay presents a co.   ⌐f an important aspect
of the French Enlightenment, discussing its de.   ⌐g characteristics, internal
dynamics and historical transformations. The *Companion* discusses the most
influential reinterpretations of the Enlightenment that have taken place during
the last two decades, reinterpretations that both reflect and have contributed
to important re-evaluations of received ideas about the Enlightenment and the
early modern period more generally.

Daniel Brewer, Department of French and Italian, University of Minnesota, has
published widely in the area of eighteenth-century French literature and culture.
He is author of *The Enlightenment Past: Reconstructing Eighteenth-Century
French Thought* (Cambridge, 2008) and co-editor of *L'Esprit Créateur*, an
international journal of French and Francophone literature and culture.

A complete list of books in the series is at the back of the book

THE CAMBRIDGE
COMPANION TO
THE FRENCH
ENLIGHTENMENT

EDITED BY
DANIEL BREWER

CAMBRIDGE
UNIVERSITY PRESS

CAMBRIDGE
UNIVERSITY PRESS

University Printing House, Cambridge CB2 8BS, United Kingdom

Cambridge University Press is part of the University of Cambridge.

It furthers the University's mission by disseminating knowledge in the pursuit of education, learning and research at the highest international levels of excellence.

www.cambridge.org
Information on this title: www.cambridge.org/9781107626140

First published 2014

Printed in the United Kingdom by Clays, St Ives plc

A catalogue record for this publication is available from the British Library

Library of Congress Cataloguing in Publication data
The Cambridge companion to the French enlightenment / edited by Daniel Brewer.
pages cm
Includes bibliographical references and index.
ISBN 978-1-107-02148-8 (hardback)
ISBN 978-1-107-62614-0 (paperback)
1. Enlightenment – France. 2. France – Intellectual life–18th century.
3. Philosophy, French–18th century. I. Brewer, Daniel.
B1925.E5C36 2014
944'.034–dc23 2014020419

ISBN 978-1-107-02148-8 Hardback
ISBN 978-1-107-62614-0 Paperback

CONTENTS

Notes on contributors   *page* vii
Chronology   xi
Acknowledgements   xvi

1   The Enlightenment today?   1
    DANIEL BREWER

2   Private lives, public space: a new social history of the Enlightenment   14
    ANTOINE LILTI

3   Anthropology   29
    ANDREW CURRAN

4   Commerce   44
    PAUL CHENEY

5   Science   60
    J. B. SHANK

6   Political thought   78
    DAN EDELSTEIN

7   Sex and gender, feeling and thinking: imagining women as intellectuals   91
    JULIE CANDLER HAYES

8   Religion   105
    CHARLY COLEMAN

CONTENTS

9 Art and aesthetic theory: claiming Enlightenment as
   viewers and critics   122
   JENNIFER MILAM

10 Enlightenment literature   137
   THOMAS DIPIERO

11 *Philosophe*/philosopher   153
   STÉPHANE VAN DAMME

12 Music   167
   DOWNING A. THOMAS

13 Architecture and the Enlightenment   184
   ANTHONY VIDLER

14 Medicine and the body in the French Enlightenment   199
   ANNE VILA

15 Space, geography and the global French Enlightenment   214
   CHARLES W. J. WITHERS

   Guide to further reading   233
   Index   240

CONTRIBUTORS

DANIEL BREWER is Professor of French at the University of Minnesota. He has published on such topics as theories of knowledge and the critique of institutions, visual representation and art criticism, the project of Enlightenment, literary history and social formation and the figure of the intellectual. His books include *The Discourse of Enlightenment: Diderot and the Art of Philosophizing* and *The Enlightenment Past: Reconstructing Eighteenth-Century French Thought*. He has co-edited volumes on the *Encyclopédie* (with Julie Candler Hayes) and on French wars (with Patricia Lorcin), and he is co-editor of *L'Esprit Créateur*.

PAUL CHENEY teaches history at the University of Chicago. Prior to receiving his Ph.D. at Columbia University, he studied political economy at the New School for Social Research. He is the author of *Revolutionary Commerce: Globalization and the French Monarchy*. Several of his articles on the economy of France and its colonial empire in the eighteenth century appear in journals such as *Past & Present*, *Dix-huitième Siècle*, *The William and Mary Quarterly* and *The Radical History Review*. His forthcoming book, *Cul de Sac: Economy and Society in Eighteenth-Century Saint-Domingue*, examines France's plantation complex in its final decades.

CHARLY COLEMAN is Assistant Professor of History at Columbia University. In addition to articles in *The Journal of Modern History* and *Modern Intellectual History* on the intersections of religion and philosophy in eighteenth-century France, he has published *The Virtues of Abandon: An Anti-Individualist History of the French Enlightenment*.

ANDREW CURRAN is Professor of French at Wesleyan University. He has published a number of articles on topics related to scientific academy debates, the history of anthropology, the science of French empire and Denis Diderot. He is also the editor of a collection of essays, *Faces of Monstrosity in Eighteenth-Century Thought*, and the author of two books: *Sublime Disorder: Physical Monstrosity in Diderot's Universe* and *The Anatomy of Blackness: Science and Slavery in an Age of Enlightenment*.

THOMAS DIPIERO is Professor of French and of Visual and Cultural Studies at the University of Rochester, where he is also Dean for Humanities and Interdisciplinary Studies. He is the author of *Dangerous Truths and Criminal Passions: The Evolution of the French Novel, 1569–1791* and of *White Men Aren't*. He is also co-editor of *Illicit Sex: Identity Politics in Early Modern Europe*. The author of numerous articles on seventeenth- and eighteenth-century French literature, his research focuses on prose fiction, particularly depictions of human bodies as representative of diverse modes of Enlightenment thought.

DAN EDELSTEIN is Professor of French and (by courtesy) History at Stanford University, where he is also the W. Warren Shelden University Fellow in Undergraduate Education. He is the author of *The Terror of Natural Right: Republicanism, the Cult of Nature, and the French Revolution* and of *The Enlightenment: A Genealogy*. He has also edited a volume of essays on *The Super-Enlightenment: Daring to Know Too Much*, and he is a principal investigator for the Mapping the Republic of Letters project at Stanford.

JULIE CANDLER HAYES is Professor of French and Dean of the College of Humanities and Fine Arts at the University of Massachusetts Amherst. Her research focuses on literary and philosophical texts of the French Enlightenment; she has also written extensively on contemporary literary theory and the history and theory of translation. Her most recent book is *Translation, Subjectivity, and Culture in France and England, 1600–1800*. Her earlier books study French theatre and Enlightenment concepts of systematicity in literature, philosophy and science. She co-edited two volumes, *Using the Encyclopédie: Ways of Reading, Ways of Knowing* (with Daniel Brewer) and *Émilie du Châtelet: Rewriting Enlightenment Philosophy and Science* (with Judith Zinsser). Her current scholarly work looks at seventeenth- and eighteenth-century women moral philosophers.

ANTOINE LILTI is Directeur d'Études (Professor) at the École des Hautes Études en Sciences Sociales (Paris). He published *Le Monde des salons, sociabilité et mondanité au XVIIIe siècle* and has just finished *Figures publiques: célébrité et modernité*. He also co-edited (with Céline Spector) *Commerce, civilisation, empire: penser l'Europe au XVIIIe siècle*.

JENNIFER MILAM is Professor of Art History and Eighteenth-Century Studies at the University of Sydney. Her interdisciplinary interests seek to identify unconventional visual processes stimulating and directing the production and reception of art in the intersecting fields of art history, intellectual history and eighteenth-century studies. She has published articles in journals such as *Art History, Eighteenth-Century Fiction, Eighteenth-Century Studies* and *Curator: The Museum Journal*. Her books include *The Historical Dictionary of Rococo Art, Fragonard's Playful Paintings: Visual Games in Rococo Art* and *Women, Art and the Politics of Identity in Eighteenth-Century Europe*.

J. B. SHANK is Associate Professor of History and Director of the Center for Early Modern History at the University of Minnesota, where he is also a founding coordinator of the Theorizing Early Modern Studies Research Collaborative. His research focuses on early modern European intellectual and cultural history with special emphasis on the emergence of the modern sciences after 1400. Recent publications include *The Newton Wars and the Beginning of the French Enlightenment* and 'A French Jesuit in the Royal Society of London: Father Louis-Bertrand de Castel and Enlightenment Mathematics, 1720–1744' (*Journal of Early Modern Studies*). His most recent book is *Before Voltaire: Making 'Newtonian?' Science in France around 1700*.

DOWNING A. THOMAS is Professor of French and currently serves as Associate Provost and Dean of International Programs at the University of Iowa. He has published two books (*Aesthetics of Opera in the Ancien Régime, 1647–1785* and *Music and the Origins of Language: Theories from the French Enlightenment*) and has co-edited *Operatic Migrations: Transforming Works and Crossing Boundaries in Musical Drama* (with Roberta M. Marvin). He has served on the Executive Committee of the Eighteenth-Century French Literature division within the Modern Language Association. In 2007 he was President of the Association of Departments of Foreign Languages.

STÉPHANE VAN DAMME, Professor of the History of Science at the European University Institute, examines the origins of early modern scientific knowledge and European culture between 1650 and 1850 by looking at essential elements overlooked by historians of science, such as scientific centres, founding fathers, paradigmatic disciplines and imperial projects. His publications include *Descartes: essai d'histoire culturelle d'une grandeur philosophique (XVIIe–XXe siècle)*, *Paris, capitale philosophique de la Fronde à la Révolution*, *Le Temple de la sagesse: savoirs, écriture et sociabilité urbaine (Lyon, 17–18e siècles)*, *L'Épreuve libertine: morale, soupçon et pouvoirs dans la France baroque* and *Métropole de papiers: naissance de l'archéologie urbaine à Paris et à Londres*. His latest book, *À toutes voiles vers la vérité: une autre histoire de la philosophie au temps des Lumières*, is an attempt to produce a cultural history of early modern philosophy.

ANTHONY VIDLER is a historian and critic of modern and contemporary architecture specializing in the Enlightenment and the present. He is Professor of Architecture at The Cooper Union. As designer and curator, he installed the permanent exhibition of the work of Claude-Nicolas Ledoux in the Royal Salt Works of Arc-et-Senans (Franche-Comté, France). He has received awards from the Guggenheim Foundation and the National Endowment for the Humanities. His publications include *The Writing of the Walls: Architectural Theory in the Late Enlightenment*, *Claude-Nicolas Ledoux: Architecture and Social Reform at the End of the Ancien Régime*, *The Architectural Uncanny: Essays in the Modern Unhomely*, *Warped Space: Architecture and Anxiety in Modern Culture*, *Histories of the Immediate Present: The Invention of Architectural Modernism* and *The Scenes of the Street and Other Essays*.

ANNE VILA is Professor of French at the University of Wisconsin-Madison. Her publications include *Enlightenment and Pathology: Sensibility in the Literature and Medicine of Eighteenth-Century France* (1998) and the edited volume *The Cultural History of the Senses in the Enlightenment* (2014). She is completing a book entitled *Singular Beings: Passions and Pathologies of the Scholar in France, 1720–1840* and a re-edition (with Ronan Chalmin) of Tissot's *De la santé des gens de lettres*. Her current research explores the cultural history of 'extraordinary' psychic states such as ecstasy, catalepsy and magnetic somnambulism during and after the eighteenth century.

CHARLES W. J. WITHERS is Ogilvie Chair of Geography at the University of Edinburgh and a Fellow of the British Academy. His books include *Placing the Enlightenment: Thinking Geographically about the Age of Reason, Geography and Science in Britain, 1831–1939* and, as co-editor, *Geographies of Nineteenth-Century Science*. He has research interests in the historical geographies of science, travel and the Enlightenment. Forthcoming works include a study of the travel imprint of John Murray publishers, 1773–1857, and a book on the historical geography of the prime meridian.

CHRONOLOGY

1637	René Descartes, *Discours de la méthode* (*Discourse on the Method*)
1685	Revocation of the Edict of Nantes, which guaranteed freedom of religion to Protestants
1697	Pierre Bayle, *Dictionnaire historique et critique* (*Critical and Historical Dictionary*)
1715	Death of Louis XIV, ascension of Louis XV, regency of Philippe, duc d'Orléans
1717	Jean-Antoine Watteau, *L'Embarquement pour Cythère* (*The Pilgrimage to the Island of Cythera*)
1719	Jean-Baptiste du Bos, *Réflexions critiques sur la poésie et sur la peinture* (*Critical Reflections on Poetry and Painting*)
1721	Charles-Louis de Secondat de Montesquieu, *Lettres persanes* (*Persian Letters*)
1727	Anne-Thérèse de Marguenat de Courcelles, marquise de Lambert, *Réflexions nouvelles sur les femmes* (*New Reflections on Women*)
1731	Antoine-François Prévost, *Histoire du chevalier Des Grieux et de Manon Lescaut* (*Manon Lescaut*)
1731	Pierre Carlet de Chamblain de Marivaux, *La Vie de Marianne* (*Marianne*)
1733	Louis XV commissions Jacques Cassini to produce a map of France, completed in 1744

1734	Voltaire (François-Marie Arouet), *Lettres philosophiques* or *Lettres anglaises* (*Philosophical Letters*)
1736–8	Claude Prosper Jolyot de Crébillon *fils*, *Égarements du cœur et de l'esprit* (*Strayings of the Heart and Mind*)
1737	Salon exhibitions instituted as regular events in Paris and reviewed biennually by Denis Diderot from 1759 to 1781
1747	Julien Offray de La Mettrie, *L'Homme machine* (*Man a Machine*)
1747	Françoise de Graffigny, *Lettres d'une Péruvienne* (*Lettres from a Peruvian Woman*)
1748	Jean-Baptiste de Boyer, marquis d'Argens, *Thérèse philosophe*, one of the eighteenth century's best-selling libertine works
1748	Charles-Louis de Secondat de Montesquieu, *De l'esprit des lois* (*The Spirit of the Laws*)
1749–88	George-Louis Leclerc, comte de Buffon, *Histoire naturelle, générale et particulière* (37 vols.) (*Natural History*)
1750	Jean-Jacques Rousseau, *Discours sur les sciences et les arts* (*Discourse on the Sciences and Arts*)
1751–72	Publication of *Encyclopédie, ou dictionnaire raisonné des sciences, des arts et des métiers* (*Encyclopedia; or, A Systematic Dictionary of the Sciences, Arts and Crafts*) (17 vols. of articles, 11 vols. of plates), edited by Denis Diderot and Jean-Baptiste le Rond d'Alembert
1752–4	The *Querelle des bouffons* opposing partisans of French music and of Italian music
1753	Translation with commentary of Isaac Newton's *Philosophiæ naturalis principia mathematica* (*Mathematical Principles of Natural Philosophy*) by Gabrielle Émilie Le Tonnelier de Breteuil, marquise du Châtelet
1755	Jean-Jacques Rousseau, *Discours sur l'origine et les fondements de l'inégalité parmi les hommes* (*On the Origin of Inequality*)

1756	Victor de Riqueti, marquis de Mirabeau, *L'Ami des hommes* (*Friend of Man*)
1756	Voltaire (François-Marie Arouet), *Essai sur les mœurs et l'esprit des nations* (*An Essay on Universal History, the Morals and Manners of Nations*)
1758	Claude Adrien Helvétius, *De l'esprit* (*Essays on the Mind*)
1759	Voltaire (François-Marie Arouet), *Candide*
1760–3	Critics and playwrights produce pamphlets and plays critical of the *philosophes*
1761	Jean-Jacques Rousseau, *Julie, ou la nouvelle Héloïse* (*Julie; or, The New Heloise*)
1763	End of the Seven Years' War, with France regaining Guadeloupe and Martinique in the Caribbean and ceding Canada and land east of the Mississippi to Britain
1764	Jeanne Julie Éléonore de Lespinasse opens her salon
1765	Jean-Baptiste Greuze, *La Bonne Mère* (*The Good Mother*), *Le Mauvais Fils puni* (*The Bad Son Punished*) and *La Malediction paternelle* (*The Father's Curse*)
1766	Anne-Robert-Jacques Turgot, *Réflexions sur la formation et la distribution des richesses* (*Reflections on the Formation and Distribution of Wealth*)
1766	Louis Antoine de Bougainville sets sail from France on a voyage to circumnavigate the world
1767	Jean-Honoré Fragonard, *L'Escarpolette* (*The Swing*)
1769	Denis Diderot, *Le Rêve de d'Alembert* (*D'Alembert's Dream*)
1770	Paul Henri Thiry, baron d'Holbach, *Système de la nature* (*System of Nature*)
1770	Guillaume Thomas François Raynal, *Histoire des deux Indes* (*A History of the Two Indies*)
1772	Denis Diderot, *Supplément au voyage de Bougainville* (*Supplement to Bougainville's Voyage*)

1775–8	Claude-Nicolas Ledoux designs the Royal Saltworks at Arc-et-Senans
1778	Pierre-Augustin Caron de Beaumarchais, *Le Mariage de Figaro* (*The Marriage of Figaro*)
1782	Pierre Choderlos de Laclos, *Liaisons dangereuses* (*Dangerous Liaisons*)
1784	Immanuel Kant, *Was ist Aufklärung?* (*What Is Enlightenment?*)
1785	Jacques-Louis David, *Le Serment des Horaces* (*The Oath of the Horatii*)
1785–9	Thomas Jefferson succeeds Benjamin Franklin as US Minister to France
1789	Beginning of the French Revolution (convocation of the Estates-General, Declaration of the Rights of Man and of the Citizen, assault on the Bastille, march on Versailles forcing the court back to Paris)
1791	Constantin-François de Chasseboeuf, comte de Volney, *Les Ruines, ou méditations sur les révolutions des empires* (*Ruins; or, Meditations on the Revolutions of Empires*).
1791–1804	Slave revolt in the French colony of Saint-Domingue (Haiti)
1791	Donatien Alphonse François, marquis de Sade, *Justine, ou, les malheurs de la vertu* (*Justine; or, the Misfortunes of Virtue*)
1792	Proclamation of the French republic
1793	Execution of Louis XVI
1793–4	Reign of Terror under Maximilien Robespierre and the Jacobin party
1795	Nicolas de Caritat, marquis de Condorcet, *Esquisse d'un tableau historique des progrès de l'esprit humain* (*Sketch for a Historical Picture of the Progress of the Human Mind*)
1799	Anne Louise Germaine de Staël-Holstein, *De la littérature considérée dans ses rapports avec les institutions sociales* (*The Influence of Literature on Society*)

1804   Proclamation of the First Empire under Napoleon Bonaparte

1815   Bourbon restoration

ACKNOWLEDGEMENTS

As Denis Diderot and Jean le Rond d'Alembert well knew, knowledge production is best understood as a collective enterprise. I'm pleased to acknowledge first of all the contribution made by the authors in this volume not only in the form of their individual chapters, but also through their stimulating and energetic participation (face-to-face and virtually) in a two-day workshop on new disciplinary approaches to the French Enlightenment. Held at the University of Minnesota, that workshop was made possible by the support of the TEMS collaborative (Theorizing Early Modern Studies) and the College of Liberal Arts. Invaluable technical support was provided by my research assistant Sean Killackey.

My own contribution to this volume benefitted from the opportunity to present it in lecture format during my stay at the University of Kent as a Leverhulme Visiting Professor and to discuss questions of historicity and temporality with members of the School of European Culture and Languages. My thanks go as well to Linda Bree at Cambridge University Press for her initial invitation to design this Cambridge Companion, her valuable editorial suggestions and her confidence throughout. I'm grateful to Anna Bond and Emma Walker at Cambridge University Press for their timely assistance in steering the project to port, and to Emma Wildsmith and Liz Hudson for their sharp-eyed technical work on the manuscript.

I

DANIEL BREWER

The Enlightenment today?

For long, the Enlightenment has been seen as the cornerstone of modern Western intellectual and political culture. Whether as historical period, philosophical and intellectual movement or social and political event, the Enlightenment has been equated with the beginnings of modernity, a past that betokens the present, a moment that in some sense is also our own. But what do these moments share, and how are the Enlightenment past and present joined? We can begin to answer this question by noting that the Enlightenment took shape in attempts to place knowledge on new foundations, to know things differently. This regrounding of knowledge involved nothing less than a redefinition of human existence, values and action. The term 'Enlightenment' would thus come to signify a set of ideas, ideals and cultural practices that grew out of an existing intellectual and socio-political order, sometimes by resisting it from without, but often enough by working to reconfigure it from within, and that gradually gained prominence and power during the eighteenth century. Over the following two centuries these ideas, ideals and practices would come to define fundamental aspects of modern political and social life in a liberal, democratic society, on the level of both individual existence and collective action.

Ultimately, the term 'Enlightenment' would designate the following aims and values: the autonomy of essentially rational individuals; the progressive function of the State to which individuals give up their freedom in return for increased collective well-being; the pre-given rationality of a natural order made accessible through scientific investigation, the knowledge resulting from experimental practice and technological applications of science designed to improve material existence; and, finally, the potentially just nature of collective social relations. Thus defined, the Enlightenment designates not a past moment but a goal to be realized, a programme reflecting the desire to reform and regulate individual behaviour and collective social relations. Reformist, progressivist and emancipatory, the Enlightenment project is fundamentally future-oriented, even to the point of seeming impossibly utopian. Rising up on a constantly receding horizon, it represents a worthy goal, yet perhaps a constitutively and forever unrealizable one.

To approach the Enlightenment not simply as period but also as project means that the question of the Enlightenment cannot be posed solely in the past tense. Michel Foucault suggests as much when he asks, 'What is this event called Enlightenment that has determined, at least in part, what we are, what we think and what we do today?'[1] With this question, posed in 1984, Foucault revived another question that had been formulated some two centuries earlier by Immanuel Kant in his celebrated essay 'An Answer to the Question: What Is Enlightenment?'. In this short essay, Kant suggested that Enlightenment is the emergence from a self-incurred immaturity or tutelage (*Unmündigkeit*), a state marked by the inability to use one's own understanding without being guided by another or directed by tradition and unexamined beliefs. Instead, Enlightenment involves the courage to establish a new relation to knowing, a relation encapsulated in the phrase Kant borrowed from Horace, *sapere aude* (dare to be wise, dare to know). The chapters in this volume examine the French Enlightenment from numerous disciplinary perspectives, yet they all address what it was that men and women of the French eighteenth century 'dared to know', how they did so and with what results.

The present chapter opens this volume by recalling Foucault's contemporary return to Kant's question in order to stress what Foucault takes to be, for us today, the inescapability of the Enlightenment question. We are bound to the Enlightenment, which bequeaths to us its haunting legacy and challenges us to realize its emancipatory project. The attempt has been made, however, to loosen, if not undo, that bind, which links us to an Enlightenment associated with darker events in the history of the West. This Enlightenment has been denounced for being implicated in capitalist expansion, in the rise of fascism and in colonial exploitation. This Enlightenment is a more sombre one, in which reason seems to be in eclipse, promoting ways of knowing human subjects that instrumentalize and institutionalize them, transforming them into objects of a masterful power/knowledge.[2] It is entirely understandable that we might wish to forget such a past, or recall it only partially, in other words in bits and pieces, but also prejudicially and in service of particular interests. Our relation to this Enlightenment is a critical one, an Enlightenment both crucial to who we are yet one in need of vigilant critique. This critical relation is driven by the wish to free ourselves finally from this shadowy past, to believe we have developed ways of knowing that are more scientific, more rational and ultimately more just. Yet in subjecting the Enlightenment to such a critique, we subject ourselves all the more to the double bind of Enlightenment, for we cannot escape using what

Kant called courageous thinking, an unfettered and self-reflexive form of questioning, in order to critique precisely the Enlightenment thought from which we might seek to free ourselves. Herein lies the ensnaring double bind of Enlightenment, the impossibility of engaging in modern critical thinking except in relation to, and perhaps by using the terms of, the Enlightenment itself.

But this version of the Enlightenment is only one of many, for numerous modern moments have defined themselves in relation to the particular 'Enlightenment past' they construct.[3] Seldom, however, has this modernity been theorized with the unflinching self-reflexivity that Foucault enjoins us to adopt. In the idiom of intellectual history, for example, the story of Enlightenment is told in less problematic terms. Here, an advent narrative recounts the development of a modern way of knowing, one conventionally located in the work of René Descartes. Author of *Discours de la méthode* (*Discourse on Method*) and *Méditations métaphysiques* (*Metaphysical Meditations*), Descartes also wrote a dialogue (published posthumously in 1701) entitled *La Recherche de la vérité par la lumière naturelle*. The 'light' figured here stands for a way of knowing that is distinct from both religion and scholastic philosophy, faith and tradition, as the work's complete title indicates: *La Recherche de la vérité par la lumière naturelle, qui toute pure, et sans emprunter le secours de la religion ni de la philosophie, détermine les opinions que doit avoir tout honnête homme touchant les choses qui peuvent occuper sa pensée et qui pénètrent dans les secrets des sciences les plus abstraites* (*The Search for Truth by Means of the Natural Light That, Entirely Pure, and Unaided by Either Religion or Philosophy, Determines the Opinions That Every Honest Man Must Hold Concerning Things That May Occupy His Mind and That Enter into the Secrets of the Most Abstract Sciences*). This inner 'light' no longer needs to be in harmony with divine or scholastic revelation, and the truths it reveals found a more reliable and scientific knowledge of the world.

Although Descartes's scientific writings would be criticized in the next century as fanciful, overly systematized and ungrounded in empirical experience, his philosophical position was received more positively. The intuitive and innate 'natural light' of Cartesian philosophy would be rephrased as human reason, a universally shared faculty of the mind that frees the rational thinker from shadowy and unexamined superstition and dogma. In the eighteenth century, light becomes lights, as the abstract principle of reason is made visible in multiple ways of knowing. The philosophical spirit of the Enlightenment submits received truths as well as empirically experienced reality to critical examination, as the enlightened subject maps the world anew, guided by his or her own reason. This remapping occurs in numerous domains, notably in the scientific realm, in the path-breaking works of what we now classify as natural history, biology, chemistry, anthropology, art history and medicine. But new forms of aesthetic experience share in this remapping as well. Perhaps most famously, in Voltaire's *Candide* the tale's eponymous hero constantly tests his received view of the world, analysing it against what he comes to know of it through experience. But in countless eighteenth-century novels as well, from the sentimental to the libertine and even the erotic, the reader's experience of reading doubles the hero or heroine's experience of the world, as fiction becomes a way for readers to feel newly in sync with the world, both critically and empathetically, to know it through aesthetic imagination.[4]

The shape this 'new' knowledge takes need not mirror divine order, claim the Enlightenment writers. This position has led scholars to view the Enlightenment as driven by the imperative of rational scientific analysis, whose by-product is a demystifying process of secularization. In this view, scientific rationalism of the eighteenth century resulted in delegitimizing what Max Weber in the next century would call an 'enchanted' and sacred world view, in which spiritual beliefs infuse institutions and give meaning to action. Scientific rationalism was seen to depart from the sacred view of things, following a strategy of resistance to the sacred that was frequently experienced as heady liberation from unreason. The nineteenth-century philosopher of science Auguste Comte pursued this distinction, promoting 'positive' science as the source of empirical, quantifiable and ultimately objective knowledge. Yet this objectivity was seen to have come at a steep price. C. P. Snow, writing in the mid twentieth century, worried that the rise of 'modern scientific thought', for all its benefits, led not to the certainty of a totalizing epistemological viewpoint but rather to fragmented, contradictory and irreconcilable ways of knowing. There existed 'two cultures', Snow claimed, two ways of knowing, with that of 'the sciences' set against that of 'the humanities'.[5] Philosophers would investigate this rift further, grappling with the question of technology's impact upon society and its implications concerning the essence of humanity.[6] At present, the rift seems only to have widened, as the current debate in higher education suggests, in which 'the STEMs' (science, technology, engineering and mathematics) are cast as pitted irreconcilably against 'the liberal arts'.

The opposition between 'enchanted' knowledge and scientific knowledge need not be drawn in such inflexible terms, however, at least not in the case of the Enlightenment. The narrative that sets static and benighted tradition against a more dynamic, secularizing and modernizing Enlightenment – in which modernization stands as the outcome of secularization – is not the only way to explain the Enlightenment's approach to knowledge production.

The dividing line between the religious and the scientific, the enchanted and the secular, was not always a simple one to draw in the eighteenth century. Exploring the complex crossovers between reason and emotion in Enlightenment scientific discourse, historians of science have shown that Enlightenment science is less scientific than we might think, or rather that it is scientific but only once framed in terms other than those of an inexorable march to modernity.[7] The thesis of scientific rationalism, the keystone of the modernizing narrative, may reflect not so much how things actually happened in the eighteenth century but rather how a later moment configured its past as pre-scientific. Exploring the French version of such a reconfiguration, we can see its deep roots in the rancorous political and ideological debates leading to the establishment of the nineteenth-century Third Republic, which pitted partisans of religion against those of secularism or *laïcité*, the hallmark of which was the secular state.

It is doubtless not possible to rid ourselves fully of the lens of the present when reading the texts of the past. Nor perhaps should we, at least if treating the Enlightenment historically means understanding it as part of the present's inevitable project of constructing, if not the past itself, then at least its own past. Consequently, in returning to the Enlightenment we need to keep in mind that various intellectual debates, as well as political and ideological battles (from the French Revolution onwards, and including the battle to bring about modernity), were not necessarily those of the Enlightenment writers themselves, however much they and their writings can be, and indeed were, pressed into service in those debates. The question thus arises, how might we read the Enlightenment otherwise than in terms of an oppositional, demystifying, secularizing and modernizing narrative?

Consider, for instance, the *Encyclopédie* and how its writers grappled with the ordering of knowledge. As Diderot concedes in the article 'Encyclopédie', divine knowledge provides the most perfect of epistemological ordering principles. But he approaches the question of encyclopedic order not so much in oppositional terms as in pragmatic ones. However desirable that divine knowledge of things might be, he observes, it ultimately remains unattainable. So, for the encyclopedist, to know something one must dare not to know everything. Better instead is to order knowledge on a human scale, organizing it the way the mind works in interacting with the world. This principle was the one that Diderot and his co-editor Jean le Rond d'Alembert adopted in the *Encyclopédie*. The articles of this compendious scale model of Enlightenment are organized and interconnected according to the branches and sub-branches of the 'tree of knowledge', whose divisions reflect the way the encyclopedists assumed the mind worked in processing sensation and organizing knowledge; these divisions also mark the still unruly beginnings of the modern disciplines – and disciplining – of knowledge.[8] In this way the encylopedists can claim to found their knowledge not on God but on 'man', the subject they put at the centre of their work. The term 'man' refers in their writings to the universal rational subject, or so implied the lettered men of a certain social privilege who readily saw themselves represented in such a construct. But even if encyclopedic knowledge is not all-encompassing and universal, it nonetheless remains workable, providing strategic and provisional knowledge because it is knowledge on the human scale, designed to be used in human time. Arbitrary as it is, and however much it might be mediated and limited by pragmatic self-interest, this form of knowledge remains a more useful tool, and a more powerful weapon, in the enterprise in which the encyclopedists willingly enlist, namely, as Diderot defines the goal of the *Encyclopédie*, 'to change the common way of thinking'. To be sure, much of the knowledge the *Encyclopédie* contains is quaintly out of date today. The encyclopedists themselves worried that even in their own time both philosophical and technological innovation would outstrip their ability, and that of language, to keep up with change. It is in this vast work's relation to knowledge, rather than in the knowledge it conveys, that the *Encyclopédie* creates a more modern way to conceive of, produce, disseminate and use knowledge, in a manner that is at once critical, disciplinary and collective.

Since the 1970s, scholars have taken renewed interest in the social and cultural history of the Enlightenment. With this shift, the 'ideas' of the 'high Enlightenment' on which intellectual historians previously had focused were seen instead as being contextually embedded, materially determined and characterized by their rich cultural density. From the perspective of this newer history, the Enlightenment was no longer the continuation and popularization of a 'modern' science that emerged in the seventeenth century. Nor was it the ideological, class-based expression of a rising bourgeoisie, as Marxist historiography had claimed. Instead, hybrid historiographical models were developed to explain social and cultural transformation otherwise. From a cultural perspective, the Enlightenment writer's identity and activity were seen to be shaped by complex negotiations and interactions in a world characterized by an array of scholarly institutions (such as the Académie Royale des Sciences or the Académie Royale des Beaux-Arts), as well as more social ones (such as Mme de Geoffrin's salon or d'Holbach's 'coterie').[9] The story of this Enlightenment was less about ideas than about communication, a lens that brought a new Enlightenment world into focus. If historical change was driven by anything, it was not by the insufficiently contextualized ideas of intellectual history, nor by an overly determined theory of class conflict dear to Marxist historiography. Rather, what drove change during the Enlightenment were forms of exchange and patterns of politeness and sociability, the defining features of an elite society in which privilege could coexist with the principle of merit and civic equality.[10] As César Chesneau Dumarsais suggests in his *Encyclopédie* article 'Philosophe', Enlightenment writers readily imagine themselves to be citizens of the greater Republic of Letters, as belonging to an enlightening elite whose members are committed to striving to realize the greatest happiness of the largest number of men and women.

The world of this French Enlightenment was centred in such places as the salons, coffee houses, print shops and libraries of Paris, yet it was marked by a powerful centrifugal impulse that opened it up to a world outside of France. A writer such as Voltaire, for example, was keenly aware of how broadly his readership spread across Europe. Perhaps the first Enlightenment celebrity in the modern sense of the term, he took great care to construct and manage his image beyond French borders, as if he knew that this celebrity would serve as a strategic weapon in his defence of victims of fanaticism. Enlightenment writers just as intentionally participated on an international stage, as did Voltaire and Diderot in their individual relations with Frederick the Great of Prussia and Catherine of Russia. More broadly, Enlightenment writers were active members of international networks of exchanges involving scholarly societies, newspapers, journals and reference volumes (such as Melchior Grimm's *Correspondance littéraire* [*Literary Correspondence*] or Guillaume Thomas François Raynal's *Histoire des deux Indes* [*History of the Two Indies*]). The cosmopolitan world of these communication networks was experientially real, which means we can reproduce it in an empirical sense by generating, for instance, the membership list of the Prussian Royal Academy of Sciences (whose first president was the Frenchman, Pierre-Louis de Maupertuis) or the geographical reach of one of the thousands of Voltaire's letters.

But that empirical world also possessed a symbolic dimension. Participation in these communication networks was a form of self-fashioning, a way of moving up the ladder of prestige, leaving the world of 'Grub Street' that Robert Darnton has analysed, and becoming a writer, a critic, a man of science.[11] In a broader, more social and political sense, participation in these networks created what Jürgen Habermas called *Öffentlichkeit* or the 'public sphere'.[12] A non-courtly space, set apart in significant ways from the State, this space was discursive in nature, characterized by the public discussion and debate that took place there. In coffee houses, reading rooms and salons, this discussion was spurred by the growing variety of critical genres, including newspaper articles, public speeches, scientific reports, encyclopedia articles and novels. Participation in this public space created a community of enlightened citizens whose reasoned discussion and critical debate were perceived as a process that gave voice to public opinion. Producing a form of civic identity independent from religion or royal power, the public opinion located in the public sphere was also seen as possessing a regulative power over state authority. For Habermas, the development of this public sphere parallels no less than the rise of democracy.

While some social and cultural historians highlighted the public dimension of Enlightenment life, others turned to its more private sides. Not so much an 'age of reason' as an 'age of affect', this other Enlightenment was one that promoted the development of intimate relations and new forms of identity (such as family, domesticity, maternity or sentimentality). In contrast with a public courtly space whose prestige and power were in decline, private space allowed new forms of subjectivity to emerge via experiential modes such as conversation and reading. A privileged genre of such experience was the 'new' novel, not that of previous centuries' pastoral romance, for example, but rather the urban, sentimental, domestic novel. Epistolary novels, fictional memoirs and autobiographies, all flourishing genres in the eighteenth century, were especially important in making reading into an experience of intimacy by proxy. Finally, this newly emerging private space was also a gendered space. Here, the experience of intimacy that reading afforded gave rise to a sense of the gendered self, in a process that cultural and literary historians of the Enlightenment have explored in great detail.[13]

Whether considered in its intellectual, social, cultural or political dimension, the French Enlightenment was soon overtaken by historical events. From 1789 onwards, the French Revolutionaries struggled to bring about a new, autonomous and legitimate modernity; reshaping cultural practices and remaking institutions, they aimed to produce a modern political subject. For long, historians have debated whether, to what extent and in what fashion the Enlightenment can be said to have prepared, perhaps even brought about, the French Revolution, either in its initial and more progressive version (1789) or its more radical and bloody one (that of Robespierre and the Reign of Terror of 1793–4). To be sure, the connections between the French Enlightenment and the French Revolution are rich and complex. Yet a teleological model of cause and effect, based on the notion of origin, is likely not the best way to explain these connections. As Roger Chartier has noted, following Michel Foucault, origins are not pre-given but rather after-effects, something produced after the fact. Consequently,

> when history succumbs to 'the chimera of origins', it burdens itself, perhaps unconsciously, with several presuppositions: that every historical moment is a homogeneous totality endowed with an ideal and unique meaning present in each of the realities that make up and express that whole; that historical

becoming is organized as an ineluctable continuity; that events are linked together, one engendering another in an uninterrupted flow of change that enables us to decide that one is the 'cause', another the effect.[14]

Instead of supposing a causal relation between the Enlightenment past and the Revolutionary present, Chartier asks (productively albeit counter-intuitively) whether it was not the Revolution that invented the Enlightenment.

This revolutionary invention involves putting in place a new *régime d'historicité*, a new way of configuring the historical subject's relation to past, present and future. Consider the well-known example of the Revolutionary calendar, for instance, in which 22 September 1792 became the beginning of Year One. The Revolutionaries' calendar created a violent temporal break designed to reset not just calendar time but social, political and cultural time as well. Subjected to the temporal disjunction that this new calendar produced, individuals underwent a collective beginning, which marked the political subject's existential 'regeneration' as citizen. For that process to work though, and the Revolution itself, the Revolutionaries had to position the Revolutionary present in relation not just to a past with which they broke but to a past of their own construction. Consequently, this new and imaginary past, the Ancien Régime, was less a reflection of what had been than a projection of what had to have been. That past was a kind of screen that made legible the conflicts, contradictions and drives shaping the Revolutionaries' own present. Thus, if the Revolution invented the Enlightenment, argues Chartier, it was 'by attempting to root its legitimacy in a corpus of texts and founding authors reconciled and united, beyond their extreme differences, by the preparation of a rupture with the old world'.[15] In this sense, the Enlightenment may well be located at the origin of our modernity but an origin that comes into view retrospectively. As a result, the 'Enlightenment question' is not about what the Enlightenment actually was so much as how we construct it and make use of it. Interpretations of the Enlightenment, as of any intellectual or cultural phenomenon, are best understood as being contextually embedded in the moment of their production. They are produced, received and have their impact in particular contexts, whose determining role must not be forgotten, papered over or repressed but instead identified and brought to light. Three examples of such embedding and its recall are particularly illustrative.

Few books have shaped succeeding generations' understanding of the Enlightenment as extensively as Ernst Cassirer's *Philosophy of the Enlightenment*, published in German in 1932 and in English translation in 1951. In retrospect, the impact of Cassirer's work can be seen to lie not only in its neo-Kantian understanding of the Enlightenment but also in the way this interpretation was entwined with the intellectual, cultural and political context of the times. In 1932, Cassirer held a professorship at the University of Hamburg. The following year, Hitler became Chancellor, and Cassirer left Germany in exile. In his 1932 introduction to the volume, Cassirer refers implicitly to the darkening clouds of unreason on the horizon, suggesting how crucial was the return he sought to an eighteenth century of reason, tolerance and free thought. 'Instead of assuming a derogatory air', he wrote,

> we must take courage and measure our powers against those of the age of the Enlightenment, and find a proper adjustment. The age which venerated reason and science as man's highest faculty cannot and must not be lost even for us. We must find a way not only to see that age in its own shape but to release again those original forces which brought forth and moulded this shape.[16]

Rejecting German Romanticism's 'derogatory' dismissal of Enlightenment, Cassirer sought a way to revive the Enlightenment in the threatening pre-war fascist present. The American translation of Cassirer's work a few decades later has an equally significant contextual dimension to it, for its commercial success and academic impact can be read as reflecting the wish in the USA to reconstruct post-war Europe. Cassirer's Enlightenment, whose beginnings he locates in England and France but whose ultimate culmination he situates in Germany with Kantian philosophy, meshes remarkably well with the post-war goal of rebuilding European intellectual and cultural unity.

If Cassirer's Enlightenment is a hopeful one, Max Horkheimer and Theodor Adorno's *Dialectic of Enlightenment* is far gloomier. Originally published in German in 1947 in the aftermath of the devastation that Cassirer anticipated, this work analyses the negative dialectical unfolding of an Enlightenment characterized by a reason whose internal logic and historical development reflect the attempt to master the real. In the process though, reason negates itself, working upon subjects as if they were objects. This reason produces an objective knowledge, but one that is also objectifying, for it promotes the dehumanization of human subjects through a powerful brand of knowledge that undergirds the technological expansion of the totalitarian state. Adorno and Horkheimer's Enlightenment begins with the Greeks, but the French eighteenth century occupies a privileged place in the story they tell. What should we make of this juxtaposition of Cassirer and Horkheimer and Adorno? For Michel Delon, it is a politically dated conflict that opposes two bygone ideologies, with Cassirer standing for a hopeful liberalism and Horkheimer and Adorno voicing an intransigent Marxist critique of advanced capitalist societies.[17] Can we escape from this bipolar situation, Delon asks, in which the choice seems to be either to identify uncritically with Enlightenment values or to decry their constitutive illusions? Or, rather, rephrasing Delon's alternatives slightly, is it sufficient to reveal the ideological determination of past versions of the Enlightenment, as if present versions (including one's own) remained untouched by such determination? But of course no understanding of the past can claim such objectivity, to be a view from nowhere, situated somehow outside the very history it seeks to reveal. We can measure the consequences of such a situation in relation to a third version of the French Enlightenment.

For historian Daniel Roche, the quintessential eighteenth-century experience was that of *désenclavement* or the opening up of bordered spaces.[18] Roche's image of *désenclavement* calls up the multiple ways in which physical, psychological and symbolic barriers are broken down, borders are crossed (or limits transgressed), isolation is overcome, patterns of exchange and circulation are created and greater connectedness is established between places, ideas, things and people. This opening up to the world, both real and imaginary, involved the encounter with others outside one's own enclaves. One master concept for making sense of the opening up was cosmopolitanism. As concept and ideal, cosmopolitanism allowed Enlightenment thinkers to imagine ways of overcoming local and national limits, establishing connections beyond a single time and place and becoming members of an ideal, transnational and transhistorical community, the Republic of Letters. But there were other concepts that were related to this experience of *désenclavement* during the eighteenth century, notably the expansion of commerce, colonization and enslavement. A good deal of current scholarship on the eighteenth century investigates the period in spatial terms, whether focusing on empirical or on imaginary spaces. This 'spatial turn' has not occurred by chance, in a contemporary moment when the term 'global' freights powerful connotations, both positive and negative, raising crucially important questions involving social policy, cultural transformation, identity formation and ethics (to mention only these). By exploring the forces at work in this opening up of the eighteenth century, scholars are working to understand a crucial aspect of the Enlightenment past, as well as its belated significance for the present moment.

In conclusion, a word in the mode of a user's guide to this volume. The overarching aim of this collection of chapters on the French Enlightenment is to pursue the question of the Enlightenment today in a way that is both comprehensive and innovative. Each of the subsequent fourteen chapters presents a concise and unified view of an important aspect of the French Enlightenment, discussing its defining characteristics, internal dynamics and historical transformations. Each approaches the French Enlightenment from a specific disciplinary perspective, ranging from philosophy, religion and literature, to art, medicine, anthropology and architecture. The choice of these disciplinary perspectives is not arbitrary. These perspectives represent the areas of scholarship in which some of the most influential reinterpretations of the Enlightenment and, more broadly, the early modern period have taken place during the past two decades. Each chapter explicitly takes into account its own disciplinary position and the contemporary state of knowledge concerning the French Enlightenment, discussing how current scholarship has critically reworked received ideas about the Enlightenment, revising earlier paradigms of interpretation and offering new ones. Each chapter thus presents a particular aspect of the rich and complex object called the French Enlightenment, at the same time basing its presentation, and at times the debate with which it engages, on the ways contemporary disciplines of knowledge shape how we know this object called Enlightenment. Hopefully it is this double perspective on the French Enlightenment that will make this Companion both innovative and timely.

NOTES

1 Michel Foucault, 'What is Enlightenment?', in Paul Rabinow (ed.), *The Foucault Reader* (New York: Pantheon Books, 1984), pp. 32–50, at p. 32.
2 See Max Horkheimer, *Eclipse of Reason* (New York: Seabury Press, 1974) and *Critique of Instrumental Reason* (New York: Seabury Press, 1974).
3 For an analysis of this process over the past two centuries, see Daniel Brewer, *The Enlightenment Past: Reconstructing Eighteenth-Century French Thought* (Cambridge University Press, 2008).
4 See David Marshall, *The Surprising Effects of Sympathy* (University of Chicago Press, 1988). See Lynn Festa's relating of sentimentalism to commercial expansion and colonialism, *Sentimental Figures of Empire in Eighteenth-Century Britain and France* (Baltimore, Md.: Johns Hopkins University Press, 2006).
5 C. P. Snow, *The Two Cultures* (1959) (Cambridge University Press, 2001).
6 Martin Heidegger, *The Question Concerning Technology and Other Essays* (New York: Harper & Row, 1977).
7 Jessica Riskin, *Science in the Age of Sensibility: The Sentimental Empiricists of the French Enlightenment* (University of Chicago Press, 2002).
8 Martine Groult, *L'Encyclopédie, ou la création des disciplines* (Paris: CNRS, 2001). See Robert Darnton, 'Philosophers Trim the Tree of Knowledge: The Epistemological Strategy of the *Encyclopédie*', in *The Great Cat Massacre and Other Episodes in French Cultural History* (1984), rev. edn (New York: Basic Books, 2009), pp. 191–213.
9 Dena Goodman, *The Republic of Letters: A Cultural History of the French Enlightenment* (Ithaca, NY: Cornell University Press, 1994); Antoine Lilti, *Le Monde des salons: sociabilité et mondanité à Paris au XVIIIe siècle* (Paris: Fayard, 2005). See Alan Charles Kors, *D'Holbach's Coterie: An Enlightenment in Paris* (Princeton University Press, 1976).
10 Daniel Gordon, *Citizens without Sovereignty: Equality and Sociability in French Thought, 1670–1789* (Princeton University Press, 1994).
11 Robert Darnton, *The Literary Underground of the Old Regime* (Cambridge, Mass.: Harvard University Press, 1982); Darrin M. McMahon, *Enemies of*

the Enlightenment: The French Counter-Enlightenment and the Making of Modernity (Oxford University Press, 2001).

12 Jürgen Habermas, *The Structural Transformation of the Public Sphere: An Inquiry into a Category of Bourgeois Society*, trans. Thomas Burger (Cambridge, Mass.: MIT Press, 1989).

13 Dena Goodman, *Becoming a Woman in the Age of Letters* (Ithaca, NY: Cornell University Press, 2009); Erica Harth, *Cartesian Women: Versions and Subversions of Rational Discourse in the Old Regime (Reading Women Writing)* (Ithaca, NY: Cornell University Press, 1992); Londa Schiebinger, *The Mind Has No Sex? Women in the Origins of Modern Science* (Cambridge, Mass.: Harvard University Press, 1991).

14 Roger Chartier, *The Cultural Origins of the French Revolution*, trans. Lydia G. Cochrane (Durham, NC: Duke University Press, 1991), pp. 4–5.

15 Ibid. p. 5.

16 Ernst Cassirer, *The Philosophy of the Enlightenment*, trans. Fritz C. A. Koelln and James P. Pettegrove (Princeton University Press, 1951), pp. xi–xii.

17 Michel Delon, 'Enlightenment (Representations of)', *Encyclopedia of the Enlightenment* (London: Fitzroy Dearborn, 2001), pp. 457–62.

18 Daniel Roche, *France in the Enlightenment*, trans. Arthur Goldhammer (Cambridge, Mass.: Harvard University Press, 1998).

2

ANTOINE LILTI

Private lives, public space: a new social history of the Enlightenment

Is it possible to write a social history of the Enlightenment? What connections should be drawn between the works, ideas and authors that brought great changes to the intellectual and political landscape in France during the long eighteenth century – commonly called the Enlightenment – and the social changes that occurred during this period? The question has long been debated by historians. When social history played a predominant role in French historiography, dividing up society into various categories, it was tempting to rely on aspects of the social structure to explain the innovations and limits of the French Enlightenment. The rise of the bourgeoisie, the importance of the administrative nobility, the resistance (if not the feudal reaction) on the part of the landed nobility – these were obvious categories to adopt for anyone wanting to escape from a disembodied history of ideas. Marxists were not alone in seeing bourgeois ideology in the Enlightenment. The basic tenet of any social history consisted of conceiving of society as a set of distinct and coherent social groups (whether they were called orders or classes) characterized by different, even conflicting, values and beliefs. Offering a social interpretation of the Enlightenment involved ascribing the intellectual changes at work to specific social groups, which were defined with various degrees of refinement.

Since the late 1970s, the social history of the Enlightenment has undergone extensive renewal, brought about by adopting another way of conceiving of a society's driving forces. Divisions according to 'social groups' defined by legal status or economic situation have given way to a more flexible view of Ancien Régime society, one more focused on practices, interactions, exchanges and networks and forms and categories of experience. This shift brought about a new way of understanding the Enlightenment's social dimension. The emblematic case of written culture provides a telling example. Instead of counting the library holdings of the aristocracy and the commercial bourgeoisie, or comparing the literacy rates of workers and servants, historians have investigated reading practices, the spaces of private withdrawal that books promoted, the forms of sociability produced by these forms of reading, the uses of correspondence, the distribution of printed works in public space and the diversity of their forms and uses.

New ways of interpreting these cultural practices thus emerged, which often classified these practices according to a private/public paradigm that extended from intimacy to public space and displayed the full range of forms of sociability. The history of private life, of sociabilities, of public space – these categories have generated fruitful publishing ventures and research agendas. Although they were based on often very different historiographical projects, these new ways of articulating social experiences and cultural practices thoroughly transformed how the Enlightenment was understood.

Forms of privatization

In a text written in 1983 and published as the introduction to the volume of *Histoire de la vie privée* (*The History of Private Life*) devoted to the Enlightenment, Philippe Ariès advanced the hypothesis that traditional frameworks of experience underwent a deep-seated transformation during the eighteenth century. Prior to the previous centuries, individuals in villages and large cities had lived under the constant gaze of others, whether neighbours or strangers, with no distinction whatsoever between private and public. During the eighteenth century, according to Ariès, social experience was gradually restricted to private and family life, a withdrawal that occurred as forms of ordinary, informal conviviality became more complex and the State grew relentlessly. The result of this double movement was an autonomous political sphere, henceforth freed from domestic forms of power, and privatized social life, reduced essentially to the family unit and the ideal of intimacy.[1] Although Ariès did not make the point explicitly, this analysis obviously led to an interpretation of Enlightenment: was not this encounter between the individual and sovereignty, the intimate and the political, at the very heart of the European modernity the Enlightenment was supposed to have engendered? Instead of seeking the roots of Enlightenment in political philosophy, Ariès proposed to decipher its most material forms.

Numerous scholars have pursued this hypothesis, examining 'the birth of intimacy'.[2] From this perspective, it is material living conditions that first of all underwent a deep-seated transformation. In the houses of the urban elites, the model of a single, multi-purpose room gradually gave way to more complex living spaces where the bedroom was increasingly distinct from shared spaces, such as the dining and reception rooms. In the private mansions of Paris, with their increasingly differentiated spaces, especially at the height of the Rococo period, numerous rooms created a sense of separation and intimacy: bedchambers, study rooms (*cabinets*) and bathrooms. The boudoir is the most important of these spaces, which explains the significant role it plays in the libertine literature of the Enlightenment.[3] But this transformation involves essentially the elites and pertains only marginally to popular spaces, even in Paris where the most frequently found space is the single multi-purpose room, which was used as sleeping room, common space and kitchen. Intimacy remained limited in this space.[4]

The more complex interior spaces, which offered greater room for intimacy, were also more richly furnished and decorated. The eighteenth-century world underwent a deep-seated transformation with regard to material culture. Objects that previously had been limited to the aristocratic elites, such as furniture, undergarments, mirrors, handkerchiefs and cutlery, began appearing much more frequently in the urban interiors of the commercial and artisanal bourgeoisie. Even working-class households slowly became less impoverished, to the point that one could speak of a first consumer revolution affecting even certain rural sectors, such as farmers in the region of Paris. The eighteenth-century world is no longer one of scarce and precious items, especially in cities. The probate inventories of working-class Parisian households reveal that many objects had actually become 'everyday things', whereas among the more well-off strata the English ideal of 'comfort' was spreading.[5] No longer was it a question of the ostentatious luxury that characterized the court nobility, completely focused on prestige; what had taken shape instead was an intimate relation to objects, to the decoration of rooms and to the arrangement of living spaces.

Chief among once-rare objects whose possession was becoming commonplace we find books. In the cities of western France, one-third of probate inventories mention books. Even the working class reflects this trend. At century's end in Paris, forty per cent of the servants own books, as do thirty-five per cent of the workers. The practice of reading was changing as well. No longer an exclusively scholarly activity, limited to the elites and performed in designated spaces such as a library, reading becomes more common, familiar and mobile. New figures emerge, such as the female reader of novels. Silent and intimate reading becomes the norm, even though it would be an exaggeration to speak of a reading revolution, as some have done, since older practices persisted for quite some time, opposing scholarly reading, on the one hand, and oral and collective reading, on the other.[6]

It is not surprising that the family is one of the major themes in eighteenth-century moralist literature, since it emerges as a haven of conviviality and affectivity. Paternal and maternal love is expressed with new energy, as is tender friendship between spouses. The family does not appear only as an economic unit but as a special place for discovering a way of life supposedly free from the constraints of social life, that is, a 'private life', a laboratory of affectivity and sentiment. An entire body of eighteenth-century French painting bears witness to this new way of life, which stresses intimacy, the comfort of private life and the gentleness of family life. Genre painting, as opposed to history painting or religious scenes, seems to be in step with this new society. In his *Jeune fille lisant* (*Young Girl Reading*), Fragonard depicts a reader comfortably seated, leaning against several pillows and completely absorbed in reading the small book she holds in her right hand and that the viewer imagines to be a novel. In *Le Déjeuner* (*Morning Coffee*), Boucher paints a family having morning coffee in the gentle tranquillity of a living room richly decorated with a mirror, a clock and knick-knacks. Family members are enjoying the fashionable new drinks of chocolate and coffee, drunk from porcelain cups. Affectionate gazes are exchanged. The children, one of whom is holding a doll, are obviously pampered. As for Greuze, although the village dwellings he paints are clearly starker and more rustic, his major works, such as *Le Père de famille expliquant la bible à ses enfants* (*A Father Explaining the Bible to His Children*), *L'Accordée du village* (*The Village Bride*) or *La Piété familiale* (*The Paralytic*), are all designed to move the viewer by presenting the family as a refuge of morality and feeling.

The age of sociabilities

The hypothesis that Ariès proposed was that certain forms of sociability declined during the eighteenth century in favour of a direct encounter between family life (the space of privacy, intimacy and affectivity) and political life (monopolized by the State and its representatives). This diagnosis was refuted by numerous studies of the history of forms of sociability, which showed the richness of the kinds of social and associative life found in the eighteenth century. The very notion of sociability emerged as a historiographical concept in the work of Maurice Agulhon, who revealed the intensity of social relations during the Enlightenment in southern France, where Masonic lodges seem to have taken over from penitent brotherhoods.[7] This form of sociability paved the way for a large-scale political mobilization in this region, first during the Revolution and later the Republic.

Even though few historians of the Enlightenment have pursued the hypothesis of a specific regional temperament or that of the directly political effectiveness of sociable practices, the notion of sociability, on the other hand, has enjoyed exponential success. Using this notion, numerous social configurations could be examined, from the most institutionalized (such as academies) to the most informal (such as correspondence between friends). These various configurations all promote a strong network of social interactions and intellectual exchanges, located in a space neither of family life nor of politics and commerce. Whether as cafés, salons, clubs, conversation circles or Masonic lodges, these spaces all resist being categorized according to the binary division public/private. They define an in-between space, much more broadly open than domestic and family life, yet based on assimilation. This space, which in the eighteenth century was called 'society', is based on an ideal type of codified exchanges, both intellectual and social, that nurtures conversations in all its various forms.

Provincial academies multiplied during the eighteenth century, enabling a moderate version of Enlightenment thought to spread among the notables who favoured both the advancement of knowledge and a certain social and political stability. As Daniel Roche has shown, it was in the provincial academies that Enlightenment values (scientific progress, the cult of reason, religious toleration, etc.) were espoused by the social elites, which included members of the nobility and the clergy, under the auspices of a monarchy that both supported and protected academic institutions. These academies provided shelter for a 'disorganized yet real alliance between forms of knowledge and power'.[8] Here sociability became a value in its own right, in a revived version of the Republic of Letters where the aim was less to contribute to scientific progress in a learned and scholarly way than to gather together as people of merit and goodwill in order to encourage progress in general. This is the sense in which we can also understand the development of academic competitions, which animated intellectual life, gave rise to impassioned debates and sometimes revealed promising authors, the most famous of whom was Jean-Jacques Rousseau, prize-winner in a competition sponsored by the Académie de Dijon in 1750.[9]

Unlike academies, salons did not enjoy official recognition. They were not monarchical institutions, possessing statutes and a stable membership list. They were based on forms of hospitality practised by the urban elites: a hostess and occasionally a host opened their house on certain days and received a group of regular guests, more infrequent visitors who had already been introduced and newcomers who needed to have received a formal invitation. These salons played an important role because they resembled both the court (because of the essential role played by the upper nobility and the importance of a logic of social distinction) and a cultural coterie (because of the presence of writers and philosophers, most often, and even of artists). Freer than the court, since no one would think of applying the rules of etiquette, these salons were governed by the implicit yet binding rules of politeness and decorum and by the art of conversation, which is, above all, an art of shining in society. This fashionable Enlightenment sociability enabled Parisian nobility to redefine its social prestige by displaying its refined and cultivated lifestyle, which distinguished it both from the new financial elites and from provincial nobility. But this sociability also provided certain writers with a means of access to the lifestyle of these elites, to their generosity and their protection, all the while allowing these writers to affirm themselves as true men of the world. 'One must be a man of the world before being a man of letters', wrote Voltaire to Mme du Deffand, expressing a slogan for the *philosophes* that also served to flatter members of high society. Perpetuating the previous century's salons, those of the eighteenth century thus were also a privileged space in which social, political and cultural elites could mix.[10] Like the academies, they prompt us to question the well-known interpretation proposed by Tocqueville, who saw in the French Enlightenment a thriving literary current that existed in complete separation from social and political realities.[11] In reality, in the salon of Julie de Lespinasse as in the Academy, the leaders of the *Encyclopédie* project, grouped around d'Alembert or Condorcet, associated actively with the ministry of Turgot (1774–6).

In the dynamics of Enlightenment sociability, what was essential was the diversity of practices and the fascination on the part of urban elites for all forms of conviviality in which cultural pleasures were compatible with the distinction of remaining among one's own. Beyond the conventional figures of incidental poetry or drawing-room theatre, the taste for painting, music or science was also a powerful vehicle for sociability, giving rise to imitation and cooperation. The tradition of cabinets of curiosities was compatible with new forms of scholarly sociability, which were rooted in academic institutions, international networks of scholarly life and new spaces of experimentation or teaching.[12] Art connoisseurs met at the house Claude-Henri Watelet owned in Moulin-Joli to discuss their collections, exchange engravings and produce drawings themselves. This sociability was far from being closed in upon itself for it influenced the world of art through the Royal Academy of Painting and Sculpture, where 'amateurs' enjoyed a special status. Its impact was also felt in the context of patronage, as well as in the production and circulation of new forms of knowledge.[13]

Salons and academies existed before the eighteenth century, but it was during this century that Freemasonry arose and enjoyed a remarkable development. In France, the first official lodge was established in 1725, and on the eve of the Revolution there were 900 lodges and approximately 50,000 Freemasons. A dense set of interconnections existed in the kingdom: there were numerous lodges in the provincial capitals, parliamentary cities and ports, but lodges were found in the smaller cities as well.[14] With its secret rituals, Freemasonry gave rise to all manner of phantasms, especially in the early nineteenth century, when counter-revolutionary figures, such as the abbé Barruel, were convinced that the Revolution represented a conspiracy against the social and political order. In its modern form and supported by sociology and history, this idea enjoyed a long afterlife, especially as disseminated by Augustin Cochin. In this view, Masonic lodges promoted a new form of sociability that was egalitarian, staunchly committed to Enlightenment ideas and sensitive to having to work in secret. This sociability was thus seen as a free-standing form of democratic experimentation situated within a society of orders but one that accustomed Enlightenment elites to secret action and unanimity. These views, popularized not only by French historian François Furet and his students but also by German historian Reinhardt Koselleck, have given way today to a much more measured interpretation of Masonic sociability. Although some Masonic lodges may certainly have brought powerful minds together, especially in the francophone community in Holland, most were spaces devoted to conviviality and entertainment, in a way perfectly paralleling the social norms of the Ancien Régime. As Pierre-Yves Beaurepaire has shown, Freemasonry was not the place for a democratic form of sociability; rather, it largely reproduced the practices of social distinction, shared identity and exclusion prevailing in other spaces of urban sociability. In the larger cities, a kind of social Freemasonry existed, which was openly integrated into upscale social life, and which organized concerts and plays, charitable activities and dinners. A select lodge such as the 'Assembled Friends' welcomed tax farmers, aristocrats, financiers and rich foreigners, conceiving of itself as an English-style club and holding its summer meetings in the chateau de la Chevrette.

Moreover, this is also why, prior to the Revolution, the authorities never perceived Freemasonry in France as a real danger. Nonetheless, the egalitarian and cosmopolitan ideals proclaimed by Masonic lodges doubtless contributed to familiarizing the Ancien Régime elites with the principles of a form of sociability that was much less rigidly codified than the principles imposed by distinctions of order. These ideals also contributed to creating interconnections of sociability at the European level by facilitating movement and encounters.

Enlightenment individuals and ideas infiltrated existing structures (academies, salons, cafés) and created others (Freemasonry, reading circles, clubs); certain of these structures were explicitly devoted to an intellectual or scholarly ideal (agricultural societies), whereas others were involved with the entertainment of urban elites (salons). Overall, these spaces and practices contributed to accelerating the circulation and social transmission of enlightened themes, even in an attenuated form, as well as to embedding the Enlightenment in Ancien Régime society, albeit indirectly, even if these themes cannot be associated with specific socio-economic groups. This situation explains why such a broad segment of the nobility, especially in Paris and certain large cities, was affected by Enlightenment ideas. The ideal of sociability, which was initially a philosophical concept dear to the proponents of natural law (people's natural ability to live in society), but one easily used by the educated elites in defence of cultivated *otium* or leisure time, symbolizes this alliance perfectly.[15] Sociable life, as led by urbane writers, amateurs of art and music, the Parisian nobility and financiers, seems to its apologists to represent a process of civilization that made Paris the capital of Europe. 'Earthly paradise is where I am', wrote Voltaire in *Le Mondain* (*The Man of the World*).

What is public space?

De Toqueville's lesson, which sharply distinguished between Enlightenment and State, was based on the assumption that 'public' referred above all to the action of the State and its administration. Similarly, Ariès opposed the space of the private and the family to two notions of the 'public': on the one hand, the State, and on the other, collective and anonymous life in the streets, public gardens and open spaces. In both cases, reading, intellectual exchange and amicable conversations belonged to the private side. The reception of Jürgen Habermas's enormously important *The Structural Transformation of the Public Sphere* thoroughly modified the conception of the public, sparking considerable research. Translated into French in 1978 but not discussed substantially by Enlightenment specialists until it was translated into English in 1986, Habermas's book was based on a new definition of the public, conceived as a group of private individuals making public use of their reason. In this conception, inspired by Kant and his celebrated essay of 1784, *Was ist Aufklärung?* (*What Is Enlightenment?*), the public sphere is constituted outside of the State; it is at once the principle (publicity) that involves public, rational and critical discussion and a set of places and institutions (coffee houses, lodges and newspapers) where individuals, regardless of their social status or political responsibilities, can participate in such discussions. In this view, it was the combination of this demand for the public examination of shared questions with the social transformations of the conditions in which critique can be exercised that gave rise to the modern figure of public opinion. Having appeared in the early eighteenth century in connection with literary and artistic debates, the public sphere rapidly became politicized, making public opinion into a legitimate tribunal, as opposed to the absolutist will of the king.[16]

In the wake of this reinterpretation of the cultural and political history of the Enlightenment, numerous scholars have re-evaluated the importance of the notion of public opinion in pre-revolutionary political culture, stressing its normative coherence and its rhetorical uses.[17] Historians of the book have related the development of print and new reading practices to the creation of this public sphere in which all questions – from the rules of tragedy to the grain train, from Jansenism to the American War of Independence – would henceforth be debated publicly. What all these debates had in common, along with the public controversies they fuelled, was readers' belief that they were participating in a common space of discussion. The small number of public libraries was offset by the existence of reading rooms, where it was possible to subscribe to and read newspapers and the latest publications.

The ideal of publicity involved flexibility concerning the conditions under which information was published and circulated. Even if censorship rules officially remained strict, the system of tacit permission to print made it possible to publish without obtaining official approval. Certain books were available throughout the kingdom, especially books and gazettes written in French and published in Geneva, Amsterdam and London, or even in the principality of Bouillon. In many respects, the explosion of pamphlets and longer works in the two years prior to the opening of the Estates-General can be seen as the direct consequence of a continuous expansion of the public sphere.

Far from reducing the public sphere to that of print, Habermas associated it with social spaces, from the coffee house to the lodge, in which these writings could be read and discussed. In his wake, several studies sought to reinterpret traditional spaces of sociability from the perspective of the public sphere.[18] The numerous limits of this approach have been revealed.[19] On the one hand, a conception of the public sphere centred on the practices of high society and the intellectual elite excludes other forms of participation from public discussion, including those that perhaps voice protest most strongly. Women, who were excluded from official institutions in the Republic of Letters and from Masonic lodges, sought out other forms of participation. Similarly, popular sociability, especially the kind found in the street or the marketplace, enabled another form of public opinion, which was closely monitored by the police and found expression in improper speech and rumours, occasionally leading to revolts or riots.[20] Events of the 1770s clearly reveal the gap between debates within the enlightened public sphere that supported liberalizing the grain trade and the circulation of rumours about a plot designed to starve the people, which was connected to a moral economy of the crowd and a deep-seated popular sociability.[21]

In addition, the Habermasian model, which projects onto the eighteenth century an idyllic vision of the public sphere as a normative counterpoint designed to expose its subsequent decline, would be questioned for its tendency to idealize the effects of sociability and to overestimate the latter's critical and public dimension. The thick network of forms of sociability defines a space that is neither a public space of critical deliberation nor a private, familial and intimate space but rather a mixed and hybrid space, that of life in 'society'. This term refers to a set of social experiences that go well beyond the more traditional forms of social divisions, implying new forms of distinction, social prestige and even power. An entire body of Enlightenment literature echoes these various social experiences in which a society redefines its divisions and categories in spaces that are simultaneously open and closed, spaces that declare their openness so that the effects of closure can be felt all the more intensely. From Montesquieu's *Persian Letters* (1721) to Laclos's *Dangerous Liaisons* (1782), the French epistolary novel was especially well equipped to reveal the underlying stakes of a frivolous and cruel Enlightenment sociability.

The dynamics of publicity

The process of privatization and the emergence of the public sphere appear to be phenomena that are not only distinct but opposed. This impression is reinforced by the fact that these phenomena have been examined according to different historiographical models: on the one hand, a social history model that focuses on everyday practices, material culture and spaces of intimacy; on the other, a cultural and political history model that valorizes investigating the growing power of modernity and the questioning of absolutism. However, Jürgen Habermas sought to show that the Enlightenment public sphere was based on the autonomization of a space that belonged to the private. But this space, in his view, resulted above all from the socio-economic development of a bourgeois form of life that was consistent with what the philosophical tradition designated as 'civil society'. Furthermore, these new conceptions of the public were closely connected to the recognition of private interiority, a new relation to intimacy. Private and public were not polar opposites. Instead, they formed a linked pair that developed jointly during the eighteenth century, on the level of practices and representations.

Prior to the seventeenth century, the term 'public' referred to the group of individuals who lived under the same form of sovereignty in so far as this group constituted a political body. By extension, the public referred to the State since the State proceeded from this sovereignty and ensured the existence of the political community. As a juridical and political entity, this public stood in opposition to *'particuliers'*, that is, individuals who did not exercise specific functions in the political order. In the eighteenth century, whereas the notion of society was coming to designate small groups based on conviviality and association, as well as the overall community of individuals, the pair public/private became an increasingly useful structural principle. Private life did not refer to a particular condition but rather to something that fell outside of public life. Initially, private life corresponded to a statesman's voluntary retreat from society and renunciation of power. This meaning endured and became more general in the eighteenth century: private life did not exist in and of itself, for it was defined by its opposition not only to the sphere of publicity and of power but also to the sphere of the social scene that became increasingly important as one of the essential dimensions of city life. Gradually, the entirety of social life was divided between a public dimension, which was subjected to others' inspection, and hence to discussion and commentary, and a private dimension, which was legitimately removed from inspection and discussion because it concerned intimate and family life.

The two notions of private and public, then, are intimately connected. Together they offer a framework for understanding the conditions of social life, with each reacting to changes in the other. The development of the public sphere, through the press, books and urban entertainment, makes all the more pressing the call for the intimacy and solitude that pre-Romantic sensibility thrives on at the end of the century, heightened by the impact of Rousseau's *Julie, ou la nouvelle Héloïse* (*Julie; or, the New Heloise*) (1761) in particular. And the claim made by all, even rulers, to benefit from a private life feeds curiosity and provokes prying eyes. Marie Antoinette, queen of Louis XVI, offers an illustrative example of this trend. Royal etiquette, which implies that the king and queen live constantly under the gaze of courtiers and are thoroughly public figures, in the double sense of embodying the State and having a life that is completely a spectacle, was something to which Louis XIV could adapt quite well, but it became unacceptable for Marie Antoinette. Consequently, she developed an intimate, private life, sheltered from the gaze of others, a life symbolized by the Trianon Palace at Versailles. But this need for intimacy, perfectly in line with the new values of the end-of-century social elites, in turn aroused an unbridled curiosity on the part of the public, that is, journalists, polygraphs, pamphlet authors and probably everyone who avidly bought up whatever was written about the Queen, to the point that the royal police had to intervene on several occasions to make so-called revelations concerning 'the Queen's private life' disappear.[22]

Publicity is therefore essential to understanding the Enlightenment's social and cultural transformations, provided that it is taken not simply as a principle of enlightened, critical discussion concerning literary or political questions but also as the dynamic force by which private or intimate topics are subjected to public display. Three examples will allow us to see this more clearly.

For some time, literary historians have noted the emergence of a new genre of writing, namely, texts written in the first person that departed from the classical model of the account book or the life story centred on public and political life. These 'stories of private lives', as historians have called them, describe the evolution of a subjectivity, its torments, hopes and doubts. The diary acquires its long-standing function as 'the soul's barometer', thus becoming, from the early nineteenth century on, a widely practised form of writing.[23] With his *Confessions* (completed 1769), Jean-Jacques Rousseau celebrated a form of autobiographical writing centred on interiority and intimate feelings. The chief characteristic of this type of writing is its affirmation of the sovereignty of an inner self that is transparent to itself and that delights in solitary meditation, a writing that at the same time makes this aspiration to intimacy public, turning the adventures of subjectivity into a public spectacle.[24]

Similarly, ordinary individuals who were involved in judicial matters had their private life laid out for all to see during sensational trials that spurred lawyers' eloquence and zeal. These are the *causes célèbres* that Sara Maza has analysed.[25] The 'memoranda' that were written up by lawyers and originally intended for judges became best-sellers, printed in several thousand copies and snatched up by the public. These texts make excessive use of sentimental rhetoric, borrowed mainly from bourgeois drama, but also from a moral eloquence à la Rousseau, in order to present their clients as the symbols of social and political injustice and to appeal to the judgement of public opinion. These affairs contributed to shaping a new political culture, one that treated with equal scorn both ministerial despotism and aristocratic corruption by opposing them to the moral virtues of family order and the dignity of ordinary people. To that end, the private life of unknown individuals had to be transformed into a public story, sometimes even recounted in instalments. The family life, marital misfortunes and financial difficulties of these affairs' protagonists became their 'private life' in the very gesture that made them public and transformed them into a spectacle for an urban readership that avidly sought out these reports. The public repercussion of these cases conjoins three evolutions: publicity concerning strictly private affairs; the politicization of questions linked to the family and sexuality; and the emergence of a public consisting of individuals as 'public opinion', in other words, a legitimate tribunal.

Finally, the private life of public persons becomes a specific object of investigation and even an editorial genre in itself.[26] These 'private lives' are based on a double presupposition. On the one hand, the public exhibition of certain famous individuals, such as writers, criminals and actors, arouses the public's curiosity for anecdotes of their private and even intimate life. Thus, the author of *La Vie de Joseph Balsamo, connu sous le nom du comte Cagliostro* (*The Life of Joseph Balsomo, Known as Count Cagliostro*) writes, 'Since for some time he has attracted everyone's attention, his origin, the events of his life, the web of his duplicities and the proceedings that recently and likely forever have determined his destiny, excite general curiosity: it is all but certain that his private life will be eagerly received.'[27] On the other hand, it was held that the private life of public figures, political ones in particular, reveals the hidden motifs of their actions. Beginning in the 1770s, and then during the Revolution, narratives of the private lives of Louis XV, Mirabeau or Marat multiplied. For some time these texts were studied from an exclusively political angle, through the theme of the desacralization of the monarchy. More recently they have been re-evaluated as testifying to a change in the balance between private and public that grants slander a new place in the repertory of political action.

In 'What Is Enlightenment?', Emmanuel Kant did not just define Enlightenment as humanity's gradual emanicipation from a 'self-incurred tutelage'. He made the public use of reason the condition of this emancipation. But, as many commentators have pointed out, Kant employed a complex definition of this public use, referring more to freedom of conscience than to freedom of action. This claim of totally free reasoning was not incompatible with a form of social conservatism, at least as prudent political obedience. At the same time, writers, lawyers and philosophers in France made appeals that were much more insistent and daring, for they went further than their predecessors in pressing for a militant reformism that would lead, sometimes to their great surprise, to revolutionary radicalism. In its different forms, the horizon of the public is intrinsic to the Enlightenment. It is in this sense that the Enlightenment can be distinguished from the humanist or rationalist tradition. Beyond all doctrinal differences, the Enlightenment was an intellectual movement whose unity lay in a militant desire and the will to spread knowledge, advance useful reforms and abolish forms of superstition and abuse.

Here, the intellectual history of the Enlightenment turns out to be inseparable from social history. For the 'public' that Kant as well as Condorcet invoked is not a straightforward socio-political concept. It also refers to a set of social realities, and it is rooted in a complete transformation of the social experience of eighteenth-century men and women, whether in their relation to domestic intimacy, to the conditions of intellectual communication or to the exercise of power. Through this 'public', historians are encouraged to investigate these new divisions of the social world.

The history of private life, forms and networks of sociability, public space: these are the three areas that renewed the social history of the Enlightenment by revealing the connections between new patterns of social experience and the conditions of intellectual and artistic life. Established originally as autonomous research fields based on potentially differing assumptions, these three areas now overlap in such a way that the conceptual pair of private/public has become one of the key ways of understanding the Enlightenment. This pair should not be understood in terms of a continuous spectrum of forms but rather according to a problematic tension. The emergence of a critical public space was based on social conditions that allowed for solitary reading and independent reflection, while the new ideal of individual subjectivity took shape in reaction to the demands of sociability and to multiple forms of publicity. Publicity in turn jeopardized the ideal of the private, which existed only in so far as it was constantly in danger of being displayed publicly. These ambivalences define the field of heterogeneous forces on which Enlightenment culture thrived.

NOTES

Translated from the French by Daniel Brewer.

1 Philippe Ariès, 'Introduction', in Philippe Ariès and Georges Duby (eds.), *A History of Private Life*, vol. III: *Passions of the Renaissance*, ed. Roger Chartier, trans. Arthur Goldhammer (Cambridge, Mass.: Harvard University Press, 1993), 'Introduction', pp. 1–11.

2 Annick Pardailhé-Galabrun, *La Naissance de l'intime, 3000 foyers parisiens, XVIIe–XVIIIe siècles* (Paris: Presses Universitaires de France, 1988).

3 Michel Delon, *L'Invention du boudoir* (Paris: Zulma, 1999).

4 Daniel Roche, *Le Peuple de Paris: essai sur la culture populaire au XVIIIe siècle* (Paris: Fayard, 1982).

5 Joël Cornette, 'La Révolution des objets: le Paris des inventaires après décès (XVIIe–XVIIIe siècle)', *Revue d'Histoire Moderne et Contemporaine*, 36 (1989): 476–86; Daniel Roche, *A History of Everyday Things: The Birth of Consumption in France, 1600–1800*, trans. Brian Pearce (Cambridge University Press, 2000).

6 Roger Chartier, *Lectures et lecteurs dans la France d'Ancien Régime* (Paris: Seuil, 1987).

7 Maurice Agulhon, *Pénitents et francs-maçons dans l'ancienne Provence: essai sur la sociabilité méridionnale* (Paris: Fayard, 1966).

8 Daniel Roche, *Les Républicains des lettres: gens de Lumières et de culture* (Paris: Fayard, 1988), p. 15. See especially Daniel Roche, *Le Siècle des lumières en province: académies et académiciens provinciaux (1680–1789)* (La Haye: Mouton, 1978).

9 Jeremy L. Caradonna, *The Enlightenment in Practice: Academic Prize Contests and Intellectual Culture in France, 1670–1794* (Ithaca, NY: Cornell University Press, 2012).

10 Antoine Lilti, *Le Monde des salons: sociabilité et mondanité à Paris au XVIIIe siècle* (Paris: Fayard, 2005).

11 Alexis de Tocqueville, *The Old Régime and the Revolution*, trans. Stuart Gilbert (New York: Anchor Books, 1955).

12 Stéphane Van Damme, *Paris, capitale philosophique, de la Fronde à la Révolution* (Paris: Odile Jacob, 2005).

13 Charlotte Guichard, 'Taste Communities: The Rise of the Amateur in Eighteenth-Century Paris', *Eighteenth-Century Studies*, 45(4) (2012): 519–47.

14 Pierre-Yves Beaurepaire, *L'Espace des francs-maçons: une sociabilité européenne au XVIIIe siècle* (Presses Universitaires de Rennes, 2003).

15 Daniel Gordon, *Citizens without Sovereignty: Equality and Sociability in French Thought, 1670–1789* (Princeton University Press, 1994).

16 Jürgen Habermas, *The Structural Transformation of the Public Sphere: An Inquiry into a Category of Bourgeois Society*, trans. Thomas Burger (Cambridge, Mass.: MIT Press, 1989).

17 Keith Michael Baker, *Inventing the French Revolution: Essays on French Political Culture in the Eighteenth Century* (Cambridge University Press, 1990).

18 For a view of the salon as a place of women's access to the Republic of Letters and the public sphere, see Dena Goodman, *Republic of Letters: A Cultural History of the French Enlightenment* (Ithaca, NY: Cornell University Press, 1994).

19 Stéphane Van Damme, 'Farewell Habermas? Deux décennies d'études sur l'espace public', available online at http://dossiersgrihl.revues.org/682 (accessed 20 May 2014).

20 Arlette Farge, *Dire et mal dire: l'opinion publique au XVIIIe siècle* (Paris: Seuil, 1992). Arlette Farge and Jacques Revel, *Logiques de la foule: l'affaire des enlèvements d'enfants, Paris 1759* (Paris: Hachette, 1988).

21 Steven Laurence Kaplan, *Le Complot de famine: histoire d'une rumeur au XVIIIe siècle* (Paris: Armand Colin, 1983).

22 Chantal Thomas, *La Reine scélérate: Marie-Antoinette dans les pamphlets* (Paris: Seuil, 1989); Simon Burrows, *Blackmail, Scandal, and Revolution: London's French Libellistes, 1758–92* (Manchester University Press, 2006); Robert Darnton, *The Devil in the Holy Water, or, The Art of Slander from Louis XIV to Napoleon* (Philadelphia, Pa.: University of Pennsylvania Press, 2009).

23 Pierre Pachet, *Les Baromètres de l'âme: naissance du journal intime* (Paris: Hachette, 2002).

24 Jean-Marie Goulemot, 'Literary Practices: Publicizing the Private', *The History of Private Life*, vol. III, *Passions of the Renaissance*, ed. Roger Chartier, trans. Arthur Goldhammer (Cambridge, Mass.: Harvard University Press, 1993), pp. 363–95. Antoine Lilti, 'The Writing of Paranoia: Jean-Jacques Rousseau and the Paradoxes of Celebrity', *Representations*, 103 (2008): 53–80.

25 Sara Maza, *Private Lives and Public Affairs: The Causes Célèbres of Prerevolutionary France* (Berkeley, Calif.: University of California Press, 1993).

26 *Dictionnaire des vies privées (1722–1842)*, Olivier Ferret, Anne Marie Mercier-Faivre and Chantal Thomas (eds.), Studies on Voltaire and the Eighteenth Century, 2011:02 (Oxford: Voltaire Foundation, 2011).

27 *Vie de Joseph Balsamo* (Paris: 1791), p. iii.

3

ANDREW CURRAN

Anthropology

In its widest scope, the contemporary use of the term 'anthropology' refers to the study of the human as a physical and social being. To the extent that anthropology is still considered a unified discipline, this field of study is the most capacious of the social sciences, encompassing both forensic palaeontologists analysing the mitochondrial DNA of ancient hominids at one end of the spectrum and urban anthropologists engaging in comparative ethnography and linguistics at the other. And yet, despite the astonishing breadth of contemporary anthropology, there is perhaps one thing that brings together the discipline's practitioners. More so than other social scientists, anthropologists today understandably tend to distance themselves from the work of their intellectual predecessors, be they Nazi Germany's infamous, race-oriented theorists or the legions of nineteenth-century craniologists, pseudo-evolutionists and classification-oriented writers who codified the zoological construction of race.

Enlightenment-era anthropology (or proto-anthropology) appears even more remote to current scholars. In addition to the fact that early practitioners undertook their study of the human from a dizzying number of perspectives that were often linked to history and philosophy, not to mention Scripture or religious beliefs, the term 'anthropology' itself did not yet have the same meaning it does now. Indeed, depending on the specific European tradition, the concept of 'anthropology' often hovered awkwardly between two competing epistemologies. In French, this can be readily seen in the often-republished Jesuit *Dictionnaire de Trévoux* (*Trévoux Dictionary*) (1704). The first entry for this term defined '*anthropologie*' as the 'science that leads us to knowledge of Man', particularly as it related to human anatomy.[1] The second defined '*anthropologie*' as a particular way of anthropomorphizing God himself, as a rhetorical trope that was 'necessary in order to speak of God, and to pass on many ideas [about the Deity]'.[2]

Despite this lexical confusion, many of the preoccupations and innovations associated with 'anthropology', as it emerged in the nineteenth century, came into being during the Enlightenment era. In fact, most specialists who study the eighteenth century believe that the sine qua non of anthropology – the quest for a practicable method of interpreting the human in both physical and social spheres – is actually synonymous with Enlightenment itself. This was the era, after all, when Pope famously declared in his *Essay on Man* (1734) that 'the proper study of mankind is man'.[3] It was also a time of great change when (a) naturalists increasingly interpreted human customs and minds as the products of causal forces acting on humankind's physical essence; (b) the human was placed within the larger category of the animal; (c) speculative deep-time histories of humankind displaced long-standing biblical narratives; and (d) race-based anatomy and classificatory schemes were increasingly superimposed on more supple understandings of human differences.

Studying the eighteenth century's understanding of anthropology is a daunting task. The century's numerous meditations on humankind extend untidily over various disciplines and genres. Comments and speculation on human diversity, human origins, human comportment, human anatomy and (supposedly different types of) human minds appeared in a wide variety of works, not only in first-person travelogues, travel compilations, medical texts and works of natural history, as might be expected, but also in a wide variety of 'secondary sources' that included works of comparative religion, mercantilist texts, novels, poetry and even women's periodicals and children's books. Indeed, textualized Africans, Indians, Laplanders, Asians and Patagonians wove themselves into the fabric of eighteenth-century thought.

Some of the newness of seventeenth- and especially eighteenth-century anthropology was simply quantitative. While Renaissance-era travellers had transformed the basic medieval understanding of the world by recounting their encounters with West Africans and New World peoples, their tales were episodic and fragmentary, much like the era's overall knowledge of non-European spaces and humans. By 1600, however, Europeans (and European travelogues) had begun to fill in many of these gaps. Travelogues recounting landfalls in Asia, Africa and the New World had proliferated to the point where editors were able to synthesize centuries of isolated ethnographic accounts into coherent collections (from the relative comfort of Amsterdam, Bologna, Paris or London). Inspired by early collections of travelogues, including Giovanni Battista Ramusio's *Delle navigationi et viaggi* (*On Travels and Voyages*) (1550–9), Giovanni Botero's *Relationi universali* (*Universal Relations*) (1595), Richard Hakluyt's *Principal Navigations, Voyages, Traffiques and Discoveries of the English Nation* (1598) and Samuel Purchas's *Purchas, His Pilgrimage; or, Relations of the World and the Religions Observed in all Ages* (1613), seventeenth- and eighteenth-century writers produced ever greater collections of travel writing and proto-ethnography. In French, it was the abbé Prévost who produced the most significant Enlightenment-era collection of travel writing, his voluminous *Histoire générale des voyages* (*A General History of Travels*) (15 vols., 1747–59). Based initially on a translation of the Englishman John Green's four-volume *A New General Collection of Voyages and Travels* (1745–7), Prévost's *Histoire* contained a wide-ranging synthesis of travelogues from Africa to Asia.[4] First published in a luxury edition filled with sumptuous engravings supplied by Jacques-Nicolas Bellin, the *Histoire* served as critical reference for Diderot, Voltaire, Helvétius, Rousseau, Raynal and Buffon, among others.

Scholars have long emphasized the critical role that proto-ethnography and cultural relativism played in the high Enlightenment's re-evaluation of the human condition. It was Leibniz's correspondence with Jesuit missionaries in China, who were fascinated with the country's secularizing and universalist philosophy, that prompted him to situate the origins of the era's 'emancipation of reason' in Asia.[5] Similarly, John Locke's consultation of American travelogues convinced him that New World 'savages' represented an early chapter in an overall history of humankind, which led him to assert that 'in the beginning all the World was America'.[6] Among French thinkers, it was Montesquieu who effectively pioneered the use of proto-ethnography as a means of attacking reigning orthodoxies and obscurantism. Early in his career he consulted a series of travelogues, including the *Voyages de monsieur le chevalier Chardin en Perse et autres lieux de l'Orient* (*The Travels of Sir John Chardin in Persia and the Orient*) (1711), to create his satire of Parisian society and the despotism of the harem (and thus French monarchy) in his *Lettres persanes* (*Persian Letters*) (1721). Some twenty-five years later, Montesquieu again drew from a much wider corpus of travelogues to create his pioneering geography- and climate-based assessment of the world's different political systems (*De l'esprit des lois*) (*The Spirit of the Laws*) (1748). Rousseau, too, often looked to non-European peoples as the point of departure for his writings. Most famously, in his *Discours sur l'origine et les fondements de l'inégalité parmi les hommes* (*On the Origin of Inequality*) (1755), Rousseau's text-based knowledge of hunter-gatherer societies allowed him to recount humankind's supposed downfall from happy, simple forest-dweller to dehumanized city denizen. Voltaire, who ridiculed this conjectural history of humankind, was no less a 'user' of the era's travelogues and ethnography. His corpus, which included political writings, plays and novellas, was infused with countless recastings of proto-ethnography culled from the era's travel literature and compilations. In short stories such as 'L'Ingénu' ('The Sincere Huron'), Voltaire conjured up 'foreign' peoples whose naivety was designed to mock religious dogma and the illogic of French customs. More ominously, in texts including his *Essai sur les mœurs et l'esprit des nations* (*An Essay on Universal History, the Morals and Manners of Nations*) (1769), Voltaire cited negative stereotypes derived from travelogues as well as the era's anatomy as 'proof' that non-European human races were so divergent from the norm that they must have had (biological) origins that were distinct from those of the superior white 'species'.[7] Like Voltaire, Diderot also actively engaged with the era's ethnography throughout his career. In 1746, he published the orientalist (and libertine) *Les Bijoux indiscrets* (*The Indiscreet Jewels*), a satire of (French) royal life projected into the court of the sultan Mongogul; in his early (c. 1750) *Encyclopédie* entries, Diderot also produced 'ethnographic musings' of a different sort, for example on cannibalism or the royal pomp of the king of Benin. Later in his career, in his *Supplément au voyage de Bougainville* (*Supplement to the Voyage of Bougainville*) (1772), Diderot conjured up an imaginary Tahitian sexual economy (a system based on the rules and logic of nature) as a means of ridiculing European 'abstractions' such as shame, chastity, abstinence, *coquetterie*, marriage, legal systems and religion. Some eight years later, as an anonymous contributor to abbé Raynal's *Histoire des deux Indes* (*A History of the Two Indies*) (2nd edn, 1774; 3rd edn, 1780), his reprocessing of the era's ethnography became part of one of the most ideologically engaged and progressive anti-colonial readings of the eighteenth century.

The extent to which the high Enlightenment bathed in proto-ethnography can also be seen in the library of the militant atheist baron d'Holbach. According to the inventory of his estate, d'Holbach owned approximately 3,000 works dedicated to theology, jurisprudence, philosophy, metallurgy, chemistry, astronomy, astrology, mythology, rhetoric, belles-lettres, works from Antiquity, history and a 'belle suite de voyages'. Within this sizeable corpus, d'Holbach held hundreds of works containing information on non-European peoples. In addition to a number of indispensable works of geography from Antiquity (including Pomponius Mela and Strabo), d'Holbach owned basic reference works such as d'Anville's dictionary-like synthesis of place names and peoples, his *Géographie ancienne abrégée* (*Compendium of Ancient Geography*) (1763). More important, d'Holbach had purchased a number of important travel compilations. In addition to Prévost's *Histoire générale des voyages*, d'Holbach's library contained Pierre Bergeron's 1735 *Voyages faits principalement en Asie* (*Asian Voyages*) (a compilation of medieval and Renaissance writings on Asia, as well as a history of Sarassins and Tartares); de Brosses's 1756 *Histoire des navigations aux terres australes* (*History of Southern Voyages*) (with a wide variety of redacted accounts including Narborough's, Magellan's and Dampierre's); and Olfert Dapper's 1686 *Description de l'Afrique* (*Description of Africa*) (an astonishing and relatively open-minded processing of hundreds of Dutch travelogues into synthetic chapters). D'Holbach had also purchased (and would draw from) a number of stand-alone travelogues that were household names during his time. These included Dampier's *Nouveau voyage autour du monde* (*Voyage around the World*) (1751), Cook's *Journal during the First Voyage around the World* (1773), *Les Voyages de [Jean-Baptiste] Tavernier en Turquie* (*Tavernier's Voyages in Turkey*) (1703), *Les Voyages de Jean Struys en Moscovie, en Tartarie et en Perse* (*Jean Struys' Voyages in Moscovy, Tartary and Persia*) (1681); *Voyages de monsieur le chevalier Chardin en Perse* (*Voyages of Sir John Chardin in Persia*) (1735); Bosman's *Voyage de Guinée* (*Voyage to Guinea*) (1705); *Voyages du Baron de la Hontan dans l'Amérique septentrionale* (*The Voyages of Lahontan in Northern America*) (1703); *Relation abrégée d'un voyage fait dans l'intérieur de l'Amérique méridionale* (*A Shorter Description of a Voyage in Southern America*) (1745); Lafitau's *Mœurs des sauvages amériquains* (*Customs of the American Indians*) (1724), de Pauw's *Recherches philosophiques sur les Américains* (*Philosophical Investigations on the Americans*) (1768) and Charlevoix's *Histoire de l'Isle Espagnole, ou de Saint-Domingue* (*History of the Island of Espagnola*) (1733) as well as his *Histoire du Japon* (*History of Japan*) (1754). D'Holbach also owned a number of works that were specifically dedicated to the world's diverse creeds and superstitions, one of the major 'ethnological' concerns of his era. In addition to studies of one specific subject, for example *La Religion des Mahométans* (*The Religion of the Muslims*), *Catechismus judæorum* (*Jewish Catechism*) and *Conformité des coutumes de Indiens orientaux avec celles des Juifs, et des autres peuples de l'antiquité* (*A Comparative Study of the Customs of the Eastern Indians with Those of the Jews and Other Peoples of Antiquity*), d'Holbach possessed (and cited) more comprehensive works of comparative religion, chief among them Bernard Picart's beautifully illustrated *Cérémonies et coutumes religieuses de tous les peuples du monde* (*Religious Ceremonies of the World*) (1723).

   While d'Holbach's extensive collection of travelogues, compilations and works of comparative religion may seem difficult to parse, taken as a whole the corpus actually reflects three key facts regarding the era's understanding of ethnography. First is the obvious prominence of the genre of travel literature itself, which had become more popular than theology in d'Holbach's lifetime. Second, the specific works of travel literature that d'Holbach held (and ultimately his synthesis of such material in his own works) extended well beyond the contemporary era; indeed, in keeping with standard practice, the *philosophe*'s library (and conception of non-Europeans as well) was perhaps as historical as it was ethnographic, based as it was on works from Antiquity as well as contemporary travelogues. Third, d'Holbach's library was an international collection, filled with translations of travelogues and compilations first written in English, Dutch and Portuguese, among other languages; this last fact accurately reflects the massive transnational circulation of ethnographic stereotypes taking place during the pre-modern era, an exchange of ideas reinforced both by translators and by the era's plagiarists.

Not surprisingly, one of the most striking features of eighteenth-century ethnography is the remarkable recycling of essentialist ideas that seemed to move uncritically and easily from era to era (and from country to country). While there was perhaps more scepticism vis-à-vis this ethnography than contemporary scholars have indicated, much of the era's unsubstantiated stereotyping clearly had the status of fact. This can be heard in the dogmatic tone used to describe different ethnicities in the era's ethnographic writing, be it first-hand or recycled. On Black Africans, for example, the geographer Didier Robert de Vaugondy claimed that they have 'laws [that] have no other principals than those of an aborted morality and no other consistency than that produced by indolent and blind habits'.[8] Voltaire's view on the same subject was similar: 'the majority of blacks, all the Caffres, are submerged in ... stupidity and will remain huddling there for a long time'.[9] Laplanders were also seen as similarly backwards (or degenerated), dirty and unintelligent, with a 'physiognomy' as savage as their behaviour. As the *Grand dictionnaire géographique* (*Geographical Dictionary*) put it, the Laplander's errant existence in the northern snows had transformed these 'ugly and bent' people into an 'angry', 'brutal', 'superstitious', 'cowardly' and 'fearful' group of humans.[10] Eighteenth-century thinkers generally portrayed Amerindians in a more ambivalent fashion. Some, like the Jesuit missionary and cultural comparatist Jean-François Lafitau, emphasized the merits of this 'pre-civilized' society; others painted a bleak portrait of stupid, crude and retrograde people with no history.[11] Perhaps the only ethnicities to receive generally positive views were the Persians and Chinese (especially the higher classes of these groups). The Chinese, in particular, fascinated the French; Prévost's *Histoire générale des voyages*, for example, contains numerous anecdotes (such as the Pope's Legat Archbishop Carlo Ambrogio Mezzabarba's fascinating audience with the Kangxi Emperor in 1720) that emphasize the sophisticated aspects of a civilization which was seen as rivalling that of Europe. This admiration was conveyed in the *Histoire*'s many Chinese plates, which feature aesthetically pleasing images of Quang-Cheu-Fu (Canton), the Porcelain Tower of Nanking, fleets of Chinese ships, well-ordered royal processions with elephants and the Great Wall.

Scholars interested in the study of race have understandably underscored the prevalence of unshakable xenophobic stereotypes within the era's travel literature. Nonetheless, it is important to note that many of the era's writers repackaged the ethnography found in such 'primary sources' with a variety of intentions in mind. This varied reappropriation of ethnographic 'data' was particularly evident in debates related to the status of the most vexing and economically important category of non-European, the Black African or so-called *nègre*. If all thinkers interested in the Black African 'variety' or 'race' had access to the same basic corpus of travel literature – much of which portrayed the Black African as hypersexual, animalistic, lacking basic cognitive skills and living solely in the present – their reaction to these 'facts' diverged considerably. Jacques Savary, mercantilist author of the often republished *Le Parfait Négociant* (*The Perfect Merchant*) (1675), clearly consulted African travelogues and written accounts from the Caribbean, including ethnographic writing, in order to codify existing trade practices and to reduce this type of human to an African commodity like any other. The Dominican priest and plantation manager Jean-Baptiste Labat put forward a slightly different view in his 1722 *Nouveau voyage aux isles de l'Amérique* (*A New Voyage to the American Islands*). While Labat's overall presentation of the African overlapped with that of Savary's, the Dominican spent much more time explaining how black Africans (whom he described as initially 'idolatrous' and prone to all kinds of sorcery, magic and dealings in 'poison') not only became more docile once converted but that their resulting Christian mentality corresponded perfectly to a life of servitude.[12] Such religious and mercantile views differed markedly from what we find among the thinkers associated with the high Enlightenment. In *De l'esprit des lois* (*The Spirit of the Laws*) (1748), Montesquieu hinted not only that peoples living in torrid zones (Asia and Africa) suffered from physiological and moral shortcomings – such as lax 'fibres' and sloth – but that they might be, alas, more suitable for slavery. In an entirely different context, the proto-physiocrat Victor de Riquetti, marquis de Mirabeau, also engaged with African ethnography within the context of his population-based 'economic' evaluation of the colonial system in his best-selling *L'Ami des hommes* (*The Friend of Man*) (1756). Like the physiocrats who came after him, Mirabeau vilified African chattel slavery and the plantation system as economically illogical and morally corrupt. The paradox of Mirabeau's 'enlightened' position, however, was that it was based, in part, on a brutal disparagement of the African as a poor worker whose 'species' and 'instinct' were distinct from those of Whites. As for the aforementioned atheist baron d'Holbach, neither the natural history of the African nor the fate of African slaves was of any interest to him. What intrigued d'Holbach, not surprisingly, were

African religious practices themselves, which he compared with brutal irony to European monotheism:

> The Laplander who loves a rock, the Negro who prostrates himself in front of a monstrous serpent, at least they see what they venerate: the Idolater gets on his knees in front of a statue in which he believes resides a hidden power ... but the subtle reasoner that we call a theologian, by dint of his unintelligible science, believes that he has the right to mock the Savage, the Laplander, the Negro, and the Idolater ... yet he does not see that he himself is on his knees before a being that only exists in his own mind.[13]

D'Holbach's highly idiosyncratic portrait of Laplanders and Africans is a prime example how 'standard' ethnography was consistently filtered through distinct ideological prisms.

To a large extent, the new and divergent ways that savants were able to interpret non-Europeans during the eighteenth century can be attributed to the freedom afforded by the era's increasingly naturalist orientation. Naturalism not only allowed thinkers such as d'Holbach to desacralize the basic understanding of what it meant to be human but also blurred the barriers between man and machine and man and animal. Perhaps most significantly, it raised profound questions about the origins and status of non-Europeans. Where did Africans and Indians come from, given that the story of Adam and his three sons was no longer a convincing explanation of humankind's origins? What was one to make of Laplanders' minds now that theoreticians including John Locke and Condillac had affirmed that all ideas (culture) came from the senses? Indeed, what were the status and physiology of non-European brains and bodies, both of which often came to maturity in torrid zones, on the frozen tundra or in sparsely populated forests?

While versions of these questions had been posed before the eighteenth century (some during Antiquity), the quest to provide an entirely material explanation of the human species reached new heights during the Enlightenment era, particularly after the 1740s. Not surprisingly, much of this speculation began with the overall re-evaluation of human reproduction. One of the most important works to take up some of these questions was Maupertuis's *Vénus physique* (*The Earthly Venus*), which appeared anonymously in 1745.[14] A freethinking text that conjured up scabrous ideas including aesthetic-based human cross-breeding, *Vénus physique* also put forward what was then a new theory of reproduction (generation) that interjected the possibility of chance and dynamism into the narrative of humankind's origin. According to Maupertuis's vibrant understanding of human reproduction, the different races of men living on the planet could be attributed to curious mutations – like albinos – that became numerous enough that entire tribes were driven off by the more populous and 'original' white race.[15]

It was George-Louis Leclerc, comte de Buffon (working with the imprimatur of Louis XV as the keeper of the Royal Garden), who refined this speculative and admittedly uncertain genealogy of the human in his 1749 'Variétés dans l'espèce humaine' ('Varieties of the Human Species'). At first glance, this hugely influential chapter of the *Histoire naturelle* appears to be a simple pigmentation map of the world's peoples coupled with reductive ethnographic snapshots. And yet, appended to this list of the world's different 'varieties' is what was perhaps the single most influential reconceptualization of the human species during the eighteenth century, Buffon's theory of humankind's monogenesis (or single origin) and subsequent degeneration into different 'types' of humans in diverse climates. Buffon summed up this process best in the fourteenth volume of the *Histoire naturelle*:

> As soon as mankind began to move around the world and spread from climate to climate, man's nature was subject to various alterations; these changes were minimal in temperate regions, [lands] that we presume to be the place of his origin; but these changes increased as man moved farther and farther away and, once centuries had passed, continents had been crossed, offspring had degenerated due to the influence of different lands, and many [people] had decided to settle in extreme climates and populate the desert sands of southern lands and the frozen regions of the north, these changes became so significant and so apparent that it would have been understandable to believe that the *nègre*, the Laplander, and the White constituted different species ... [But] these markings are in no way original [or distinct]; these natural alterations, these differences, being only on the exterior are only superficial. It is [in fact] certain that all humans are nothing more than the same man who has been adorned with black in the torrid zone and who has become tanned and shrivelled by the glacial cold at the Earth's pole.[16]

More so than anyone before him, Buffon explained the existence of non-Europeans within a degenerative chronology according to which human variation was a climate-induced accident produced by an unthinking nature. Not only did the French naturalist free the story of the human species from a biblical framework, he also inserted humankind into a deeper narrative that emphasized a slow, progressive change that was anything but adaptation. This particular view of humankind had significant implications within the history of proto-anthropology. By emphasizing human migration, mutation, miscegenation and racial reversibility, Buffon implicitly rejected a zoological breakdown of humankind into strict categories or 'races'.

Regardless of Buffon's stance on taxonomy (a point to which we will return), eighteenth-century anthropology is now very much associated with the birth of racial classification, clearly the most nefarious expression of what Michel Foucault called the 'Age of the catalogue'.[17] Seemingly more indicative than the thousands of (unstudied and often mind-numbing) pages of descriptive testimony about Laplanders and Africans, the era's human taxonomies function as persuasive emblems of the race-based politics of oppression that was operative in overseas colonies. What is more, eighteenth-century racial schemes also provide fertile hunting-grounds for those historians of race who seek out the antecedents of polygenist theory – the belief that different races of humans came into being separately, had different origins and should be treated accordingly.

The history of racial classification is usually presented (particularly in anthologies) as part of a somewhat linear genealogy. Aristotle had, of course, classed animals into *genera* and species and created a hierarchy according to which man was at the summit.[18] Late medieval and Renaissance classifiers followed suit, but humans, for reasons having to do with man's special status within God's kingdom, were excluded from such taxonomies during the 'age of the bestiary'.[19] Man's reintroduction into taxonomical schemes began in the seventeenth century. In 1684, François Bernier (often called the 'father' of race) published a short article in the widely read *Journal des Sçavans* that divided humankind into four geo-ethnic blocks; he sometimes used the word 'race' and at other times 'species' to refer to the different types of humans he had encountered in his travels. Much more famously, in 1735, Carl Linnaeus published his (then) pamphlet-length *Systema naturae* (*The System of Nature*). Unlike earlier naturalists, Linnaeus took (existing) comparative anatomy studies of humans and animals (apes in particular) and incorporated them into a comprehensive taxonomical framework, a radical move that broke down epistemological and conceptual barriers separating the human from the rest of the world. In the *Systema*, humankind was classed under the category of anthropomorpha, identified by an ability to reason (*sapiens*) and further broken down into racialized categories: *Homo sapiens europaeus albus, americanus rubescens, asiaticus fuscus* and *africanus niger*. While Linnaeus refined this classification in subsequent years by adding both new categories to anthropomorpha and humoral tendencies to his racialized breakdown of humankind, the next well-known intervention in the areas of classification came in 1775, when Johann Friedrich Blumenbach published his *Generis humani* (*On the Varieties of Mankind*).[20]

When considering the history of race, it is critical to bear in mind the huge span of time separating significant attempts at classification. Forty years separate Bernier from Linnaeus; another forty went by between Linnaeus's first edition of the *Systema* and Blumenbach's *Varieties*. Not only did teleological histories of classificatory thought tend to ignore the relative absence of human taxonomies until the last quarter of the century, such narratives also confuse the creation of the category of race with the muddy story of how the category itself took shape. The early 'pioneer' François Bernier, for example, may have anticipated the 'zoological' categorization of human phenotypes in the late seventeenth century, but he lived in an era before (specious) scientific data on different ethnicities allowed naturalists such as Blumenbach and Kant to flesh out the categories and give them an entirely different status from the early unempirical attempts at classing the human. Although Bernier has enjoyed a new and prominent place in the study of race, eighteenth-century naturalists saw his article (although it was certainly cited from time to time) as being closer to idiosyncratic travelogue than to science. Surprisingly enough, a similar remark might be made about Linnaeus's very schematic mid-century rendering of the human race as well, particularly in France. Attacked by Buffon and in the *Encyclopédie* as being arbitrary and reductively schematic, Linnaeus's breakdown of the *Homo sapiens* got little traction in France until much later in the century (c. 1770).

Rather than look at the incremental history of classification schemes themselves, it is perhaps more useful to see how naturalists progressively claimed the right to produce real and meaningful categories based on what they deemed to be unimpeachable evidence. It was, in fact, the increasing materiality and naturalist explanation of the human that set the stage for the zoological construction of race after mid-century. Like many other epistemological shifts during the eighteenth century, the movement towards a more material construction of ethnicities became particularly important during the 1740s. Building on the research of seventeenth-century anatomists including Malpighi and Littré, anatomists such as Pierre Barrère began looking for elemental and race-specific structures within non-Europeans.[21] As a surgeon in Guyana, Barrère dissected African slaves and sought out and 'discovered' an elemental difference in Africans on the level of blood and bile, maintaining that both substances were much darker than in Whites. Several years later, Johann Friedrich Meckel conducted similar (spurious) research on African brains and pineal glands, affirming that they were dark and ashy.[22] Many of these so-called 'discoveries' (along with other anatomical 'findings' identified in subsequent decades) echoed in various scientific journals for more than fifty years.

Anatomical research on human varieties – almost exclusively Black Africans – had a terrific impact on the understanding of humankind's origins more generally. Incrementally but significantly, physiological discoveries prompted naturalists to refashion the aforementioned Buffonian understanding of monogenetic degeneration theory (the belief that one group of humans moved across the globe and degenerated as a function of climate, etc.). Writing in French, the hugely important (and neglected) Dutch naturalist Cornelius de Pauw refined Buffonian degeneration by affirming in his 1768 *Recherches philosophiques sur les Américains* that Africans had undergone a terribly damaging shift that was inscribed in their seminal fluid, a hereditary determinism that belayed any hope of redemption. These views were adopted readily by a number of French thinkers, including the famous naturalist Jacques Valmont de Bomare who, while a Buffonian vulgarizer, nonetheless hinted at a very different type of degeneration theory in his often-republished *Dictionnaire d'histoire naturelle* (*Dictionary of Natural History*) (and presumably in the Paris natural-history classes that he taught).

By the 1770s, the human narrative, which had seemed quite open-ended under Buffon's pen, was being overlaid not only with rigid anatomical structures but also with notions of racial permanence. The French, who had been comparatively wary of classification schemes, were slow to realize the implications of their own research. In Germany, however, naturalists including Blumenbach pored over the works of French and German anatomists and asserted that they had enough evidence for real categories. (Blumenbach initially asserted the existence of four races in his 1775 *On the Varieties of Mankind*.[23]) By the early 1780s, the French had followed in the footsteps of Blumenbach and the other German forerunners in this area (who included Immanuel Kant, Johann Christian Polykarp and August Wilhelm von Zimmermann), putting forward their own zoological classifications, based largely on their reading of the Germans.

The rise of classificatory thought during the last quarter of the eighteenth century is often confused with the rise of anthropology itself. But the status of 'anthropology' during the last decades of the century is difficult to reduce to a simple narrative. Indeed, the way various 'anthropological subjects' were interpreted during this time shifted dramatically as a function of the extreme political forces that were unleashed after 1789, be they the imperatives of the French Revolutionary government, English incursions in the Caribbean or the political manoeuvres of the decidedly pro-colonial Napoleon at the end of the century. What makes Revolutionary-era anthropology even more difficult to grasp is that, to a large extent, ongoing (published) debates on the human species declined considerably for a decade. While some new ethnography in the form of travelogues appeared (and Buffon's *Histoire naturelle* was republished by Deterville), the pre-Revolutionary era's intense discussion of non-Europeans was displaced by other matters.

In retrospect, the only real anthropological 'subject' to remain truly active – and hotly debated – during the Revolutionary era was the ethnology of the Black African. This too can be attributed to the politics of the era. In the first place, members of the Société des Amis des Noirs (c. 1788–93) put the status of France's African slaves on the Revolutionary agenda, lobbying (unsuccessfully) for a cessation of the slave trade. Perhaps more important, in 1791 tens of thousands of African slaves revolted against their French masters on what was then the world's most prosperous island colony, Saint-Domingue (Haiti). Judging from the published accounts of these uprisings, much of the French public clearly entered into an era of increased anxiety about the Caribbean colonies, much of it racialized. This anxiety only intensified twelve years later in 1803, when, after various treaties, betrayals and (under Napoleon) a failed mission to take back the island, the former African slaves living on Saint-Domingue defeated the last of the French colonial forces at Vertières. The loss of this colony, which is rarely acknowledged in contemporary France, can be compared to the American defeat in Vietnam. Small wonder, then, that, with the notable exception of abbé Grégoire's 1808 *De la littérature des Nègres* (*The Literature of Blacks*), French writers during the era of Napoleon tended to turn on the Black African, producing some of the most virulent anti-black 'natural history' ever to appear in print. While perhaps the culmination of the properly racialized views of Africans that had begun in the 1770s, this backlash heralded a new era in anthropology. Not only had benevolent anti-slavery writings (such as those associated with Diderot, Condorcet and Frossard) all but disappeared, early nineteenth-century writers were also far less willing to challenge long-standing and powerful ethnographic beliefs regarding non-Europeans.

As is the case for many other eighteenth-century issues, the legacy of the Enlightenment's anthropology is both complex and ambiguous. During the Enlightenment era, a nexus of institutional, political, colonial and epistemological forces effectively canonized Western civilization in general and an increasingly biologically based notion of a *civilized man* in particular. Indeed, like no era before it, the Enlightenment put forward a new historical understanding of the human that, in addition to producing a secular narrative of humankind that asserted white primacy and non-white degeneration, assumed and explained the historical inevitability of European superiority. Although the precise 'anthropological' explanations of white pre-eminence varied widely, most eighteenth-century thinkers (the primitivist Rousseau included) believed that the majority of non-European human varieties either were trapped in an earlier stage of existence, continuing to regress or were suffering from anatomical liabilities brought on by brutal climates. Little wonder, then, that European powers soon asserted that they had not only the power and intelligence but also the moral obligation to intervene in the rest of the world.

Students of the Enlightenment tend to conflate the era's anthropology and anthropocentrism. While the two may have gone hand in hand during the eighteenth century, they were actually two very distinct sides of Enlightenment thought. Anthropocentrism in its loftiest sense tended towards the study of a universal man, whereas the Enlightenment's anthropology produced a very different type of human geography. Indeed, as a subcurrent of eighteenth-century thought, anthropology often runs *contrary* to the traditional narrative of Enlightenment. It is the very area of enquiry where the era's thinkers confronted the fundamental limits of their more theoretical belief in a universal human condition.

NOTES

1 'Anthropologie', *Dictionnaire universel françois et latin: contenant la signification et la définition des mots de l'une et de l'autre langue la description de toutes les choses naturelles, l'explication de tout ce que renferment les sciences et les arts*, 5 vols. (Paris: F. Delaulne, 1721), vol. I, p. 439.
2 Ibid.
3 Alexander Pope, 'An Essay on Man', *The Major Writings*, ed. Pat Rogers (Oxford University Press, 2008), pp. 270–308, at p. 270.
4 John Green and Thomas Astley, *A New General Collection of Voyages and Travels Consisting of the Most Esteemed Relations, Which Have Been Hitherto Published in Any Language: Comprehending Everything Remarkable in its Kind, in Europe, Asia, Africa, and America*, 4 vols. (London: Thomas Astley, 1745–7).
5 Birgit Tautz, *Reading and Seeing Ethnic Difference in the Enlightenment: From China to Africa* (New York: Palgrave Macmillan, 2007), p. 8.
6 'Thus in the beginning all the World was America, and more so than that is now; for no such thing as Money was anywhere known. Find out something that hath the Use and Value of Money amongst his Neighbors, you shall see the same Man will begin presently to enlarge his Possessions.' John Locke, *Two Treatises of Government* (1689) (Cambridge University Press, 1967), p. 319.
7 Earlier titles and versions of the *Essai* include an unauthorized version, the 1745 *Abrégé de l'histoire universelle* and a version revised by Voltaire, the *Essai sur l'histoire générale et sur les mœurs et l'esprit des nations* (1756). It received its final title in 1769.
8 Didier Robert de Vaugondy, 'Afrique', *Encyclopédie méthodique ou par ordre de matières*, 216 vols. (Paris: Panckoucke, 1782), vol. I, p. 18.
9 Voltaire, 'Essai sur les mœurs et l'esprit des nations et sur les principaux faits de l'histoire depuis Charlemagne jusqu'à Louis XIII', *The Complete Works of Voltaire*, ed. Theodore Besterman (Oxford: Voltaire Foundation), vol. LIV, p. 96.
10 Bruzen la Martinière, *Le Grand dictionnaire géographique et critique*, 10 vols. (Venice: Jean-Baptiste Pasquali, 1737), vol. VI, p. 62.
11 Joseph-François Lafitau, *Mœurs des sauvages amériquains comparées aux mœurs des premiers temps*, 2 vols. (Paris: chez Saugrain l'aîné, 1724).
12 Jean-Baptiste Labat, *Voyage aux Isles: chronique aventureuse des Caraïbes, 1693–1705* (Paris: Phébus Libretto, 1993), p. 152.
13 Pierre-Henry Thiry, baron d'Holbach, *Système de la nature*, 2 vols. (London: 1780), vol. II, p. 238.

14 A large portion of *Vénus physique* was originally published under the title *Dissertation sur le nègre blanc* in 1744.

15 Embryologically oriented speculation also had an unexpectedly significant influence on conceptions of non-Europeans. In the first place, new theories of reproduction (generation) interjected the possibility of chance and dynamism, a 'discovery' that opened the door for more material explanations of varietal or 'racial' difference. Maupertuis's musings on human reproduction were based, for example, on the existence of accidental monsters; these became a metaphor for the contingencies and vagaries of the human species in general.

16 Georges-Louis Leclerc comte de Buffon, *Histoire naturelle, générale et particulière*, 36 vols. (Paris: Imprimerie Royale, 1749–88), vol. XIV, p. 311.

17 Michel Foucault, *Les Mots et les choses* (Paris: Gallimard, 1966), p. 143.

18 Aristotle suggested that there were eleven levels on the 'ladder of life'. Plants occupied the bottom rungs, while reptiles and amphibians were on the middle levels. Mammals were highest in the hierarchy, with humans being at the top. The form of the creature at 'birth' determined its place in the ranking, as sprouts and hatched eggs were deemed lower than live-birthed beings. See Aristotle, *Generation of Animals* (London: William Heinemann, 1943).

19 See Florence McCulloch, *Medieval French and Latin Bestiaries* (Chapel Hill, NC: University of North Carolina Press, 1962) regarding the relationship between beast and human in earlier eras.

20 The number of races increased from four in 1775 to five in the 1781 edition of the *Generis humani*. Blumenbach coined the expression 'Caucasian' in 1795.

21 A famous microscopist, Marcello Malpighi (1628–94) made a fundamental skin-related discovery in 1655: he identified a third and separate layer of gelatinous 'African' skin located in between the outer 'scarf' skin and the inner 'true' skin. Alexis Littré, a prolific member of the Académie Royale des Sciences de Paris, was the first Frenchman to test Malpighi's hypothesis that the black colour of the reticulum was caused by a thick, fatty black liquid.

22 Johann Friedrich Meckel, 'Recherches anatomiques sur la nature de l'épiderme, et du réseau, qu'on appelle Malpighien', *Histoire de l'Académie royale des sciences et belles lettres de Berlin*, 25 vols. (Berlin: Ambroise Haude, 1753), vol. XI, pp. 79–113.

23 Blumenbach's 1775 *Varieties*, in particular, drew from de Pauw in order to assert that, in addition to what he deemed to be the white prototype race, one could distinguish three other degenerate races or general varieties. *The Anthropological Treatises of Johann Friedrich Blumenbach* (London: Longman, Green, et al., 1865), pp. 105–6.

4

PAUL CHENEY

Commerce

Eighteenth-century France was a predominantly rural, agrarian nation whose intellectual and political classes were fascinated by the sometimes halting transformation to a modern economy taking place in their midst. As Guillaume Thomas Raynal wrote in the opening lines of his *Histoire philosophique … des deux Indes* (*A History of the Two Indies*), this process was upending the material, cultural, intellectual and political order of France, Europe and the wider world:

> there has never been an event so important for the human race in general, and for the people of Europe in particular, as the discovery of the new world and the passage to the Indies by the Cape of Good Hope. From that point forward there began a revolution in the commerce, the power of nations, the customs, the industry and the government of all peoples.[1]

For eighteenth-century observers, 'commerce' became an organizing concept of the French Enlightenment, even if the causal role of capitalism in shaping this movement has remained controversial among historians.

Since historical views of the French Enlightenment have been crucially shaped by the historiography of the French Revolution, it is little wonder that the decline of Marxist interpretations of the Revolution has made it more difficult to explain how commerce should fit into our understanding of the Enlightenment. The fate of one landmark text in the modern historiography of the Enlightenment, Jürgen Habermas's *The Structural Transformation of the Public Sphere*, is a case in point. Habermas himself attributed the birth of the public sphere very clearly to the growth in early modern Europe of 'early finance and trade capital'; here the symbiosis between a state hungry for tax receipts and regular loans from bourgeois merchants paved the way for a freer flow of mercantile information and, eventually, critical assessments by the public at large of the State's economic management. The dialogue between state and society so characteristic of Enlightenment social thought, in which the respective forces, influences and

rights of each were carefully weighed against the other, was the result of
the rise of the 'early capitalist system', which 'turned state administration
into a public affair'.[2] But subsequent historians would view the causal role
of capitalism somewhat differently. Keith Michael Baker and others relied
upon key elements of Habermas's thesis – in particular the centrality of public reason in Enlightenment intellectual culture – but the overall thrust of
the 'political culture' model developed by Baker was to reject the sociology,
which pitted bourgeois against aristocrats, that went into many analyses of
Ancien Régime intellectual conflicts. Adherents of the political-culture model
went much further, however, denying that disagreements over authority and
sovereignty were connected to the growing incompatibility between state
and society caused by economic changes operating over the *longue durée* in
France and in Europe as a whole.[3] Generational lassitude with social history
and real weaknesses in the sociology that underpinned Marxian interpretations of the Enlightenment and Revolution encouraged historians to focus
on ideas and representations; but recent attempts to account for developments in the history of Ancien Régime France raise the possibility that, for
at least two reasons, cultural and intellectual historians of the 1980s and
1990s went too far in dismissing the broad material contexts for understanding the origins and development of the French Enlightenment.

First, as historians have exposed in great detail, political economy was
central to many of the constitutional debates – the same debates that have
fascinated intellectual historians working in the political-culture mould –
that dominated intellectual life in Ancien Régime France. No assessment
of the proper form that the French government should take – republic, constitutional monarchy or enlightened despotism – could be plausibly detached from European social evolution since the discovery of the
Americas. Rousseau may have deplored the 'universal dependence' to which
civilized men seeking tranquillity and the 'conveniences of life' submitted
themselves, but, citing Montesquieu, he agreed that modern men who lived
by and through commerce could not be expected to renounce their comfort
and private liberty in exchange for the austere pleasures of direct, popular
government.[4] The pattern of linking constitutional questions to economic
forces was set quite early on in the French Enlightenment when critics such
as Fénelon, Vauban and Boisguillbert urged agrarian reform as a means of
achieving a wider moral regeneration of French state and society. Political
economy was an essential, perhaps even dominant, element of the political
culture of Enlightenment France.

Second, understanding the Enlightenment entails an appreciation of the
material contexts that changed over the course of the long eighteenth century, a period notable for the expansion of domestic luxury industries, the

construction of an astonishingly profitable plantation complex in the Antilles and an expanding trade that linked metropolitan France to Europe and the wider world. The most reliable figures we now possess suggest that the French economy as a whole grew at an annualized rate of 1.2 per cent between 1701 and 1795; foreign trade grew at about twice the annual rate, 2.4 per cent, over roughly the same period, while specifically extra-European trade registered a 3.3 per cent increase. European nations bulked large in France's foreign-trade statistics, but the root of this growth lay in the French Antilles, the source of copious re-exports of sugar, coffee and cotton, and the outlet, in turn, for a host of French products, in particular high-value textiles. Put another way, between 1716–20 and 1787–9, the value of France's European commerce increased by 412 per cent, while its colonial commerce expanded by 1,310 per cent. Because of its role in linking diverse sectors of the economy and in attracting investment capital, foreign trade contributed to growth rates out of proportion to its actual weight in the economy. At between 5.5 and 8 per cent of the economy, foreign trade to all countries contributed between 8.5 and 13 per cent of growth; extra-European trade was even more dynamic, accounting for 4 and 4.74 per cent of GDP but between 6 and 7.5 per cent of overall growth, much of this concentrated in industrial sectors.[5]

Naturally, the tonic effects of foreign trade were most keenly felt in the largest of France's port cities. It is no coincidence that the more successful port cities – Nantes, Bordeaux and Marseille – served as principal ports for economically diverse hinterland areas (Normandy, Brittany, Languedoc and Aquitaine), stimulating manufacturing and agricultural output from these regions. Perche, a small town located in Basse-Normandie, furnishes one example of industrial growth stimulated deep in the hinterland by colonial trade: here, proto-industrial workers produced canvas destined for sailcloth and crude slaves' attire, as well as more elegant muslin fabrics worn by owners, as well as city-dwellers in the luxury-hungry provincial capitals of the French managers Antilles. Bordeaux and Aquitaine held a particularly privileged position in agricultural exports: wines and eaux de vie had ready markets all over Europe and in the French Antilles; as the eighteenth century wore on, moreover, Bordeaux became an important exporter of grains to hungry island colonies. Naval construction and sugar-refining sustained growth in industrial production, rounding out the regional economy and its Atlantic exchanges. While colonial re-exports supplied the most magnificent profits, cross-investments in agriculture and industry served the economic and social ends of a mercantile bourgeoisie that sought to mitigate risk in the fragile environment of colonial commerce while ensuring its social ascent.

The implications for France of this expanding world of commerce were widely discussed among *philosophes*, but no less central to the impact of commerce on the French Enlightenment were the ways in which an increased circulation of goods and accumulation of wealth transformed the habitus of urbanized men and women in France. The French Enlightenment was not simply an intellectual movement but a cultural one whose material aspects influenced a wide range of attitudes and practices. In France, Paris was the centre of these transformations. During the regency of Philippe, the duke of Orléans (1715–23), the centre of court life moved to Paris, where aristocratic courtesans increasingly were constructing sumptuous townhouses (*hôtels particuliers*) from which to assert their wealth, power and cultural authority. Early in the century, much of the wealth that built up the chic *faubourgs* of western Paris came from traditional sources – land, *rentes* (bonds) and royal sinecures – but, particularly after the Seven Years' War, wealth from the West Indies contributed to the luxury construction boom in Paris.[6] The ruinously expensive war for prestige within the plutocratic kernel of the Parisian elites provoked a never-ending process of innovation and refinement that consistently set the French luxury trades ahead of their European competitors. Dressmakers, such as Rose Bertin, established a name for themselves by catering to spendthrift courtesans; on house calls or in their carefully appointed Parisian shops, ever-solicitous *marchands de mode* hunted smaller but more plentiful game, luring socially ambitious or merely bourgeois with the latest refinements. And this competition was not restricted to clothing: houses, interior decor, carriages, hunting paraphernalia, pleasure gardens, wines and gastronomic fantasy were all subject to cycles of refinement, diffusion and renewal.[7] Paris and its elites were at the summit of Europe's new consumer economy, and fashions were diffused socially downward and geographically outward from this privileged centre; the power and intellectual prestige of the French Enlightenment developed in tandem with other forms of Parisian taste-making.

In moving from Versailles to Paris, the court aristocracy carved out a space from which to assert its political and cultural autonomy; in so doing, it helped to create the public sphere, which, along with the market for all sorts of cultural goods, including paintings, grew in size and social inclusiveness. The retreat to Paris helped to fuel the rise of Rococo painting, which was based upon an explicit rejection of official standards of taste promulgated by the Royal Academy of Painting, which stressed the sort of history painting that drew upon edifying, regime-friendly classical subjects. Aristocrats newly arrived from Versailles adorned their townhouses and chateaux with works by Antoine Watteau, François Boucher and Jean-Honoré Fragonard, whose canvases depicted a closed, often mysterious world of eroticism and leisure that reflected the *art de vivre* this class was refining through its private, conspicuous consumption. These works also reflected the values of aspirants to this group, who purchased them in quantity. Although these paintings drew upon popular forms of theatre that were on the rise in Paris – Watteau's famous harlequin Pierrot provides one example – their significance for the development of a more broadly based, highly politicized public sphere lay elsewhere. The growth in the market for aristocratic confections was only part of a wider trend, in which the creative energies and commercial potential of genre painting – still life, portraiture, landscapes – were unleashed in the salons, shops and ateliers of Paris. For a number of reasons, these paintings and their public called forth a whole new apparatus of art expertise and criticism: genre paintings offended the official canons of taste established by the Royal Academy; they were purchased by a public unsure of its right to assert aesthetic judgements; and they were acquired through new, more explicitly commercial channels.[8] Works by painters such as Jean-Baptiste Siméon Chardin depicted socially modest individuals with sensitivity and grace, investing their faces, activities and the objects of their domestic surroundings with dignity and meaning. Material objects themselves, these paintings demonstrate the valorization of everyday life made possible by widely experienced improvements in material life.[9] Others, like Jean-Baptiste Greuze, one of Rousseau's favourite painters, took a more didactic route onto the psychological terrain of sensibility. *Philosophes*, seeking aesthetic alternatives to aristocratic decadence and the brittle grandeur of the absolutist state, advanced these burgeoning forms of artistic expression through their critical writings. Even if art critics such as Denis Diderot did not call upon an oppositional public opinion so much as they sought to create one through their writings, the existence of a well-developed critical apparatus by the 1780s demonstrates the manner in which the expansion of consumer markets, in this case for art, helped to produce publics and forms of criticism characteristic of the French Enlightenment.[10]

The rise of genre painting, and its thematic and commercial extension beyond the closed world of privilege, suggests that while the aristocracy may have provided a necessary cultural and economic stimulus, its values were not entirely dominant and only partly defined new patterns of consumption. Even the male wig – symbol if ever there were one of the dominance of courtly style in seventeenth- and eighteenth-century France – was subject to modern notions of comfort and naturalness that contravened the constraint and formality of courtly fashion. The loss of popularity of the full-bottom wig worn by Louis XIV and the spread of the shorter, more comfortable and easily maintained bag wig symbolized a broader cultural reorientation in France after the Regency. Personalized experiences of pleasure, beauty and comfort (*commodité*) began to trump the overtly status-bound norms of consumption that characterized the high aristocracy. Tellingly, while the huge full-bottom wig was baptized the 'folio', the more convenient bag wigs were called 'quarto', 'octavo' and 'duodecimo' – a nod to the more portable, cheaper and hence more accessible book formats that were being produced for an expanding eighteenth-century readership.[11] The adoption in 1783 by none other than Marie Antoinette of an uncossetted, loosely draped muslin dress called a *gaulle* shows the degree to which naturalness and comfort began to inform elite notions of elegance.[12] In the home, dishware, furniture (including beds) and heating technology began to emphasize comfort, utility and privacy over the constraining norms of aristocratic display.[13] The comfortable, unostentatious and morally unobjectionable comfort that some commentators called 'luxe de bienséance' (seemly luxury) was the product of an *embourgeoisement* of French cultural norms over the eighteenth century.

The spread of one tropical commodity, coffee, encouraged new forms of consumption and sociability in Enlightenment France. Cafés were a fixture of Parisian life since the seventeenth century, as Jacques Savary des Brulons observed in his *Dictionnaire universel de commerce* (*Universal Dictionary of Commerce*): 'The Parisian cafés are for the most part magnificently decorated spaces, adorned with marble tables, mirrors and shining crystal where respectable city people [*d'honnêtes gens de la ville*] get together for the pleasure of conversation, to learn the news, and to sip this drink.'[14] Up until the mid eighteenth century, Paris cafés combined and reinforced three growing categories of consumption in a novel social milieu: luxury goods (Savary's mirrors, marble and crystal); the periodical press (papers and *libelles* were read aloud and circulated hand to hand); and the stimulants (coffee, chocolate and sugar) coming from American colonies. At first, these cafés attracted the *beau monde* of Paris, and, in contrast to London, women of quality freely entered them. But, as coffee production increased and the price of this beverage fell within reach of the 'populuxe' consuming classes, the social significance and dynamic of Parisian café life changed: after mid-century, cafés were increasingly regarded as male, proletarian places to be avoided by people of quality – especially women. Café sociability further segregated more strictly along social and occupational lines: *philosophes* such as Franklin, Rousseau, Voltaire, Diderot, and d'Alembert met for serious discussion at the Procope, while merchants and artisans gathered at their own occupationally defined haunts to exchange professional gossip or news. Later in the century, the Palais-Royal, home to many shops and cafés, came under the ownership of Philippe d'Orléans, the future Philippe d'Egalité. Because the immunity from police scrutiny granted to a prince of the blood extended to his property, the Café de Foy, located in the Palais-Royal, began to attract a highly politicized clientele who could converse more freely there.

Consequently, the Café de Foy earned the sobriquet 'Estates-General of the Palais-Royal' during the Revolution. Respectable members of the upper crust retired to their homes, continuing to consume coffee in small groups or privately, accompanied by elaborate serving paraphernalia – yet another niche of luxury and 'populuxe' production in eighteenth-century France. In the case of coffee, a widening circle of consumption helped to expand production in the Antilles and to push down prices, bringing coffee within the reach of still more consumers in what were initially mixed spaces of sociability and consumption. But this materially and socially democratizing market logic, widely celebrated by scholars of the consumer revolution, was neither inevitable nor durable: social hierarchies – some old, some more recently evolved – reasserted themselves relatively quickly.

The history of consumption has enabled historians to widen their view of Enlightenment culture and therefore of the people who might have had access to it; moving beyond the world of arts and letters, moreover, invites a more experiential analysis of the modes of Enlightenment. The shift in perspective to material culture makes possible a more precise description, in certain domains, of the linkages between commercial expansion and cultural transformations. To those who had access, the sensorium of the new consumer economy – a self-renewing spectacle of sights, sounds, textures and tastes – dignified daily life in a way that reinforced the celebration of utility, comfort and material progress found in the pages of the *Encyclopédie*.[15] But even as the market liberated urban consumers by breaking down certain social hierarchies and opening up new forms of cultural expression, it also subtly enforced existing hierarchies or brutally asserted new ones. The same may be said of France's eighteenth-century Republic of Letters, which grew thanks to realignments within a modestly expanded elite rather than to a process of wholesale cultural democratization as we might conclude from the recent historiographical emphasis upon a new consumer economy. Robert Darnton describes the transformation, by the final decades of the eighteenth century, of France's literary and scientific public sphere into a greasy pole, with members of the high Enlightenment establishment dominating the salons and academies, enjoying state protection and sinecures by dint of close – and therefore necessarily scarce – ties to Parisian ruling classes.[16] Turning to the famous salons, the *locus classicus* of the French Enlightenment's democratized sociability, Antoine Lilti has found instead a world utterly dominated by traditional elites, in which dependent *philosophes* served as chic accessories, the new must-haves in a constantly evolving world of competitive display.[17]

Although literate elites and those who surrounded them in Paris and in provincial capitals both reflected upon and inhabited a world transformed by commerce, the French economy as a whole remained rural, agrarian and traditional. Until well into the mid nineteenth century, agricultural production outweighed other sources of wealth, including trade and industry; rates of urbanization, occupational structures and demographic patterns reflected this basic fact. On the eve of the Revolution of 1789, 78 per cent of France's 29 million inhabitants lived in the countryside, and 87 per cent of these rural dwellers (and 67 per cent of the population as a whole) made their living primarily from agricultural pursuits.[18] Although Paris and certain Atlantic port cities enjoyed some population growth in the eighteenth century, France's rate of urbanization remained essentially static. Demographic growth occurred mainly in the countryside – precisely the pattern one would expect in a traditional, agrarian economy where low crop yields strictly limit the possibility of growth among urban, non-agricultural populations. The situation was much different in Great Britain, which experienced galloping population growth *and* urbanization throughout the eighteenth century, thanks to industrialization accompanied by gains in agricultural productivity; London nearly doubled its already immense population to about a million, while flourishing port and new industrial cities such as Manchester, Bristol, Glasgow and Dublin grew like fungi, from virtually nothing to rich agglomerations that concentrated industry, trade and banking in one urban centre and its hinterland. This pattern had existed in the Low Countries and in Italy for some time, although these regions experienced comparative declines in the eighteenth century. Despite some signs of consolidation and centralization, France's urban system remained characteristic of the great agrarian monarchies where juridical, administrative and, naturally, fiscal cadres were distributed relatively evenly among urban centres situated close to primary agricultural producers. Paris did not grow at the expense of large provincial cities such as Lyon and Bordeaux, but it profited by reinforcing the links between central and peripheral nodes of the French urban system.[19]

The persistence of rural, peasant France was mirrored in the absolutist state and in the elites that simultaneously served and exploited country-dwellers through the management of estates, the administration of justice, the maintenance of order and the dispensation of charity. Logically enough, land remained the source of social and political power among the First and Second Estates (the clergy and the nobility) and attracted investment by risk-averse and socially ambitious bourgeois. Landed wealth also ensured the existence of a large and so-to-speak rural bourgeoisie – the army of pettifogging lawyers, estate stewards and tax collectors necessary to sort out the baroque array of rents, dues and taxes to which a single plot of land might be liable, and which enriched the Church, the State and noble landlords.

France's seigneurial system on the eve of the Revolution was an immense source of wealth for landholding elites and a veritable permanent employment act for petty officialdom, but not necessarily an efficient conduit for agricultural surplus or a forcing ground of dynamic mercantile elites.

The comparatively high shipping cost, low value and short shelf-life of many agricultural products ensured that they were usually consumed locally, so that intermediate economic activities such as rough manufacture, transportation and food-processing also remained evenly distributed among the provinces, resisting the funnelling into large cities more natural to financial operations, high-value manufacture and, later, industrialized production. In contrast to England, where comparatively higher rates of industrialization and urbanization favoured lower ages of marriage and growing birth rates, France's peasantry remained stubbornly 'Malthusian' in its habits, limiting family size in order to prevent the division of agricultural land that large cohorts of children and relatively egalitarian inheritance customs produced. France's population grew by 30 per cent over the course of the eighteenth century, while Great Britain's leaped by 71 per cent.[20] In the absence of large productivity gains, even this comparatively modest increase in population put pressure on the incomes of rural dwellers, who struggled with land hunger, increasing rents and a burden of taxation that penalized non-privileged landholders in the form of the *taille*, France's land tax.[21] Rural workers, representing the overwhelming mass of the French population, were excluded by poverty from participating in the new consumer economy. The situation among the urban working classes is much less clear-cut: inflation unquestionably ate away at real wages over the course of the century, but there is ample evidence from other sources that many workers held their own and were thus able to afford new 'populuxe' goods and enjoy the new forms of sociability they engendered. But even if urban participation in the consumer economy was more broad-based than pessimistic accounts of the eighteenth century have led us to believe, France nevertheless remained polarized between, on the one hand, a numerically small urban world that was stimulated by thriving Atlantic commerce, a world-leading luxury industry, consumers with disposable income who helped to shape taste and, on the other, a preponderating rural world that, despite some pockets of growth and dynamism, generally remained cut off from the material and cultural advances that characterized the French Enlightenment.

In an era when economic progress was supposed to be entirely remaking Europe and its colonial periphery, the spectacle of two incommensurate and in some senses opposed worlds made commerce a persistent topic of discussion in Enlightenment France.[22] For some it was a question of asserting the value of past social forms and habits of material life; but for the overwhelming majority of *philosophes*, men of state or merchants, the problem of political economy – or what was often termed 'the science of commerce' – was how best to reconcile commercial and agrarian France into a wealthy and progressive, but politically and socially stable whole. Two related circumstances raised the stakes of this discussion and helped define it. First, France's commercial expansion took place against the backdrop of escalating conflict with another commercial power, Great Britain. Early modern commercial dynamos such as the United Provinces and Great Britain posed economic threats, but the implication that commercial prosperity was the result of ostensibly republican political and social forms posed another sort of menace to the monarchical nations that would imitate them. *Philosophes* sought a more systematic understanding of the circuits of production, exchange and consumption through the science of commerce, but they also addressed broader questions of political and cultural identity. Second, rivalry between commercial empires became exceedingly costly as the eighteenth century progressed; France's agrarian economy seemed, in contrast to that of Great Britain, unable to meet the expenses of conflicts such as the War of Spanish Succession (1700–13), the War of Austrian Succession (1740–8), the Seven Years' War (1756–63) and the American War of Independence (1776–83). Disagreements among French elites over war finance and taxation sharpened over the course of the century, leading some to question the desirability and affordability, for France, of modern commercial empire. In this context, the *philosophes* developed approaches to political economy that can be divided into three broad categories: republican, physiocratic and a final camp that argued for commercial monarchy. Few writers advanced these approaches in their pure form, but these three ideal types provide useful points of triangulation for navigating the highly varied *topos* of intellectual responses to the rise of commerce.

When republican political thinkers in eighteenth-century France considered the rise of commerce in modern states, their approach was informed by a rejection of two widely shared premises of early modern political economy: first, materialist utilitarianism; and, second, the belief that the market was capable, as the English man of letters Bernard Mandeville put it, of turning the 'private' vice of greed into the 'publick benefits' of prosperity and civility.[23] Republican political thinkers only ruefully accepted a third premise: the economy had come to occupy a central place in modern statecraft. Rousseau's *Encyclopédie* article 'Économie or Œconomie' counter-intuitively sought to redefine the fundamental question of political economy not as production of wealth but as the maintenance of 'virtue': 'the greatest power [*ressort*] of public authority lies in the hearts of citizens'.[24] Far from calming egoistic passions and redirecting individual desires for gain towards the public good, the market favoured the polarization of wealth and the 'tyranny of the rich' against the poor, who, deprived of property and liberty, became 'evil slaves' who cravenly subverted the public good. A well-managed polity did not encourage the accumulation of wealth but rather kept it within strictly defined limits in order to prevent inequality and corruption: 'the word *economy* is best understood as the wise management of what one has, rather than the means of acquiring what one doesn't'.[25] Only an equality of poverty – some republicans merely insisted upon a moderation or 'médiocrité' of fortunes – could assure the reign of virtue. Although Rousseau believed in the necessity of property for subsistence and public order, his republican political economy was premised fundamentally upon the denigration of production, exchange and consumption. For republicans such as Rousseau, the sphere of needs was to remain subordinate, lest it encroach upon and corrupt the domain of freedom: politics. If by political economy one means the re-evaluation of the role of the economy in statecraft, and its promotion to a position of equality or even primacy above traditional territorial, dynastic or spiritual claims, republican political thinkers were profoundly *un*economic in their point of view. This somewhat abstract description is worth insisting upon because it helps one to differentiate thinkers such as Rousseau from the many *philosophes* who were in no sense republican but who nevertheless criticized the tendency to luxury in modern commercial societies and preached respect for wholesome agricultural pursuits. Such a description also helps explain the flexibility of republican political economy: while Rousseau and the abbé Mably sought an alternative social model in the supposed egalitarianism of the Roman republic, others used the language of republicanism to assert the rights of France's military aristocracy, whose position had been eroded by the rise of commerce among European states. Republican political economy offered a way of looking backwards, or at least of finding an alternative to a thoroughly modern France whose values and social structure were determined by commerce.

Although the physiocrats argued insistently that France should play upon its natural strengths by emphasizing agriculture over commerce, this prescription was commonplace by the time François Quesnay, the founder of physiocracy, began writing publicly in the *Encyclopédie* in 1757. In his seminal articles 'Grains', 'Fermiers' ('Farmers'), and 'Impôts' ('Taxes'), Quesnay set forth a programme for a dynamic sort of agricultural capitalism that had nothing to do with the misty-eyed elegies to bygone rural virtue proffered by Fénelon in his urtext of Enlightenment pastoralism, *Les Aventures de Télémaque* (*The Adventures of Telemachus*) (1699). The highly commercialized system of agriculture the physiocrats envisioned had no room for the small peasant proprietor who was both exploited and protected by France's seigneurial system; the key words in this forward-looking order were scale, specialization, investment and *laissez-faire*. Indeed, as Tocqueville would later remark, while the physiocrats were hardly self-conscious Revolutionaries, the ensemble of the physiocratic reform programme implied the complete demolition of the system of privilege that characterized Ancien Régime France. For the physiocrats, France's economic problems were fundamentally political: the countryside of an inherently rich nation was largely sunk in misery, while the State and the mercantile interests to which it was captive pursued illusory profits in overseas commerce. Both of these facts resulted from France's feudal heritage, and the way forward, according to the physiocrats, was a system of law that respected property, productivity and freedom of contract.

But the physiocrats distinguished themselves by more than their insistence that only agriculture was the source of value and hence the true basis for a prosperous economy; they couched their economic doctrine in a highly rigorous, deductive language that admitted of no interpretation or variation. Two consequences flowed from canonizing Quesnay's famously eye-strain-inducing *Tableau économique* (*Economic Table*) as the centrepiece of physiocratic economic science. In so doing, first, the physiocrats constituted themselves as a group (some called them a sect) that could flaunt the same epistemological coherence and rigour as the natural sciences: this strategy ensured respect from an enlightened reading public that saw genuine social progress as premised upon scientific discovery and application. Second, if the conclusions of the *Tableau économique* were derived by a special scientific procedure valid in all places and in all times, it put the physiocrats' policy prescriptions beyond the ineffectual wrangling that characterized economic reform efforts in eighteenth-century France. When Quesnay adopted the term 'enlightened despotism' (*despotisme éclairé*), he did so in a deliberately provocative gesture against aristocratic republicans in the *parlements* who opposed the Crown's reform efforts in the name of freedom from despotism. In this context, Quesnay's call for 'economic government' (*gouvernement économique*) meant de-politicizing governance, converting it into a form of rational administration according to timeless laws of nature. Economic government also meant the affirmation, utilitarian in essence, of individuals' material well-being as the origin and final end of statecraft; the protection of property, which derived from the individual's natural right to ensure survival by appropriating the fruits of nature, was the only universally verifiable basis for government and defined its scope: 'it is sufficient for government to see to the growth of profits out of the kingdom's wealth, not to harass industry and to leave to citizens the capacity to follow their investment choices [*de laisser aux citoyens la facilité et le choix des dépenses*].'[26]

Quesnay and his followers' appeal to science, combined with their lucid insistence that every route to widespread prosperity must pass through the French countryside, ensured them a wide and appreciative audience, but others envisioned the modernization of France's economy and society along quite different lines.

For most contemporary observers, commercial monarchy was a *fait accompli* in eighteenth-century France; those who approved this fact affirmed two things that were rejected by republicans *and* by most physiocrats. First, France had arrived historically at a point where luxury and the commerce that supported it were necessary for widespread prosperity and the maintenance of France's international stature; they also thought this was a positive development. Such was the position of Jean-François Melon, whose *Essai politique sur le commerce* (*Political Essay on Commerce*) (1734) remained widely cited throughout the eighteenth century, and of Voltaire, who issued a direct riposte to anti-luxury republicans in *Le mondain* (*The Man of the World*) (1736):

> Others may with regret complain
> That 'tis not fair Astrea's reign,
> That the famed golden age is o'er
> That Saturn, Rhea rule no more:
> Or, to speak in another style,
> That Eden's groves no longer smile.
> For my part, I thank Nature sage,
> That she has placed me in this age:
> ...
> I love the pleasures of a court;
> I love the arts of every sort;[27]

Second, although many advocates of commercial monarchy saw room for economic reforms that would help France compete against nations like Great Britain, they accepted the social hierarchies upon which Ancien Régime France was based. This situation meant several things simultaneously: a society of orders that divided all people into status groups – the nobility, the clergy and the third estate; a corporate society in which groups and the individuals that belonged to them enjoyed rights based on the inheritance, purchase or conferral of privileges; and a society marked by sometimes extreme inequalities of wealth.

No advocates of commercial monarchy denied the importance of agriculture in France; however, they maintained the entirely plausible conviction that the two Frances – based on agriculture on the one hand and commerce and industry on the other – must develop simultaneously as they had in Great Britain. *Philosophes* such as Montesquieu conceived of this fusion between the two Frances in broadly social and political terms rather than in purely sectoral ones. For Montesquieu, promoting this fusion meant encouraging the development of French commerce by freeing it from the heavy hand of the absolutist state, whose rent-seeking behaviour distorted markets and threatened the financial system upon which modern commerce rested and states depended. The collapse of John Law's financial system in 1721 was one such event that informed Montesquieu's *De l'esprit des lois* (*Spirit of the Laws*) (1748). But for Montesquieu the corollary to this proposition was that the French nobility – along with its odious and admittedly artificial privileges – should be protected from the democratic, socially levelling tendencies at work in commercial societies: commerce should be left to merchants and government to aristocrats. Maintaining the nobility and their privileged institutions of governance (the *parlements* and *états* of Ancien Régime France) would protect *all* French people against monarchical despotism; moreover, Montesquieu argued, preserving aristocratic *mœurs* (customs, manners) would help France maintain its edge in the production of luxury goods. Other writers in this tradition, like the abbé Gabriel François Coyer, believed that nobles should be allowed and even encouraged to participate in commerce, and that the Crown should promote commerce by ennobling successful merchants. Coyer disagreed with Montesquieu on certain points, but in using ennoblement as an enticement, like Montesquieu, he proposed to reorient the institutions, manners and hierarchies of Ancien Régime France away from the pursuit of military conquest towards commercial prosperity while avoiding disruptive social changes. The circle of economic writers surrounding Vincent de Gournay, France's intendant of commerce from 1751 to 1758, articulated this basic position from numerous perspectives, advocating reforms, gently criticizing the French state (often from within) and probing the manner and degree to which France could plausibly imitate its closest commercial rivals while maintaining its coherence and identity as an Ancien Régime monarchy.

In this respect, Montesquieu and members of the Gournay circle represented the consensus position on commerce in Enlightenment France. The material benefits of commercial expansion were disputed and fretted about in certain quarters, but never seriously called into question: the lively spectacle of Paris and provincial capitals, enriched by commerce and projecting an unprecedented cultural prestige, ensured this result. Most observers were aware of the impasses that stood in the way of integrating the other, rural France fully into this new economic system, and they feared the loss of France's commercial empire and the internal political divisions that could result. The Seven Years' War gave a heady foretaste of both threats. But the basic question for most *philosophes* was not whether but *how* commerce should be integrated within the traditional structures of French society. The element of socio-political critique that was ever-present in French political economy – particularly in its physiocratic and republican variants – issued from an essentially self-confident, prosperous and increasingly comfortable nation.

NOTES

1 Guillaume Thomas Raynal, *Histoire philosophique et politique des établissements et du commerce des Européens dans les deux Indes* (Amsterdam: 1773), vol. I, p. 1.
2 Jürgen Habermas, *The Structural Transformation of the Public Sphere*, trans. Thomas Burger (Cambridge, Mass.: MIT Press, 1989), pp. 20, 24.
3 Keith Michael Baker, *Inventing the French Revolution: Essays on French Political Culture in the Eighteenth Century* (Cambridge University Press, 1990), pp. 171–2.
4 Jean-Jacques Rousseau, 'Discours sur l'origine et les fondements de l'inégalité parmi les hommes' (1755), *Œuvres complètes* (Paris: Gallimard, 1964), vol. III, pp. 153, 187 and 282–3.
5 Guillaume Daudin, *Commerce et prospérité: la France au XVIIIe siècle* (Paris: Presses Universitaires de l'Université Paris-Sorbonne, 2005), pp. 24, 397, 406 and 415. The statistical ranges given indicate the admitted imprecision of Daudin's estimates.
6 Allan Potofsky, 'Paris-on-the-Atlantic from the Old Regime to the Revolution', *French History*, 25 (1) (2011), 89–107.
7 Natacha Coquery, *L'Hôtel aristocratique: le marché du luxe à Paris au XVIIIe siècle* (Paris: Publications de la Sorbonne, 1998), chaps. 2–3. On the plutocratic kernel of the aristocracy, see Guy Chaussinand-Nogaret, *The French Nobility in the Eighteenth Century: From Feudalism to Enlightenment* (Cambridge University Press, 1985), pp. 52–9.
8 Andrew McClellan, 'Watteau's Dealer: Gersaint and the Marketing of Art in Eighteenth-Century Paris', *The Art Bulletin*, 78 (3) (1996): 439–53.
9 Daniel Roche, *France in the Enlightenment*, trans. Arthur Goldhammer (Cambridge, Mass.: Harvard University Press, 1998), p. 610 passim.
10 Thomas E. Crow, *Painters and Public Life in Eighteenth-Century Paris* (New Haven, Conn.: Yale University Press, 1985), chap. 4.
11 Michael Kwass, 'Big Hair: A Wig History of Consumption in Eighteenth-Century France', *The American Historical Review*, 111 (3) (2006): 631–59.
12 Caroline Weber, *Queen of Fashion: What Marie Antoinette Wore to the Revolution* (New York: H. Holt, 2006), pp. 160–3.
13 Daniel Roche, *A History of Everyday Things: The Birth of Consumption in France, 1600–1800*, trans. Brian Pearce (Cambridge University Press, 2000), chaps. 7–8.
14 Jacques Savary des Brulons, 'Caffe', *Dictionnaire universel de commerce* (Paris: 1741), vol. II, p. 30.
15 Roche, *A History of Everyday Things*, pp. 250–5; Roche, *France in the Enlightenment*, chap. 19.

16 Robert Darnton, 'The High Enlightenment and the Low-Life of Literature in Pre-revolutionary France', *Past and Present*, 51 (1) (1971): 81–115.

17 Antoine Lilti, *Le Monde des salons: sociabilité et mondanité à Paris au XVIIIe siècle* (Paris: Fayard, 2005), chap. 5.

18 P. M. Jones, *The Peasantry in the French Revolution* (Cambridge University Press, 1988), p. 4; for comparable figures, see Daudin, *Commerce et prospérité*, p. 28.

19 Bernard Lepetit, *The Pre-industrial Urban System: France, 1740–1840* (Cambridge University Press, 1994), pp. 82–91; Jan de Vries, *European Urbanization, 1500–1800* (Cambridge, Mass.: Harvard University Press, 1984), p. 91; Paul Bairoch, 'Une nouvelle distribution des populations: villes et campagnes', in Jean-Pierre Bardet and Jacques Dupâquier (eds.), *Histoire des populations de l'Europe*, vol. II: *La Révolution démographique, 1750–1914* (Paris: Fayard, 1997), pp. 139–229.

20 Bairoch, 'Villes et campagnes', p. 197.

21 Jones, *Peasantry*, pp. 30–45.

22 The notion of two Frances is explored in Edward Whiting Fox, *History in Geographic Perspective: The Other France* (New York: W. W. Norton, 1971).

23 These phrases come from the title of Bernard Mandeville's famous polemic, *The Fable of the Bees; or, Private Vices, Publick Benefits* (1723) (Indianapolis, Ind.: Liberty Fund, 1988).

24 Jean-Jacques Rousseau, 'Économie ou œconomie', in Denis Diderot and Jean-Baptiste le Rond d'Alembert (eds.), *Encyclopédie, ou dictionnaire raisonné des sciences, des arts et des métiers, par une société de gens de lettres* (Paris: Briasson, 1751–88), 17 volumes of articles, 11 volumes of plates, vol. V, pp. 340–1. Available at http://encyclopedie.uchicago.edu (University of Chicago: ARTFL Encyclopédie Project, spring 2013 edn, ed. Robert Morrissey) (accessed 21 May 2014).

25 Rousseau, 'Économie ou œconomie', pp. 342, 345.

26 François Quesnay, 'Grains', *Œuvres économiques complètes et autres textes*, ed. Christine Théré, Loïc Charles and Jean-Claude Perrot (Paris: Institut National d'Études Démographiques [INED], 2005), vol. I, pp. 161–212, at p. 204.

27 From *The Works of Voltaire*, ed. Tobias Smollett and trans. William Flemming (New York: E. R. Du Mont, 1901), vol. XXXVI, pp. 84–5.

5

J. B. SHANK

Science

There was no such thing as science in the French Enlightenment, and this is a chapter about it.[1] There were, of course, sciences in Enlightenment France, many of them, and they were essential to the Enlightenment no matter how we define the term (as a historical period, a cultural or philosophical movement, a normative agenda, etc.). But since science in the portentous singular is a creation of the late nineteenth century, only by shearing the term 'Enlightenment' of many of its most important referents – not least its attachment to the eighteenth century – can we sustain the category 'Enlightenment science' as a singular, monolithic concept.

The *Encyclopédie* edited by Denis Diderot and Jean-Baptiste le Rond d'Alembert illustrates the point, for, while this most scientific of Enlightenment tomes has an entry on 'science', the article defines the term traditionally as secure and reliable knowledge in any domain, not as some separate kind of extra-reliable knowing. Within this un-modern understanding, talk of a science of poetry or a science of painting could proceed without generating any dissonance, and apparent sciences such as engineering or medicine could be placed outside the sciences proper because of their reliance on artful craft. D'Alembert's 'Système figuré des connaissances humaines' ['Figurative System of Human Knowledge'], which taxonomically opens the *Encyclopédie*, illustrates the modernizing changes afoot around 1750, since many of the fields we would call 'science' appear under his rubric of 'Reason', while poetry, painting and the literary arts are all grouped separately under the rubric of 'Imagination'. This is the division we would expect. But a third category, 'Memory', challenges our sense of order by including both planetary science and the literary art of the memoir. 'Reason' also includes rhetoric, grammar and the other 'arts of communication', together with seemingly scientific fields such as mathematics. In short, any attempt to find our modern disciplinary divisions in d'Alembert's tree, or in the *Encyclopédie* more generally, is doomed to frustration.

The noun '*scientifique*', which is the French equivalent of the English word 'scientist', also does not appear in the *Encyclopédie*, nor in the thousands of eighteenth-century French texts contained in the database of the American Research Treasury of the French Language. This absence is not surprising, for the word denoting a specialist practitioner of disciplinary scientific research is a nineteenth-century neologism coined to describe the new professional scientific researchers found in the new universities born in that era.[2] Science pursued by specialized professional scientists did not emerge in the familiar modern form until after 1815, and the use of such terms as '*savant*', '*philosophe*' and '*gens de lettres*' in the *Encyclopédie* to describe people we would today call '*scientifiques*' makes clear that science in the contemporary unified and disciplinary sense was not a part of the eighteenth-century Enlightenment's conceptual apparatus.

So there was no singular modern science in the French Enlightenment, and we must question any firm binary that isolates art, literature and other seemingly unscientific pursuits from some imagined monolith called Enlightenment science. But since there were many influential Enlightenment sciences, and science in the Enlightenment was composed of them, how should we handle this terminological anachronism? Is the solution simply to add an 's' at the end of this chapter's title and then move on? Yes and no. Pluralizing the sciences of the French Enlightenment allows us to see the various ways that scientific practices, values and results were crucial to the French Enlightenment as a period, a movement and a historical agent. Yet simply to shift to the plural and speak of the many sciences in Enlightenment France is not enough, given the influence of an important tradition of Enlightenment scholarship that makes the anachronistic slippage into the portentous singular a foundation for its understanding of Enlightenment. In this tradition, which is anything but moribund in Enlightenment scholarship today, modern science is said to have been born in the eighteenth century, and Enlightenment finds its interpretive unity as the progenitor of this consequential world-making force.

This tradition begins in the Enlightenment itself with the twin German philosophical pillars of Kant and Hegel. The former isolated universal *Wissenschaft* – the specific Enlightenment science of Newtonian mathematical physics was what Kant actually had in mind – as the pure, critical ground upon which all other categories of knowledge (metaphysics, morality, religion, aesthetics) should be built. Kant's critical project laid the foundation for the new disciplinary machinery of modern scientific knowing by drawing clear lines between science proper (objective, universal knowledge) and the subjective, emotional domains of literature and the arts. Hegel reinforced this foundation by giving universal science an appropriately universal history that made the isolation of *Wissenschaft* after 1650 the crucial agent in the modern mind's progressive leap forward. The Kantian–Hegelian philosophical conception of Enlightenment science was reiterated in the nineteenth century in a French key by Auguste Comte, who made the invention of 'positive science' – neutral, objective, fact-based empirical inquiry – the foundation of civilizational progress. The tradition was further consolidated around 1900 when a range of thinkers – including Nietzsche, Weber, Husserl and Heidegger – made the new singularity that Kant and Hegel called *Wissenschaft*, and Comte '*la science positive*', a guiding force determining the contemporary fate of world civilization. From this perspective, science was not only singularly influential in making the modern world, it was also responsible for its values and its normative direction.

A classic strand of twentieth-century Enlightenment scholarship was built upon this philosophical understanding. As a Hegelian, Ernst Cassirer set out after the First World War to chart the historical steps by which *Wissenschaft* came to define modernity ('*die neuere Zeit*'). As a Kantian, he found the central step forward to be a new conception of eighteenth-century scientific reason, namely, Newtonian mathematical physics.[3] Cassirer's 1932 *Die Philosophie der Aufklärung* (*The Philosophy of the Enlightenment*) articulated this argument as a history of Enlightenment, using the French mathematician and *encyclopédiste* d'Alembert to personify the science that for him defined the essence of this modernity-making epoch.[4] Cassirer's work anchored an entire programme of Enlightenment scholarship devoted to the historical excavation of the scientific rationality that was said to define this world-historical moment. His influence persists in the commonplace conception of Enlightenment as a historical mindset or world view connected in one way or another to 'Newtonian scientific reasoning'.

Theodor Adorno and Max Horkheimer, influential members of the German Frankfurt School, shared Cassirer's Hegelian historical outlook, but they saw in the historical advent of *Wissenschaft* a much less sanguine prospect. In *Dialectic of Enlightenment*, dictated feverishly above the beaches of Malibu, California, as the two post-war émigrés worked to reassemble the shards left by the mid-century collapse of Western civilization, Adorno and Horkheimer isolated an eighteenth-century 'factual mentality' derived from the period's veneration of Baconian experimentalism and instrumental empiricism as the core Enlightenment ethos.[5] *Dialectic of Enlightenment* made the pursuit of value-neutral, instrumental empiricism the essence of the eighteenth-century scientific mind and the source of its destructive pathologies, and in this they echoed Comte while turning his happy conception of human perfectibility on its head. The morality of the marquis de Sade marked for Adorno and Horkheimer the natural product of this sort of

Enlightenment instrumental reason, and they found the same pedigree in the dehumanizing instrumentalism of National Socialism and the camps.

The shared, if discordant, equations of Enlightenment with a certain monolithic understanding of 'modern science' in the work of Cassirer, Adorno and Horkheimer are emblematic of how a retrospective philosophical understanding of science, Enlightenment and modernity has shaped scholarship in the field. To take another classic example, the reason why the widespread popular devotion to Franz Anton Mesmer's theories of animal magnetism marks the 'end of the Enlightenment' in historian Robert Darnton's influential 1968 account is that Darnton takes the Enlightenment to stand for a particular kind of scientific rationality whose demise results from a countervailing triumph of anti-scientific values such as imagination, fantasy, emotionalism and the rule of the passions.[6] Darnton's view divides the eighteenth century into two competing cultures, one rooted in reason and the other in emotionalism and sentiment. This split mirrors another classic divide, the one separating the eighteenth-century Enlightenment (reason and science) from nineteenth-century Romanticism (emotion and the arts), and contemporary scholarship continues to bear witness to the ongoing power of these conceptual and disciplinary dualisms.

The most recent scholarship has begun to dissolve these classic binaries in fruitful ways. In Jessica Riskin's Enlightenment, for example, reason and emotion, along with the mind and the passions, couple and cohabitate in ways that explode Kant's rigid distinction between science and the arts.[7] Other recent scholarship has also emphasized the impossibility of sifting science from literature when analysing the print culture of the period. The Enlightenment sciences circulated in all sorts of literary forms, with mathematics and natural history appearing in epistolary texts and the latest thinking in the life sciences finding an audience through libertine pornography. Traditional genres such as dialogues and utopian fantasies also continued to be deployed, even as more narrowly technical scientific treatises became widespread. Overall, Enlightenment science appeared in every textual corner of the eighteenth century, even if no single home for it existed.

Such revisionist reconfigurations, which recognize the varied manifestations of science in the French Enlightenment, are the norm within the most recent anglophone scholarship. A particular French tradition of Enlightenment scholarship derived from a particular French tradition of the history of science has also been incorporated into these reconfigurations. Given the lexical preference in French for plural understandings of science – it has always been the Académie des Sciences in France, and singular understandings of '*la science*' generally are imported idioms – francophone scholarship on the modern sciences has always stressed the pluralism of the scientific assemblage. The foundational interwar encounter between German and French philosophy, which produced everything from Merleau-Ponty's phenomenology to Sartre's existentialism and the many strands of 1960s post-structuralism, also created a particularly fertile climate in France for critical historical studies of the emergent modern sciences. For these and other reasons, France also became a leader in the formation after the First World War of the new international discipline of the history of science. By the 1930s, these intellectual and institutional changes were converging in the creation of a new climate conducive to the formation of a new tradition of French Enlightenment scholarship.

Three examples can stand in for the many figures in this nexus. Daniel Mornet was educated as a *littéraire*, defending a thesis in 1909 on 'le sentiment de la nature' in eighteenth-century French literature. A professor of the history of French literature at the Sorbonne from 1924 to 1945, Mornet produced books such as *Les Sciences de la nature en France au XVIIIe siècle* (*The Natural Sciences in France in the Eighteenth Century*) that exemplified the interwar fusion of literary history, intellectual history and the history of science that proved so fecund in France.[8] Contemporaries of Mornet such as Paul Hazard, and post-war scholars such as Jean Ehrard and Jacques Roger, built on this literary historical foundation, producing seminal work on the scientific character of the French Enlightenment grounded in the synthetic study of texts and discourses.[9] Peter Gay's two-volume *The Enlightenment: An Interpretation*, first published in the late 1960s, mirrored this literary 'history of ideas' approach, and, by entitling one of his two magisterial volumes *The Science of Freedom*, Gay stood with his French counterparts in framing Enlightenment as an epoch when literary-textual production attested to widespread scientific ferment.[10]

Mornet also pointed Enlightenment scholars towards a second point of entry: the material and social history of Enlightenment institutions. Aligning himself with the serial and materialist historical methods of the first generation of *Annales* historians, a pioneering group of French scholars linked to the journal *Annales – économies, societies, civilisations* (*Annales – Economies, Societies, Civilizations*), Mornet used notarial records and library inventories to trace the reception and popularity of Enlightenment French books. This archival work led to *Les Origines intellectuelles de la révolution française* (*The Intellectual Origins of the French Revolution*), a seminal account of Enlightenment and its influence.[11]

Enlightenment science in the socio-material intellectual mode of Mornet and the *Annales* is neither a period zeitgeist nor a textually encapsulated form of embodied cogitation; it is, rather, a manner of being and doing whose pervasiveness is evinced by the discourses and artefacts – especially books – preserved in the archive. Daniel Roche's scientific Enlightenment is emblematic of this second French tradition.[12] Roche finds Enlightenment in the widespread social urges towards reform and improvement in the eighteenth century and in the concretization of these impulses into innovative and provincially diffuse scientific academies and societies. Roche's scholarship on Enlightenment science is also linked to the wider turn towards publicity and the public sphere in Enlightenment studies more generally, a trend catalysed by the reception of German social theorist Jürgen Habermas's *Structural Transformation of the Public Sphere*. In the Habermasian frame, Enlightenment science is found less in the ideas, texts, authors, discourses or concepts of the period themselves than in the practices of public scientific activity itself and the transformative material and institutional dynamics it generated.

The third scholarly thread descended from French history of science is Michel Foucault's seminal scholarship on science and Enlightenment. His work might be imagined as a critical meeting of the literary-textual and socio-material/institutional threads just discussed. Educated within the post-war milieu that brought German philosophy together with the new French history of science, Foucault eschewed any single monolithic conception of 'modern science' when conceiving Enlightenment even as he found its modernizing potency in an infinitely diffuse array of scientific and technological micro-mechanisms. Foucault found Enlightenment in the new *savoirs et techniques* that together remade knowledge and institutions in the eighteenth century, and he focused attention on the new eighteenth-century sciences of political economy, demography, psychology, clinical medicine and public hygiene that remade the world by remaking the languages and institutions governing life in eighteenth-century France. Foucault's scientific Enlightenment ultimately resides in composites of scientific discourse and institutional concretization, and his work has been widely influential among students of Enlightenment scientific languages, institutions and practices alike.

Given the directions that scholarship on science and Enlightenment have taken over the past century, what are its trajectories for the future? One of the most significant accomplishments of recent scholarship has been to split the monolithic notion of 'Enlightenment science' into a multiplicity of sites of Enlightenment scientific discourse and practice. Two major questions arise from this break-up: 'What is the role of the eighteenth-century sciences in the making of the French Enlightenment?', and, conversely 'What is the role of Enlightenment in the making of the eighteenth-century sciences?'

The dynamic between these two entangled questions can be explored by looking at two personae central to each: the French Enlightenment *philosophe* and the proto-modern eighteenth-century scientist. The latter is an anachronism, yet historians of science seeking the first beginnings of this modern form have found many reasons to locate them in eighteenth-century France. For example, if one of the traits of the modern specialized scientist is a narrow disciplinary focus on specialized scientific work to the exclusion of other pursuits, then the beginnings of this conception are certainly connected to the Académie Royale des Sciences, which from 1699 organized members into disciplinary classes (*astronomie, chimie, géométrie*, etc.) according to meritocratically defined ranks (*adjoint, associé, pensionnaire*) that held each member to an institutional ideal promoting singular, intensive research in pursuit of a particular expertise. All similar institutions of disciplinized modern science were founded in emulation of the French Academy, and the eighteenth century was a watershed moment in the creation of this recognizably modern form of specialized, professional science. Many of the luminaries of French science in this period also exemplified this particular French Enlightenment institutional formation.

Alexis Claude Clairaut illustrates the point. A child prodigy who presented his first mathematical paper before the Académie Royale when barely a teenager, Clairaut grew into the new role of specialized mathematical physicist (the name for the identity came later) because of the French royal academic system that made his career possible. He was admitted to the Academy in his early twenties, travelled with the team to the Arctic Circle in the 1730s to measure the arc of the earth's curvature and then spent his middle years (he died at the age of fifty-two) pursuing highly specific questions in mathematical physics with singular and narrow assiduousness. Perhaps his crowning achievement was predicting to within thirty days the return of Halley's comet in April 1759. Overall, Clairaut's career exemplified the new technical scientific identities created by the emergence of proto-professional institutions of science in Enlightenment France.

Initiating what historians of science call the eighteenth-century 'chemical revolution', Antoine Lavoisier also illustrates this shift. He pursued the mathematical and experimental work integral to his new discipline, modernizing chemical nomenclature and a theory of combustion in specialized laboratories supported by the French Académie Royale. Lavoiser was also a *fermier général* (one of forty financiers appointed by the Crown to oversee tax collection) and an important state administrator. Dividing his life between experimental and mathematical chemistry on some days and royal fiscal administration on others, Lavoisier personified the emerging bifurcations of the sciences that isolated specialized practice from other pursuits. Like Clairaut, who was a founder of the new Enlightenment discipline of mathematical physics, Lavoisier helped define the modern discipline of chemistry by establishing specialized practices and foundations that isolated it from other, more amateur pursuits.

To call Clairaut and Lavoisier emblematic 'Enlightenment scientists' is to equate Enlightenment scientific modernity with this new proto-modern specialization and disciplinization of scientific knowledge. It is also to link Enlightenment science with the eighteenth-century absolutist state, since the latter was the impetus behind these proto-professional urges. Historically speaking, French Enlightenment science can be defined this way, so long as one's goal is telling teleological stories about the birth and growth of modern specialized, professional science. But confusions arise if this understanding is conflated with another very different conception of Enlightenment science that was equally crucial to the fabric of eighteenth-century life.

The provincial academies studied by Roche illustrate this other current, for they were rarely frequented by specialized scientific practitioners such as Clairaut and Lavoisier, nor were they linked to the Académie Royale de Sciences in Paris like provincial satellites in some national network of disciplinary scientific expertise. Nothing so systematic was assembled until the Napoleonic regime, and eighteenth-century provincial academies were very different institutions from the Royal Academy in the capital. In the provinces, scientific academies were assemblies of local notables who came together out of devotion to the practice and promise of scientific inquiry. Provincial academies were also autonomous, possessing neither formal ties with the royal scientific academies nor any of the financial support afforded to royal institutions. Regional academies were often little more than sociable clubs of elite men, many of whom were involved with political administration. What they shared with the Royal Academy in Paris was a passion for science and a belief in its value as a modernizing force in society. Not subject to the rigour imposed at the Royal Academy, provincial savants worked in informal, pragmatic ways that contrasted strongly with the proto-professional disciplinary practices of their compatriots in Paris. In Lavoisier's case, it was his work as a tax farmer, and his efforts to rationalize royal fiscal administration, that linked him with the work of provincial scientific academicians far more than his rigorous instrumental experiments in pursuit of his theory of combustion.

In short, the Enlightenment science that Roche finds in the provincial academies of eighteenth-century France is simply not the same Enlightenment science that Clairaut and Lavoisier exemplified in their scientific work. In the second case, the modernizing trajectory of Enlightenment science is found in the narrow, disciplinary specialization of scientific practice and the organization of these practices into proto-professional institutional networks of technical expertise. In the case of Enlightenment science as found in the provincial academies, its modernity lies in the deployment of scientific learning towards projects of sociability, utilitarian service and reform-minded improvement. Both cases are emblematic of the modernity-making character of Enlightenment science, and we will return to the science of the provincial academies in a moment. But first, let us complete our understanding of the other conception, the one engendered by the absolutist state through its Enlightenment programme of institutionalized scientific specialization and disciplinary expertise.

A host of features of Enlightenment science resulted directly from the governmental organization and deployment of science within eighteenth-century royal institutions. The French state, for example, had a strong interest in controlling land and sea, which generated support for quantification projects in oceanography and civil engineering, and in precision mapping and instrumentation programmes generally, aims that also shaped tendencies in other sciences ranging from astronomy and cartography to demography and political economy. What has been called the 'quantifying spirit' of Enlightenment science was in many ways an outcome encouraged by these state impulses. When Isaac Newton formulated his theory of universal gravitation using the precisely quantified data in astronomy, geodesy and mechanics he obtained from those he called 'the measuring Frenchmen' (he was referring to the pensioned astronomers and mathematicians of the Académie Royale), he was building upon an evidentiary edifice created by strong state interests in precisely this kind of narrow, technical scientific work.

Imperial maritime states such as France also sent ships and *savants* around the world in search of discoveries, and the loot assembled from these voyages, both material and conceptual, generally found its way back home to royal scientific depots such as the Jardin Royal. Once relocated to these new institutional sites, imperial acquisitions were transformed into the data from which botany, natural history and the emerging human sciences of geography and anthropology would be built. Maritime exploration and colonization thus directly fed Enlightenment scientific inquiry. The Baconian urge, so often seen as a foundation of Enlightenment science, to restrict sound scientific reasoning to rigorous inductions made from large accumulations of empirical data was easiest to satisfy in the royal archives of nature assembled by state scientific institutions, and it is no coincidence that the paradigmatic eighteenth-century taxonomic projects of Buffon were sustained by the count's fifty years of royal support as superintendent of the French Royal Garden. Supporting his work were teams of research assistants made available to him through royal scientific patronage, and an institutional environment that encouraged rigorous specialization and the establishment of professional disciplinary hierarchies. Buffon's ascent to the pinnacle of royal French science began in 1732 because of the prospects that his early scientific research on wood held for improving French shipbuilding, and even at the end of his life, when he was pioneering the modern evolutionary life sciences, his work was entangled with the absolutist state and its scientific institutions.

The new governmental sciences emphasized by Foucault also grew from the same state nexus. The new eighteenth-century political economy of the physiocrats, for example, was incubated within the *bureaux* of the royal fiscal administration. Enlightenment political economy overall was saturated with state influences, and the pioneering turn towards quantifying fiscal and commercial activities, which is one of its hallmarks, along with its impulse to accumulate and deploy statistical data, were all stimulated, and sometimes even directly provoked, by absolutist urges towards scientific governmental management and improvement. Demography, another distinctive Enlightenment social science, has a similar origin, as does the new eighteenth-century professionalization of engineering, a trend manifest in the foundation of royal schools where a new kind of scientized civil servant was trained through specialized courses in mathematics, physics, chemistry and other newly disciplinized sciences. Napoleon would solidify these changes into the widely emulated system of polytechnical education characteristic of France today.

The new proto-professional disciplinary experts produced by the royal scientific institutions illustrate one crucial dimension of Enlightenment science. But alongside and sometimes entangled with them, another equally significant exemplar of scientific Enlightenment existed. The group of *encyclopédistes* responsible for Diderot and d'Alembert's *Encyclopédie* exemplified this other community. These scientific *savants* were rarely the proto-professional knowers of the Royal Academy, although they were often members of the wider network of royal state scientific institutions of which the academy system was part. The *encyclopédistes* emerged from the different scientific milieu of the provincial academies, and although most resided in Paris, the scientific locales they inhabited were outside the Royal Academy in the public lecture halls, reading rooms, salons, cafés and other sites of non-official public scientific ferment, which expanded in number and influence throughout the eighteenth century. The Enlightenment man of science from this world, the one behind the thousands of technical scientific articles in the *Encyclopédie*, was not a narrow scientific expert, and, while his identity was often captured by labels such as 'homme de lettres' or 'savant', the term that most often described this characteristic persona of Enlightenment science also carried larger significance, that of the *philosophe*.

D'Alembert was rare in inhabiting both identities at once, for, when he attended meetings of the Académie Royale des Sciences and debated questions in mechanics and astronomy with Clairaut and other academicians, he was a specialist mathematician personifying one brand of Enlightenment science. But when he presided over meetings at the Académie Française, where he was secretary, or attended the salon of Julie de Lespinasse to discuss theatre or the arts, or corresponded with Voltaire about the politics of the *Encyclopédie*, he was engaging in Enlightenment scientism of another sort, one that was just as influential as specialized mathematical physics in making Enlightenment science, even if it had no direct connection to it.

D'Alembert's case was an exception – a specialized Enlightenment scientist who was also an Enlightenment *philosophe*. Classic Enlightenment scholarship leads to confusion in so far as it conflates these two roles, as Cassirer does in making d'Alembert's mathematical science the essence of Enlightenment *tout court*. In fact, d'Alembert was the exception that proves another rule since these two scientific identities were almost never combined in this way in eighteenth-century France. There were Enlightenment scientists such as Clairaut and Lavoisier, and the *philosophes* often admired them, even if they occasionally mocked their esoteric detachment from the pleasures of the world. Then there were *philosophes*, who admired the science practised by disciplinized savants such as those at the Académie Royale but who pursued a completely different vocation. The *philosophes* also called the focus of their own activity by a different name, *philosophie*, and, while *philosophie* was connected to the eighteenth-century sciences, it would be inaccurate to equate the two, or to call Clairaut and Lavoisier Enlightenment *philosophes* simply because they were leading Enlightenment scientists.

What then was the role of the sciences in the Enlightenment if Enlightenment is defined by the activities of the *philosophes*? Four themes characterize these activities. The first is utility. The *philosophes* saw themselves above all as servants of the public good, for, as Dumarsais wrote in the *Encyclopédie* entry 'Philosophe': 'For [the *philosophe*], civil society is, as it were, a divinity on earth; he flatters it, he honours it by his probity, by an exact attention to his duties, and by a sincere desire not to be a useless or embarrassing member of it.'[13] This desire to be useful to society allied the *philosophes* strongly with the Baconian strand of the new sciences that emphasized nature as a reservoir of powers to be harnessed in the service of man and science as a practical and empirical activity, not an exercise in abstract theorizing.

Experimental empirical inquiry, which was the essence of utilitarian science of this sort, constitutes the second theme of the *philosophe*'s scientific sensibility. To be useful to society, science needed to be clear, concrete and publicly demonstrable. The *philosophes* were eager to support those sciences that made universal truths acceptable to all in clear and evident ways. They were also critical of abstractions, including scientific abstractions, which were not sufficiently grounded in evident empirical fact. The familiar *philosophe* rant that described the vortical cosmological system of Descartes as a vain scientific fantasy devoid of empirical veracity illustrates this tendency, as does the *philosophes*' general critique of philosophical systems and hypothetical-deductive reasoning. Scientific knowing for the *philosophes* began and ended with clear and visible empirical demonstrations, a value illustrated by their celebration of the rustic, common-sense, pragmatist Benjamin Franklin as the model Enlightenment man of science.

Voltaire's practice of Newtonian science, and his imagined association with the expert mathematical Newtonians of the Paris Académie, were crucial for his formation as a *philosophe*. But he was never really an associate of these expert practitioners or a scientist in any proto-modern sense. Nonetheless, the Enlightenment sciences shaped his identity in crucial ways. Perhaps the best example of their influence was his vigorous advocacy of smallpox inoculation. Here was a clear vehicle for social improvement, discovered and demonstrated through empirical research and experiment, which was being withheld from the public because of ignorance, fear and superstition. A plan to construct a system of running water linking every building in the city of Paris, which appeared in the public media circuits of the 1760s and was then realized in fictional form in Mercier's novel *L'An 2440* (*The Year 2440*), was also representative of the *philosophe* scientific sensibility. Such utilitarian projects of public improvement required the deployment of the latest scientific expertise, but just as important to the *philosophes* who advocated for them was the reform-minded zeal necessary to channel abstract scientific theorization towards the amelioration of human life. *Philosophe* scientism always championed the second and disparaged the first, at least as a goal in itself, and it was regarding scientific projects of social reform that the *philosophe* most fully showed his true scientific colours.

A third theme of the *philosophe*'s scientific sensibility is critical scepticism. While Galileo, Bacon and Descartes possessed radically different scientific epistemologies, each shared a deeply sceptical stance that became the universal hallmark of the new sciences of the seventeenth century. The *philosophes* were good scientists in this respect since they submitted everything to critical scrutiny and advanced only those truths that had withstood every critical challenge. This devotion to critical scepticism, sometimes as an end itself, anchored the *philosophes*' well-known hostility towards system-building and demonstrative rationalism, and it even separated them on occasion from the specialized practitioners of Enlightenment academic science.

Voltaire and Maupertuis, for example, each personified the *philosophe* stance when they defended the Newtonian theory of universal gravitation not by demonstrating why it was right but by dismantling the arguments of those who held it to be a patent absurdity. In taking this critical approach to scientific argument, these two practitioners of scientific Enlightenment were not asserting and defending a particular scientific thesis so much as skewering the epistemological pretensions of those who claimed to know with certainty what they had in fact uncritically taken for granted. Such sceptical and critical scientism was representative of the *philosophe* brand of Enlightenment science.

The marquis de Condorcet, a protégé of d'Alembert, and like him a hybrid figure who combined expert mathematical work in the Académie Royale with *philosophe* scientism in the public sphere, exemplifies how these tendencies could be synthesized in distinctive Enlightenment ways. As an academic scientist, Condorcet concerned himself with the challenge of deriving sound empirical inductions from indefinite empirical data, a research programme that led him to develop mathematical models of probability capable of overcoming sceptical challenges to induction. The development of mathematical probability and its specialized application to the problem of empirical induction was one of the great achievements of French Enlightenment mathematics, astronomy and physics. Condorcet also directed probabilistic mathematical induction towards questions of political and social reform, using probability to theorize the rationality of democratic voting practices and pioneering quantitative approaches to political economy and social policy that laid the foundations for contemporary rational choice theory. It was in this second field that Condorcet worked as a *philosophe*, using his Enlightenment scientific expertise to promote social reform and utilitarian public service.

With Condorcet, sceptical rationalism was used to undermine claims to dogmatic certainty so as to lay a rigorous though probabilistic foundation for developing socially useful knowledge. This kind of social-scientific argumentation defined the *philosophes*, even if very few bridged the worlds of the academy and the public reform movements the way Condorcet did. Much more common were the manoeuvrings of Maupertuis, who would circulate in the public in one guise then reclaim his identity as an Enlightenment academic scientist on other occasions by pursuing expert mathematical work in mechanics and astronomy. Voltaire's brilliant partner Émilie de Breteuil, the marquise du Châtelet, illustrates the inverse of the same pattern. She was excluded from the academy because of her sex and frequented exclusively the public spaces inhabited by the *philosophes*. But from these public spaces she also cultivated an identity as expert scientific practitioner, publishing her own treatise on physics in 1740 and a still unsurpassed French translation of Newton's *Principia* published posthumously in 1753. Voltaire was du Châtelet's partner in many ways, but never in her specialized mathematical work, and in the difference between the scientific Enlightenment of Voltaire and the *philosophes* and the Enlightenment science of du Châtelet, Maupertuis and Clairaut, the dual strands of Enlightenment science are visible.

The work of Maupertuis also illustrates the fourth and final theme of *philosophe* science: sensationalism and *sensibilité*. In his final published writings, Maupertuis turned his attention to questions in what we would today call biology (human and animal reproduction, hereditary inheritance, physiology, sexuality, etc.), areas that had not yet been institutionalized as disciplinary sciences but which were central to eighteenth-century *philosophie*. Maupertuis's studies of animal generation and albinism were certainly mainstream works of eighteenth-century science, and they drew upon widely circulated public experiments, such as those performed by Trembley on the auto-regeneration of the polyp. Maupertuis's theories also deployed the studies of male seminal fluid that were a feature of early microscopy. Yet, if Maupertuis's *Dissertation physique à l'occasion du nègre blanc* (*Physical Disquisition Concerning the White Negro*) and *Vénus physique* were scientific books, they were also materialist philosophical tracts supporting the pejorative definition of the *philosophe*, still powerful in the eighteenth century, as a libertine subversive who used critical reason to undermine the foundations of established moral order.

What linked Enlightenment life science with Enlightenment *philosophie* was *sensibilité* or 'sensationalism', a term that referred to the scientific domain of the senses, the role of sensate experience in constituting human consciousness, and the new philosophies of the body that equated life and self with the motion of material bodies. *Sensibilité* in this complex sense therefore circulated, depending on the discourse and its context, simultaneously as a scientific term (either the seat of sensory perception or the active agent at work in organic processes of life) and as a category in libertine materialist philosophy (the active agent animating matter in materialist anthropology). Separating the eighteenth-century science of *sensibilité* from its circulation in Enlightenment materialist philosophy is simply not possible in the way that Voltaire's *philosophe* scientism can (and should) be distinguished from the Enlightenment mathematical physics of du Châtelet, Maupertuis and Clairaut.

Electricity, arguably the French Enlightenment science par excellence given its combination of sophisticated mathematical theorization and overwhelming public notoriety and influence, illustrates perfectly the characteristic hybrids that this multiform dynamic of French Enlightenment science produced. Inside the Académie Royale, electrical phenomena were subjected to increasingly specialized regimes of measurement, quantification and instrumental experimental control, ultimately producing the late-century work of such academicians as Charles-Augustin de Coulomb and André-Marie Ampère who laid the foundations for the specialized modern science of electrodynamics. Outside the academy, electricity passed through other Enlightenment circuits. It was the show-stopping favourite of the public physics demonstrators who established experimental physics as a new Enlightenment public science. Abbé Jean-Antoine Nollet illustrates this public path to Enlightenment scientific authority, for he earned his initial scientific credentials as a popular electrical showman, electrifying in one famous performance a chain of 100 Capuchin monks before the royal court at Versailles. But after securing his position of public fame he went on to become a respected member of the Académie Royale and the holder of the first French university chair in experimental physics, a position created especially for him.

Nollet illustrates how science in the Académie Royale was often transformed by the very different science circulating around it in the wider public sphere. Electricity also flowed along other influential Enlightenment circuits that bypassed academic science altogether. The shock felt by Nollet's electrified monks became a commonly invoked item of scientific evidence supporting materialist notions of the *sensibilité* of living matter. Long before Mary Shelley made the electric spark of life a centrepiece of *Frankenstein*, her modern tale of horrific scientific generation, electro-physiology was also circulating widely in the Enlightenment public sphere, producing everything from new electro-materialist cosmologies and remedial therapies to sentiment-provoking 'love machines' and the craze for Mesmer's spiritualist animal magnetism. The link Benjamin Franklin and others established between the charge found in electrical wires and the natural phenomenon of lightning also made the lightning rod a new and widely recognized emblem of utilitarian science in the service of Enlightenment reform. Among the historical figures who entered the public eye as a result of this characteristic dimension of Enlightenment social scientism was a young Savoyard lawyer named Maximilien Robespierre, who gained public notoriety after trying a well-publicized case concerning the safety and preventive validity of home lightning rods.

Pulling the strands of the discussion together, we can best view the modern influence of French Enlightenment science in terms of a twofold legacy. On the one hand, if we consider the new specialized scientific disciplines born and instituted in eighteenth-century France, it seems natural to posit the Enlightenment as the beginning of narrow, disciplinary science that we today associate with unified science *tout court*, a domain distinct from art and literature and essential to modernity through its claim to offer objective, expert knowledge. Viewed from this perspective, the modernity of Enlightenment science resides in the crystallization of this new, narrow and disciplinary conception of science in eighteenth-century France and the emergence of the professionalized social field that supported it. The first specialized, technical journal addressed solely to disciplinary experts, the *Journal de physique*, was indeed established in France in 1764, and a defining difference between the grand *Encyclopédie* of Diderot and d'Alembert and its successor, the *Encyclopédie méthodique*, was a shift from an alphabetical organization to one determined '*par matières*' or by newly demarcated disciplinary categories. These examples mark a dynamic push within the French Enlightenment towards disciplinary specialization and the advent of science in the portentous singular, along with the first split dividing the imagined two cultures of art and science.

But French Enlightenment science was both more than and different from proto-professional, institutionalized, disciplinary knowledge-making. It also included the new life sciences and especially the new human sciences of psychology, political economy, anthropology and history. When these sciences found their place alongside the so-called natural sciences in the new scientific research universities of the nineteenth century, the founders of these new disciplines looked back to the eighteenth century as the originating moment of their endeavours. Yet, unlike mechanics or astronomy, the eighteenth-century human sciences were anything but narrow, specialized sciences with professionalized disciplinary networks. The life sciences remained entangled with older traditions of libertinism and materialist philosophy, and they were found as much in the boudoirs of Enlightenment France as in its academic laboratories. Political economy emerged when government bureaucrats theorized the practices of royal administration in terms of the new scientific models of the period, creating a new science of the laws of society and human nature. It was a long time before these Enlightenment human and social sciences became the institutionalized disciplines of economics, sociology and political science. Psychology, anthropology and history were likewise anything but coherent disciplinary sciences in the eighteenth century, and they are better described as clusters of philosophical discussion and debate within the public discourse of the eighteenth-century Republic of Letters. Only in the nineteenth century, through a process of anachronistic retrofitting, were these discursive clusters recognized as the first incarnation of the disciplinized social sciences of modern times.

Yet, even if the Enlightenment did not create the modern social and behavioural sciences in the direct way that it made modern mathematical physics, the Enlightenment human sciences must be recognized as serving an equally crucial role in shaping modern science today. Born out of an urge to reform society, with impulses that favoured the useful while abhorring vain abstraction, Enlightenment social scientism gave birth to the characteristically modern fact-value question with respect to modern scientific understanding. As Lorraine Daston and Peter Galison have shown, the value of disinterested scientific objectivity did not emerge consubstantially with science but was a specific product, like singular science itself, of the mid nineteenth century.[14] The objectivity that crystallized after 1815 was in fact the epistemological glue that fused all the particular sciences into one portentous monolith. Yet, when viewed through the prism of Daston and Galison's history of objectivity, the history of the Enlightenment human sciences reveals how these eighteenth-century scientific pursuits constituted a potential alternative to the exactitude, rigour and analytic precision of the 'objective' pure sciences. The Enlightenment human sciences came together via the *philosophes'* programmes of reform, and, from their inception, they were always a method for changing the world in an interested fashion as much as a programme for knowing it in a disinterested way. Utilitarian and reform-minded scientism as practised by the *philosophes* has always been at the heart of the Enlightenment conceived as a project, and this legacy too was bequeathed to the scientific complex of the modern world.

So we return to where we started. If there was no science in the French Enlightenment, there were still many new sciences that helped lay the foundation for modern science as it developed later. But there were also sciences that stood outside the unification of science in the portentous singular after 1815, and they too shaped the fabric of our scientific world today. The legacy of French Enlightenment science, therefore, lies not in one or the other of these two modes of science by themselves but in their knotty entanglement. *Philosophe* scientism opened a critical space that channelled scientific reasoning and practice towards social and political reform even as institutionalized French mathematics and physics created the architecture for something completely different: disinterested, objective natural science as a universal standard of knowing. Each was modernizing in its own way, but neither was (or is) essentially connected to the other. Enlightenment science is not reducible to either conception exclusively, and in the end it is perhaps more in the historical tension between them than in either conception alone that one finds the most important influence of French Enlightenment science on our modern scientized world today.

NOTES

1   I appropriate here the opening sentence of Steven Shapin, *The Scientific Revolution* (University of Chicago Press, 1996), p. 1.

2 The first appearance of the noun '*scientifique*' in a French dictionary describing '*ceux qui s'occupent des sciences*' (those dealing with sciences) occurs in the sixth edition of the *Dictionnaire de l'Académie Française* published in 1835. This early nineteenth-century neologism denoting a specialist who practises professional, disciplinary research is mirrored in English by the invention of the word 'scientist' by William Whewell in 1834. See the article 'Scientist' in the *Oxford English Dictionary*.

3 Ernst Cassirer, *Das Erkenntnisproblem in der Philosophie und Wissenschaft der neueren Zeit*, 3 vols. (Berlin: Verlag Bruno Cassirer, 1920–2).

4 Ernst Cassirer, *Philosophy of the Enlightenment*, trans. Fritz C. A. Koelln and James P. Pettegrove (Princeton University Press, 1951).

5 Theodor Adorno and Max Horkheimer, *Dialectic of Enlightenment*, trans. Edmund Jephcott (Palo Alto, Calif.: Stanford University Press, 1947).

6 Robert Darnton, *Mesmerism and the End of the Enlightenment in France* (Cambridge, Mass.: Harvard University Press, 1968).

7 Jessica Riskin, *Science in the Age of Sensibility: The Sentimental Empiricists of the French Enlightenment* (University of Chicago Press, 2002).

8 Daniel Mornet, *Les Sciences de la nature en France au XVIIIe siècle* (Paris: Armand Colin, 1911).

9 Paul Hazard, *The Crisis of the European Mind, 1680–1715*, trans. J. Lewis May (New York: New York Review of Books Classics, 2013); Paul Hazard, *European Thought in the Eighteenth Century, from Montesquieu to Lessing*, trans. J. Lewis May (Gloucester, Mass.: Peter Smith, 1973); Jean Ehrard, *L'Idée de nature en France dans la première moitié du XVIIIe siècle* (Paris: Albin Michel, 1994); Jacques Roger, *The Life Sciences in Eighteenth-Century French Thought*, ed. Keith R. Benson and trans. Robert Ellrich (Palo Alto, Calif.: Stanford University Press, 1997).

10 Peter Gay, *The Enlightenment: An Interpretation*, 2 vols.: *The Rise of Modern Paganism* and *The Science of Freedom* (New York: W. W. Norton, 1995).

11 Daniel Mornet, *Les Origines intellectuelles de la révolution française* (Paris: Armand Colin, 1933).

12 Daniel Roche, *Le Siècle des lumières en province: académies et académiciens provinciaux, 1680–1789*, 2 vols. (Paris: Éditions de l'École des Hautes Études en Sciences Sociales, 1978).

13 César Chesneau Dumarsais, 'Philosopher', in *The Encyclopedia of Diderot and d'Alembert Collaborative Translation Project*, trans. Dena Goodman (Ann Arbor, Mich.: Michigan Publishing, 2002). Available online at http://hdl.handle.net/2027/spo.did2222.0000.001 (accessed 14 November 2013). Trans. of 'Philosophe', in Diderot and d'Alembert, *Encyclopédie*, vol. XII.

14 Lorraine J. Daston and Peter Galison, *Objectivity* (Brooklyn, NY: Zone Books, 2010).

6

DAN EDELSTEIN

Political thought

In a famous portrait by Maurice Quentin de la Tour, Madame de Pompadour sits in her study, surrounded by symbols of culture. Among these feature a number of elegantly bound volumes: the curious viewer can even make out the titles of Voltaire's *Henriade*, Montesquieu's *De l'esprit des lois* (*The Spirit of the Laws*) and Volume IV of Diderot and d'Alembert's *Encyclopédie* (which had been published only a few months before the painting was displayed at the salon of 1755). While the presence of these works contributes to Pompadour's self-presentation as a patron of the arts and letters, they present a puzzling choice of props. Montesquieu's study had been placed on the Vatican's Index of Prohibited Books, and the first two volumes of the *Encyclopédie* had been suppressed by the Royal Council. Yet here they were, prominently visible on the desk of the King's mistress.

In many respects, this painting can serve as an allegory of the relation between the French government and the *philosophes*. Put simply, the intellectual, social and cultural movement we know as the French Enlightenment would not have been possible (or would have taken a very different form) without the close alliance between 'enlightened' (*éclairés*) authors and the ministers, aristocrats and, yes, a royal mistress who gravitated around the seat of the French power. To be sure, not every royal official looked favourably upon the philosophical books printed in eighteenth-century France and neighbouring countries. Accordingly, the *philosophes* were not always immune from official punishment: many saw their works condemned, even burned, and quite a few spent time in prison. But they still enjoyed a remarkable degree of protection from the highest levels of the French state.

Recognizing this alliance is essential to understanding the political thought of the *philosophes*. It allows us to make sense of the apparent contradiction that they could be ferocious critics of the French government while refraining from calling into question its legitimacy. They would rail against the French judiciary, the *parlements* in particular, but these courts were also a thorn in the side of the monarchy. Although the French Revolutionaries would adopt the *philosophes* as their own founding fathers, they were far from revolutionary themselves. They may instead best be viewed as 'subversive conservatives'. This label is not meant to be oxymoronic: opposed to sudden, radical change, the *philosophes* also prodded and needled political authorities and institutions to mend their ways. They articulated self-consciously 'progressive' political agendas but to a large degree remained fairly conformist.

This chapter sketches a synoptic picture of French Enlightenment political thought, focusing on the common threads and overarching frameworks of the *philosophes'* writings. While I also try to indicate the singularity of certain key texts, my approach is primarily designed to give the reader the contextual knowledge needed to explore individual works in greater detail.

Crossing the Channel; or, When English political thought became French

The simplest observation one can make about French political thought in the Enlightenment is that it picked up where seventeenth-century English political thought left off.[1] In many respects, the *philosophes* had little choice: their immediate French predecessors, writing under the blinding Louisquatorzian sun, offered them few options for questioning the status quo (two exceptions are Fénelon and Boulainvilliers). But this observation also points to some of the difficulties in assessing and interpreting the political arguments of the *philosophes*. When ideas and theories are transplanted from one culture to another, do they retain the same meaning? Do they make it to their destination intact, or do some parts get lost along the way? The challenge for the historian of political thought is not to be duped by the appearance of familiarity. Oftentimes the *philosophes* can sound as though they are speaking the same political language as their English predecessors, when upon closer analysis it becomes evident that they have a different understanding of the terms they are using to address different problems.

The two main political frameworks that the *philosophes* inherited from the English are natural right theory and classical republicanism, each of which I examine in more detail in subsequent sections. Both of these discourses came to the forefront of political debates in England during the turbulent period between 1642 and 1689, when such canonical works as Thomas Hobbes's *Leviathan* (1651), James Harrington's *Commonwealth of Oceana* (1656), Marchamont Nedham's *Excellency of a Free State* (1656), Algernon Sidney's *Discourses Concerning Government* (published posthumously in 1698, fifteen years after his death) and John Locke's *Two Treatises of Government* (published in 1689) were written.

This particular historical context, however, should also highlight the reason why English writers might be read very differently in eighteenth-century France. Let us recall that, between 1589, when Henri IV became king, and 1715, the year of Louis XIV's death, France witnessed the direct succession of a mere three monarchs, all issued from the same dynastic family. This long seventeenth century was not without its moments of political instability, due in part to two regencies, unpopular ministers and rebellious nobles; moreover, in later years, Louis XIV's religious policies attracted plenty of hostile (largely Protestant) critics.[2] But these challenges pale in comparison with the turmoil experienced during the same period across the Channel, where, between 1603, when James I acceded to the throne, and 1715, England was ruled by nine different heads of state, underwent five dynastic shifts and experienced four different political regimes. Most dramatically, the English lived through the political chaos and experimentation of the Civil War and the Commonwealth. When Louis XIV was facing the frightening, but ultimately rather disorganized, rebellion known as *La Fronde*, Charles I was being led to the scaffold.

These different political experiences are key to understanding the reception of English political thought in France, where the fundamental question of sovereignty – Who has the right to rule? – was rarely raised as directly as it was in England. The English Civil War had pushed this question to the forefront of practical, as well as theoretical, concerns: once it became evident that Charles I, even in defeat, would not abandon his absolutist pretensions, his opponents had to devise an alternative system of government. They did not come to an easy agreement, as the Putney Debates made clear, but different groups built strong defences for their respective arguments. Most of the English works cited above developed and refined these arguments to portray republican, popular or (in the case of Hobbes) absolutist government as the most legitimate form there was.

In France, by contrast, the debate about who had a legitimate right to rule had largely simmered down since the polemical age of the Wars of Religion. If Henri de Boulainvilliers was still defending a form of aristocratic sovereignty in the 1720s, the heated argument over his *thèse nobiliaire* about the origins of elective Frankish kingship (as opposed to the *thèse royale*, according to which French monarchy was a continuation of the Roman Empire) largely devolved into an academic quarrel in the eighteenth century. When Montesquieu, in *The Spirit of the Laws*, waded into this debate to attack the thesis recently advanced (*contra* Boulainvilliers) by the abbé Jean-Baptiste du Bos, his historical conclusions did not lead him to advocate for any constitutional changes.

There were, of course, some exceptions to this general trend, the most famous being Rousseau's argument that sovereignty could only ever reside in the body of the people. Rousseau's claims would be echoed and amplified by others, notably Guillaume-Joseph Saige, in his *Catéchisme du citoyen* (*Citizen's Catechism*) (1775). Another defender of popular sovereignty could be found in Gabriel Bonnot de Mably, in a work that would be published posthumously only in 1789, *Des droits et des devoirs du citoyen* (*The Citizen's Rights and Duties*). Also arguing for republican government beyond the grave was Claude Adrien Helvétius, in *De l'homme* (*On Man*) (published 1773).

But these works were exceptions, just as their authors were exceptional. Rousseau was a Genevan citizen who was born in one of the few actual eighteenth-century republics; Mably was a Frenchman who often sounded more like an Englishman (his mouthpiece is named 'Stanhope'). Neither Saige's nor Helvétius's books were widely read or much noticed at the time. It would take the fiscal crisis of the late 1780s to put the question of legislative sovereignty back on the table of French political thought. For most of the eighteenth century, the claim that 'the principle of all sovereignty resides in the Nation' (as stated in Article 3 of the Declaration of the Rights of Man and of the Citizen) was simply too far removed from reality to be seriously contemplated.

The politics of nature

Given the different political routes that France and England followed from the 1640s onward, is it really a surprise that the *philosophes* shied away from questioning their monarch's right to rule? One reason why we might have expected the *philosophes* at least to raise the issue is that they commonly viewed politics through the lens of natural right theory. This was a philosophical, theological and juridical framework for examining the relations between civil society and positive legislation, on the one hand, and the laws of nature, natural rights and the state of nature, on the other. The key articulation between these two states, natural and civil, was the social contract, a pact between willing members to constitute a new polity.

Natural right theory was hardly an eighteenth-century invention: in its modern incarnation, it can be traced back to sixteenth-century theologians and philosophers. Nor was it a specifically English political framework: some of the most famous 'jusnaturalist' authors were Spanish (Francisco de Vitoria), Italian (Alberico Gentili), Dutch (Hugo Grotius), German (Samuel von Pufendorf) and Swiss (Jean Barbeyrac, best known for his annotated translations of the preceding two).[3] But seventeenth-century English history gave natural right theory a unique role both in practical debates (especially during the Civil War) and in works of political philosophy, most famously those of Hobbes and Locke. It was no accident that Mably presented his ideas about natural right in the voice of an Englishman.

The French reception of this complex tradition is itself quite complex. Many historians have long assumed that the *philosophes* largely derived their ideas about natural right from their seventeenth-century predecessors, Locke in particular. While Locke clearly was well known and studied by some of the leading *philosophes* (notably Rousseau, Diderot, Mably and d'Holbach), there is a tendency to exaggerate his influence. Voltaire, for instance, does not appear to have read Locke's *Second Treatise of Government*, nor for that matter does Montesquieu. What's more, those French writers who were familiar with the *Second Treatise* did not follow its precepts: Rousseau, the *philosophe* most closely associated with natural right theory in the French Enlightenment, offers a radically different theory of the social contract, positive legislation and political procedure. As many have noted, including in his own time, Rousseau's theory of sovereignty bears a much greater resemblance to that of Hobbes, whose influence on the French Enlightenment – and particularly on its materialist thinkers, such as Diderot, Helvétius and d'Holbach – was arguably much greater than that of Locke (at least where the latter's political writings are concerned).

In addition, the *philosophes* held most of their jusnaturalist predecessors in remarkable contempt. Among other reasons, their biggest bone of contention was that the former relied excessively on reason and philosophy, whereas natural right in their eyes was more a matter of sentiment and intuition. As Lynn Hunt has argued, we may detect here traces of the literary 'cult of sensibility' that washed over eighteenth-century French writers and that led them to appeal to their readers' sense of empathy and pity.[4] In any event, this epistemological substitution – sentiment in lieu of reason – had widespread ramifications for the genre and style of natural right theory. Where jusnaturalist authors tended to write dense, erudite and lengthy tomes, often in Latin, the *philosophes* pioneered a much more 'worldly' style of argument, which could just as easily find outlets in poetry (see Voltaire's *Poème sur la loi naturelle* [*Poem on Natural Law*]) and in essays (such as Rousseau's *Discourse on Inequality*). The short, accessible and French-language Declaration of the Rights of Man and of the Citizen owes a great deal to these 'generic' innovations.

For the most part, the *philosophes* also shied away from some of the more dangerous elements of natural right theory. As we already saw, few were keen to address the issue of sovereignty. What this meant in practice was that they did not dwell on – and sometimes did not even mention – the primal scene of the social contract, that critical moment when all gathered to form a polity and decide on its government. Instead, most authors simply assumed that the people were already together, either through an accident of history or through some other, organic nation-building process.[5] They may have taken their lead from Fénelon, who, in his immensely successful and widely read political epic, *Les Aventures de Télémaque* (*The Adventures of Telemachus*) (1699), imagined various utopian societies (most famously, Boetica) in which the inhabitants were always already associated and lived according to the laws of nature, as during the Golden Age. Later in the century, this vision of a natural society would reappear in the works of the physiocrats, an influential group of economists grouped around François Quesnay. In his account, societies seamlessly grow out of family tribes, without ever requiring a contractual agreement.

This omission is important, as it transformed natural right theory, in the hands of the *philosophes*, from a political discourse into a legal one. Rather than focus on *who* has the right to make the laws – an unavoidable question when discussing the social contract, as Rousseau makes clear – most of the *philosophes* preferred to concentrate on *what* a good law should be in the first place. Indeed, when one surveys the many references to 'natural right' or 'natural law' in French Enlightenment texts, they overwhelmingly concern the quality of the law, not the person of their author. 'Civil law should merely articulate the law of nature', Diderot wrote in a characteristic passage of his *Supplément au voyage de Bougainville* (*Supplement to Bougainville's Voyage*) (written c. 1772). By tactfully avoiding questioning the legitimacy of the ruler, the *philosophes* could direct their energy towards reforming the State: 'it is always necessary to uproot everything in a state that is contrary to natural right', Victor Riqueti de Mirabeau proclaimed in his influential *L'Ami des hommes* (*The Friend of Men*) (1756).[6] In this process, the ruler was more likely to be an agent than an obstacle. This was precisely the argument of the physiocrats, who sought to turn the monarch into a 'legal despot' charged with aligning natural and positive law.[7] Unsurprisingly, these arguments tended to be met favourably by heads of state.

Another crucial aspect of natural right theory that failed to implant itself across the Channel was the right of resistance. Even the *philosophes* who quoted and knew Locke well usually avoided bringing up this most 'revolutionary' dimension of his thought.[8] No discussion of legitimate resistance appears, for instance, in the numerous *Encyclopédie* articles that lengthily cite (without attribution) Locke's *Second Treatise*. This omission was most likely a conscious avoidance, as Diderot explicitly rejects the right of resistance in his article 'Autorité politique' ('Political Authority') (perhaps the most famous political article of the *Encyclopédie*). Its absence is equally striking in Rousseau's *Social Contract*, a text that includes chapters on such apparently Lockean topics as 'the abuse of government' and 'the death of the political body' but no reflections whatsoever on legitimate resistance.[9]

This unwillingness to condone popular resistance, even against a tyrannical ruler, is emblematic of the *philosophes*' critical yet cautious attitude towards political power. Even Rousseau, the most democratic of the *philosophes*, warned against revolutionary change, arguing that if subjected peoples 'attempt to shake off the yoke, they move all the farther away from freedom [...] their revolutions almost always deliver them up to seducers who only increase their chains'.[10] In the *Supplément au voyage de Bougainville*, Diderot elaborates on the reason why he refused to consider resistance: 'Anyone who on the strength of his own personal authority violates a bad law thereby authorizes everyone else to violate the good.'[11] Voltaire even refused to give the name of philosopher to any writer 'who ever roused the people to rebel, who joined in an attack on a king's life, who ever troubled society'.[12]

Republican ideals during the French monarchy

If Rousseau avoided even discussing the right of resistance in his political masterpiece, it was also because he did not think about government solely in terms of natural right. His analysis of how and why states dissolve focused instead on their inevitable decay and on the degeneration of governmental forms. These concerns were not traditionally part of natural right theory but instead harked back to an older tradition of political thought, which would come to be identified as 'republican'.

Rousseau was one of the few explicitly republican authors in eighteenth-century France, a commitment that stemmed in part from his own status as a 'citizen of Geneva' (an identity he proudly proclaimed on the title page of many works). At the same time, Rousseau's ideas about republics, like those of his contemporaries, came less from experience than from books. In his *Confessions*, Rousseau describes how at a young age he read Livy's and Plutarch's accounts of ancient republican heroes, with whom he so identified that he 'became the character whose life [he] read'.[13] It was only later in life, when living in Paris, that he underwent his own republican 'conversion', after which he abandoned modern, worldly and urban society in favour of a more Roman-like, 'virtuous' and austere lifestyle.[14]

Rousseau's case was certainly anomalous. If a few other eighteenth-century French readers shared his political predilections, most were able to distinguish between republican imagination and monarchic reality. In part, this reality check was the result of a commonplace assumption about republics, namely that they were unsuitable for large countries: 'There can only be small republics', affirmed Diderot, repeating a well-worn mantra.[15] Another widespread belief about republics was that they were incompatible with commercial activity, a hallmark feature of modern economic activity. This sense that republics required personal austerity and economic equality was cemented by Montesquieu, whose portrayal of republics in *The Spirit of the Laws* firmly associated them with a simpler, bygone age (with the exception of the commercial republics in the Low Countries, Geneva and 'the nation where the republic is hidden under the form of monarchy', that is, England).[16] In his influential account, monarchy emerged as the form of government best suited for modern times.

Despite the paucity of actual republicans in eighteenth-century France, many authors nonetheless adapted arguments and claims about politics that can be described as republican, or, to use the label preferred by historians, 'classical republican'.[17] This label is confusing though, since classical republican theory was neither classical in its origins, nor was it always republican in its goals. What its name really reflects is the fact that this discourse was elaborated with examples of ancient republics in mind, Rome in particular (its canonical expression is Machiavelli's *Discourses on Livy* [1531]). In the eighteenth century, however, authors embraced this mode of political thought more as 'a discourse of political diagnosis rather than a model of an ideal regime of government', as Keith Baker has shown. In this respect, classical republicanism became 'a language of opposition to an increasingly administrative state that simultaneously fed and was fed by the individualism of a modern commercial society'.[18]

At the heart of classical republican complaints about modern society were the binary opposites of virtue and corruption. For Montesquieu, virtue was the defining principle of republics, without which they would inevitably degenerate, in large part due to corruption. But critics of modern France similarly lamented the loss of virtue, and the pursuit of common good, in commercial affairs. As a kind of constitutional patriotism (what Montesquieu calls 'the love of one's country's laws'), political virtue of this sort was equally at home – and, for some, equally as necessary – in monarchies as in republics.[19]

The strong tie between virtue and law underscores another important feature of classical republicanism, which is its theory of the separation of powers. This theory grew out of the classical ideal of mixed government, as praised by Aristotle and Polybius in antiquity. Machiavelli revived it in his discussion of the Roman republic, whose strength, he argued, derived from its fusion of monarchy (the consuls), aristocracy (the senate) and democracy (the tribunes).[20] Under the English Commonwealth, this way of thinking about divided sovereignty took a new form: Nedham, followed by Harrington, began to speak about 'legislative and executive powers', as embodied in the Parliament and the Lord Protector, respectively. In his famous chapter on the English Constitution, Montesquieu described the separation of these powers, to which he added the judiciary, as the only barrier to despotism.[21] While he did not object to the legislative and executive powers being combined in a single person or institution, as they were in France, it was the judiciary (of which Montesquieu had himself been a member) that he believed must remain independent. The Ottoman court, he suggested, offered an example of what happened when it was not, though some (including Voltaire) found that Montesquieu protested too much, and that his references to 'oriental despotism' were really veiled attacks on the French Crown. When Louis XV's minister, René Nicolas Charles Augustin de Maupeou, tried to replace the *parlements* with a new court system of salaried officials, Montesquieu's warnings against despotism at home seemed prescient and would be remembered.

Underlying these different republican arguments was a renewed faith and interest in the ideal of political liberty (also known as *liberté publique*). This was perhaps the *philosophes'* most important contribution to eighteenth-century political thought: they insisted that every man had the right to live free, even in a monarchy. Usually what they meant by 'free' was 'in accordance to established laws', though Rousseau took this argument further and defined freedom as living in accordance to laws of one's own making.[22] Political liberty was often coded as an ancient, republican quality: 'Where are the generous defenders of public liberty, who chased kings and tyrants out of their land?' wrote the curé Jean Meslier in his posthumous *Mémoire*.[23] But it came to be viewed as wholly compatible with monarchic government as well; indeed, Montesquieu would even go so far as to argue that liberty was *more* compatible with monarchy than republicanism.[24] The demand for greater political liberty would be one of the motifs of the *Cahiers de doléances* (lists of grievances), prepared for the meeting of the Estates-General in 1789.

The subversive power of modest ideas: public opinion and the road to revolution

The political legacy of the *philosophes* was such that, from a distance, it may easily appear as the foundation for the French Revolution. The *philosophes* refashioned natural right theory to make it more amenable to the sort of declaration that the National Assembly would issue in August 1789; they advocated for the separation of (executive and judicial) powers and railed against despotism; and they led the chorus demanding greater liberty.

But these commonalities tell only a small part of the story. Most critically, in addition to the numerous differences we have seen, there is the simple fact that the political ideas discussed above played little part in the crisis that broke out in 1787–89. The origins of the crisis were economic, not political. And once the crisis became politicized, it rapidly evolved along lines that would have terrified the *philosophes* (and did frighten those who were alive to witness it).

In conclusion, then, another question arises: was there *any* connection between the political ideas put forward by Enlightenment writers and the outbreak of the French Revolution? More particularly, was the sudden shattering of royal sovereignty completely unrelated to the intellectual ferment of the previous half-century? This question may perhaps best be answered by standing on the ruins of royal sovereignty and looking backwards. How did the National Assembly come to declare that the 'principle of all sovereignty resides essentially in the Nation'?[25] The decree that transformed the Third Estate into a National Assembly on 17 June 1789 had invoked the need to 'interpret and present the general will of the nation'.[26] This language inevitably calls to mind Rousseau, but the theory of the general will found in the *Social Contract* was significantly different. For Rousseau, the general will could be determined only through the majority vote of *all* citizens, not that of their representatives.[27] Moreover, the general will was not something to be 'presented' (here, to the King) but rather was to constitute the law itself. In fact, what the nascent Assembly seems to have been expressing, in Rousseauist language, was the older idea that the king should know the thoughts and opinions of his people. This had been one of the original purposes of the Estates-General. Traditionally, these consultations were supposed to be private, for the king's eyes and ears only. But over the course of the eighteenth century (and especially after 1750), they were increasingly aired in public. The Parisian Parlement blazed the path by publishing its '*remonstrances*' (a kind of forceful rebuttal) to the King, but the *philosophes* latched onto this idea as well. Public opinion was 'the measure [*la règle*] of government', which should modify its actions accordingly, Guillaume Thomas Raynal argued in his 1770 *Histoire philosophique ... des deux Indes* (*Philosophical History of the Two Indies*).[28] Voltaire put the matter more succinctly: 'L'opinion publique est une arme puissante' (Political opinion is a powerful weapon).[29]

The rhetorical deployment of the category 'public opinion' was not dependent on a social reality: whether or not 'public opinion' really existed, or really leaned in one particular direction, would not prevent the *philosophes* from invoking its authority. But they were far from alone in appealing to this source. In the run-up to the French Revolution, government ministers sought to convince the 'Notables' of the kingdom (mostly the high aristocracy and clergy) to accept administrative and fiscal changes; these innovations would eradicate the abuses responsible for fiscal distress, and which had, in the words of the Controller-General Charles-Alexandre de Calonne, 'resisted up to the present moment the condemnation of public opinion'.[30]

In the years immediately preceding the French Revolution, then, the monarchy itself had come to accept the idea that the opinion of the nation should be heard and respected. The King's ministers even sought to institutionalize this belief by creating new provincial assemblies (in the so-called *pays d'élection*, provinces without provincial Estates), which would regulate the new land tax proposed by the government. This plan included some of the features that would provoke a fiery debate in early months of the Revolution: Calonne's successor, Étienne-Charles de Loménie de Brienne, proposed that representatives of the Third Estate in these provincial assemblies should have their number doubled, and that all votes be counted by head, rather than by order – two demands that the King would begrudgingly grant in 1789 for the national Estates-General.

The transformation of the pre-Revolutionary fiscal crisis into a Revolutionary political crisis was thus in large part brought about by the monarchy itself. It was the King's own ministers who sought to find a lasting political solution that guaranteed the Crown higher revenues (through a new form of taxation) but that also offered the people a clearer conduit through which to voice their complaints. To be sure, the government had few other options: the Paris Parlement had repeatedly refused its entreaties to raise taxes. The new plan was a desperate attempt to shift fiscal authority to a different institution. But the plan also bore a strong resemblance to a proposal made in better times by another minister, Anne-Robert-Jacques Turgot. In his *Mémoire sur les municipalités* (*Memoir on Municipalities*), written in 1775, Turgot had similarly suggested that a new structure of provincial assemblies, connected at the centre by a 'general municipality', be put into place to distribute taxes more fairly (among other goals). Turgot defended his proposal as being driven by 'enlightenment and equity' (*les lumières et l'équité*), arguing that 'there can be no grounds for perpetuating institutions created without reason'.[31] He had made this claim before, in his anonymous *Encyclopédie* article on 'Foundations', published in 1757.[32] With Turgot, the reforming spirit of the French Enlightenment literally became embodied in the French state.

There is, to be sure, an important difference between consultative assemblies and legislative ones. For Turgot, it was never a question of giving assemblies legislative power: the king, he maintained, was the absolute legislator of the realm. But the fact remains that it was these reformist proposals, inspired by Enlightenment principles that were not overtly 'radical', that paved the way for the eventual breakdown of the monarch's legislative sovereignty in 1789. The government already claimed that the king wanted only the best for his people (a point his ministers ceaselessly repeated); once it also accepted the principle of national consultation on a representative basis, it only took a fairly small conceptual leap to grant these representative assemblies a legislative power. This last step was by no means inevitable and, if small from a conceptual standpoint, was symbolically huge. But in the end, it was the conservative nature of Enlightenment political thought that made it so subversive.

NOTES

1 Keith Michael Baker, *Inventing the French Revolution: Essays on French Political Culture in the Eighteenth Century* (Cambridge University Press, 1990), p. 182. I would distinguish here between the genealogy of political thought in the French Enlightenment, which one can trace back to England, and the genealogy of the idea of the Enlightenment, which one should not. See Dan Edelstein, *The Enlightenment* (University of Chicago Press, 2010).
2 Lionel Rothkrug, *Opposition to Louis XIV: The Political and Social Origins of the French Enlightenment* (Princeton University Press, 1965).
3 Throughout this section, I use the term 'jusnaturalist' (from the Latin *jus naturae*, that is, natural law or right) to refer to these sixteenth- and seventeenth-century authors and their eighteenth-century commentators (such as Barbeyrac).
4 Lynn Hunt, *Inventing Human Rights: A History* (New York: Norton, 2007).
5 On the emergence of a national sentiment during this period, see David A. Bell, *The Cult of the Nation in France: Inventing Nationalism* (Cambridge, Mass.: Harvard University Press, 2001).
6 Victor Riqueti de Mirabeau, *L'Ami des hommes, ou, traité de la population* (Avignon, 1756), book 3, chap. 5, p. 237.
7 Le Mercier de la Rivière, *L'Ordre naturel et essentiel des sociétés politiques* (Paris, 1767).
8 Two exceptions to this trend are the baron d'Holbach, *Système social* (Paris, 1773), and abbé Gabriel Bonnot de Mably, *Des droits et devoirs du citoyen* (Paris, 1789).
9 Jean-Jacques Rousseau, *The Social Contract*, ed. Victor Gourevitch (Cambridge University Press, 1997), book 3, chaps. 10–11.
10 Jean-Jacques Rousseau, *Discourse on Inequality*, in *The Discourses and Other Early Political Writings*, ed. Victor Gourevitch (Cambridge University Press, 1997), p. 115.
11 In *Political Writings*, trans. and ed. John Hope Mason and Robert Wokler (Cambridge University Press, 1992), p. 74.
12 *Questions sur l'Encyclopédie*, see 'Superstition', in *Complete Works of Voltaire*, vol. XLIII, ed. Nicholas Cronk and Christiane Mervaud (Oxford: Voltaire Foundation, 2013), pp. 301–20, at p. 319.
13 Jean-Jacques Rousseau, *The Confessions*, trans. Christopher Kelly, in *The Collected Writings of Rousseau*, ed. Christopher Kelly, Roger D. Masters and

Peter G. Stillman, 12 vols. (Hanover, NH: University Press of New England, 1995), vol. V, p. 8. For the French, see *Les Confessions* (Paris: Gallimard, 1973), p. 38.

14 Rousseau, *Collected Writings*, vol. V, p. 295; *Les Confessions*, p. 431.

15 Denis Diderot, *Réfutation suivie de l'ouvrage d'Helvétius intitulé 'L'Homme'*, in *Œuvres complètes*, 20 vols., ed. Jules Assézat (Paris: Garnier, 1875), vol. II, p. 390. Accordingly, Voltaire could look favourably on republicanism in Geneva. See Peter Gay, *Voltaire's Politics: The Poet as Realist* (New Haven, Conn.: Yale University Press, 1988).

16 Charles-Louis de Secondat de Montesquieu, *Spirit of the Laws*, ed. Anne M. Cohler, Basia C. Miller and Harold S. Stone (Cambridge University Press, 1989), book 5, chap. 19.

17 See John G. A. Pocock, *The Machiavellian Moment: Florentine Political Thought and the Atlantic Republican Tradition* (1975) (Princeton University Press, 2003); and Keith Michael Baker, 'Transformations of Classical Republicanism in Eighteenth-Century France', *Journal of Modern History*, 73 (2001): 32–53.

18 Baker, 'Transformations of Classical Republicanism', p. 35.

19 Montesquieu, *Spirit of the Laws*, 'Avertissement'. More generally, see Marisa Linton, *The Politics of Virtue in Enlightenment France* (New York: Palgrave, 2001), and Bell, *The Cult of the Nation*, chap. 5.

20 Niccolò Machiavelli, *The Discourses on Livy*, trans. L. J. Walker and B. Richardson (London: Penguin, 2003).

21 Montesquieu, *Spirit of the Laws*, book 11, chap. 6.

22 For the first definition, see the 'Avertissement' to Montesquieu's *Spirit of the Laws*; for the second, see Rousseau, *Social Contract*, book 1, chaps. 6–8.

23 Jean Meslier, *Mémoire des pensées et sentiments de Jean Meslier*, in *Œuvres complètes*, ed. Roland Desné, 3 vols. (Paris: Anthropos, 1970), vol. III, p. 142.

24 Montesquieu, *Spirit of the Laws*, book 11, chap. 6.

25 The wording for this article was first proposed by Lafayette on 11 July 1789. In *Archives parlementaires de 1787 à 1860*, ed. Jérôme Mavidal, Émile Laurent and Louis Claveau et al., 127 vols. (Paris: Librairie Administrative de P. Dupont, 1862–), vol. VIII, p. 222.

26 Ibid., vol. VIII, p. 127.

27 Rousseau, *Social Contract*, book 3, chap. 15.

28 Guillaume Thomas François Raynal, *Histoire philosophique et politique des établissements et du commerce des Européens dans les deux Indes*, 6 vols. (La Haye, 1774), vol. VI, book 18, pp. 393–4.

29 Voltaire, *Don Pèdre*, in *Œuvres complètes de Voltaire*, ed. Marie-Emmanuelle Plagnol-Diéval, Theodore E. D. Braun, et al. (Oxford: Voltaire Foundation, 2011), vol. LII.

30 In *The Old Regime and the French Revolution*, ed. Keith Baker (University of Chicago, 1987), p. 128.

31 In 'Memoir', ibid., pp. 98, 117.

32 'Fondation', in Diderot and d'Alembert (eds.), *Encyclopédie*, vol. VII, p. 75; translation available in Baker, *Old Regime*, pp. 89–97.

7

JULIE CANDLER HAYES

Sex and gender, feeling and thinking: imagining women as intellectuals

The abbé de la Porte begins his five-volume *Histoire littéraire des femmes françoises* (*Literary History of French Women*) (1769) with a Virgilian quotation and a burst of enthusiasm for his subject.

> *Quid Femina possit.*
>
> The purpose of this work is expressed in the epigraph: to show what a woman is capable of in the path of knowledge, once she sets herself above the prejudice that forbids her to develop her mind (*esprit*) and perfect her reason.[1]

La Porte's condemnation of prejudice and endorsement of education indicate his enlightened philosophical commitments. His appreciation of women's literary achievements is, to be sure, an extension of appreciation for women in all their attractiveness. He promises his readers they will see that 'a mind is not incompatible with beauty' and that women, 'whose charming faces destine them to please, may also aspire to the glory due to talent and thereby gather as many laurels as myrtle; that we can be as happy to hear them as to see them, to read their works as to contemplate their charms' (I, v).

While hardly to contemporary taste – or to that of many eighteenth-century women – La Porte's flirtatious praise is evidently sincere, as is his call for women's education and full participation in the Republic of Letters: 'We cannot denounce too strongly the injustice of those who require that women make no use of their minds' (I, vi). The *Histoire littéraire des femmes françoises*, with hundreds of articles compiled from a variety of sources and excerpts from the works of women both famous and forgotten, is an impressive accomplishment and a useful tool for scholars today. Its inherent tensions and contradictions are no less evident. While the work itself is framed as a series of letters addressed to a woman, 'Madame', the preface is written for a male audience. A cultivated woman's mind, he tells his readers, 'can be for us a source of instruction and pleasure and prepares for them an agreeable future and resources for the time when they are no longer able to please' (I, vi). Women writers, however distinguished, are inevitably judged by the pleasure they give men: reading their works, as La Porte says, is another way of contemplating their *attraits*.

The epigraph to which he called attention in his first sentence emblematizes the problematic status accorded women: 'What woman can do' (*ce que peut une femme*) is but a partial quotation of an oft-cited phrase, 'furens quid femina possit' from the beginning of *Aeneid*, Book 5: 'what woman can do in a frenzy'. The reflection comes as Aeneas and his men are sailing away from Carthage; they look back to see smoke rising; while they do not know that it is from Dido's funeral pyre, they fear the worst. La Porte repurposes the phrase as an affirmation of women's abilities, but it is also a reminder of women's unruly passions.

La Porte and many others saw women's social role – 'their presence in society, to which they are admitted at an early age, the freedom that they enjoy, the commerce between the sexes and women's need to please' – as a particular feature of French national culture and a key element of Enlightenment (I, vi–vii). Despite complaints by some that women's influence and 'frivolity' had weakened French culture, women's presumed sensitivity to feelings, interpersonal relations and language was seen as integral to social life.[2]

Much has been written, in the eighteenth century and in the present, on the notion that women were especially 'sensitive' and had a particular affinity with the nuanced sensations of their physical world. In his 1775 *Système physique et moral de la femme* (*The Physical and Moral System of Women*), physiologist Pierre Roussel argued that women's sensitivity was incompatible with an 'immoderate desire for learning' and could only weaken their fragile constitutions.[3] Roussel's work crystallized a number of ideas already in circulation, in particular the triumph of the 'two-sex model', according to which women's bodies were held to be distinct from and incommensurate with those of men. As Roussel put it, sexual difference 'is not limited to a single organ, but extends … to each and every part'.[4] Emerging in the late seventeenth and early eighteenth centuries, this model replaced notions prevalent since Antiquity that the female was in effect a variant of the male.[5] The displacement of the one-sex model with the two-sex model was accompanied – and to a certain extent shaped – by an increasing cultural emphasis on sentimental domesticity and an insistence, inspired by Rousseau and others, on separate spheres of activity for men and women. It is worth pointing out that the 'two-sex' model rarely gives equal attention to both sexes and is most frequently a 'one-sex' theory, that of femaleness. Masculinity is the unmarked norm; femininity is the marker of difference and, as such, requires explanation. The Enlightenment had its (often implicit) theories of maleness; but 'le sexe' referred to women.

The significance of both sociability and sensibility in Enlightenment discourse and their entwinement ensure the pervasiveness of the 'woman question'. Sociability and sensibility are both simultaneously 'natural' and 'cultural': while social existence would be juxtaposed to a hypothetical state of nature in order to call attention to its constructedness and contingency, humankind was as frequently thought to be inherently social. And while sensibility was by definition rooted in the body, which provided its sensorial interface with the world, many commentators believed that civilized existence, especially in the refined comforts afforded the upper classes, encouraged hypersensitivity to the point of moral and physical weakness. Women lived at this chiasmus of nature and culture.

In keeping with the overall purpose of this volume, my focus here will be on women's explicit participation as writers and intellectuals in the ongoing work of les lumières, or the 'Enlightenment project' as we have referred to the process more recently. Prior to the eighteenth century, to be a 'writer' was still an emergent concept, and 'woman writer' was even less clearly articulated. The phrase 'femme auteur' comes into usage only in the latter part of the eighteenth century, as does the expression 'femme de lettres'; 'gens de lettres' continued to refer to male writers. In part, this phenomenon is linked to the gradual evolution of the modern notion of authorship, which offset the potential social stigma incurred by professionalization by incorporating concepts of honour and honnêteté from polite society.[6] Germaine de Staël would point out that the Ancien Régime stigma of professionalization was magnified for women: 'nevertheless it was difficult for women to bear the reputation of author with nobility'.[7] Although excessive intellectual effort might be seen as potentially harmful to both sexes, 'no group suffered more acutely from the perceived peculiarity of the thinker than did women intellectuals', particularly as the two-sex model of human nature gained credence.[8] Women's role in intellectual life could therefore never be taken for granted.

Women and the production of knowledge

For writers of the eighteenth century, the previous era helped shape women's role in cultural life. The seventeenth century was viewed as having been particularly hospitable to women's intellectual ambitions. 'There once were houses where one was permitted to speak and to think, where the Muses kept company with the Graces', wrote Mme de Lambert in 1727.[9] Her sentiments were echoed nearly a century later by Stéphanie de Genlis: 'In the time of Louis XIV ... there were numerous women writers of every sort; and not only did men of letters not attack them and rail against women writers, but they were pleased to recognize their worth and pay homage to them'.[10] While contemporary scholars have differed on the degree to which women's role in shaping Enlightenment sociability should be viewed as an intellectual or political contribution, it is clear that the rise of woman-guided salons provided a stimulus to elite women's intellectual influence and role in cultural production.

A second key element of the seventeenth-century legacy comes in the strain of Cartesian thought most famously associated with Poullain de la Barre, the notion that 'the mind has no sex'. Such radical feminism found itself at odds with the eighteenth century's increasing emphasis on sex, sensibility and a bodily mediated understanding of the world. However, many writers were capable of holding both views. Thus, the mid-century anthologist Pons-Augustin Alletz begins his compilation *L'Esprit des femmes célèbres* (*The Mind/Wit of Celebrated Women*) by staunchly affirming that 'sex in and of itself produces no difference among minds', only to propose the opposite view in the same paragraph:

> It is true that [women] do not usually possess that mental strength that invents and creates, or the firm judgment that prevents one from going astray. But on the other hand, they possess an extreme facility that enables them to conceive the most difficult things; a mental clarity [*netteté*] that leads them to perceive things in their natural order; a delicate taste, a finesse that we would dispute in vain, an easy expression and graces that we can only imperfectly imitate.[11]

From one point of view, the notion of sexless minds might be considered an older residual concept, coincident with and gradually yielding to emergent concepts of sensibility and embodied minds. Yet the equality of the sexes was never an unquestioned, culturally dominant view, and the two-sex model of the intellect did not develop specifically in opposition to it. The 'naturalizing' of women's intellect underwent a sea change during the period due to shifting views of nature. Although nature was initially viewed as a legitimizing force, women's supposed proximity to nature was ultimately seen as an inability to accede to higher, masculinized, forms of reason. At the same time, as Lorraine Daston puts it, 'The early modern mind was a crowded place, crammed with separate but not always wholly distinct faculties that together orchestrated the life of mind and heart.'[12] Just as 'woman' does not automatically belong wholly to either nature or culture, so 'reason' does not align neatly with a polarizing view of sex or gender.[13]

The full explication of women's role in early modern French intellectual life lies beyond the scope of this chapter. Recent scholarship points to a European network of learned women even prior to the emergence of the distinctive concept of the 'woman author'.[14] Linda Timmermans has argued that female authorship held a positive value in the seventeenth century, and she distinguishes the period's 'intellectual feminism' from the increasingly pejorative connotations attached to the expression *femme savante*.[15] By the early eighteenth century, however, personal and institutional memories of earlier female intellectual networks were fading. Admiring references to iconic women scholars such as Anne Dacier and Anna Maria van Schurman continue to be found, but even among women writers – as seen in the remarks by Lambert and Genlis cited above – women's cultural production in the seventeenth century is couched in terms of salon life, rather than the Republic of Letters. The Enlightenment brought in new models of cultural and intellectual production and participation, as *gens de lettres* and *philosophes* took the place of humanist *érudits*; new literary genres emerged; men's and women's roles, associational practices and communication protocols shifted.

Woman, reason and the world of letters

Within the crowded place of this complex conceptual territory concerning women's intellect, women claimed their right to both feeling and reason. I view the intellectual projects of the women discussed here as feminist in so far as they contribute to a female intellectual tradition and a space for women's participation in the public sphere. They themselves represent a wide range of views, not all compatible with one another; many would be at odds with contemporary notions of feminism and female agency, and not all of them viewed themselves in terms of a female tradition. Thus we need to consider them with a broad, inclusive approach.

Anthologies of literary women by La Porte and others play a significant role in the construction of female authorship. One can trace the origins of the genre in Renaissance 'catalogues' of famous women and in seventeenth-century portrait books and 'galleries'. The genre also owes something to the eighteenth-century love of dictionaries, anthologies and other sorts of educational self-help tools. Over the course of time there are two significant shifts: from lists of 'famous women' to compilations of 'women writers' and from male-authored anthologies to the female-authored literary histories of Louise de Kéralio, Fortunée Briquet and Stéphanie de Genlis.[16] Literary historians Joan DeJean and Faith Beasley have argued that many of these anthologies played an important role in mythologizing *le grand siècle* and shaping the male-centred literary canon.[17] Nonetheless, and in a less teleological view, we should note that while intellectual networks of learned women may have receded in importance, eighteenth-century anthologies such as those of Lambert, Alletz and La Porte – and all the more so those of Kéralio, Briquet and Genlis – offer a compelling construction of women writers as a distinct group with a distinct history. The existence of such works thus enables the consolidation of the notion of woman writer, whether to be decried or defended, in the modern era.

Given the pervasiveness of the woman question in Enlightenment France, discussions of women's mental constitution and social role cut across the genres from history to fiction, scientific treatise to private correspondence. The question of female intelligence surfaced in all of these domains, but I would underscore the significance of a particular form of intellectual intervention, the moralist essay. Moralist writing possessed cultural capital derived from classical antiquity and from illustrious modern writers: Montaigne, La Rochefoucauld, La Bruyère. For eighteenth-century critics, the 'feminine' genre par excellence was epistolary writing, followed closely by the novel; both forms were associated with what William Reddy calls 'the new interiority' to which women's spontaneity and exquisite awareness of feelings presumably gave privileged access.[18] Moralist writing, however, had long been a site for anatomizing the human heart, and, hence, it was compatible with certain of the goals of the sentimental revolution. Furthermore, the persona of the moralist asserts the power of observation and disinterested spectatorship. By writing in this mode, women writers lay claim to a distinguished tradition and to their own right to observe and analyse.

I will focus primarily on works by four women whose lives spanned the long eighteenth century: Jeanne-Michelle de Pringy (fl. 1694–1709); Anne-Thérèse de Marguenat de Courcelles, marquise de Lambert (1647–1733); Marie-Geneviève-Charlotte Thiroux d'Arconville (1720–1805); and 'Madame de Verzure' (fl. 1766). Of these, Mme de Lambert was indisputably the best known in her day as she is in ours; all, however, analysed the paradoxes and constraints confronting women writers, and all strove to reconcile body and mind, intellectual ambition and female condition.

Written in the moralist genre made popular by Jean de la Bruyère, Jeanne-Michelle de Pringy's *Les Différens Caractères des femmes du siècle* (*The Different Characters of Women of Our Time*) (1694) exemplifies the complexity of the debate on women's intellect.[19] Pringy first sets forth six 'characters' representing moral and intellectual failings among her contemporaries: *les coquettes, les bigottes, les spirituelles, les économes, les joueuses, les plaideuses* (women who are coquettish, hypocritical, pretentious, avaricious, gamblers, argumentative). Each defective character has its corresponding virtue: *la modestie, la piété, la science, la règle, l'occupation* and *la paix* (modesty, piety, true learning, orderliness, industriousness, tranquillity). Readers are expected to recognize themselves in the first set, then correct themselves through the edifying descriptions of the second. The second half of the work, however, reminds us that the path to enlightenment is less than certain, given the pervasiveness of *amour-propre*, the source of every vice.

Although Pringy does not cite Molière, 'Les Spirituelles' closely resemble his *femmes savantes*: they wish to appear clever, but their learning is superficial and disorganized. 'They make a confused mixture of everything that they know; this heap of confused facts fills their heart as poorly as their mind. Opinion spoils the will, while the wandering heart confirms the mind's errors and prevents it from changing again' (86). As she explains in the chapter on *amour-propre*, these women's innate capacity to discern truth is blinded by the deceptions of pride, which is all-knowing with respect to external objects, but ignorant of itself. The problem thus lies not in a lack of intellectual ability but in moral failure. Indeed, as she declares in the opening passage of the corresponding essay, 'La Science': 'Mind belongs to each sex' (88). Women are constituted differently from men; their *vivacité* leads them to grasp sublime truths with unusual immediacy, but it can also distract them. Therefore, women need education in a particularly profound way: education offers the mental discipline that provides the framework not only for knowledge but for moral advancement through the eradication of *amour-propre*: 'To know much, one must love oneself little' (91).

Pringy's account of the feminine condition has produced opposite reactions in contemporary critics, some of whom see her as misogynistic, while others as feminist.[20] The charge of anti-feminism seems misplaced. Pringy shares a certain neo-Augustinian view of human fallibility that is widespread among her contemporaries, both male and female. To see *amour-propre* as 'dominant' in women is not to claim that men are exempt from it; the inverse relation between *amour-propre* and true learning both points to the reason for this domination in women and provides an argument in favour of women's education.

One of the most admired women of the Enlightenment, the marquise de Lambert took aim squarely at the questions of women's mental aptitude and their role in public culture in her *Réflexions nouvelles sur les femmes* (*New Reflections on Women*). Circulated in manuscript and published without her permission in 1727, the *Réflexions* examine two distinct, but inter-related, questions: men's unnatural and unjust authority over women and the entwinement of sentiment, imagination and taste in the constitution of understanding. Women have lost a sense of themselves, she argues, because social prejudice attaches as much opprobrium to female learning as to vice: 'all shame being equal, one may as well choose that which pleases the most, and so they have given themselves over to pleasure'.[21] Women are trapped within a conflicting network of demands: their education is neglected in favour of an injunction to please, yet they are condemned when they pursue an inclination for pleasure. 'It is time to decide: if we wish them only to please, then do not forbid them to employ their charms; if we wish them reasonable and thoughtful, then do not abandon them when that is their only merit' (30). What do you want from us? she asks. If men wish to have companions who are both wise and virtuous, then they must allow women to study and perfect their reason. If men wish for women to cultivate those qualities that give pleasure, then they should not complain if women seek pleasure themselves.

The ideal social world would clearly be something akin to the great salons of the past century, 'where the Muses kept company with the Graces', and that Lambert has sought to emulate (14). The final pages of the *Réflexions* explore her 'metaphysics of love', in which such mixed-sex gatherings enable thought and feeling to unite in a manner that escapes the dichotomy between *estime* and *agrément* in the form of a non-purposive desire, thoroughly pleasurable and morally irreproachable.

That world is made possible because of the distinct cast of women's minds, when they are allowed to develop them. Lambert turns to the philosopher Nicolas Malebranche, whose work she had long known and esteemed but whose opinions on women's intellect were problematic. As he declared in his *De la recherche de la vérité* (*On the Search for the Truth*):

> The greatest delicacy of inner fibres is usually to be found in women; it gives them their profound understanding of whatever relates to the senses. Women decide on style, judge language, discern proper appearances and manners. They have greater knowledge, subtlety and finesse than men in such matters. All questions of taste fall to them, but in general they are incapable of penetrating truths that are even slightly hidden. Abstractions are incomprehensible to them.[22]

Lambert tones the passage down considerably in her citation: 'A very respectable author concedes to women all the pleasures of the imagination. *All matters of taste*, he says, *fall to them, and they are the judges of the perfection of language.* This is no mediocre advantage' (18).

Lambert deftly turns the philosopher's analysis on its head here. Although she shares Malebranche's form of Cartesianism whereby the mind is influenced by embodied experience, she argues that the experience of women does, in fact, offer certain advantages beyond those that he sought to trivialize. She proceeds through an analysis of taste, understood as a subtle and complex interaction of sentiment/sensation and inner rectitude (*'justesse de l'esprit'*). Unlike Pringy, who saw taste, *le goût*, as a manifestation of a will weakened by the deceptions of *amour-propre*, Lambert views taste as a non-discursive intuition of the right path. It would be incorrect, she argues, to claim that women's propensity to 'sentiment' obscures their ability to think;

rather, sentiment provides a shorter, more immediate pathway to the truth: 'I do not believe that sentiment impairs understanding; it furnishes new insights that enlighten us in such manner that ideas present themselves in a more lively fashion, clearer and less confused' (25).

If the mind has a sex, says Lambert, then it points to women's 'effortless feminine cognitive excellence'.[23] Lambert's juxtaposition of *réflexion* and *sentiment* as two different means to arrive at truth echoes the tensions between traditional erudition and the more worldly, spontaneous and fluid approach to social interaction known as the code of *honnêteté*. While aristocratic in its origins, the worldly or *honnête* appeal to the natural would of course come to have a considerably broader attraction, and, as we have seen, the advantage Lambert granted to women would often be lost from view.[24] In his commentary on the *Réflexions*, Gayot de Pitaval responded to her denunciation of women's double bind by quoting La Bruyère: 'Why, he asks, blame men that women are not more learned? By what Laws, what Edicts, what orders have we forbidden them to open their eyes?'[25]

As in the case of Pringy, women writers sometimes judge other women harshly, and not all viewed social life as conducive to women's mental growth or agency. The mid-century moralist, historian and woman of science Marie-Geneviève-Charlotte Thiroux d'Arconville offers little quarter in her essay 'Sur les femmes' ('On Women'): 'Men have pride, but most women have only vanity.'[26] As the essay unfolds, however, it is clear that d'Arconville's irritation at her sex does not stem from a sense of women's immutable nature but rather is directed at what women become when they conform to social expectations. As women's role is inevitably smaller, more constricted than that of men, so too are their expectations and desires: rather than pride, they display vanity; rather than praise, they seek flattery. D'Arconville reserves her most scathing indictment for the social-sexual compact that denies women any positive role whatsoever:

> In the private sphere, a woman assumes no role with impunity. Is she flirtatious? She is despised. Does she engage in intrigue? She is dreaded. Does she display learning or wit? If her works are bad, they are mocked; if they are good, others take credit for them, and she is left with only the ridicule of having claimed to be an author.[27]

These lines apparently struck a chord, and they were much cited throughout d'Arconville's lifetime and beyond, often without attribution (or misattributed), and were seen by her biographers as the explanation for her steadfast adherence to anonymous publication.[28]

While the essay portrays women as insipid creatures given to thoughtless love affairs, it also makes it clear that few other avenues are open to them.

Later, in the preface to her translation of Alexander Monro's *Anatomy*, she again attacks the frivolity of society women:

> Not satisfied with the power that grace and beauty provide, the women who set the style even for the things they understand the least, attempt to exercise their empire over Medicine. A physician who thinks only of his art is incapable of pleasing them, for he disdains little niceties and puerile language strewn with supposed witticisms, the usual recourse of mediocrity.[29]

Londa Schiebinger interprets this passage as a diatribe 'against women who wished to study medicine'.[30] But d'Arconville directs her ire not at women with a sincere desire to learn, but at those who take no interest in science at all and dismiss anyone who cannot play the social game.

In her moralist writings, d'Arconville gives no indication that women are constituted differently from men: both sexes suffer the burden of the human condition, which is to be blinded by *amour-propre* and driven by desire. Detachment from desire, the inner contentment furnished by profound friendships and intellectual pursuits, represents the greatest good. Her moral philosophy strives to weave connections between what are usually regarded as opposite views: on the one hand, a naturalistic view of moral development rooted in the passions; on the other, a voluntaristic view of virtue as the result of conscious choices. Like Lambert, she recognizes the inconsistent demands that society places on women, but she holds them responsible for their choices. While she herself does not attempt to map this approach onto a theory of knowledge, her blending of naturalism and voluntarism, embodiment and consciousness, is analogous to Lambert's account of the body's inflection of mental activity and the search for truth.

Even their views on sociability are less different than might at first appear. Lambert's preference for mixed-sex gatherings where carefully cultivated sentiment never strays from virtue's path is echoed in d'Arconville's account of friendship as 'the commerce of souls' and friendship between men and women as 'the most agreeable relation of all'.[31] It is clear, however, that whereas salon culture – at least the salon culture of the previous century – provided the grounds for Lambert's social ideal, d'Arconville's perfect friendships exist in a more intimate, private setting, away from what she saw as the superficiality of worldly social relations.

D'Arconville's dislike of worldly sociability reminds us that, while salon culture clearly offered certain women a site for agency and intellectual engagement, not all women experienced it in this way. Émilie du Châtelet too saw a profound disjuncture between her worldly activities and her decision to commit herself to the quest for knowledge: 'I am happy to have renounced in mid-course frivolous things that occupy most women for their entire lives; I wish to spend what time I have left to cultivate my mind.'[32]

Women who chose to engage in serious study were not universally admired, as evinced by the misogynist tone of Anne Dacier's interlocutors during the *querelle d'Homère*, or Mme du Deffand's venomous portrait of du Châtelet.[33] Unlike the 'republic of women' of the previous century, female intellectuals of the Enlightenment all too often pursued their ambitions alone or in the company of men only.

One of the most solitary was a woman identified by nineteenth-century bibliographers as 'Madame de Verzure'.[34] The abbé de la Porte expressed his admiration for the anonymous author of *Réflexions hazardées d'une femme ignorante* (*Chance Reflections of an Ignorant Woman*): 'Wit, taste, good sense and judgment reign; a profound and extensive knowledge of the heart and of the world put to rest the term *ignorant woman*.'[35] The reviewer of the *Correspondance littéraire* (December 1765), on the other hand, dismissed the work with an airy witticism: 'The title leaves nothing further to say.'[36] Like d'Arconville and others, Verzure preferred anonymity: 'A woman who takes it upon herself to write, who dares risk publication, should hide herself with care.'[37] She describes her enterprise as the result of intense self-scrutiny, away from the eyes of the world and 'scarcely known even to those that I frequent the most' (I, xv). In one of her essays, she describes 'the study of oneself' as one of the best ways of employing one's time, since 'at every instant, one makes new discoveries' (I, 191). Her essays on the interior life – 'Notions sur l'âme' ('Thoughts on the Soul'), 'Sur le cœur' ('On the Heart') and 'Sur les désirs' ('On Desires') – thus take us on a journey not unlike that of Descartes's *Meditations*, as she endeavours to define the basic elements of the mind through self-examination. Less concerned than Descartes with pursuing an unassailable basis for truth, Verzure seeks to explicate the strands of her thought and to consider the connections among them.

While clearly informed by nearly a century of discussion of 'the new interiority', Verzure charts her own course in the epistemology of feeling. In 'Quelques notions sur l'âme', she argues that the self (*âme*) is composed of both heart (*cœur*) and mind (*esprit*), but the ramifications of each and their interrelations are complex. The heart is the seat of taste, preference, appetite; its choices are instantaneous, unreflective and ineluctable: it is never neutral. However, it is subject to the enlightened judgement of the mind, which in turn determines the direction of the will (*volonté*). 'Taste' and 'sentiment' are both 'movements' of the heart; unlike philosophers who subordinate heart or embodied existence to mind or disembodied abstraction, Verzure sees the heart as 'ennobling' the senses and on an equal footing with the mind. She observes that reason cannot determine taste or sentiment but only marshal our will and prevent us from acting on our impulses. In the essay's final section, the interrelation between impulsive sentiment and reflective judgement is complicated anew by imagination, as unconstrained and immediate as sentiment and yet governed by reason, whose 'vivacity and grace' depend on its freedom.

As she pursues her thinking in the following essay, 'Sur le cœur', Verzure underscores the positive, creative dimension of the heart. Ultimately, the heart is present in all our actions and all our thoughts. The mind has feeling, she tells us, and that feeling is the heart. While reason has the capacity to control our actions, the heart is never indifferent and may govern us without our conscious knowledge. Verzure is less inclined than other moralists to condemn the subterfuges of the heart or even of *amour-propre*, however, and therein lies her originality. Her cartography of the intersection of thoughts and feelings is remarkably nonjudgemental. Verzure's commentary on gender is no less real for being implicit: as she reminds us on multiple occasions, her analysis is drawn from self-analysis. Describing herself as 'the only woman who has dared deviate from the normal path', she pursues her reasoning to its conclusion, in defiance of 'received principles and prejudices' (II, 101). Her sense of intellectual mission and her decision to publish exemplify her participation in the advancement of *lumières*.

The stereotypes that philosophically minded women of the eighteenth century contested would not soon disappear, but they made their voices heard. In the early years of the nineteenth century, Stéphanie de Genlis would reflect on the history of women writers in France and dissect the incoherence and stereotyping in their treatment. Looking back to Mme de Lambert, Pauline de Meulan would approve both her prose style and her personal reticence: 'Discretion is a woman's armor.'[38] Less inclined to gloss over the shortcomings of the pre-Revolutionary era, Germaine de Staël nevertheless found that the status of the woman writer had not improved: 'In monarchies, women must fear ridicule; in republics hatred.'[39]

As we have seen, the ambiguity of La Porte's epigraph, *Quid femina possit*, translates itself into a series of mixed messages for women intellectuals. Emboldened by new ideas, avid for educational opportunities and desiring to 'deviate from the normal path', women often encountered obstacles if not outright mockery. Defining themselves as writers required them to consider the question of gender and to define authorship on their own terms. Over the course of the long eighteenth century, they advanced arguments in favour of women's learning and developed theories of what it might mean to consider the heart in reflections on the mind and the desiring body as a component of the soul.

Sex and gender, feeling and thinking

NOTES

Joseph de la Porte, *Histoire littéraire des femmes françoises*, 5 vols. (Paris, 1769), vol. I, p. v. All translations are my own. Further references are given by volume and page number in the text.

2 Edme Ferlet, *Sur le bien et le mal que le commerce des femmes a fait à la littérature* (Nancy, 1772), p. 49.

3 Pierre Roussel, *Système physique et moral de la femme* (Paris, 1775), p. 104.

4 Ibid. p. 2.

5 Thomas Laqueur, *Making Sex: Body and Gender from the Greeks to Freud* (Cambridge, Mass.: Harvard University Press, 1990), pp. 8, 149–54.

6 Alain Viala, 'The Theory of the Literary Field and the Situation of the First Modernity', trans. Michael Moriarty, *Paragraph*, 29 (1) (2006), pp. 80–93; Gregory Brown, *A Field of Honor: Writers, Court Culture, and Public Theater in French Literary Life from Racine to the Revolution* (New York: Columbia University Press, 2002).

7 Germaine de Staël, *De la littérature*, ed. Axel Blaeschke (Paris: Garnier, 1998), p. 327.

8 Anne C. Vila, 'Ambiguous Beings: Marginality, Melancholy, and the Femme Savante', in Sarah Knott and Barbara Taylor (eds.), *Women, Gender, and Enlightenment* (New York: Palgrave MacMillan, 2005), pp. 53–69.

9 Anne-Thérèse de Marguenat de Courcelles, marquise de Lambert, *Réflexions nouvelles sur les femmes* (Paris, 1727), p. 14.

10 Stéphanie de Genlis, *De l'influence des femmes sur la littérature française*, 2 vols. (Paris: 1826), vol. I, pp. li–lii.

11 Pons-Augustin Alletz, *L'Esprit des femmes célèbres* (Paris, 1767), pp. iv–v.

12 Lorraine Daston, 'The Naturalized Female Intellect', *Science in Context*, 5 (2) (1992), pp. 209–35, at p. 213.

13 On the 'changing fortunes of Cartesian philosophy' for women, see Jacqueline Broad, *Women Philosophers of the Seventeenth Century* (Cambridge University Press, 2002).

14 Carol Pal, *The Republic of Women: Rethinking the Republic of Letters in the Seventeenth Century* (Cambridge University Press, 2012).

15 Linda Timmermans, *L'Accès des femmes à la culture sous l'ancien régime* (1995) (Paris: Champion, 2005), pp. 19–86.

16 Louise-Félicité de Kéralio, *Collection des meilleurs ouvrages français composés par des femmes*, 14 vols. (Paris, 1786–9); Fortunée Briquet, *Dictionnaire historique, littéraire et bibliographique des Françaises et des étrangères naturalisées en France* (Paris, 1804), and Claude-François Lambert, *Histoire littèraire du regne de Louis XIV*, 3 vols. (Paris: Prault, 1751).

17 See also Joan DeJean, 'Classical Reeducation: Decanonizing the Feminine', in Joan DeJean and Nancy K. Miller (eds.), *Displacements: Women, Tradition, Literatures in French* (Baltimore, Md.: Johns Hopkins University Press, 1991), pp. 22–36; Faith Beasley, *Salons, History, and the Creation of Seventeenth-Century France* (Aldershot: Ashgate, 2006), pp. 184–99.

18 William M. Reddy, *The Navigation of Feeling* (Cambridge University Press, 2001), p. 91.

19 Jeanne-Michelle de Pringy, *Les Différens Caractères des femmes du siècle, avec la description de l'amour propre*, ed. Constant Venesoen (Paris: Champion, 2002). Further references to Pringy are given by page in the text.

20 Eliane Viennot, *La France, les femmes et le pouvoir*, 2 vols. (Paris: Perrin, 2008), vol. II, p. 370; Timmermans, *L'Accès des femmes à la culture*, pp. 209, 335.

21 Lambert, *Réflexions*, p. 6. Further references to Lambert are given by page in the text.

22 Nicolas Malebranche, *De la recherche de la vérité*, 4th edn, 2 vols. (Paris, 1678), vol. I, p. 192.

23 K. J. Hamerton, 'A Feminist Voice in the Enlightenment Salon: Madame de Lambert on Taste, Sensibility, and the Feminine Mind', *Modern Intellectual History*, 7 (2) (2010): 209–38.

24 Timmermans, *L'Accès des femmes à la culture*, pp. 169–70.

25 Gayot de Pitaval, *Esprit des conversations agréables, ou nouveau mélange de pensées choisies*, 3 vols. (Paris, 1731), vol. III, p. 437.

26 Marie-Geneviève-Charlotte Thiroux d'Arconville, 'Pensées et réflexions morales', in *Mélanges de littérature*, 7 vols. (Amsterdam, 1775), vol. I, p. 398.

27 D'Arconville, *Mélanges*, vol. I, pp. 370–1.

28 Julie Candler Hayes, 'From Anonymity to Autobiography: Mme d'Arconville's Self-Fashionings', *Romanic Review*, 103 (3–4) (2013): 381–97.

29 D'Arconville, *Mélanges*, vol. III, pp. 195–6.

30 Londa Schiebinger, *The Mind Has No Sex? Women in the Origins of Modern Science* (Cambridge, Mass.: Harvard University Press, 1991), p. 249.

31 D'Arconville, *Mélanges*, vol. I, pp. 330, 336.

32 Gabrielle Émilie le Tonnelier de Breteuil, marquise du Châtelet, 'Préface du traducteur' (of Mandeville's *Fable of the Bees*), *Studies on Voltaire, with Some Unpublished Papers of Mme du Châtelet*, ed. Ira O. Wade (Princeton University Press, 1947), p. 136.

33 Judith P. Zinsser, *La Dame d'Esprit: A Biography of the Marquise du Châtelet* (New York: Viking, 2006), p. 237.

34 The *Correspondance Littéraire*'s reviewer identified the author as Mme Bontemps (Friedrich Melchior, baron von Grimm, *Correspondance littéraire* [December 1765], ed. Maurice Tourneux [Paris: Garnier, 1877], vol. VI, p. 455). A plausible candidate for authorship, Marie-Jeanne de Châtillon, or Mme Bontemps (1718–68), was a minor *salonnière* and the translator of James Thompson's *Seasons*. Following established usage, I refer to the author as Verzure.

35 De la Porte, *Histoire littéraire des femmes françoises*, vol. IV, p. ix.

36 Von Grimm, *Correspondance littéraire*, vol. VI, p. 455.

37 Verzure, *Réflexions hazardées d'une femme ignorante*, 2 vols. (Amsterdam: 1766), vol. I, p. v. Further references to Verzure are given by volume and page in the text.

38 Pauline de Meulan, 'Des femmes qui ont écrit, et de Mme de Lambert en particulier', in J. B. A. Suard (ed.), *Mélanges de littérature*, 5 vols. (Paris, 1804), vol. IV, p. 255.

39 Staël, *De la littérature*, p. 325.

8

CHARLY COLEMAN

Religion

We often think of the Enlightenment and religion as antithetical. Voltaire's repeated exhortation to 'Crush the vile thing!' (*Écrasez l'infâme!*) – the obscurantist, despotic character of spiritual authority – suggests as much. The sentiment is writ large in triumphalist histories of the period, with their claim that the *philosophes* heralded the emergence of secular modernity. They sought, in the name of 'modern paganism', to strip society of its Christian trappings.[1] In place of faith, they turned to reason as the standard for judging between true and false, moral and immoral. To persecuted religious minorities, they promised toleration, although this courtesy did not necessarily extend to those deemed intolerant themselves. Jettisoning a theocentric view of creation, they instead designated the human person as the measure of all things.[2]

This portrait resembles neither the intellectual dynamics within the Enlightenment nor the prevailing religious conditions of the eighteenth century. Philosophers, no less than kings and queens, had grown weary of the confessional strife that had ravaged Europe during the Reformation and the Thirty Years' War. In England, Prussia and Austria, and among Catholics, Lutherans, Calvinists, Pietists and Jews, champions of 'religious Enlightenment' sought to reconcile the dictates of faith with the operations of reason. They advanced the cause of peaceful pluralism against doctrinal absolutism, as part of a thoroughly pragmatic, moderate movement that garnered support from solicitous monarchs as well as the broader public sphere.[3]

France, once considered the cultural epicentre of eighteenth-century Europe, has been somewhat marginalized in recent scholarship on these developments. In contrast to kingdoms across the English Channel or the Rhine, the French body politic found itself besieged by a particularly virulent strain of anti-clericalism, while conflict was waged within the Church itself. Violent quarrels broke out between members of the Society of Jesus, who offered a relatively optimistic vision of the soul's capacity to participate

105

in its own salvation, and the staunchly Augustinian, pro-Gallican followers of Cornelius Jansen (or Jansenists), who denied this possibility. The latter's positions on issues such as original sin, the power of grace and ecclesiastical organization sharpened the *parlements'* rhetoric against abuses of royal power. Such criticisms, as much as those launched by the likes of Voltaire, eroded the legitimacy of the Ancien Régime, precipitating its eventual collapse in 1789.[4] Clashes between Jesuits and Jansenists also sabotaged attempts at rapprochement between the Church's intellectual elites and the *philosophe* movement. It proved difficult for partisans in one camp to make peace with the Enlightenment if the attempt exposed them to charges of impiety from their opponents. Feeling under siege, the *parti dévot* at court, the faculty of the Sorbonne and other bastions of traditional authority denounced the *philosophes* in apocalyptic tones, as harbingers of a debased, violent and godless future.

This chapter will survey the middle ground between religious culture and Enlightenment thought that emerged despite such challenges. The terrain was treacherous, not least because the fault lines between 'sacred' and 'secular' were never as definitive as the *philosophes* or their enemies at times asserted. Nevertheless, the absence of a full-fledged religious Enlightenment in France did not prevent clerics and *philosophes* from sharing similar convictions or making common cause against mutual adversaries. Theologians proved receptive to ideas and intellectual methods promoted by the *philosophes*, and the latter, even the most irreligious among them, remained acutely interested in matters pertaining to the identity of God, the nature of the soul and the status of revelation. In particular, thinkers of all stripes together struggled with a long-standing theological problem, that of fixing the relationship between the divine and temporal spheres. For moderate theologians and *philosophes*, the recognition of God's transcendence, or distance from creation, made it possible to recast the world as an independent domain, and humans as autonomous subjects within it. In contrast, radical mystics and materialists denied the purported separation between individual persons and the omnipresent forces thought to control them, whether identified as God or nature. When the dispute over transcendence is taken into account, the French Enlightenment takes on a markedly different aspect – as a movement that arose within the world of 'religion' rather than as a definitive departure from it.

The spiritual order of the Ancien Régime

As J. B. Shank points out in the case of science, it is misleading to speak of religion as a distinct category in eighteenth-century France.[5] Although both the Enlightenment and the Church prepared the way for such an outcome, it was never fully realized in the period's theory or practice. Religion had not yet been reduced to a neutral category of cultural comparison or to a matter of subjective choice. Even the *Encyclopédie*'s articles on the topic – such as 'Religion (Théolog.)' and 'Religion chrétienne' – deny that faith could remain merely a private affair. Among the vanguard in the drive to change this view were Cartesians and Jansenists. They argued that the insurmountable barriers between the worldly and otherworldly spheres necessitated the formation of concepts and institutions that functioned independently of divine dictates. Their calls for the sequestering of religion, while influential, proved difficult to reconcile with venerable traditions that endowed every facet of human existence, whether individual or social, with a pervasive spiritual aura.[6]

Absolutist politics demonstrate the degree to which the sacred and the secular remained intertwined under the Ancien Régime. According to Jacques Bénigne Bossuet – former tutor of the dauphin, bishop of Meaux and relentless defender of Catholic orthodoxy – the monarch enjoyed quasi-divine status. As he observed in *Politics Drawn from the Very Words of Holy Scripture*, kings are the 'ministers of God, and his lieutenants on earth'. As the personification of divine authority, the monarch's public, eternal body, which lives on despite the mortal end of each successive reign, encompasses the whole of his kingdom. 'The prince', Bossuet remarked, 'is not considered as an individual; he is a public personage, all the state is comprised in him; the will of the entire people is included his own.'[7] His will, which in Bossuet's time radiated from the Sun King's court at Versailles, must prevail over any subordinate, whether individual or institutional. God alone was competent to judge whatever errors the king made or crimes he committed.

These principles were reflected in political practice. A king was anointed with oil at his coronation in a ceremony invoking biblical tradition as well as admission into Holy Orders. He took communion in both bread and wine, a privilege enjoyed only by members of the clergy. He was even thought to wield a supernatural power to heal victims of scrofula. In ecclesiastical affairs, the Crown appointed men to powerful, often lucrative positions within the Church. The king swore to eradicate heresy, and his courts and administration served as formidable bulwarks against lapses in doctrinal discipline. Indeed, the absolute powers claimed by the reigning Bourbon dynasty stemmed in part from a tacit guarantee that it would quell the confessional strife that had wreaked havoc during the Wars of Religion. Louis XIV believed himself to be honouring this commitment by outlawing Protestantism in 1685, before launching a pyrrhic campaign against

Catholic Jansenists that continued, with disruptive effects, into his successors' reigns.

The monarch who ruled over men and women was thought to exist within a divinely ordained hierarchy. As the jurist Charles Loyseau explained in his *Treatise on Orders*, 'In all things there must be order, for the sake of decorum and for their control.' Men as a species governed the 'sublunary world'. As for the French kingdom, it comprised distinct but interdependent ranks, including the clergy, the nobility and the members of the Third Estate.[8] The heavens were organized into ascending classes of saints and angels, with Christ and the Virgin Mary at the pinnacle of a chain of being that extended to God the creator. According to this vision, the boundaries between civil and spiritual authority remained fluid. Kings routinely named prelates to the highest offices in the kingdom. More generally, the French state drew on the Gallican church not only for moral legitimacy and administrative expertise but also for financial support. Although the reach of the former's power gained at the expense of the latter over the course of the eighteenth century, their symbiotic relationship came to an end only with the Ancien Régime's demise.

If the monarch was exalted as a godlike being, he was also very much a mortal man. Louis XIV, for all his grandeur and apparent piety, was criticized as a warmonger who cravenly sought glory for himself while his people suffered. His successor, once acclaimed as 'the Well-Beloved', became reclusive in his later years. Sullied by charges of despotism and dissipation, Louis XV, along with the monarchy itself, began to lose some of their sacred lustre. This did not necessarily mean, however, that the Crown lost all associations with divinity. If, as Bossuet had asserted, God manifests political power indirectly, through the king, then what might stop an earthly prince from conducting himself in an analogous manner, by exercising authority through the State apparatus? In other words, if there is a transcendent, 'hidden God', why not a 'hidden king'? The Bourbons had long made considerable use of *intendants* (royal commissioners sent to enforce the king's will in the provinces) and other functionaries, so that Louis XV's reserved style further hastened the depersonalization of royal governance. As we shall see, these tendencies corresponded to broader shifts in how theologians and philosophers gauged God's proximity to creation.

Grounding the terrestrial sphere

The disaggregation of the worldly sphere from the divine took place over the religious *longue durée*. The origins of modernity can be located in nominalism, which unsettled the notion of providence with the claim that an all-powerful God would have no reason to consider the needs or aspirations of humankind in the act of creation. This argument was itself an effort to resolve a problem inherited from the ancient world, that of accounting for evil. Augustine famously responded by distinguishing the City of God from its inferior modulation, the City of Man. The former is the locus of perfection, the latter a consequence of original sin. Accordingly, God governs the earthly city with different standards, rules and ends than those that prevail in Heaven. However, Augustinian theology bequeathed vexing difficulties of its own. How does one reconcile the idea of God's omnipotence and omniscience – and its corollary that no soul can be saved without divine foreknowledge – with an equally strong emphasis on human wilfulness in and accountability for sin? Moreover, if the two cities operate according to their own distinct principles, then it is conceivable that they lack any resemblance to each other.

In the chasm between the divine and terrestrial cities, there emerged a conceptual space for asserting the independence of the latter from the former. Descartes exemplifies this outlook in *Meditations on the First Principles of Philosophy*, where he recounts how he arrived unaided at a secure knowledge of his own existence and that of God. Despite his awareness of a source of perfection outside himself, he realizes that it will remain unattainable to his own mind. Since divine knowledge is impossible for mere humans to comprehend, it is absurd to blame God for one's foibles on the basis of a preconceived, anthropocentric notion of justice. Descartes makes a similar point in the *Discourse on Method*. If natural philosophers could not grasp the rationale behind God's act of creation, they could nevertheless reproduce it, by imagining 'what would happen in a new world, were God now to create enough matter to compose it, somewhere in imaginary spaces'. In so doing, they could discover the purely physical laws by which the divine 'let nature act'. This knowledge, in turn, formed the basis of a 'practical philosophy' geared towards human needs, the aim of which would be to 'render ourselves, as it were, masters and possessors of nature'.[9]

Descartes's view was taken up by Jansenist moral philosophers seeking to account for social relations in a debased world. Blaise Pascal expressed their anthropological pessimism with characteristic incisiveness. Reflecting on God's 'overwhelming power', he invited human creatures to 'consider what we are, compared to what is in existence' and thus 'see ourselves as lost within this forgotten outpost of nature'. Humankind, he added, remains stranded by sin between its original innocence and its present corruption, tortured by knowledge of a happiness it cannot achieve.[10] If men and women cannot help but act in self-interested, vicious ways, then how is a well-ordered society possible? Another Jansenist luminary, Pierre Nicole, developed an influential argument in response. Humans, once alienated from God, fall under the tyrannical sway of self-love, which compels them to seek out the praise and esteem of others. Men form societies not through the exercise of virtue but by engaging in deceitful flattery. Their urge to dominate others is checked only by the fear of being dominated. The mutual attachment that binds them to their fellows is all the more powerful in being motivated by self-interest. Enlightened self-love thus provides a seemingly counter-intuitive, yet perfectly sound, basis for peaceful coexistence.

Cartesianism's mechanistic vision and the Jansenist theory of social forces remained touchstones, if not direct sources of influence, for theologians and *philosophes* alike. While Voltaire, d'Alembert and other thinkers associated with the Enlightenment's mainstream came to prefer Newton to Descartes, they retained the principle that nature operates without divine vigilance and that it can be manipulated for human ends. This instrumental approach was predicated on the depersonalization of physical phenomena, as Voltaire suggested in a dialogue staged between a philosopher and nature. 'I can certainly measure some of your planets, know their routes, and assign to them laws of movement', the philosopher noted, 'but I cannot know who you are' – whether active or passive, spiritual or material. Yet he could be certain of 'a supreme intelligence that presides over your operations', even if its reason for being remained unclear.[11]

In a series of works, Voltaire further stressed that humans live 'under the hand of this invisible master', who has furnished them with resources – material, moral and mental – to subsist without his immediate intervention. They carry the mark of the 'divine seal' that God imprinted on their being, such as the gifts of 'reason', a 'head capable of generalizing ideas' and a 'tongue supple enough to express them'.[12] It was sacrilege, therefore, to belittle either human or divine powers, just as it was foolhardy to overstate their scope. Voltaire rebuked Pascal for his unjustifiably pessimistic account of the human condition.[13] He likewise lashed out against fellow *philosophes* who sought to reduce humans to inert, unthinking matter. The author of the *Treatise of the Three Impostors*, one of the most notorious atheistic tracts of the century, struck him as a fool who wrongly blamed God for the evils perpetrated in his name. True religion, he argued, is not based on prescribed forms of worship. This 'sublime system' also buttresses the 'sacred bond of society' that provides a 'check on the villainous' and the 'hope of the just'. Despite his passion to *écraser l'infâme*, he avowed that 'If God did not exist, it would be necessary to invent him.'[14]

Deistic sensibilities prevailed among the moderate *philosophes*. According to Montesquieu's *Spirit of the Laws* (1748), 'God is related to the universe' through his implementation of laws, or the 'necessary relations deriving from the nature of things'.[15] This claim struck critics as a conduit to Spinozism, an accusation that Montesquieu dismissed outright. His aim had been to refute the likes of Spinoza and Hobbes, whose understanding of necessity deprived God of agency and men of an intuitive knowledge of justice. On the contrary, he affirmed the intelligence of the supreme being and humankind's native virtues, as well as Christianity's standing as a 'divine institution'.[16] In additions made to an earlier work, the *Treatise on Duties*, Montesquieu sketched his position on the relationship between humankind and its creator. God revealed himself to be 'a charitable being', not only 'because he gave us life' and 'the sentiment of our existence' but also by employing his 'infinite force' to arrange the universe in a providential manner. Rejecting God thus entailed surrendering any sense of order – indeed, any sense of self. As evidence for his assertion, Montesquieu pointed to Spinoza, whom he castigated for reducing human beings to 'a mere modification of matter'. If this were true, one individual could no longer be 'distinguished from any other' but would be reduced instead to 'a drop of water in the sea'.[17]

Christian apologists echoed these sentiments while maintaining that Enlightenment *philosophes* had neglected the mysteries of revealed religion. For instance, the Jansenist Guillaume Maleville shared with Montesquieu and Voltaire an abiding respect for the advantages that God had bestowed on humankind. 'Without the fear of God', 'faith in providence' and 'natural law', unregulated passions would subject men 'to all manner of disorder'. While Maleville upheld the absolute value of justice and temperance, he also appealed to social utility. One should follow the dictates of nature, because they are 'a fecund source of good for men'. At the same time, he acknowledged that obedience did not lead invariably to happiness. A perfect correlation between virtue and contentment would require 'miracles without cease', a level of involvement that contravened God's decision to govern 'by general means, and not by the rules of a particular providence'. However, humans had been endowed with sufficient powers to make their way in the world, including 'memory, intelligence, and will'. Catholic doctrine, while supplemented by revelation, was 'founded on solid proofs' and displayed 'evident qualities of truth' that even unaided minds could grasp. 'God did not give us reason' only to 'contradict it' in matters of religion. However reasonable, this state of affairs still rested on God's 'perfect liberty and independence'.[18] Although nothing could have prevented the Creator from denying human beings free will, active consciousness and rational faculties, Maleville was convinced that he had chosen not to do so.

Montesquieu, Voltaire and other apostles of the moderate Enlightenment kept traditional religion at arm's length. Their scepticism brought them into conflict with spiritual and political authorities. Nevertheless, they shared two axioms with adversaries such as Maleville. First, God's existence as the creator of a well-ordered universe did not require knowing the precise ways in which divine causes produce natural effects. Second, the human person possesses an active, sensitive mind capable of directing itself and its actions according to both personal desires and the common good. These principles were logically related. A hidden God is largely an absent one. It made sense, then, to focus on identifying physical and social laws. In other words, the magnitude of divine transcendence compelled theologians and philosophers to conceive of the world as an enclosed domain, within which the individual self acts as a creative, knowledge-generating subject. This view in turn pre-cipitated the development of intersecting spheres of human activity – social, cultural, political and economic – each with its own dynamics.

Many of the Enlightenment's master ideas can be considered as aftershocks of this seismic shift in the conceptual terrain. At the most fundamental level, Keith Baker has argued, the need to establish moral standards in the absence of a regulator-God led to the invention of society as the ultimate grounding of human thought and experience.[19] Henceforth, utility – and, by extension, physical and existential fulfilment – would reign supreme as the measure of value. According to the *Encyclopédie*, the *philosophe* looks to society as a 'divinity on earth', with the understanding that rational behaviour involves careful consideration of the needs and desires of one's fellows.[20] In a similar vein, Montesquieu served as a chief proponent of *doux commerce*, a theory arguing that trade and other forms of exchange have a potentially civilizing effect on those who engage in them. Attempts to apply natural law to all social interaction led to novel forms of economic reasoning such as physio-cracy, which its founder, François Quesnay, claimed to have discovered in a flash of divine illumination. Along with the physiocrats, merchants, admin-istrators and agronomists of various persuasions applied their expertise to thorny political tasks, such as the liberalization of the grain trade or gauging the consequences of global commerce.

The spectre of the hidden God continued to haunt French politics down to the Revolution and beyond. In 1775, the reform-minded controller-general of finances, Anne-Robert-Jacques Turgot, commissioned his deputy, the physiocrat Pierre-Samuel Dupont de Nemours, to prepare a *Memorandum on Local Government*. The document claimed that rationalizing the admin-istration would allow the King to 'govern like God', according to 'general laws'.[21] If Bossuet had once imagined that the monarch's transcendence stemmed from his exercise of quasi-divine forces, Turgot attributed the same transcendence to all-too-natural principles grounded in self-interest and utility. His plans, however, failed to overcome resistance from privileged elites. Looking beyond the collapse of the Ancien Régime, David Bell has argued that the modern idea of the French nation emerged from a need to reconfigure the social order given God's unfathomable distance. During the Revolution, political leaders drew on the time-honoured Catholic practices of theatre and festivals in their efforts to regenerate the body politic as a purely secular entity, divorced from links to Christianity.[22]

Taken together, these examples indicate how Enlightenment thought developed from pre-existing theological difficulties related to God's transcendence. Moderate *philosophes* formulated new conceptions of self, society and nature, emphasizing their relative freedom from divine interference. They were not alone in this enterprise. In addition to royal administrators, magistrates of the *parlements* and other advocates of reform, professional theologians also proved eager to join the fray. While often clashing with the *philosophes* on a range of issues, they also held the human subject's powers in high regard. Moreover, the two factions both sought to neutralize attacks on the self's capacity for independent thought and action. It is to these critics – and the arguments marshalled against them – that we now turn.

Mystics, materialists and the challenge of the radical Enlightenment

It might seem surprising, given the French Enlightenment's associations with anti-clericalism and the hostility shown by mitre and crown towards its leading figures, that Montesquieu and Voltaire broke ranks with the more subversive of their fellows. Such manoeuvres were not merely tactical countermeasures intended to preserve the credibility of the movement as a whole. On the contrary, the *philosophes* found themselves deeply divided over fundamental issues related to the attributes of the human person and its relationship to God and nature. While the Enlightenment's mainstream advanced a platform espousing natural religion and the prerogatives of the individual, an equally vocal faction called these ideals into question. Its partisans implicitly rejected the equation of divine remoteness with terrestrial autonomy and asserted that the self ultimately remains beholden to nature, a determining power beyond its control. While moderate *philosophes* held positions on the self's status analogous to those of theologians of transcendence, their radical brethren recalled the views of heretical mystics, who had taught that the soul must submit itself to a fully immanent God without reservation.

If the French eighteenth century was an age of theological controversy as well as Enlightenment, this axiom holds true not only for Jansenism but also for quietism, a controversial mystic doctrine named for its valorization of spiritual repose or quietude. The so-called Quietist Affair of the 1690s brought Bossuet into contention with his fellow prelate, François Fénelon.

The influence both men enjoyed among the court's inner circle drew Louis XIV and Pope Innocent XII into their debate, which also captivated much of the ecclesiastical establishment. In defending the notorious mystic Jeanne-Marie Guyon, who had become his mentor, Fénelon elaborated a sophisticated vision of spiritual abandon, which held that the soul's personal existence was a mere figment to be subsumed within the divine. His devotional writings charted the experiences leading to this outcome, culminating in what he called the 'prayer of union', whereby the soul loses its particular will and 'lives only by divine life'.[23] As he explained to Guyon, 'God opens [the soul] to himself by pushing out the love of ourselves that once occupied the space. To be in God is to be entirely dispossessed of one's will', which is reduced to a function of 'purely divine movement'.[24] Accordingly, one should reject every personal longing for recompense – including for salvation itself. The reason is that God becomes manifest only in the 'loss of all gifts' and 'the real sacrifice of oneself after having lost every interior resource'.[25]

The danger posed by Fénelon and his allies, according to Bossuet, stemmed from their denial of the soul's necessary interest in spiritual goods. The doctrine inculcated a 'new mysticism', as Bossuet called it, which 'extends the scope of indifference to include the eternal possession of God'.[26] Furthermore, the heresy obviated the desire to procure happiness through salvation, thus compromising moral agency in this life. Quietists exalted a state of absolute detachment, a sort of mystical sleep in which the soul lost all control of, and therefore accountability for, its thoughts and actions. Against this doctrine Bossuet asserted the orthodox virtues of spiritual activity. Not unlike Descartes, he distinguished 'the empire of will' from the passivity of the body, as a power 'by which man makes himself master of many things', including the imagination and the passions.[27] According to this taxonomy of transcendence, the divine moves the heavens, spirit directs matter, and, as we have seen with Bossuet's political writings, monarchs reign over their kingdoms. Quietism thus posed a scandalous threat to all forms of authority, including the soul's powers of self-control. As pressure on Fénelon mounted, he was driven from Versailles, and the affair was placed in the hands of Innocent XII, who, in March 1699, issued a brief condemning him.

Despite papal censure, Fénelon's views continued to attract attention, not only in a series of clerical trials and scandals but even in the writings of the *philosophes*. Suspected quietists faced prosecution before the *parlements* in Dijon and Aix. During the 1720s and 1730s in Paris, a sect of mystic Jansenists, known as the *convulsionnaires*, shocked contemporaries with their bizarre practices, such as inducing violent states of convulsion (hence their name), in an effort to render themselves living symbols of God's designs for his church. Their horrified co-religionists denounced them as victims of spiritual enthusiasm who, as harbingers of a 'renewal of Quietism', witlessly fell prey to 'transports that deprive them of all use of free will to such a degree that even if they lapse into grievous sin, they nonetheless are not at all inwardly culpable'.[28] D'Alembert treated the episode in the *Encyclopédie*, describing the *convulsionnaires* as 'fanatics' who did grave damage to the Jansenist cause with their outrageous displays and prophesies.[29]

D'Alembert's response was typical of the mainstream Enlightenment. For instance, Montesquieu's character Rica in *Persian Letters* is informed by a particularly candid monk that mysticism referred to a 'delirious state of devotion', while a quietist is 'nothing other than a man at once mad, devout and a libertine'.[30] In *The Age of Louis XIV*, Voltaire dismissed the *convulsionnaires* as part of a lost remnant of the population still resistant to 'the progress of reason'. Likewise, he belittled Fénelon's fellow mystic Guyon as 'a woman without credibility', whose 'heated imagination' left her susceptible to 'mystic reveries'. If one were to take to heart her views on 'the silence of the soul' and the 'annihilation of all its powers', the fear of divine punishment would no longer provide a motive for moral behaviour.[31] These judgements reflect the negative image against which moderate *philosophes* defined themselves. Mystic abandon suspended reason and will. Its sufferers lost control of their aberrant impulses, which, in turn, drove them to still greater excesses. A true adherent of the Enlightenment, in contrast, led a life of self-mastery and social purpose.

The materialists and atheists who problematized these ideals of selfhood tellingly took up the rhetoric of quietism. The reputation of heretical mystics for sexual experimentation features prominently in *Thérèse philosophe* (1748), one of the eighteenth century's best-selling libertine works. Its purported author, the marquis d'Argens, exploited their notoriety not only to ridicule revealed religion but also to convey his own message. If 'all our actions are necessarily determined', then there is no such thing as sin. Indeed, 'we are no more free to think in this or that fashion, or to have this or that will, than we are free to have or not have a fever'.[32] Quietists made fitting surrogates for such lessons, even if their claims to disinterestedness deviated from d'Argens's message that human beings are creatures of pleasure. Their teachings infused Christian devotion with eroticism, and their exploits were widely known. Morever, they claimed that the self's thoughts and desires were not, properly speaking, its own, but emanations of divine will. By replacing God with nature, one could arrive at a fair approximation of a key tenet of radical materialism.

Denis Diderot, co-editor of the *Encyclopédie* and one of the leading figures of the French Enlightenment, offers a still more arresting case of a *philosophe*'s engagement with the mystic tradition. His article 'Delicious' describes a manner of existential fulfilment during which one only relates unconsciously to sentiment, 'through a wholly passive ownership, without being attached to it'. He likened such a 'moment of enchantment' to a 'delightful *quietism*' that promises, despite its fleetingness, 'the greatest and purest happiness that humanity could imagine'.[33] Given the fraught status of the doctrine among both orthodox clerics and moderate *philosophes*, Diderot would not have used such a designation lightly. He chose to do so because it captured a specific dynamic, one that he would explore further in his materialist account of existence, *D'Alembert's Dream* (1769). In the dialogue, unpublished until 1831, the character d'Alembert endures a night of delirious sleep. During his ravings, it dawns on him that the human person is a mere assemblage of particles, adrift in the 'vast ocean of matter' that constitutes nature. What the waking d'Alembert had once believed to be 'individuals' now appear as transitory compounds of shifting elements. 'There is but one great individual', he realizes, 'and that is the whole.'[34] To arrive at this radical conclusion, the slumbering d'Alembert must surrender control of himself, thereby offering a physical demonstration of the metaphysical insight his character ultimately embraces. Deviating from the image of the attentive, observant, self-possessed *philosophe*, Diderot speculated on the revelations to be gained from states of altered consciousness, when ideas stray and darkness clouds the mind. In d'Alembert's case, he becomes aware of the extent to which one's thoughts, actions and even identity are determined by overwhelming forces that reign both within and beyond oneself.

Theological critics were quick to exploit the materialists' denials of human agency as well as their problematic treatment of nature. The eminent Christian apologist Nicolas-Sylvestre Bergier took such an approach in refuting the baron d'Holbach's *System of Nature* (1770), a treatise influenced by Diderot's thinking. Unlike his comrade, d'Holbach wore his atheism on his sleeve. Nonetheless, Bergier noted, he 'put nature in the place of God' by endowing it 'not only with force, energy, and action, but also laws, rules, foreknowledge, and goodness'.[35] D'Holbach's professed desire to demystify creation concealed an abiding faith in 'absurd and contradictory dogmas'. Bergier saved his most cutting remark for last. Not only were philosophical renegades like d'Holbach theists despite themselves, but their deification of matter also gave rise to 'a being more *mystical*, stranger and more inconceivable than a spiritual God'.[36] Even by the rational standards they claimed to live by, Bergier implied, their position was ultimately self-defeating. It was now up to Christian apologists to save reason, morality and nature itself from the dangerous speculations of atheistic materialists.

To Bergier and other critics, the allusion to mysticism was a perfectly apt manner of undermining the position of their opponents. As he noted in the *Encyclopédie méthodique*, quietists taught that 'it is necessary to annihilate oneself in order to be united with God', by entering into a 'state of passive contemplation'. Bergier likewise upbraided d'Holbach for his assertion that 'Man is, in each instant of his life, a passive instrument in the hands of necessity.'[37] Voltaire lodged similar complaints. D'Holbach had argued, like Diderot, that man is 'a being formed by nature and circumscribed by it', so that 'there exists nothing beyond the great whole of which he is a part'. God is thus a figment of the human imagination; uncreated, 'eternal elements' configure themselves to produce 'all the marvels on which we meditate and reason'.[38] To counter these views, Voltaire professed his faith in a divine 'architect' who had designed the universe with foresight and care. Since humans likewise possess self-consciousness and will, it stands to reason that they owe these attributes to their maker. Without an idea of a 'remunerative and vengeful God', there would be only 'calamities without hope' and 'crime without remorse'.[39]

The position taken by Bergier and Voltaire against materialists such as d'Holbach and Diderot is indicative of deeper fissures within the Enlightenment as a whole. Mainstream theologians and *philosophes* held that the self related to the world as a subject to an object. Human autonomy, on this view, mirrored the divine. Spiritual and philosophical radicals reversed this formula: the self was submitted to the dictates of a totalizing power capable of supplanting one's personal will and identity. For Christian mystics such as Fénelon and Guyon, this entity was God, located not in a distant sphere but in a position so immanently close to all creatures as to efface their independent existence. Radical materialists like Diderot and d'Holbach proceeded further still, by dethroning God along with the self. In their writings, the forces once concentrated in the divine redounded to nature, now conceived as a self-generating, ubiquitous web within which all things are inextricably bound.

Conclusion: resacralizing the French Enlightenment

There are compelling reasons to question the once canonical view of the eighteenth century as an age of scepticism and declining belief. Scholars have begun placing stronger emphasis on the role of religion in the emergence of what were once regarded as unambiguously secular ideas and institutions. Much of their work has focused on the influence exerted by Jansenist theology and, in particular, the Augustinian distinctions it posed between the City of Man and the City of God. Yet we still have much to learn about the relationship between the French Enlightenment and Catholicism and about the lines of demarcation between the temporal and spiritual domains during the eighteenth century. In so far as a religious history of the Enlightenment is no longer considered a contradiction in terms, it will be necessary to address questions concerning the nature and function of God as intently as the *philosophes* themselves. Even d'Holbach, despite his atheism, showed a keen interest in biblical exegesis and sacred history.[40]

Viewing the Enlightenment from a theological perspective yields crucial insights into the period. The writings of radical mystics and materialists reveal a far-reaching anti-individualist counter-current in thinking about the self. Their insistence on the determined and divisible character of personhood struck terror into the hearts of opponents, who feared that it undermined the basis for moral agency and intellectual autonomy. It also cast doubt on the image of the *philosophe* as an independent, rationally calculating, self-governing subject. Diderot himself took aim at this ideal by portraying his former collaborator d'Alembert in feverish slumber, his mind at the mercy of his rambling thoughts. Scandalized, he later asked that the manuscript of *D'Alembert's Dream* be destroyed.[41]

It is equally significant that an editor of the *Encyclopédie* would choose to develop his views on states of altered consciousness with reference to quietism. Of course, Diderot himself did not share Fénelon's views on God. But his allusion to a mystic heresy known to attenuate the self's powers and prerogatives offered a means of defining a position outside both the theological and the philosophical mainstreams. Historians who emphasize the differences between moderate and radical factions of the Enlightenment often associate the former with a willingness to compromise with spiritual authority and the latter with its complete repudiation. Yet, in certain cases, radical *philosophes* were even more iconoclastic than this characterization implies, hence Bergier's attack on d'Holbach as a self-deluding heretic. To the extent that one can speak of a 'Christian Enlightenment' in France – or at least an enlightened Christianity – it is on the basis of apologists such as Maleville and Bergier, who offered themselves as the only credible defenders of the ideals that the *philosophes* disingenuously claimed to uphold.[42]

More generally, the striking analogues between mystics and materialists point to an alternative account of secularization during the eighteenth century. Historians have often argued that the period witnessed a gradual disenchantment of political, social and intellectual life. The work of philosophers such as Descartes and theologians such as Nicole could be regarded as contributing to this development, by explaining the world not through otherworldly frameworks but as the interplay of human and physical agents. Fénelon, Diderot and d'Holbach offered a very different perspective. Instead of stressing the distance between the sacred and the profane, they understood God and nature as forces that existed in intimate proximity to the human person and acted upon it with complete dominion. Thus, if the world was seen as increasingly desacralized in some quarters, it came to be resacralized in others. The French Enlightenment, harbouring both tendencies, fostered not so much a decline in spiritual belief but rather its proliferation in newly charged conceptions of the self, nature and the body politic.

NOTES

1 Peter Gay, *The Enlightenment: An Interpretation*, vol. I: *The Rise of Modern Paganism* (New York: Knopf, 1966–9).
2 See also Paul Hazard, *The Crisis of the European Mind, 1680–1715*, trans. J. Lewis May (London: Hollis and Carter, 1953).
3 David Sorkin, *The Religious Enlightenment: Protestants, Jews, and Catholics from London to Vienna* (Princeton University Press, 2008), pp. 3–21.
4 See also Dale Van Kley, *The Religious Origins of the French Revolution* (New Haven, Conn.: Yale University Press, 1996).
5 J. B. Shank, *The Newton Wars and the Beginning of the French Enlightenment* (University of Chicago Press, 2008).
6 Charles Taylor, *A Secular Age* (Cambridge, Mass.: Belknap, 2007), pp. 29–41.
7 Jacques Bénigne Bossuet, *Politics Drawn from the Very Words of Holy Scripture*, ed. and trans. Patrick Riley (Cambridge University Press, 1990), pp. 58, 160.
8 Charles Loyseau, *Treatise on Orders and Plain Dignities*, ed. H. A. Lloyd (Cambridge University Press, 1994), p. 5.
9 René Descartes, 'Discourse on Method', in *Discourse on Method and Meditations on First Philosophy*, trans. Donald A. Cress, 4th edn (Indianapolis, Ind.: Hackett, 1998), pp. 24, 35.
10 Blaise Pascal, *Pensées and Other Writings*, trans. H. Levi (Oxford University Press, 1995), pp. 66.
11 Voltaire, 'Nature' in 'Questions sur l'Encyclopédie', in *Dictionnaire philosophique*, vols. XVIII–XX of *Œuvres complètes de Voltaire*, ed. Louis Moland, 52 vols. (Paris: Garnier, 1877–85), vol. XX, pp. 115–16.
12 Voltaire, 'Poème sur la loi naturelle', in *Œuvres complètes*, vol. IX, pp. 443–4, and 'Homme' *Questions sur l'Encyclopédie*, vol. XIX, p. 376.
13 Voltaire, *Letters on England*, trans. Leonard Tancock (London: Penguin, 2000), pp. 120–5.
14 Voltaire, *Épitre à l'auteur du nouveau livre: Des trois imposteurs* (n.p., n.d.), p. 1.
15 Charles-Louis de Secondat de Montesquieu, *The Spirit of the Laws*, Anne M. Cohler, Basia Carolyn Miller and Harold Samuel Stone (eds.), (Cambridge University Press, 1989), p. 3.
16 Charles-Louis de Secondat de Montesquieu, 'Défense de l'esprit des lois', in *Œuvres complètes*, ed. Roger Caillois, 2 vols. (Paris: Gallimard, 1949–51), vol. II, p. 1138.
17 Charles-Louis de Secondat de Montesquieu, 'Continuation de quelques pensées qui n'ont pu entrer dans le *Traité des devoirs*', in *Œuvres complètes*, vol. I, pp. 1137–8.

18 Guillaume Maleville, *La Religion naturelle et la révélée*, 6 vols. (Paris: Nyon, 1756–8), vol. I, pp. 67, 69–70, 74, 88, 277.

19 Keith Michael Baker, 'Enlightenment and the Institution of Society: Notes for a Conceptual History', in Willem Melching and Wygar Velema (eds.), *Main Trends in Cultural History: Ten Essays* (Amsterdam: Rodopi, 1994), p. 96.

20 'Philosophe', in Diderot and d'Alembert (eds.), *Encyclopédie*, vol. XII, p. 510.

21 Pierre-Samuel Dupont de Nemours and Anne-Robert-Jacques Turgot, 'Memorandum on Local Government', in *University of Chicago Readings in Western Civilization*, vol. VII: Keith Michael Baker (ed.), *The Old Regime and the French Revolution* (University of Chicago Press, 1987), pp. 97–117, at p. 99.

22 David Bell, *The Cult of the Nation in France: Inventing Nationalism, 1680–1800* (Cambridge, Mass.: Harvard University Press, 2001), p. 7.

23 François Fénelon, *Sentiments de piété* (Paris: François Babuty, 1713), pp. 92–3.

24 François Fénelon to Jeanne-Marie Guyon (11 August 1689), in Jeanne-Marie Guyon, *Lettres chrétiennes et spirituelles*, 5 vols. (London, 1767), vol. V, pp. 316–17.

25 François Fénelon, *Œuvres spirituelles de Messire François de Salignac de la Mothe-Fénelon*, 2 vols. (Anvers: Henri de la Meule, 1718), vol. I, p. 171.

26 Jacques Bénigne Bossuet, *Instruction sur les états d'oraison* (Paris: Jean Anisson, 1697), pp. 115, 80.

27 Jacques Bénigne Bossuet, *Introduction à la philosophie, ou De la connaissance de Dieu et de soi-même* (Paris: Robert-Marc d'Espilly, 1722), p. 210.

28 Jacques Vincent d'Asfeld, *Vains efforts des mélangistes ou discernans dans l'œuvre des convulsions* (Paris, 1737), pp. 120, 136, 142.

29 'Convulsionnaires', in Diderot and d'Alembert (eds.), *Encyclopédie*, vol. IV, p. 171.

30 Charles-Louis de Secondat de Montesquieu, *The Persian Letters*, trans. George Healy (Indianapolis, Ind.: Hackett, 1999), p. 228.

31 Voltaire, 'Le Siècle de Louis XIV', in *Œuvres complètes*, vol. XV, pp. 62, 63, 64.

32 'Thérèse philosophe', in *Œuvres anonymes du XVIIIe siècle*, ed. Michel Camus (Paris: Fayard, 1986), vol. III, pp. 107, 179.

33 'Délicieux', in Diderot and d'Alembert (eds.), *Encyclopédie*, vol. IV, p. 784 (emphasis added).

34 Denis Diderot, 'D'Alembert's Dream', in *Rameau's Nephew and d'Alembert's Dream*, trans. Leonard Tancock (London: Penguin, 1976), pp. 174, 181.

35 Nicolas Bergier, *Examen du matérialisme, ou réfutation du système de la nature*, 2 vols. (Paris: Humblot, 1771), vol. I, p. 3.

36 Bergier, *Examen du matérialisme*, vol. II, p. 232.

37 Nicolas Bergier, 'Quiétisme' in *Encyclopédie méthodique: Théologie*, 3 vols. (Paris: Panckoucke, 1788–90), vol. III, p. 310; and Paul Henri Dietrich, baron d'Holbach, *Système de la nature, ou des loix du monde physique et du monde moral*, 2 vols. (London, 1770), vol. I, p. 75.

38 D'Holbach, *Système de la nature*, vol. I, p. 1; vol. II, p. 154.

39 Voltaire, 'Dieu, Dieux', in *Questions sur l'Encyclopédie*, vol. XVIII, pp. 376.

40 See d'Holbach, *Le Christianisme dévoilé* (1756), *La Contagion: La Bible devant la critique rationaliste* (1768), *Théologie portative* (1768) and *Histoire critique de Jésus-Christ* (1770).

41 Denis Diderot to Jean le Rond d'Alembert, end of September 1769, in *Correspondance*, ed. Georges Roth, 16 vols. (Paris: Éditions de Minuit, 1955–70), vol. IX, pp. 156–8.

42 On this point, see Mark Curran, *Atheism, Religion, and Enlightenment in Pre-revolutionary Europe* (Woodbridge: The Royal Historical Society/Boydell Press, 2012).

9

JENNIFER MILAM

Art and aesthetic theory: claiming Enlightenment as viewers and critics

How interesting this age has become, causing so many artists to sigh. For a few days the countryside is abandoned; Paris comes to life; all classes of citizens come to pack the Salon. The Public, natural judge of the fine arts, already pronounces its verdict on the merit of paintings that took two years of labour to produce. Its opinions, at first tentative and uncertain, quickly acquire stability. The experience of some, the enlightenment of others, the extreme sensibility of one party and the good faith of the majority are finally able to produce a judgment all the more equitable in that the greatest liberty has presided there.[1]

The rise of the art critic is one of the most significant changes to the history of artistic reception. It is bound up in a broader understanding of the Enlightenment as process, rather than strictly as an intellectual movement. Debates about the definition of beauty, the origins of good taste and the social value of the arts occupied the Enlightenment's intellectual leaders – Voltaire, Diderot, Rousseau, Montesquieu, among others – but their theories did not inform an artistic movement. There is no Enlightenment style, and to seek out a set of criteria by which certain works of art could be claimed as a product of the Enlightenment is fraught with difficulty.[2] It is far more productive to consider how encounters with art, occasioned by the public exhibition of paintings and sculpture at the Salons, offered opportunities through which individuals could claim 'enlightenment' and thus opened up the discourse on art to a wider range of opinions and judgements that further questioned the relationship between art and society. Enlightenment was conceived as a state of mind in the reception of art, cultivated in opposition to received positions of authority in matters of taste.

In the passage quoted above from *Le Triumvirat des arts* (1783), Carmontelle intimated that the investment of authority in public opinion caused anxiety among artists: they 'sigh' in response to the judgements passed so quickly over what has taken them years to produce. Moreover, the implication of this public judgement was that the success of a work of art was no longer determined by pleasing a patron, as it had been for centuries.

Instead, success now involved some appeal to a newly formed and disparate group of viewers: some who are experienced; others who are enlightened (gifted with *lumières*); a few who have sensibility (*sensibilité*), but most of whom simply respond in 'good faith'. What is key are the distinctions between the different kinds of viewers. Although there exist a multitude of perspectives that culminate in judgements valorized as free and equitable, some viewers are described as more skilled than others. Experience, presumably, could be gained. *Sensibilité* was innate, described in the *Encyclopédie* as a 'delicate and tender disposition of the soul that makes it easily moved'.[3] How did one become an enlightened viewer? Among those at the Salons, who possessed *des lumières*?

The term *lumière* was used metaphorically in the eighteenth century to refer to the state of learning rather than to define an intellectual movement. To say that a person possessed enlightenment in a particular domain of knowledge was to recognize expertise.[4] Consequently, to be deemed an enlightened viewer at the Salons was to have gained public acknowledgement of personal expertise in matters of aesthetic taste and artistic judgement. For centuries, this expertise had been in the hands of an elite – princes and patrons. While encounters with works of art in the space of the Salon provided the opportunity to demonstrate enlightenment, art criticism and aesthetic tracts became the vehicle through which individuals claimed their status as enlightened viewers.

From 1737 onwards, when the Salon exhibitions were instituted as regular events in Paris, art became a focus of public interest. Lasting for several weeks, works produced by members of the Académie Royale de Peinture et de Sculpture were hung in the Salon Carré of the Louvre. Commentators routinely noted the vast number of people from all walks of life who flooded the main room and staircase. Prints and written descriptions of the events give a sense of the social mix: nobles, bourgeoisie, servants and working-class men and women were all seen, often standing side by side, accompanied by children and dogs. It was a levelling public space in which both contemporary art and the spectacle of its audience were on display, stimulating a range of debates around the public reception of art.[5]

For many critics, the Salons occasioned an opportunity to condemn the *goût moderne*, which was the eighteenth-century term used to describe the taste for a new style of art that emerged around 1700.[6] Sinuous line, asymmetry and the use of natural motifs are the decorative tendencies most commonly associated with this rococo style first seen in the ornamentation of French interiors. Within two decades, this ornamental idiom was transposed into figural painting through Antoine Watteau's development of the *fête galante*.[7] Perceived by the Académie Royale as a novel genre category when Watteau submitted his acceptance piece, *The Pilgrimage to the Island of Cythera* (1717), the *fête galante* epitomizes the rococo in terms of both subject and style. Beyond a general description of the scenes as depictions of leisure and love, their content remains ambiguous. Elegantly dressed figures languish in ethereal garden settings, engaged in playful diversions and the rites of courtship. There is no sense of narrative purpose to their actions.[8]

'Experienced' viewers in the eighteenth century (to use Carmontelle's term) would have been well versed in reading subject matter through the conventional narrative techniques employed by painters since the Renaissance; yet these viewers would have sought in vain to decipher the *fête galante* using these tools. Facial expressions are difficult to discern. Central figures often have their backs to the beholder, denying any possibility of reading the face. Gestures, which should have made the body's actions legible, instead lead to voids within the composition or outside the frame where no further information can be derived.[9] Instead, what captures and holds the viewer's attention are the flickering qualities of light, shimmering surfaces of fabrics and the delicate handling of brushwork and colour. Together these pictorial elements stimulate an engagement with the creative act of painting rather than the details of a story, visually told.

This self-conscious artfulness is a consistent feature of rococo art and architecture across Europe. In eighteenth-century France, however, what is much more important is the engagement of rococo painting with the manners and mores of its intended audience. While initially that audience was noble, it came to include increasing numbers of wealthy bourgeoisie who sought to emulate the behavioural codes associated with the cult of *honnêteté*. Watteau's great innovation was his development of a style that embodied the shared values of these social groups, in particular the desirable notion of an effortless and artful presentation of the self. In the hands of later artists – François Boucher and Jean-Honoré Fragonard – rococo forms and themes effectively became synonymous with an aristocratic way of life. Within the context of private spaces owned and inhabited by the nobility and wealthy bourgeoisie, such an association visually confirmed membership among a social elite. Once rococo art was decontextualized from spaces of sociability and put on view to a heterogeneous public in the space of the Salons, the values it represented became a target for social, cultural and political critique.

Watteau's paintings addressed a specific and relatively restricted audience. He was an intimate member of the circle of the financier Pierre Crozat, which included artists who were leading members of the Académie Royale, prominent collectors and published art theorists.[10] In eighteenth-century terms, Crozat was an *amateur*, defined in the *Encyclopédie* as an art lover with demonstrated taste for *les beaux-arts*.[11] Expertise in matters of artistic judgement was acknowledged through this title of esteem, allowing an *amateur* to suggest subjects and recommend improvements to a work of art without an assumption of control over the creative process. This distinguished the behaviour of the *amateur* from the conventional intervention of a patron, connecting the use of the term with an increased appreciation of artistic independence during the eighteenth century. Crozat surrounded himself with lovers of art and music, bringing together the arts in ways that prefigure the categorization that would inform aesthetic theory during the age of Enlightenment. In addition to Watteau, Crozat hosted artists and musicians, including the Venetian Rosalba Carriera, and leading academicians such as Charles de La Fosse and Antoine Coypel, who was favoured by the duc d'Orléans during the Regency and became First Painter to the King under Louis XV in 1715. Dealers and collectors (Jean de Jullienne and Pierre-Jean Mariette), as well as art and aesthetic theorists (Roger de Piles and Jean-Baptiste du Bos), were in attendance at the social gatherings that took place in the Hôtel Crozat. Mariette commented on the atmosphere at Crozat's evening salons: 'I owe what little knowledge I have acquired to the works of the great masters that we examined there and equally to the conversation of the noble persons who made up the company.'[12] The pursuit of knowledge concerning the visual arts is linked in Mariette's comment to widening forms of sociability, prefiguring the Enlightenment salons attended by the *philosophes*, who, in turn, moved their conversations out of the academy and university into the private world of the *salonnières*. In bringing together a group of practising artists and men of letters for conversations involving art and music, presumably incorporating an interest in aesthetics with the presence of de Piles and du Bos, Crozat's circle commanded a new type of authority in matters of taste and aesthetic judgement.

Crozat's gatherings represent a notable departure from earlier traditions of patronage, which located authority in the personal taste of the patron. In court circles, this meant the prince, who often set the standard and directed the tastes of his courtiers. Grand-manner painting, with its distinctive mix of baroque pomp and classical restraint, is the style most closely associated with the taste of Louis XIV. Moreover, the Académie Royale was established under the King's protection, with academic art ratified both formally and informally through this official association. As a result, academic discourse, which included the debates of the late seventeenth century over whether line or colour should dominate the art work and its appeal to the intellect or to the emotions, provided the context in which artistic standards and related issues of aesthetic judgement were debated among the artists themselves. During the Enlightenment, it would be the art-making of the previous century in France that was simultaneously celebrated and lamented as the lost Golden Age of the French School, as critics used what they framed as the decline of the arts as evidence of the social and political decadence of the French state under Louis XV.

Prior to the rise of the independent art critic in the late 1730s, theoretical writing about art in France emerged from debates that were initiated within lectures at the Académie Royale. Artists were the primary voices in these *conférences* (as Académie lectures were known), but non-artists were also present and played an active role in the development and dissemination of French art theory. Some of these men were bureaucrats with official positions at court. André Félibien was a minor nobleman and official historiographer of the Bâtiments du Roi, a part of the royal household responsible for works commissioned for the King. He wrote up the lectures that began the colour/line debates in 1667, and he edited the *Conférences* (1669). In addition, he published several texts on the history and theory of art, including his multi-volume *Entretiens sur les vies et sur les ouvrages des plus excellens peintres anciens et moderns* (*Discussions Concerning the Lives and Works of the Most Excellent Painters, Ancient and Modern*) (1666–88), which includes a definition of the 'classical doctrine' of painting as practised by Nicolas Poussin, Sébastien Bourdon and Charles Le Brun.

These artists were undoubtedly interested in the relationship between theory and practice, but their ideas circulated through personal correspondence, lectures at the Académie Royale and in unpublished notes and drawings. It must be remembered that artists are skilled in the visual communication of ideas. For the most part, the development of art theory as a form of discourse was in the hands of writers. Even so, the growing interest in writing about art theory emerged in France through the colour/line debates initiated by the artists themselves. Also known as the debate between the *Rubénistes* and the *Poussinistes* (as the proponents of colour and line became respectively known), the colour/line debates paralleled the Quarrel of the Ancients and the Moderns that took place within the Académie Française. In parallel with the Académie Royale, this institution was charged with the regulation of the French language and attended to issues of judgement in philosophy and literature. What linked the colour/line debates in painting to the Quarrel of the Ancients and the Moderns in literary matters were shared concerns over the authority of classical antiquity, upheld by the 'ancients' camp and refuted by the 'moderns'. In the visual arts, this authority was understood to mean that classical antiquity presented an ideal model, which could be equalled but not surpassed by modern artists. This position effectively restricted reception on the part of 'experts' to judgements made against a set of rules established in relation to art of the past that could not be challenged or overturned by contemporary artistic innovations. At the very heart of academic discourse, as it developed, was the contentious issue of where the authority resided (in the past or the present) to determine the standards for judgement in the visual arts. As art and aesthetic theory developed both within and outside of the academies, the role of subjective judgement in response to art became a crucial subject of interest.

Some honorary members of the Académie Royale, such as Roger de Piles, built their reputation as connoisseurs and offered advice in matters of taste to prominent patrons. When the duc de Richelieu lost his collection of paintings by Poussin in a wager with Louis XIV, he was advised by de Piles to buy works by Peter Paul Rubens. This is perhaps the most vivid example of the impact of theoretical debates on the taste of collectors, but it also demonstrates a shift of authority in matters of taste from the patron to the 'expert'. De Piles was the leading art theorist at the turn of the century. He published several treatises on art that emphasized the visual effects of painting over the purely intellectual. Like Félibien, the *conférences* that sparked the colour/line debates appear to have stimulated his interest in art theory. Five years after the *conférences* of 1667, de Piles's *Dialogue sur le coloris* (*Dialogue on Colour*) (1673) appeared. It promoted the importance of colour as the defining feature of painting that distinguished its effects from the other arts. More specifically, he based his theories of pictorial composition on issues of form and visual perception rather than on rules of expression and gesture dictated by narrative subject matter. These ideas were most fully developed in his *Cours de peinture par principes avec une balance des peintres* (*Course on the Principles of Painting, with a Comparison of Painters*) (1708), in which he argued that the effects of colour, light and shade were as important as drawing in the creation of visual unity. Moreover, he broke down the traditional genre hierarchy in his expansion of the definition of history painting to include all subject matter. The genre of landscape, for example, is celebrated for its creative potential: 'painting, which is a kind of creation, is more particularly so with regard to landscape'.[13] In responding to art, de Piles recognized the value of the imagination, enthusiasm and genius. The latter quality was something de Piles acknowledged as unusual: 'It rarely happens that a painter has a genius extensive enough to embrace all the parts of a painting' (203). According to de Piles, there were four principal parts of painting: composition, drawing, colour and expression. These are the categories against which painters of 'established reputation' were scored by de Piles on a scale of 1–20 in his 'Catalogue of the names'.

This 'catalogue' was an alphabetical list of the 'best known' Renaissance and seventeenth-century painters from Italy, the Netherlands, the Dutch Republic and France, scored numerically in columns labelled 'composition', 'drawing', 'colour' and 'expression'. As a preface to this rubric of assigned value, de Piles acknowledged the subjectivity of judgement in matters of taste: 'Opinions are too various ... to let us think that we alone are in the right. All I ask is the liberty of declaring my thoughts in this matter, as I allow others to preserve any idea they may have different from mine' (489–90). At the same time, he seized the opportunity to set himself up as a man of superior judgement:

> I must give notice, that in order to criticize judiciously, one must have a perfect knowledge of all the parts of a piece of painting, and of the reasons which make the whole good; for many judge of a picture only by the part they like, and make no account of those other parts which either they do not understand or do not relish.
>
> (492–3)

As the author who attends to all four principal parts of painting, de Piles demonstrated his own 'perfect knowledge'. Art-writing became an opportunity to display knowledge in a particular subject area, not as a patron or as an artist but as someone who had developed the capacity to pass judgement as an informed viewer.

In an institutional context, the Académie Royale brought men who were not patrons into direct contact with painters, in part to establish standards of artistic practice and in part to debate standards of taste. Through this interaction between practising artists and non-professionals who were interested in art from both a theoretical and technical perspective, issues of artistic judgement moved from the exclusive province of the princely patron into the institutional domain of the Académie Royale. Crozat's unofficial 'academy' took this process one step further and, in so doing, prepared the way for the independent voice of the critic by opening up matters of taste to unsanctioned voices of authority, who claimed expertise in matters of artistic judgement. Unlike the autonomous critic, both Félibien and de Piles were part of the art establishment, and their publications represent debates that the artists themselves initiated within the Académie Royale. Their critiques were therefore less threatening than those produced as anonymous pamphlets in response to the Salons, which were perceived by academic leaders as having the potential to damage the reputation of contemporary French artists.

The first critic to gain notoriety for these attacks on contemporary art was Étienne La Font de Saint-Yenne.[14] Of particular concern to La Font was the redirection of the arts towards the market for luxury goods. Instead of serious history painting, living artists were occupied with decorative commissions that reduced painting to 'insipid and utterly uninteresting depictions ... which required neither genius, nor invention' and that often relegated their position to inferior points within the interior (as over doors or in ceiling coves).[15] While La Font did little to advance art theory during the Enlightenment, he is significant for his contention that matters of artistic judgement required independence from the prevailing socio-political economic factors that influenced artistic production: 'It is only in the mouths of those firm and equitable men who compose the public, who have no links whatever with the artists ... that we can find the language of truth.'[16] With a statement such as this, La Font claimed that any critic who sought to speak with honesty about art would be compromised by any official association with artists, a claim that amounted to a direct attack on the authority of the Académie Royale.

Academicians responded to La Font's criticism quickly. Relying on the persuasive value of the visual as a means of communication, a number of satirical prints appeared that were designed to refute La Font's authority as a viewer: one depicts La Font as a blind man; another shows him examining a monument through a magnifying glass while a dog urinates on his leg. Teamed with the visual were actual texts produced by writers, who, like de Piles and Félibien, were closely connected to the leadership of the Académie Royale. The abbé Jean-Bernard Le Blanc was historiographer of the Bâtiments du Roi (the same post occupied by Félibien) when he wrote *Lettre sur les expositions des ouvrages de peinture, sculpture, etc. de l'année 1747* (*Letter on the Exhibitions of Painting, Sculpture, etc. of 1747*), which openly condemns the unofficial critic.[17] Boucher designed the frontispiece for this text as an allegorical depiction of *Painting Mocked by Envy, Stupidity and Drunkenness*. Such publications and some of the prints designed by academic artists and engraved by honorary members of the Académie Royale demonstrate what had become a conventional alliance between academic artists, amateurs and officials in determining matters of artistic judgement. The unofficial critics, like La Font, stood outside of this group (as did the *philosophes*) and claimed to speak on behalf of the public.

At issue for the next four decades was the source of authority that could be assumed in matters of taste. On the one hand, there was official authority, which was located with representatives of the King – members of the Académie Royale and office-holders within the Bâtiments. On the other hand were independent critics, who sought to seize authority by claiming to represent the public. Some of these men and women were intellectuals and literary figures, such as Denis Diderot; others were not. Nonetheless, they similarly sought to demonstrate personal authority in the area of knowledge that was connected with art and aesthetics.

A concern with the visual extended the major debates of the Enlightenment in ways that acknowledged the socio-political effects of art in the public sphere. The impact of art had been signalled in aesthetic writing as early as 1719, when the abbé du Bos's *Réflexions critiques sur la poésie et la peinture* (*Critical Reflections on Poetry and Painting*) was published. Du Bos, who, like de Piles, was connected to both the circles of Crozat and the Regent, argued that the relative success of art relied upon its appeal to sensation, as opposed to the intellect. In alignment with de Piles's own claims about the subjectivity of judgement, du Bos goes one step further in maintaining that aesthetic reception relied upon the feelings and emotions that a work of art aroused and that these subjective responses were more important than an objective relationship to established conventions of representation.

The *philosophes* engaged with these issues through their writings on aesthetic theory. Since the middle of the eighteenth century, prominent men of letters who are now considered to represent the Enlightenment had pondered the relationship between art and society, the definition of beauty and the formation of taste. Many of their ideas were summarized in the entries in the *Encyclopédie* on 'Goût' ('Taste') (begun by Montesquieu, taken over by Voltaire and added to by d'Alembert) and 'Beau' ('The Beautiful') (by Diderot). In their writings, good taste and the appreciation of the beautiful, as it appears in a work of art, are represented as uncommon and the result of discernment. Diderot stated that 'the educated man lends his attention only to the most perfect works'.[18] Voltaire maintained that in order to have good taste it was not sufficient 'to see' or 'to know' beauty or even 'to feel and be moved' by it; instead it was necessary to 'discern different degrees of feeling'.[19] Most exclusively, d'Alembert concluded that objects of taste are 'are destined for a small minority'.[20] In what largely amounts to an elitist stance, all three *philosophes* argued that good taste is a distinguishing feature of the enlightened man and the civilized country. Their claims in this regard are important to understanding how art put on display at the Salons provided occasions for individuals to demonstrate 'good taste' to a wider public and that, in turn, this disparate audience was crucial as a point of comparison to verify one's own status as an enlightened viewer.

Diderot's reviews of Salon exhibitions were produced from 1759 to 1781. It was in his 1760s *Salons* that he put the aesthetic debates of the period into critical practice. He celebrated works by Jean-Baptiste Siméon Chardin, Claude-Joseph Vernet and Jean-Baptiste Greuze for conveying natural truths. It must be remembered that these writings were primarily directed to a small number of titled subscribers to Melchior Grimm's *Correspondance littéraire*, in which Diderot's commentaries on the Salons originally appeared.[21] Because this publication was already shaped, through its exclusive distribution, as a vehicle of socio-political involvement, he was able to embed theoretical aesthetic concepts within his critical responses to individual works. Not only were the selected subscribers familiar with current aesthetic debates in Enlightenment circles, they were also major patrons and collectors who appreciated affirmation of their exclusive status as men and women of good taste. They were both experienced viewers and enlightened readers.

In his *Salons*, however, Diderot claimed to represent the opinions of a wider public at the same time as he advanced his personal (and subjective) aesthetic sensibilities:

> I gave my impressions time to coalesce and settle in. I opened my soul to the effects. I allowed them to penetrate through me. I collected the verdicts of old men and the thoughts of children, the judgments of men of letters, the opinions of sophisticates, and the views of the people.[22]

This passage that opens *The Salon of 1765* represents a critical shift in writing about the reception of art from the perspective of the expert connoisseur to that of the enlightened viewer. Throughout the *Salons*, Diderot does not speak as an art expert but rather as a viewer of advanced aesthetic sensibility whose superior powers of response are confirmed by the audience he describes as being around him and which is written into his criticism. For de Piles, his rubric in the 'Catalogue of Names' represented his subjective judgements, which are possible only because he is a man in possession of the ability to respond knowledgeably to the four principal parts of painting. The value of the subjective response thereby remains connected to the knowledge of the expert as a connoisseur. Diderot, in contrast, has a personal response that he then brings together with the variety of opinions that circulated (he says) among the audience at the Salons. This at once confirms both the value of subjectivity in responding to works of art as well as his personal authority as a critic capable of filtering subjectivity into cohesive judgements. Unlike de Piles, it is not Diderot's expertise as a connoisseur that gives him this authority but the occasion of the Salons that provides him with the opportunity to demonstrate his status as viewer with enlightenment.

This was the opportunity grasped by Carmontelle, but not simply to show his capacity as an enlightened viewer. For most of his life, Carmontelle was a playwright, portraitist and landscape architect in the service of the duc d'Orléans. Despite his many talents, Carmontelle was not an academically trained artist and never became an academician. The son of a boot-maker, he studied drawing and geometry before qualifying as an engineer and entering the service of high-ranking noblemen.[23] From 1763 onwards, Carmontelle created innovative works of art, garden designs and improvisational theatrical productions to entertain and delight the Orléans family and their guests. His making of art was thus directly connected with pleasing the patron whom he served. In a series of anonymous pamphlets written between 1779 and 1789, he addressed the role of the arts in society, not as a *philosophe* but from the perspective of a court artist who was exposed to liberal thought in aristocratic circles.[24] Through his critical writing, Carmontelle sought social recognition for his achievements that were largely constrained by the hierarchies of Ancien Régime society.

Far more sophisticated in his analyses of aesthetic issues than La Font, Carmontelle also foregrounded the social value of the visual arts in much of his writing:

> Let us not believe that servitude is the natural condition of man; let us be fully convinced that he should freely exercise all his faculties. Between the treacherous sociability of civilized men, who are slaves, and the fierce enmity of the savage who fears to become so, I conceive a sentiment worthy of unifying the human species; this is the passionate love for the fine arts.[25]

What is so interesting about Carmontelle's critical pieces is the extent to which they incorporate the major tenets of aesthetics as a discipline of philosophical thought developing during the Enlightenment into his responses to the Salons, which were directed at a much broader readership than those by Diderot. The practice of writing art criticism for the *philosophe* was consciously bound up with the project of the Enlightenment. For the majority of critics, however, it should be seen as part of the Enlightenment as a process in which individuals gained a voice in matters of artistic judgement through the demonstration of their personal edification. In turn, artists themselves were able to appeal to the judgement of the public, as expressed by the critics who claimed to represent its views, when official recognition from the Bâtiments or the Académie Royale was not as favourable as they would have liked. The efforts of Greuze and Jacques-Louis David are most notable in this regard.

In Greuze's case, public acclaim was unable to reverse the long-standing and hierarchical reception procedures of the Académie Royale. Greuze was initially accepted as a genre painter. He had much higher ambitions, attempting to use his public reputation to support his submission for full membership as a history painter, the only category that allowed members to be office-holders and teachers. Greuze was unsuccessful in obtaining this form of membership, but it is within the context of this ambition that his Salon entry of 1761, *The Village Bride*, stands out as an example of what enlightened art might be. It nevertheless must be acknowledged that the style and subject of this work are as much a response to market conditions that favoured a taste for Dutch genre painting as to influences of social values connected with the Enlightenment. The painting depicts a civic moment of a marriage contract with sentiment and emotion in its treatment of a family of modest means.

Greuze had already made a name for himself as a painter of 'truthful' scenes of everyday life when the marquis de Marigny, director of the Bâtiments, extended a private commission to paint a large-scale genre scene for the Salon exhibition. Marigny was undoubtedly responding to criticism about the decadent state of contemporary French art – its lack of truth to nature and decline into trivial subject matter. The commission of a major work destined for display at the Salon provided Greuze with the opportunity to distinguish himself as an enlightened artist. The resulting painting achieved this. It showed his ability to create a work that demonstrated both his knowledge of the rules of academic painting and his ability not to be constrained by them. Greuze claimed the authority of academic history painting by endowing a scene of everyday life with the moral values associated with historical subject matter – essentially rejecting traditional academic genre hierarchies and seeking to make academic art 'modern' in its engagement with a theme of contemporary life.

The Salons similarly presented David with an opportunity to establish himself as an enlightened artist, but his motivations were driven as much by his professional ambitions as by any desire to connect his art-making with the Enlightenment as an intellectual movement. Frustrated by his slow advancement and lack of recognition within the Académie Royale, David became highly skilled in manipulating the public reception of his work at the Salons to promote his status as the leading artist of the contemporary French school. Extending the familial sentiment and emotional resonance of *The Village Bride* into grand heroic subject matter, *The Oath of the Horatii* (1785) and *The Lictors Returning to Brutus the Bodies of His Sons* (1789) were enormously popular successes. Both paintings incorporate tensions between private love within the family and public loyalty to the State into subjects that convey self-sacrifice and republican virtue. While these tensions gave rise to interpretations in the public sphere that involved a political critique of the French state under Louis XVI, it must be recalled that the commissions for both works came from the Bâtiments. The intention behind the original choice of subject matter was not political critique but rather an institutional desire to return French painting to the treatment of serious historical subjects. As was well known at the time, however, David changed the subject of *Brutus* from the commission he originally received, a scene from the story of Coriolanus, shifting the focus away from subject matter that was friendly to the monarchy to one that was openly republican. While this change is telling in terms of David's desire to connect his art-making with major currents of socio-political thought, what distinguishes David's heroic history painting as 'enlightened' art is the manner by which he rejected institutional authority in all areas and replaced that authority with his own, backed by the judgements of the critics at the Salons. Famously, following the favourable reception of *Brutus* at the Salon of 1789, David asserted that while he started out making a painting for the King, in the end he made one for himself.[26] Through this statement David asserted his status as both an enlightened artist and viewer through an unmitigated subversion of institutional and princely authority.

David dismissed the combined authority of the Académie Royale (which exhibited the work), the Bâtiments (which commissioned the work), and the King (whose glory it was meant to serve) and seized it for himself, as the principal viewer. The critics, for their part, turned the exhibition of David's work to their own advantage. One piece is particularly notable in demonstrating the extent to which art criticism in the 1780s became a vehicle through which knowledge of the debates of the Enlightenment was woven into a response that incorporated sensibility and some understanding of current philosophical debates:

> This year David is exhibiting only three pictures, but any one of them alone would be sufficient to establish his reputation ... if I judge the feelings of others by my own, seeing this picture one experiences a feeling that lifts one's soul – to use J.-J. Rousseau's expression, it has something poignant, which attracts one: all the conventions are so well observed that one feels oneself transported to the early days of the Roman Republic. David's earlier works had been criticized as being too exaggerated; like a truly great man, instead of complaining about the criticism, he has profited by it.[27]

Enlightenment is found in the primacy of response – the critic to the work, responding to the feelings of others in the audience and to the aesthetic philosophy of Enlightenment; and the artist to the critics, an artist who appears, in the opinion of at least one critic, to embody that aesthetic philosophy in his works.

To what extent, then, does eighteenth-century art manifest an Enlightenment mentality? The approach taken in this chapter has been to locate the evidence of that mentality in the art criticism occasioned by the Salons. It is possible to argue that artists such as Greuze and David sought enlightenment through the occasion of producing works of art that appealed to the authority of the public over that of the Académie Royale. Essentially, they claimed their status as enlightened artists by orchestrating the popular reception of their work. Nevertheless, it cannot be argued that the Enlightenment as an intellectual movement had a direct effect on their choice of style or even subject matter, or that they conceived of their art-works as part of that movement. It is not that art was incapable of evidenc-ing Enlightenment in visual terms, but it must be recognized that the terms of debate were largely framed through art-writing, which privileged the written word over the visual. Artists certainly responded, at times reject-ing the authority seized by 'enlightened' writers to judge their works. This appears to have been the case not only with satirical prints that depicted critics as blind and ignorant but also with Baudoin's *Look What Poverty Made Me Do* and Fragonard's *Modest Model*, which responded to Diderot's claims in the Salon of 1767 that prominent artists allowed him to take the lead in imagining pictures they would later compose.[28] Greuze and David took a different approach and harnessed the idea of 'enlightened viewers' to represent their work as progressive in a direct challenge to the institutional authority of the Académie Royale and the Bâtiments as the sole arbiters of artistic success. In the end, this direct appeal to the public confirms that enlightenment is largely a matter of response – revealed more in the recep-tion than in the production of eighteenth-century art.

NOTES

1 Louis Carrogis Carmontelle, *Le Triumvirat des arts, ou dialogue entre un peintre, un musicien et un poète, sur les tableaux exposés au Louvre; pour servir de con-tinuation au Coup de Patte et à la Patte de Velours* (Aux Antipodes [Paris]: 1783), p. 3. This pamphlet and others referenced below are available in scanned form at http://gallica.bnf.fr.
2 Rémy Saisselin, *The Enlightenment against the Baroque: Economics and Aesthetics in the Eighteenth Century* (Berkeley, Calif.: University of California Press, 1992), pp. 1–6.
3 Diderot and d'Alembert (eds.), *Encyclopédie*, vol. XV, p. 52.
4 Emma C. Spary, *Eating the Eighteenth Century: Food and Science in Paris, 1670–1760* (University of Chicago Press, 2012), p. 2.
5 Thomas Crow, *Painters and Public Life in Eighteenth-Century Paris* (New Haven, Conn.: Yale University Press, 1985), pp. 1–5.
6 On the origins of the rococo, see F. Kimball, *The Creation of the Rococo* (New York: W. W. Norton & Co, 1943); Katie Scott, *The Rococo Interior: Decoration and Social Space in Early Eighteenth-Century Paris* (New Haven, Conn.: Yale University Press, 1995); and Jennifer Milam, *Historical Dictionary of Rococo Art* (Plymouth: Scarecrow Press, 2011).
7 Mary Sherriff (ed.), *Antoine Watteau: Perspectives on the Artist and the Culture of His Time* (Newark, Del.: University of Delaware Press, 2006).
8 On the cultural associations of Watteau's art, see Mary Vidal, *Watteau's Painted Conversations: Art, Literature and Talk in Seventeenth- and Eighteenth-Century France* (New Haven, Conn.: Yale University Press, 1992); and Sarah Cohen, *Art, Dance and the Body in French Culture of the Ancien Régime* (Cambridge University Press, 2000).

9 Watteau's subversion of seventeenth-century academic practice was fore-grounded in Norman Bryson, *Word and Image: French Painting of the Ancien Régime* (Cambridge University Press, 1983), chap. 2.

10 On Crozat as a patron and collector, see M. Stuffman, 'Les Tableaux de la collection de Pierre Crozat', *Gazette des Beaux-Arts*, 72 (1968): 1–144; and Barbara Scott, 'Pierre Crozat: A Maecenas of the Régence', *Apollo*, 97 (1973): 11–19.

11 'Amateur', in Diderot and d'Alembert (eds.), *Encyclopédie*, vol. I, p. 317.

12 Pierre-Jean Mariette, *Description sommaire des dessins des grands maîtres d'Italie, des Pays-Bas et de France au cabinet de feu M. Crozat* (Paris, 1741), p. ix. For a summary of the make-up of Crozat's circle, see Crow, *Painters and Public Life*, pp. 39–44.

13 Roger de Piles, 'Du paysage', *Cours de peinture par principes* (Paris: chez Jacques Estienne, 1708), pp. 200ff. Further references to de Piles are given by page in the body of the text.

14 Of bourgeois origins, Étienne La Font de Saint-Yenne was a courtier in the service of Queen Marie Leczinska from 1729 to 1737. Patrick Descourtieux, 'Les Théoriciens de l'art au XVIIIe siècle: La Font de Saint-Yenne', unpublished dissertation, Université de Paris IV, 1977–8.

15 La Font specifically refers to serial representation of the four seasons, the elements, the arts and the muses in his *Réflexions sur quelques causes de l'état present de la peinture en France* (The Hague, 1747), pp. 16–17. See Scott, *The Rococo Interior*, pp. 254–7.

16 La Font de Saint-Yenne, *Lettre de l'auteur des réflexions sur la peinture et de l'examen des ouvrages exposés au Louvre en 1746* (n.p., n.pub.), p. 206.

17 Abbé Jean-Bernard Leblanc, *Lettre sur l'exposition des ouvrages de peinture, sculpture, etc., de l'année 1747, et en général sur l'utilité des ces sortes d'expositions* (Paris, 1747).

18 'Beau', in Diderot and d'Alembert (eds.), *Encyclopédie*, vol. II, p. 178.

19 'Goût', in Diderot and d'Alembert (eds.), *Encyclopédie*, vol. VII, p. 761.

20 Ibid. p. 768.

21 As Crow has noted, the exclusive pan-European subscription list never numbers more than fifteen. 'Introduction', in John Goodman (ed.), *Diderot on Art*, 2 vols. (New Haven, Conn.: Yale University Press, 1995), vol. I, p. xii.

22 Goodman, *Diderot on Art*, vol. I, p. 3.

23 Laurence Chatel de Brancion, *Carmontelle's Landscape Transparencies: Cinema of the Enlightenment* (Los Angeles, Calif.: Getty Publications, 2008).

24 For the attribution of this anonymous series of Salon critiques to Carmontelle, see Crow, *Painters and Public Life*, p. 261, note 48.

25 *Coup de patte sur le salon de 1779: dialogue précédé et suivi de réflexions sur la peinture* (Athens [Paris]: chez Cailleau, 1779), pp. 6–7.

26 Anita Brookner, *Jacques-Louis David* (London: Chatto & Windus, 1980), pp. 83–93.

27 *Journal de Paris* (17 September 1895), pp. 1071–3. trans. Elizabeth Gilmore Holt, in *The Triumph of Art for the Public, 1785–1848: The Emerging Role of Exhibitions and Critics* (Princeton University Press, 1983), p. 29.

28 Mary Sheriff, *Fragonard: Art and Enlightenment* (University of Chicago Press, 1990), chap. 6.

10

THOMAS DIPIERO

Enlightenment literature

At the end of the eighteenth century, Germaine de Staël set out to discover the various means through which literature and the society in which it was produced shaped one another. She noted that 'the progress of literature – that is, the perfection of the art of thinking and of self-expression – is necessary to the establishment and the preservation of liberty'. She furthermore maintained that among all the developments of the human mind, 'philosophical literature, eloquence and reasoning are the things I consider to be the true guarantors of liberty'.[1] The concept of a republic composed of like-minded individuals with similar aesthetic tastes and political aspirations was not at all new in eighteenth-century France, for the term 'Republic of Letters' was already in fairly widespread use in the preceding century. However, what was new was the stipulation that universal democracy could be strengthened through the aesthetic use of language to express ideas that gained in nuance and complexity as they were circulated among citizens. Published in 1800, Mme de Staël's *De la littérature considérée dans ses rapports avec les institutions sociales* (*On Literature Considered in its Relations with Social Institutions*) provides a retrospective view of Enlightenment literature, focusing not so much on what it had been but on what roles it played in forming individual and collective identities.

Like a great many of her contemporaries, Mme de Staël held that citizens who were engaged collectively in refining complex, interrelating ideas increased shared knowledge while simultaneously forming a bond of reason and virtue among themselves. She wrote that the study of science was not sufficient to sustain freedom, largely because science contributed less to the study of morals and human passions. If one values only what can be captured in mathematical analysis, she maintained, one risks not only intellectual, but also political confinement, since profound meditation on the exact sciences causes people no longer to be interested in the events of the day. Nothing pleases absolute monarchs more, she wrote, than 'men so profoundly occupied with the physical laws of the world that they abandon it to anyone intent on taking it over' (26). Empiricism and scientific progress do not suffice to produce or guarantee freedom; philosophical literature is a necessary condition for the preservation of liberty because, Mme de Staël argues, it relates to both the human and the natural world. Synthetic connections between and among what had previously been considered disparate realms characterized Enlightenment thought, and a great many eighteenth-century literary works blended aesthetic, empirical, social and philosophical approaches to understand how thought and matter can interrelate.

Mme de Staël's characterization of Enlightenment literature displays a distinct romantic idealism in its mistrust of science, but it captures the eighteenth century's fascination with synthesizing apparently unlike things to produce new forms of thought – including intellectual and moral thought in particular – resulting from a collaborative effort among ostensible equals. Perhaps the most fundamental syntheses commonly found in French Enlightenment literature concern oppositions between, on the one hand, inert matter and sentient beings and, on the other, different types of human beings and the subjectivities they evince. Eighteenth-century literature frequently attempts to make sense of conflicting categories and confused identities. Unlike the verbal arts of the seventeenth century, which tended to test repeatedly the mettle of aristocratic and noble characters only to find them almost always undaunted, Enlightenment literature represents the totality of the contemporary social spectrum. Moreover, it frequently represented characters behaving not in character but against type: high-born landowners behaving foolishly, as well as commoners behaving nobly. Largely unbound by the rigid generic conventions that characterized seventeenth-century classicism, eighteenth-century literature investigated the different forms of knowledge – including perhaps most importantly self-knowledge – produced when ostensibly conflicting or competing ways of knowing collide. To pursue that investigation, it very often probed these forms of knowledge by looking at the problematic syntheses and indeterminate boundaries defining the material and spiritual in their most compelling and complex forms: the human subject.

To grasp the significance of eighteenth-century literature's contributions to the production of knowledge and its investigation of human subjectivities, it is important to understand the seventeenth century's commitment to traditional literary form and subject matter. Seventeenth-century French literature was, for the most part, highly rule-conscious and tightly bound to generic conventions. That was in large part because it was generally produced for a narrow segment of the population, one that promoted and consumed cultural productions that valorized nobility and aristocracy as a race, the character and valour of which were essential to the identity and survival of the nation. Adherence to the generic conventions of classical literature, especially according to the rules established by aestheticians such as Aristotle and Horace, provided this group a sense of historic continuity with a highly esteemed ancestry. Tragedy, for example, depicted highly born people in life- and identity-threatening situations that only the truly magnanimous could negotiate. Poetic verse in the seventeenth century developed complex rules of versification that prescribed highly elaborate specifications for syllabification, caesura and enjambment, meter and rhyme, including such arcane examples as the *rime couronnée* and *rime emperière*, rhymes that included multiple repetitions of final syllables at the end of a verse. Seventeenth-century French literature generally offered intricately formal self-conscious works that examined moral questions related to individuals' obligations to themselves and to their restricted social group. During the Enlightenment, however, authors generally relaxed the rigidity with which they followed aesthetic rules and conventions while simultaneously directing their attention to depicting a broad segment of the social spectrum. Correlatively, diverse reading publics that critically responded to new literary productions arose, which in turn led to the establishment of new forms of subjectivity as readers identified with the different kinds of people they read about.

Traditional literary genres

For most of the eighteenth century, the word *littérature* did not have the meaning it does today. In the dictionary of the Académie Française of 1762, the word *littérature* continued to evoke, as it had since the dictionary's first edition in 1694, personal erudition rather than a corpus of texts. The Académie illustrates the usage of the word with the sentence 'he is a man of great literature' to indicate a highly knowledgeable and refined individual. (Not until 1798 does the word also refer to 'all the literary production of a nation, a country', and in 1835 the word *littérature* begins to signify 'all the literary production of a nation, a country, a period'.) *Lettres*, or *belles lettres*, on the other hand, referred to an abstract and aesthetic use of language and ideas that was often defined either in opposition or as a complement to the sciences. Thus, expressing an idea that Mme de Staël would refine at the end of the century, the anonymous author of the article 'Lettres' in the *Encyclopédie* states that 'the principles of the sciences would be too uninviting if letters did not lend them charm'.[2] Furthermore, 'gens de lettres' (people of letters), those who have studied not only grammar but also poetry, geometry, history, eloquence, as well as philosophy, contribute to the good of the nation through the rigorous application of thought that has destroyed 'all the prejudices that infected society'. 'Gens de lettres' are people who are highly cultured and who, through intense study, especially the application of philosophy, become 'more united among themselves; they benefit more from society; they are the judges, and others are judged'.[3]

The outward turn of the concept of *littérature* from personal erudition to collections of texts illustrates the use to which the aesthetic use of language was put in the eighteenth century. Enlightenment literature was a tool for imagining, understanding and critiquing contemporary social relations. Activated in the critical capacities of writers and readers alike, literature provoked judgement and turned it outward to allow readers to engage with others, either physically (as in reasoned or other forms of public debate) or intellectually, in the form of criticism and new literary works. In both cases, the engagement with other readers that Enlightenment literature induced typically incited further critique and analysis; on occasion, however, it sometimes went so far as to engender outrage and physical altercation.

The power of Enlightenment literature to affect readers so deeply stems both from the circumstances in which literature was consumed and from the forms of literature with which readers engaged. Increased but varied access to education in France meant that close to 10 million people could sign their names by century's end. Literacy likely doubled over the course of the century, and a favourable economy helped produce a reading audience with more time to consume and to react to literature. It is not clear, however, how many of those people formed part of a heterogeneous reading public, or, indeed, whether such a public existed at all.[4] A diverse reading public required different kinds of literature and different literary forms. Enlightenment authors began to experiment more widely with form as they sought to imagine modes of thinking and being based not on the iconic religious and monarchic models that had characterized French classicism but on the exercise of individual critical judgement.

Of the traditional genres, theatre was by far the most popular and perhaps the most provocative, mainly because it brought large numbers of people together in close quarters to focus their attention on actors and actresses – living, breathing bodies ritualistically enacting scenes of love, betrayal and tragedy. Moreover, because performers and public shared the same restricted space where they participated in theatrical performances which were also highly charged social events, the public's reaction to what they saw influenced the actors and hence the production itself. While the seventeenth century witnessed the development and rapid expansion of classical tragedy, complete with its rigidly codified rules, and themes aimed at aristocratic and noble audiences, over the course of the eighteenth century theatre found ever-increasing audiences drawn from all walks of life, including labourers and people from the seamier sides of the population. The number of theatrical venues and the number of patrons they could accommodate increased enormously throughout the century. In Paris, for example, there were three public theatres serving patrons in 1750, and seven by 1789; across the country, twenty-seven theatres were constructed during that same period.⁵ The number of patrons attending theatrical productions increased at a similar rate: in 1700, Parisian theatres could accommodate roughly 4,000 spectators, with an increase to 6,000 by 1750 and 12,000 by the time of the Revolution.⁶

Enlightenment theatre occurred in a number of forms, from more or less traditional tragedy to new theatrical manifestations which included light comedy and bourgeois drama. During the first half of the eighteenth century, theatrical forms included both comedy and tragedy. Enlightenment tragedy discontinued a number of the conventions of French classical tragedy of the seventeenth century, among which perhaps the most important was the precipitous fall of a great person due either to pride or to inherent qualities such as ancestry that they could not control. Tragedy in the eighteenth century developed new manners of depicting great people brought down by introducing more foreseeable circumstances that could have been avoided, and often by having such circumstances dependent on material causes such as mistaken identities. Claude Prosper Jolyot de Crébillon was the century's first tragedian, with plays produced between 1705 and 1748. Crébillon is best known for his *Rhadamiste et Zénobie* (*Rhadamiste and Zénobie*) (1711), a violent tragedy of love and misrecognition – and not the tragic fall of a great person due to the failure to comprehend social or cultural circumstances. Voltaire, one of the century's most versatile authors, wrote a number of tragedies, including *Œdipe* (*Oedipus*) (1718), which was based largely on Sophocles' work but which introduced new characters and suggested new and controversial ways of thinking about monarchy founded not on a noble essence but on the heroic actions in which the king engages. Voltaire's best-known tragedy is the orientalist *Zaïre* (1732), another work that takes on sensitive subject matter dealing with religion and politics. In this work, religious zeal and misrecognition lead to murder and mayhem as a jealous sultan, suspecting his betrothed of infidelity, murders her because she delays her wedding after having discovered her identity as a Christian. The tragedy has been interpreted as exhibiting the striking parallels between sexual jealousy and religious evangelism, making the work a living depiction of the potential dangers of religious thought. Voltaire took on the topic of religious zeal in another tragedy, *Mahomet* (*Muhammad*) (1742), which also represents unknown familial relationships, death and political strife as consequences of unscrupulous religious enthusiasm.

Pierre Carlet de Chamblain de Marivaux, also known for his novels, was a prolific author of light comedies. Active primarily between 1722 and 1746, and generally writing in prose for the Comédie-Italienne, one of the royally supported theatres, Marivaux penned works depicting problems associated with love, inconstancy and jealousy. Representing what today might be called the lower and middle classes, as well as the aristocratic class, Marivaux's comedies introduced farcical elements, intense and rapid bantering and generally comic resolutions to the emotional duress the author put his characters through, typically in the service of determining whether their paramours' love was true. Marivaux was fond of reversing social roles in his theatre, sometimes through cross-dressing and other means of disguising identity. *Le Jeu de l'amour et du hasard* (*The Game of Love and Chance*) (1730), one of Marivaux's best known comedies, makes use of the devices of characters in disguise to determine others' true feelings, the switching of social roles and the questioning of social conventions, in particular the conventions surrounding love and marriage at the time. *La Double Inconstance* (*The Double Inconstancy*) (1723) features Silvia, a young peasant woman, who is kidnapped and held in the residence of a prince who is enamoured of her. Silvia's lover, Arlequin, is seduced by Flamina, one of the prince's confidants. The prince disguises himself as a young officer and visits Silvia and eventually wins her love. The play ends with a double wedding uniting the two couples in what turns out to be their genuine love interests. Marivaux's comedies typically ended – as indeed do most eighteenth-century comedies – with a happy resolution to the predicaments to which the social conventions under scrutiny led.

French theatre was highly politicized throughout the Enlightenment. On the one hand, the works of Marivaux, Voltaire and others meted out biting satirical tragic and comedic critiques of the monarchy, of the strictures of religious thought and of many contemporary social practices, often those pertaining to social class. On the other hand, both playwrights and spectators frequently engaged in activities that were either politically themed or that constituted outright political action. Recent scholarship has stressed the intermixing of politics and theatre throughout the French Enlightenment, and some of the most provocative work involves not what was happening on the stage but what was going on in the parterre directly in front of it. In the eighteenth century, the word parterre referred both to the frequently boisterous floor space in front of the stage as well as to the equally raucous people who occupied it. The policing of the sometimes violent parterre contributed not only to the occasional modification of theatrical works but also to the creation of a French national identity.[7] The parterre was furthermore seen as a space for the development of public criticism, as people learned from those around them how to refine their opinions and insert them into a public discourse critical of the artistic endeavours they witnessed. Jean-Baptiste du Bos, an eighteenth-century historian and critic, maintained that one did not have to be trained in the formal rules of theatre to have a critical response to it:

> With the help of their internal instincts, all men can tell, without knowing the rules, whether artistic works are good or bad … We judge them through an internal movement that we cannot explain … Without knowing the rules, the *parterre* judges a theatrical work just as well as those in the business of theatre.[8]

Du Bos's insistence that the parterre could judge 'without knowing the rules' indicates the premium he placed on reason and critical observation: there is little room, in his view, for erudition. The anonymous author of the *Encyclopédie* entry 'Parterre' went even further than du Bos, suggesting that a play's failure or success was due nearly exclusively to the judgement of the boisterous crowd; it is the members of the parterre 'who decide on plays' merits: we refer to the judgments, cabals, applause, and catcalls of the *parterre*'.[9]

The sentiment that ordinary people were capable of critically evaluating a work of art was a comparatively recent one, and it stems from the quintessential Enlightenment precept that judgement is an inherent faculty that anyone can develop through the exercise of reason. The development of critical judgement as applied to works of art was especially pronounced in eighteenth-century theatre because viewing publics consumed theatrical productions collectively and in close quarters, where shared individual responses incited almost immediate response. Furthermore, as Hans Ulrich Gumbrecht has pointed out, two other properties peculiar to the theatre encouraged the development of critical judgement. On the one hand, the actors and the audience experience the artistic production simultaneously, which leads to a 'freedom of interactions'; and, on the other hand, while the information to be conveyed in the work of art is located in the script, it comes alive only in the work's embodied performance. Thus, the theatrical experience is all the more powerful for teaching people to exercise their judgement because the theatrical experience much more closely approximates everyday experiences than does the act of reading alone.[10]

The critical exercise of judgement as undertaken through individual and collective response to theatre also had political consequences. The Enlightenment consisted, at least in part, in a dramatic shift in the form and nature of representation. That shift involved a move away from a singular and iconic mode of representation embodied by the absolute monarch to democratic – that is, representational – methods of depiction. Despite the move away from monarchic to representational politics, a comparatively small number of people continued to be political actors: that is, they allowed their representatives to engage in the work of politics. This situation might well help contextualize the work of Pierre-Augustin Caron de Beaumarchais, whose theatrical work extended from 1767 to the end of the century. Beaumarchais was involved in a great deal of contemporary politics, including offering his support to the American Revolution and participating in events surrounding and following the French Revolution. His work explores contemporary political relations through both comedy and drama, and his three most famous plays – *Le Barbier de Séville* (*The Barber of Seville*), *Le Mariage de Figaro* (*The Marriage of Figaro*) and *La Mère coupable* (*The Guilty Mother*) – offer trenchant satirical critiques of the aristocracy. In *Le Mariage de Figaro*, for example, the title character, valet to a count, is engaged to Suzanne, who is also in the count's employ. The count threatens to invoke his *droit du seigneur*, an ancient custom that would allow him to sleep with his servant's wife on her wedding night. Figaro, in one of the most famous monologues in French theatre, lambastes the aristocracy and the system of privilege based on birth: 'Just because you're a powerful lord you think you're a great intellect! ... Nobility, wealth, rank, condition – all that makes you so proud! And what have you done to have so many advantages? You took the trouble to be born, and nothing more.'[11]

For some, Figaro's on-stage diatribe against the aristocracy was merely the most straightforward manifestation of theatre's relationship to politics. Jean-François Marmontel, a noteworthy eighteenth-century playwright and critic, found that the theatre's sharpest political contribution was also its most subtle: the individual judgements it encouraged among members of the audience. Marmontel held that the parterre alone was capable of forming the kind of unified public opinion that could give identity to the nation and that such an identity would be of the people, and not of the aristocracy:

> if the *parterre* did not capture public opinion and unify it by bringing it into alignment with its own opinion, there would most often be as many different judgments of a work as there are loges in the theatre ... It is true at least that this sort of republic that composes our performances would change in nature, and that the democracy of the *parterre* would degenerate into an aristocracy.[12]

The collective critical experience of the theatre contributed both to the lambasting of traditional political views and to the imagining of new ways to live in society.

New and evolving genres

While theatre was a collective experience, the act of reading literature was primarily done in solitude, especially by the beginning of the eighteenth century. The most significant development in literary form during the eighteenth century was the novel, which, over the course of the century, developed more or less into the form of prose fiction we recognize today. The Enlightenment novel, which arguably begins in the last quarter of the seventeenth century, eschews generic convention and repudiates the formulaic, labyrinthine and wildly implausible narratives of the gigantic pastoral and heroic novels of the seventeenth century which were written by and for members of the aristocracy. Responding to existing reading publics and helping to create new ones, eighteenth-century prose fiction appeared in a wide variety of forms, including travel narratives, orientalist tales, utopian fiction, philosophical tales and libertine fiction. The tremendous variety of form and subject matter that the novel manifested across the century suggests that of all the verbal arts, eighteenth-century fiction is the most concerned with enlarging the scope of what it means to read and, as a corollary, how reading helps people find and identify with others like them and, if possible, form a community. Robert Darnton suggests that it is 'impossible to generalize about the overall literary culture of eighteenth-century France because there might not have been any such thing'.[13] Even if we rely on known quantitative data, Darnton maintains, we still do not know very much about what the French actually read during the Enlightenment. We can, however, speculate about reading based on the two types of literature extant during the Enlightenment: legal and clandestine. What the French read during the Enlightenment was determined at least in part by the way their books were published, and the publication of clandestine books was partially regulated by a system of taxes and tariffs designed to protect legitimate printers and booksellers. France's financial regulation of the production and distribution of books made it easier to produce books outside of France for smuggling into the country, and, at the same time, it paved the way for publishers to make significant profits by counterfeiting legitimate works.

Clandestine works – those produced in France and those printed abroad and smuggled into French territory – were generally those that had been deemed offensive on political or moral grounds (and sometimes on both). By the latter quarter of the eighteenth century, the harsh economic conditions that restrictions on publishing imposed on printers and booksellers led to the publication of underground works. 'Hard times forced [dealers] into lower reaches of illegality; for as they sank deeper into debt, they took greater chances in hope of greater profits.'[14] Greater chances meant more subject matter diverging from traditional literary themes, and authors of Enlightenment novels had to establish a delicate balance between writing works with greater appeal to increasing reading audiences, which led to novels that were more realistic, and eschewing the charges of immorality that accompanied that same heightened attention to realism. Irreligion, immorality and incivility became the three charges most often levelled against clandestine publications. Not all French novels were published clandestinely, of course, but it is significant that novels in general came under the same charges of immorality and irreligion that were levelled against clandestine literature in general. To understand the significance and development of the Enlightenment novel, it is crucial to consider the history of its prohibition in France.

At least as far back as the middle of the seventeenth century, novels in France were deemed morally offensive as well as politically dangerous, both because they were thought to lack a literary ancestor – contemporaries found models of tragedy and lyric poetry in ancient Greece and Rome, but they found no examples of novels in Antiquity – and because novels sometimes depicted immoral subjects, especially illicit love. Novels were also judged inferior on literary grounds: those produced up until roughly the last quarter of the seventeenth century were deemed ponderous, unrealistic and generally formally uninteresting works. In addition, a point to which we will return, they were written by and for a very small segment of the social spectrum – notable aristocrats interested in promoting the meaning and value of their way of life.

The lack of a generic ancestor had both social and aesthetic consequences for the development of the novel, and it is often difficult to separate the political and the aesthetic when dealing with Enlightenment fiction. Because novels are virtually always written in prose, the contemporary concern was that readers would confuse them with the only other literary form consistently written in prose, namely, history. While prose is often considered to be a simple lack of form – that is, it seems to be a literary mode merely stripped of the formal conventions of verse and rhyme – its historical development shows that prose developed not so much as a loss of form but as a loss of reference – reference to a tradition of visible or otherwise identifiable authority representing power or some other specific guarantor of truth. Wlad Godzich and Jeffrey Kittay have argued that prose emerged when the message delivered was deemed more important than the form it took; prose thus represented the relinquishing of form deemed in excess of the message. The written text itself assumed the authority of the agentless, disinterested message, and prose came to be seen as the transparent vehicle best suited to communicate unprejudiced truth.[15] Because history was written in prose, and because it was also almost always officially sponsored by royal authority, prose – in direct and specific opposition to verse – took on the patina of truth, even if, particularly in the seventeenth century, that truth had a decidedly noble and aristocratic edge. When new subjects began to be depicted in prose, many critics feared that the formal resemblance between novel and history might lead some to confuse fact and fiction, as well as lose sight of officially sanctioned truth. As a result, a startling new phenomenon arose: the formal resemblance between the two genres led some to speculate that new forms of truth were coming into being.

If prose stood in for neutral, disinterested truth, it was difficult for contemporaries to understand how two different literary genres could communicate alternative, sometimes competing, truths. The marquis d'Argens railed against those who made fiction that looked true: 'It is surprising that a man, however accustomed he may be to lies, would not be ashamed to pass off a novel as true history.'[16] Nicolas Lenglet Du Fresnoy compared history and the novel, finding that the novel communicated truth without necessarily being completely factually accurate:

> People may well condemn novels, but I don't find in them all these objectionable things. Nothing in novels leads me into error; and if I am seduced, it is to my advantage. When I start reading a novel, I know that everything it contains is false: I am told so, and I believe it. There is always something to gain if the novel contains truth: I can benefit from it as soon as I am made to see it. However, there is always something for me to lose when I read history as soon as a fact turns out to be false.[17]

The *vrai* that Lenglet Du Fresnoy imagines finding in a novel differs from what one would expect to find in history primarily in its relationship to facts. While the slightest error can destroy a work of history, which depends on unimpeachable accuracy, truth in fiction develops subjectively and emotionally as readers sympathize with characters and their plights. In his *Les Incas, ou, la destruction de l'empire du Pérou* (*The Incas; or, the Destruction of the Empire of Peru*) (1777), Jean-François Marmontel makes a similar point as he attempts to represent the savagery with which the inhabitants of South America were treated by people he calls religious fanatics. Announcing that his goal is to make his reader detest such fanaticism by appealing to both facts and emotions, Marmontel describes the formal means through which he attempts to move his readers, which involves combining different literary forms with different relationships to truth: 'As for the form of this work, considered as a literary production, I must confess that I do not know how to define it. There is too much truth within it for a novel, and not enough for history. I certainly did not have the presumption to write poetically.'[18]

Writers developed ingenious techniques for lending a realistic feel to their works while simultaneously – and correlatively – experimenting with techniques for representing both a broader section of the social spectrum and aspects of daily life not previously depicted. Alain-René Lesage was one of the first eighteenth-century novelists to develop literary techniques for depicting a cross-section of the population with his satirical *Diable boiteux* (*The Devil on Two Sticks*) (1707), a fantasy in which a student, having just returned from a midnight tryst, encounters a demon whose areas of mischievous expertise include arranging inappropriate marriages and introducing luxury and debauchery into society. Asmodée, the devil in question, takes don Cléofas, the student, over the rooftops of the city, allowing him to peer through their roofs and into the dwellings to observe the unguarded inhabitants in their daily activities. The devil promises Cléofas: 'In order to give you a complete understanding of human life, I want to explain what all the people you see are doing. I will show you the motives for their actions and reveal to you their most secret thoughts.'[19] The device of depicting people unaware that they were being observed was used again in 1742 by Claude Prosper Jolyot de Crébillon in his *Le Sofa*. In this orientalist tale featuring metempsychosis (a recurring eighteenth-century fascination with the transmigration of souls among different bodies), Amanzéï, a formerly promiscuous person, is punished by his Brahman god by having his soul imprisoned in a sofa until such time as two virgins dedicate their love to one another on him. In the meantime, he is offered an unprecedented, unobstructed view into the lives of numerous Parisians, observing in intimate detail their attempts at love and seduction. Crébillon's tale of passion and often despair offers a satirical view of contemporary social practices, especially as they concern people who attempt to rise in social status through the seduction of others (a topic dear to Crébillon, and one he had previously investigated in his *Égarements du cœur et de l'esprit* (*Strayings of the Heart and Mind*) [1736]).

The observation of contemporary social conventions, often in wry satiric form, animated a large number of Enlightenment novels, and it would not be an exaggeration to suggest that most fiction of the time engaged in some form of social critique. Charles-Louis de Secondat de Montesquieu modified the device of having characters observed without their knowledge in his *Les Lettres persanes* (*Persian Letters*) (1721), an orientalist epistolary novel featuring the Persian travellers Usbek and Rica who observe contemporary Parisian society from outsiders' perspectives. A wry critique of Parisian culture and of contemporary gender politics, *Les Lettres persanes* introduces philosophy and politics into the novel in a very explicit way: Montesquieu himself famously wrote that 'the author gave himself the advantage of being able to connect philosophy, politics, and morals to a novel, and to unite this ensemble by a secret and somewhat unknown chain'.[20] Some novels participated in observations of contemporary social and political life in more pointed fashion, and works such as Voltaire's *Candide* (1759) and 'Micromegas' (1752), both often referred to as philosophical fiction, performed in-depth investigations of intellectual matters such as the moral philosophy of Gottfried Wilhelm Leibniz or the critiques of religion that were engaging contemporary readers.

Various forms of Enlightenment philosophy surfaced in a great many Enlightenment novels, and forerunners of that philosophy made their way into fictional works as well. In *Le Sofa*, Crébillon experiments with metempsychosis, using it as a device to investigate the ramifications of Cartesian philosophy, a device other Enlightenment authors occasionally employed with satiric intent, perhaps most famously Voltaire in his philosophical tales 'Zadig' and 'La Princesse de Babylone'. Crébillon's *Le Sofa* pursues the radical split between thinking and extended substance – that is, mind and body – that Descartes had theorized a century before by causing Amanzéï's soul to inhabit pieces of furniture as punishment for a previous life's – the soul's – sexual indiscretions with its body. Pursuing Cartesian logic, Crébillon allows Amanzéï's soul its liberty only after two inexperienced lovers consummate their love on him – that is, unite the corporeal and sentimental components of their attachment. Crébillon's fantastic, orientalist fiction underscores in ironic detail the ramifications of considering mind and body to be separate substances while simultaneously foregrounding objective observation as the sole means for discovering the truth about contemporary erotic behaviour in society. By century's end, the marquis de Sade would experiment with dark and violent works of fiction that attempted to annihilate moral positions based on traditional notions of human subjectivity and its relationship to the body that contained it in his *Justine* (three versions published between 1787 and 1794) and *Philosophie dans le boudoir* (*Philosophy in the Bedroom*) (1795).

Depicting people unaware of being observed and enjoying a candid view into their thoughts and motivations was a way of participating in the Enlightenment's fascination with empiricism. It also permitted an investigation into the intersections and the distinctions between emotional and physiological responses to stimuli, particularly love. In marked opposition to the majority of British fiction of the same period, French Enlightenment novels depict *embodied* people in love and amorous behaviour. Not only do we get comparatively detailed descriptions of principal characters' physiognomies (as opposed to the generic portraits of conventional beauty from the previous century), we also frequently find fairly specific to highly explicit scenes of sexual encounters and their aftermaths. Noteworthy examples include Antoine-François Prévost's *L'Histoire du chevalier Des Grieux et de Manon Lescaut* (*Manon Lescaut*) (1731), a tale of the unbridled passion a young man from a prominent family has for an adventurous young woman who professes love for him but is repeatedly unfaithful, and Pierre Choderlos de Laclos's *Liaisons dangereuses* (*Dangerous Liaisons*) (1782), a libertine tale in epistolary form about two lovers who become rivals in love and sex and who use others erotically and in many cases degradingly in their attempt to achieve social ascendancy. A favourite device for representing the complexities of human emotion and the limits of philosophy to express that emotion was to show involuntary or unexpected corporeal response to desire, emotion or other forms of sentiment. Denis Diderot analysed the complex configuration of mind and body in such works as *La Religieuse* (*The Nun*) (published posthumously in 1796), which features explicit scenes of sexual relations between women in a convent and a disavowal by the first-person participant-narrator of the significance of those relations, and in *Le Supplément au voyage de Bougainville* (*Supplement to Bougainville's Voyage*) (1772), in which a failure to recognize cross-cultural erotic conventions leads to unexpected and ostensibly irrepressible sexual encounters between a priest and a young woman at the request of her family.

Not all Enlightenment novels dealing with desire and passion made use of explicit sexual depictions, although a surprising amount of non-erotic fiction articulates sentiment through the body. Jean-Jacques Rousseau's *Julie, ou la nouvelle Héloïse* (1761), the eighteenth century's most highly acclaimed sentimental novel, recounts in epistolary form the story of Julie, a young aristocrat, and her tutor Saint-Preux, who fall passionately in love but cannot marry because of their social circumstances. *La Nouvelle Héloïse* depicts the lovers at first resisting, then succumbing to their passions, and then separating; and it depicts numerous deaths, Julie's marriage to another man and finally the revelation that Julie never stopped loving Saint-Preux, a revelation that occurs only after her death. *La Nouvelle Héloïse* articulates the lovers' frustrated passions against a backdrop of rigid social conventions, religious and natural philosophy, and the wisdom of leading a simple life removed from the distractions of the city.

Recent work on *La Nouvelle Héloïse* has suggested that much of the sentimental nature of the work, with its insistence on pure, uncontaminated love, simplicity of lifestyle and devotion to ethics and natural philosophy, is articulated through and with the body of its heroine. Mary McAlpin finds that Rousseau occasionally depicts Julie's body in coarse physical detail, and that when he describes the nature of her breasts, her responses to sexual stimulation, the formation of her illnesses and even the composition of her body after death he is relating a 'physico-moral evolution' that couples nature, the human body and religious and philosophical thought into an ordered system of natural virtue.[21] More broadly, Helen Thompson and Natania Meeker have argued that novels' depictions of sensate bodies and the truths those bodies voluntarily or otherwise evinced served to provide stability of meaning in a time when meaning was anything but fixed. Rousseau, like many of his contemporaries, also pinned onto the novel the power to change words into palpable effects on the flesh. In the preface to the novel he writes, 'No chaste girl has ever read novels … She who … dares to read a single page [of this novel] is lost; but let her not attribute her downfall to this book – the evil was committed beforehand.'[22]

Rousseau's attitude towards the transformative power of reading was similar to that of many of his contemporaries: literature can have profound effects on the way people live and understand themselves, and it can help them understand their worlds in ways that other discursive forms cannot. It can, in fact, change people's lives. Whether such change would be salutary or pernicious was generally up for debate, and change was typically located in people's critical capacities, in their social affiliations or in their corporeal response to texts. Mme de Staël looked back on the century and characterized philosophical literature as the guarantor of liberty because it encouraged the art of thinking and expressing oneself. Literature differed from the empirical domains in that it allowed observation not so much of the world but of the people who inhabited it. That meant that it encouraged people not only to glean information but to infer meaning from it as well, which helped them understand how different historical and cultural circumstances caused people to evaluate their worlds differently and to live accordingly. The consumption of literature in the Enlightenment encouraged the production of critique based on facts and the debates about their meanings. Such critique enabled citizens of the eighteenth-century Republic of Letters to consider the social, political, philosophical and moral conditions under which they lived and to decide how to take action upon them, whether individually or collectively.

NOTES

1 Germaine de Staël, *De la littérature considérée dans ses rapports avec les institutions sociales* (Paris: Bibliothèques-Charpentier, 1800), pp. 23, 25. Subsequent reference to de Staël is by page in the book.
2 Diderot and d'Alembert (eds.), *Encyclopédie*, vol. IX, p. 410.
3 'Gens de lettres', in Diderot and d'Alembert (eds.), *Encyclopédie*, vol.VII, p. 600.
4 Robert Darnton, *The Literary Underground of the Old Regime* (Cambridge, Mass.: Harvard University Press, 1982), pp. 181, 16.
5 Jeffrey Ravel, *The Contested Parterre: Public Theater and French Political Culture, 1680–1791* (Ithaca, NY: Cornell University Press, 1999).

6 Logan J. Connors, *Dramatic Battles in Eighteenth-Century France* (Oxford: Voltaire Foundation, 2012), pp. 12 ff., and William D. Hoarth, *Beaumarchais and the Theatre* (London and New York: Routledge, 1995), pp. 58.

7 Paul Friedland, *Political Actors: Representative Bodies and Theatricality in the Age of the French Revolution* (Ithaca, NY: Cornell University Press, 2002).

8 Jean-Baptiste du Bos, *Réflexions critiques sur la poésie et sur la peinture* (Paris: P. J. Mariette, 1733), pp. 331–2.

9 'Parterre d'une salle de spectacle ou d'un théâtre', in Diderot and d'Alembert (eds.), *Encyclopédie*, vol. XII, p. 87.

10 Hans Ulrich Gumbrecht, 'Eighteenth-Century French Theatre As Medium for the Enlightenment', *Diogenes*, 34 (98) (1986): 98–127.

11 Pierre-Augustin Caron de Beaumarchais, *Le Mariage de Figaro*, ed. Jacques Scherer (Paris: Société d'Édition d'Enseignement Supérieur, 1966), act V, scene iii, p. 354.

12 Jean-François Marmontel, 'Parterre', *Supplément à l'Encyclopédie, ou dictionnaire raisonné des sciences, des arts et des métiers* (Amsterdam: M. Rey, 1777), vol. IV, pp. 241–2, at p. 242.

13 Darnton, *Literary Underground*, p. 181.

14 Ibid. p. 206.

15 Jeffrey Kittay and Wlad Godzich, *The Emergence of Prose* (Minneapolis, Minn.: University of Minnesota Press, 1988).

16 Jean-Baptiste de Boyer, marquis d'Argens, *Supplément, ou tome septieme des Lettres Juives* (Lausanne: Marc-Michel Bousquet, 1739), p. 175.

17 Jean-Baptiste de Boyer, marquis d'Argens, *Lettres juives* (La Haye: P. Paupie, 1738), p. 36; Nicolas Lenglet Du Fresnoy, *De l'usage des romans, où l'on fait voir leur utilité et leurs différents caractères* (Amsterdam: Veuve de Poilras, 1743), p. 59.

18 Jean François Marmontel, *Les Incas, ou, la destruction de l'empire du Pérou* (Paris: Lacombe, 1777), p. xxiv.

19 Alain-René Lesage, *Le Diable boiteux*, ed. Roger Laufer (Paris: Gallimard, 1984), p. 41.

20 Charles-Louis de Secondat de Montesquieu, *Les Lettres persanes* (Paris: Bordas, 1992), pp. 3–4.

21 Mary McAlpin, 'Julie's Breasts, Julie's Scars: Physiology and Character in *La Nouvelle Héloïse*', *Eighteenth-Century Culture* 36 (2007): 127–46.

22 Jean-Jacques Rousseau, *Julie, ou la Nouvelle Héloïse* (Paris: Garnier-Flammarion, 1967), p. 4.

II

STÉPHANE VAN DAMME

Philosophe/philosopher

Let us make a detour via Italy and borrow a phrase from the Neapolitan jurist Gaetano Filangieri who, in the 1780s, wrote in his *Science of Legislation,* 'The *philosophe* must be an apostle of truth and not an inventor of systems.'[1] The distinction between *philosophe* and philosopher has often been linked to two different spheres of activity: on the one hand, the publicist and man of letters; on the other, the scientist, scholar and natural philosopher. The intense dialogue between the history of philosophy, the history of science and cultural history now allows us to go further. The social and cultural density of philosophy in the Enlightenment is becoming apparent outside spaces where its production and reception seem the most legitimate. But Enlightenment philosophy is not confined to writings and concepts, for it can be seen at once as knowledge, social practice and a cultural object far exceeding the context of teaching in schools and universities. Can this maximal extension of the philosophical domain be explained without invoking the usual explanation of the epistemological boundaries of different fields of philosophical knowledge in the classical age? It seems imperative to shift the focus by totally abandoning a definition of philosophy in terms of disciplines in order to approach the question obliquely. Hence, this chapter will concentrate on the differentiation, the partitioning or, conversely, the blurring of distinctions.[2] Instead of taking fixed definitions as its starting point, this chapter will map the work of their production by exploring their various underlying tensions and by considering boundary objects.

Philosophy and/or science?

The first tension we must examine arises between fields of knowledge and philosophy in the Enlightenment. How should we understand eighteenth-century philosophy? Philosophical knowledge in its different aspects should be understood not as a block of disciplines but rather as a system in which statements and intellectual practices circulate between different forms of knowledge. The philosophy taught in colleges and universities was well defined within the framework of the liberal arts and quadrivium. It was integrated knowledge. It included lessons in logic, physics and metaphysics, sometimes supplemented by mathematics and geography.[3] Natural philosophy gained increasing autonomy as the different intellectual domains began to draw apart. In the second half of the eighteenth century, natural history, chemistry, botany, zoology, geology and physics gradually lost their strictly philosophical definition to become scientific disciplines in their own right. However, the shift from 'natural philosophy' to modern sciences was not linear. Many fields of knowledge were simultaneously seeking to be labelled as philosophy, a term synonymous with breadth. The linguist Ferdinand Brunot tried to measure the expansion that the concept of philosophy underwent in the eighteenth century in his *Histoire de la langue française* (*History of the French Language*).[4] Its flexibility can be seen in many expressions describing the state of knowledge at the time, including 'philosophical chemistry', 'zoological philosophy', 'economic philosophy', 'rural philosophy', 'philosophical grammar' and new terms such as 'experimental philosophy', 'moral philosophy' and 'speculative philosophy'. These designations did not correspond to the traditional representation of philosophy as an academic discipline. Instead, they indicated an identity, a new general economy of knowledge. In 'the detailed explanation of the system of human knowledge' offered by the *Encyclopédie*, Diderot is careful to make 'philosophy and science' equivalent: 'Philosophy, or that portion of human knowledge that must be linked to reason, is very broad. There is almost no object grasped by the senses from which reflective thought has not formed a science.'[5] Michel Foucault has noted the decisive mutation in the classical age concerning the field of philosophy and its objects:

> Philosophy was, precisely, the organisational system, the system that allowed knowledges to communicate with one another ... With the disciplinarisation of knowledges, in its polymorphous singularity, now leads to the emergence of a phenomenon and a constraint that is now an integral part of our society. We call it 'science'. At the same time, and for the same reason, philosophy loses its foundational and founding role.[6]

In this science, we can sense the Foucaldian episteme, understood 'as a set of relations between sciences, epistemological figures, positivities and discursive practices'.[7] The 'restricted' philosophy – as in 'restricted' rhetoric – that emerged in the nineteenth century had to work through the loss of this global knowledge, while, beyond the break imposed by modern philosophy, an older definition of philosophy as wisdom persisted.

The *philosophe*: professor or sage?

Extending this initial opposition, we must also re-evaluate the social and 'professional' status of the *philosophe*, reconsidering the identity of the teacher and the teaching of philosophy as well. While the erudite philosopher is automatically classed as a teacher, the *philosophe* is placed among the men of letters and amateurs. As heir to the 'new' philosophy of the seventeenth century, the Enlightenment was grounded in a relationship of inclusion in and opposition to the philosophy of colleges and university arts faculties.

Dictionaries first recorded this change of status and blurring of identities. In his analysis of the different meanings of the word *philosophe* in the *Dictionnaire de l'Académie française* of 1694, 1718 and 1740, Daniel Brewer notes a shift from identification with the professor of logic to the polemical definition that would become current in the mid eighteenth century: 'He is a man who rejects nothing, who constrains himself in relation to nothing, and who leads the life of a *philosophe*.'[8] With Dumarsais, the *philosophe* gained his recognition from a subversive reputation. Subsequently, in the context of the theatre, a series of plays developed new social representations of the *philosophe* and opened up a literary space of satire and critique, from Saint-Jorry's *Le Philosophe trompé par la nature* (*The Philosopher Deceived by Nature*) (1719) to the marquis de Sade's *Le Philosophe soidisant* (*The So-called Philosopher*) (1769).[9] The *philosophe* appears as an Enlightenment invention whose social portrait requires redrawing. Most of these plays were based on Marmontel's story *Le Philosophe soi-disant* (1759), from which a total of eight plays were adapted. They reflect the reworking and transposition of narrative into drama and vice versa that was common in the eighteenth century. To judge from the many theatrical adaptations produced in the years 1760–3, the story enjoyed considerable success. The theme of the self-proclaimed *philosophe*, the false *philosophe* hoodwinked and unmasked, was highly contemporary. Fréron's attacks in his journal *L'Année littéraire* (*The Literary Year*) and those of Palissot on stage were linked to an early pamphlet campaign against the *encyclopédistes*, whose cause was taken up by Marmontel. A second battle was unleashed on 2 May 1760 at the Théâtre-Français, with a three-act comedy in verse by Palissot. Another playwright, François-Georges Fouques, known as Desfontaines, adapted this play as *Le Philosophe prétendu* (*The Supposed Philosopher*), performed at the Théâtre-Italien on 6 October 1762. The various plays were primarily polemical in intent and gave visibility to new playwrights. Several elements characterize the representation of the *philosophe* in these pieces. First, he is a learned man steeped in Latin and Greek, directly based on the character of the pedantic scholar Trissotin in Molière's *Les Femmes savantes* (*The Learned Ladies*). Palissot de Montenoy's comedy represents the *philosophe* with the features of Monsieur Carondas, 'bristling with Greek and scholastic terms' (line 94). Second, the playwrights highlight his solitude and lack of socialization, pursuing a theme dear to eulogists and found in representations of the savant as unmarried and living alone.[10] It is the *philosophe*'s asocial nature that helps drive the dramatic action. A play by Destouches opens on 'a book-lined study: Ariste is seated opposite a table, on which are a writing case and pens, books, mathematical instruments and a sphere.'[11] Biographies and academic eulogies of the *philosophe* formed another genre where the man of letters or genius aspiring to immortality was to be restored to primacy, alongside the philosophy professor.[12] The ethical dimension reflects the persistence of a cynical or more broadly ancient model associating intellectual life with spiritual exercise.[13] It also permitted the links between philosophical and religious beliefs to be maintained, denials and denunciations notwithstanding. Enlightenment prophetism, the view of the *philosophe* as an apostle, clearly expresses this convergence of the messianism of progress and Enlightenment spirituality.

Individuals or communities?

These new philosophies give rise to a problem of definition and of social and collective representations. How can a form of philosophy be collectively recognized unless it is incorporated within institutions? This question is crucial to understanding how philosophies were recognized by the corporatist society of the Ancien Régime. Furthermore, we question the pertinence of a notion of identity involving arrangements and properties attached to persons. This questioning would undoubtedly involve excising part of what posterity has designated by the term *philosophes*, retaining only philosophy teachers. Three types of actors played a key role in this negative representation.

First, censorship helped to qualify the group of philosophes negatively as a sect. The affairs of libertinage offer a prime site for investigating these processes of qualifying philosophy, since they reveal a propensity among the authorities to see groups everywhere. This sectarian interpretation was often propagated by men of the Church. When Loménie de Brienne condemned the materialists in his indictment of 18 August 1770, he had no compunction about using the argument that they formed a clandestine sect:

> There has arisen among us a bold and impious sect; it has adorned its false wisdom with the name Philosophy; beneath this imposing title it claims to possess all forms of knowledge. Its supporters have set themselves up as tutors

to the human race. Freedom of thought is their cry, and this cry has echoed from one end of the world to the other. With one hand, they have sought to undermine the Throne; with the other they have tried to overturn the Altars. Their aim was to extinguish belief, to impress on minds a different teaching concerning religious and civil institutions; and, as it were, the revolution has taken place. The proselytes have proliferated, their maxims have spread: kingdoms have felt their ancient foundations tremble; and nations, astounded to find their principles obliterated, have asked what fate has caused them to become so different from themselves.[14]

Second, the police, especially in Paris, was instrumental in surveilling and identifying the philosophical threat. In the second half of the eighteenth century, libertinage was thus identified with the disturbance of public order, becoming sexualized in the language and practice of control. The geography of libertinage in Paris was not so much a geography of knowledge as a topology of pleasures. It 'contaminated' the Club du Palais-Royal reserved for the friends of the duc d'Orléans, and the Club des Arcades in the rue des Bons-Enfants, established in 1784. In August 1787, the baron de Breteuil sought to have the clubs banned, but in vain. Libertine *savoir-vivre* extended into places and settings that included the domestic spaces of high society.[15] It blossomed in boudoirs and houses of discretion which, through the fiction of plays and novels, became key places of libertine imagination. Finally, the enemies of the *philosophes*, the anti-*philosophes*, used polemics to open a discussion about the legitimacy of such intellectuals.

Knowledge, writing or practice?

Dictionary definitions also reveal a contrast between intellectual work, literary activity and behaviour in society. The *philosophe* was not merely a scholar; his art of philosophizing was rooted in the art of writing. Philosophy was completely altered as a result, since there was a shift from 'literary technology', designed to enable the communication of thought and intellectual content, to a form of heuristics in which writing was a way of practising knowledge and conducting an investigation. This shift permitted a deliberate blurring of the distinction between typical philosophical writing (essay or letters) and a wide range of genres and registers.

First, in the modern period, the concurrence of Latin with the various vernaculars turned the choice of language into an issue of philosophical communication. We know the degree to which Descartes's choices were decided by strategies of specific address and the possibility of expanding the audience for philosophy. The decline of Latin and the challenge to scholastic culture in the 1750s facilitated the emergence of vernacular philosophy. Unlike philosophers, *philosophes* wrote first in French. Beyond issues of rhetoric and language, the diversity of genres used (meditation, speech, dispute, summary, letter, ballet, comedy, etc.) rendered the literary status of philosophy problematic; it could no longer be regarded as reflecting a discipline in the manner of a taught lesson or the normative discourse implied by a treatise. Examining the rhetorical techniques used by Pierre Bayle, for example, Gianluca Mori has revealed the persistence of a libertine tradition 'of writing between the lines'. Countering the ideal of transparency upheld by philosophers, which found its most complete expression in articles and reports of experiments in learned journals, the *philosophe* continued to expand the range of literary possibilities.[16]

As a consequence of this expansion, the 'epistemic genres' dear to natural philosophy became contaminated or were reformulated. Renaissance *historia* now had to come to terms with modern history. The case studies used in medical discourse gave way to a transformative vision of nature.[17] The format of Bacon's essays was reworked by Voltaire in his *Essai sur les mœurs* (*Essay on Manners*) of 1756. Description was reformulated in eighteenth-century natural history, in the work of Buffon and Diderot, to take account of the power of images.[18] Lastly, the place given to personal speech and anecdote, and the use of fiction, turn modern philosophy into a unique literary experiment, blurring any simple distinction between literature, science and philosophy. In this way, Enlightenment philosophy tested the scholarly literary norms of institutions of knowledge, while at the same time finding certain genres such as the dictionary, encyclopedia, dialogue and essay to be more suited to intellectual flexibility, the desire for a new summation of knowledge and a culture of judgement.

Critique, judgement and public space

The *philosophe* as opposed to the philosopher not only relocated philosophical work by taking it out of the schools and knowledge institutions but refocused it on the public space. Investigations tended to become spatialized, located perfectly within the well-established tradition of Enlightenment geography.[19] Philosophy was subject to the judgements of a newly emerging audience, and philosophers of nature began to recognize this audience's presence by organizing science displays. As a result, the question of judgement, which has often been portrayed as a critical paradigm based on Kantian philosophy, became a fundamental preoccupation of the Enlightenment beginning with Pierre Bayle and his *Dictionnaire historique et critique* (*Critical and Historical Dictionary*) (1697). As Jacob Soll pointed out, 'The idea was that if established historical facts could be undermined with other established facts, the reader would have to exercise great abilities to ascertain the truth.'[20] A 'social history of truth' has sought to analyse practices of scientific judgement, basing their definition on social interaction, discussion, reception and the accuracy of what was said.[21] In the eighteenth century much philosophical activity was devoted to circumscribing and explaining the uses of reason and identifying sources of human knowledge across time and space. The theoretical approaches developed throughout the seventeenth and eighteenth centuries constantly sought to establish how to produce correct, valid reasoning. How can scientific statements be rendered universal without recourse to the art of generalities found in Aristotelian logic? One way was by redefining certainty by matching it to the vocabulary of law and of facts, or to a definition of the knowing subject, based on 'experience of oneself'. Another approach involved objectivizing objects of knowledge in order to eliminate individuality and perspectivism. By breaking down the relationship between knowledge produced and a particular place, language, culture or individual, Enlightenment scientists sought to make scientific statements more universal. This effort to clarify, mark out and situate judgement also involved defining disciplines, in which the paradigm of the sciences became a model for the identification of different types of judgement. The scientific arena saw the development of expertise directed at technical problems (urban water supplies, transportation and bridges, the risk of flooding and landslips, the relocation of cemeteries such as that of Les Saints-Innocents, the building of new hospitals such as the Hôtel-Dieu, etc.), which bound the philosophy of nature to the public sphere.

But judgement taken to the public square and intended for public opinion broke even more sharply with the logic of specialist judgement. While the *philosophes* played a specific role in the emergence of the socio-political form of the 'affair' in the eighteenth century, the iconic example being the Calas Affair, judgements proliferated at the local level in places such as salons. Intellectuals became particularly skilled at generating affairs. The long eighteenth century can thus appear as a succession of politico-religious scandals. The unfolding of the *Lettres philosophiques* scandal studied by J. B. Shank is part of a broader pre-encyclopedic context. Maupertuis had led the way in the scientific domain with his *Discours sur les différentes figures des astres* (*Discourse on the Different Figures of the Stars*) of 1732. Both Voltaire and Maupertuis were defenders of analytical mechanics. They made connections extending beyond their own interpretation of Newtonianism. By gaining recognition as the necessary mediator of Newtonian philosophy in France, Maupertuis built up his own reputation and authority within French scientific networks – the idea that France was 'Descartianized' by Voltaire is probably inaccurate. The position of Voltaire and Maupertuis was akin to self-fashioning but was not completely new. It modified commonplaces, elements that were already well-rooted in the public and critical space. But it enabled the successful deployment of a new agent, a new 'persona', the *philosophe*. The shock caused by the *Lettres philosophiques* reflected not so much the novelty of the propositions advanced as the critical style of the text, which prefigured the invention of the affair, later created by Voltaire in the context of religious scandals. Moreover, contemporaries were shocked more by the tone and style of the treatise than by its content; the generalized use of a scornful tone is often mentioned. This concern with the practice of mobilization for a cause has led some historians to concentrate on the culture of scandal and indignation during the Ancien Régime. Before the eighteenth century, few had the 'courage of truth', to borrow Foucault's phrase. For fear of parrhesia, many erudite libertines preferred to retreat or to develop an art of writing between the lines. For many men of letters it was vital to invent a range of techniques that would enable them to exercise free speech without risking imprisonment or censure. In her book *The Cynic Enlightenment*, Louisa Shea rightly focuses on the importance of this cynic culture in the world of the Enlightenment. D'Alembert himself is called 'the Diogenes of our age'. The cynicism derived from Antiquity was not very well regarded in the first half of the eighteenth century, as it contravened the norms of politeness, which themselves made plain speaking difficult. Louisa Shea shows how Diderot, who had rejected cynic strategies early in his career, reconsidered the advantages of a critical form of politeness following his incarceration in the Bastille in 1748. Through detailed analysis of the emergence of a culture of mockery and irony, other scholars have sought to reconstruct the stylistic grammar of polite critique.[22] In both the article on 'Eclecticism' in the *Encyclopédie* and in *Le Neveu de Rameau* (*Rameau's Nephew*), Diderot shows the good reasons for communication based on plain speaking.[23] The cynic tradition (in the wake of the libertine tradition) rejected alliances with the authorities and actively advocated cosmopolitanism. Rousseau portrayed himself as the defender of the motherland in his *Lettres écrites de la Montagne* (*Letters Written from the Mountain*), which were, however, cynic in intent. Far from being monolithic or holistic, the paradigm of critiques rests upon a horizontal proliferation of practices traversing Ancien Régime society, from popular rumours, art of slander and pornographic pamphlets to high Enlightenment and philosophical reflections.[24]

Interpreting and reading philosophy

In distinguishing the *philosophe* from the philosopher, we should consider the place of readers. The investigative approach of the history of reading developed out of the dead ends of classical analyses of reception. Reception in philosophy brings us face to face with the already constituted œuvres of the *philosophes*. In this category we could include Pierre Bayle's articles on numerous *philosophes*, such as the famous 'Spinoza' article, which is both the longest in his *Dictionnaire historique et critique* and one of its most famous, since it inspired many commentaries in the eighteenth century from the likes of Voltaire, Diderot, Dom Deschamps and Condillac.[25] These 'philosophical' articles form only five per cent of the 2,044 articles in the *Dictionnaire*.[26] The hermeneutic space in which the evaluation of an author became established must be seen in the context of ongoing social developments. According to Pierre Saint-Amand, the reference points changed in the mid eighteenth century. Recognition had been an object of study for moralists and *philosophes* in the seventeenth and eighteenth century, before becoming an analytical category: 'the *philosophes* of the *Encyclopédie* marked out a path that would initiate a different policy of recognition. There was a move away from the world of dignity, place and rank, towards a different, more democratic world of dignity, personal esteem and individual recognition.'[27] The jurists of the *Encyclopédie*, such as d'Alembert in his *Essai sur la société des gens de lettres et des grands* (*Essay on the Society of Men of Letters and the Great*), developed an opposition between recognition based on the distinctions of the 'société des grands' and one based on esteem. The discussion between Condorcet and Turgot on the intellectual value of Helvétius's *De l'esprit* (*Essays on the Mind*) raises the question of how to determine the quality of a scandalous work in which the philosophical register is constantly blurred by moral and political arguments.

The circulation of philosophical writings could thus create what Brian Stock has called 'textual communities' extending beyond the group and mobilized across distance through the discussion, acceptance or rejection of a text.[28] Roger Chartier notes that the letter of a text itself is never fixed in advance but remains the changeable co-production of a chain of participants (authors, publishers, readers, interpreters, translators, etc.).[29] The letter of published texts also changes. J. B. Shank notes that Newtonianism emerged in France via two communities of interpreters: on the one hand, experimenters interested in the publication of Newton's 1704 treatise on *Opticks*, which was an obvious composite of documents and experiment protocols published in the 1690s; and, on the other, mathematicians and astronomers who were readers of the *Principia*. In turn, these two communities of readers influenced the republication and transformation of both works. These co-constructions of Newtonianism by its early interpreters helped shape historiography itself, which later distinguished the eighteenth century's true Newtonians (linked to Newton the theorist) from their false counterparts linked to experimental method. More broadly, historians of the book have shown that philosophy books were well represented in urban libraries. In Paris throughout the 1750s, philosophy as a category was present in 140 libraries (fourteen per cent of the total). The list of books most frequently found in inventories places philosophical works in ninth place with Bayle's *Dictionnaire critique* and the abbé Pluche's *Spectacle de la nature*, confirming the high degree of interest in philosophy among the Parisian elites. But books read are not the same as books owned, and the proliferation of libraries in Paris, the practice of lending and the opening of reading cabinets in the years 1764–89 reflect the enthusiasm for encyclopedic works in the Parisian high society.[30]

The *philosophe*'s hand: archiving the Enlightenment

Following on from a genetic approach to philosophy, we can ask whether the use of papers forms a dividing line between *philosophe* and philosopher, distinguishing different archiving practices, often relying on institutions in the case of scientists. The idea of constituting an intellectual archive emerged gradually. In the Enlightenment century, publishers as intermediaries developed a practice of distinguishing and authenticating the hand of the *philosophe* that was close to attributionism or *connoisseurship* and enabled manuscripts to be identified.[31] This occurred in relation to a 'new' edition of Montesquieu's *De l'esprit des lois* (*The Spirit of the Laws*), which he was preparing just before his death. Two publishers, his son Jean-Baptiste de Secondat and the lawyer François Richer, claimed to have established the edition of 1757 'after the corrections that M. de Montesquieu himself gave to the publishers before his death'. However, a study of all the manuscripts and corrections indicates conversely that many corrections intended by the author were not included and that the posthumous works of 1783 were in fact based on the text of the 1748 edition. As Catherine Volpihac-Auger notes, 'The unfinished nature of these dossiers, the diversity of documents they contained and their heterogeneity itself have the remarkable advantage of revealing every stage of Montesquieu's work, captured in process, the progress of which we can thus reconstruct.'[32]

In the second half of the eighteenth century, collectors began seeking out philosophical manuscripts. This interest can clearly be seen arising out of the cult of great writers, in the cases of Voltaire and Newton for example, and with authors such as the marquis de Sade, for whom 'scribal publication' was crucial to the distribution of their work. Far from being oriented towards publication or print, these authors thought in terms of distributing their work in manuscript form. Beyond any practical imperatives, we also see the emergence of a cult of autograph letters and manuscripts. The proliferation of collections of philosophical autographs in eighteenth-century Europe transformed intellectual networks into markets within which philosophical rarity could develop. At this point we need to examine bibliophilic practices closely in order to understand how philosophy books became collectible, how their use value morphed into heritage and how collections of philosophical works were built up.

The market in autographs and manuscript collections emerged in the second half of the eighteenth century with the sale of the papers of the major Enlightenment *philosophes*. A new awareness of the cultural value of these authors turned them into heritage and led to the development of *connoisseurship* and a collector's culture around philosophical manuscripts, which became increasingly disconnected from their intellectual use.

In 1780, Diderot is said to have planned to have his entire œuvre copied in two collections, one for the publication of his complete works in Holland by the printer Marc-Michel Rey and the other for Catherine the Great. To enhance the value of the gift, Diderot sought the services of the calligrapher Roland Girbal, a former servant of Mme d'Epinay and Meister's preferred copyist for the *Correspondance littéraire*. A stable of some twenty secondary copyists was formed, including Girbal and Michel. We know that one of the manuscript collections was intended for Catherine to thank her for sending 2,000 roubles in June 1779, in order to help Diderot establish his children in society. When Diderot died in 1784, Friedrich Melchior Grimm contacted the Russian Empress. In 1785, Mme de Vandeul offered to send Catherine her father's manuscripts. Catherine's letter to Grimm states that she wanted to purchase both the manuscripts and Diderot's library. In November, thirty-two volumes were packed up and sent to Russia. The most famous acquisition is Catherine's purchase of Voltaire's library. On 21 June 1778, following Voltaire's death, the Empress quickly wrote to Grimm, his literary agent, who succeeded in acquiring the library from Voltaire's niece, Mme Denis, in September–December 1778. Voltaire's secretary, Jean-Louis Wagnière, packed the books and manuscripts and had them transported to Les Délices, near Geneva, where they remained until the spring of 1779, when they were sent to St Petersburg, to be placed in a special room in the Winter Palace.

The greatness of the *philosophe*: a deferred recognition?

Did the processes of manufacturing greatness distinguish the *philosophe* from the philosopher in the eyes of posterity? It seems likely, given the degree to which the Enlightenment century was imbued with a perception of its own historicity. In the eighteenth century, funerals were an opportunity to stage events worthy of heads of state, but in the case of Enlightenment *philosophes* they sometimes caused a scandal. Voltaire's burial in Scellières in June 1778 was watched by a large crowd, and eyewitness accounts were published:

> M. l'abbé Mignot at once showed me a letter of consent from the priest of Saint-Sulpice, signed by him, allowing the body of M. de Voltaire to be transported without ceremony; he also showed me a copy, attached by the same priest of Saint-Sulpice, of a profession of the Catholic, apostolic and Roman faith, which M. de Voltaire made in the hands of an approved priest, in the presence of two witnesses, one of whom is M. Mignot, our abbé, nephew of the penitent, and the other a Marquis de Villevieille. He also showed me a letter from the minister of Paris, M. Amelot, addressed to him and M. Dampierre d'Ornoy, nephew of M. l'abbé Mignot and grand-nephew of the deceased, in which these gentlemen were authorized to transport their uncle to Ferney or elsewhere.[33]

In reality, the priest of Saint-Sulpice had refused to authorize Voltaire's burial in Paris. So, as in the case of Descartes' tomb, the commemoration of a *philosophe* in Paris immediately after his death remained problematic due to the inherent potential for scandal. These examples contrast with the cases of Newton and Rousseau, whose respective tombs in Westminster and Ermenonville became sites of pilgrimage at the end of eighteenth century. It was not until the French Revolution that *philosophes* were granted similar recognition in the form of national commemoration, with the return of Voltaire's remains to Paris and his pantheonization in 1791.[34]

NOTES

1 Gaetano Filangieri, *The Science of Legislation*, trans. William Kendall (1784) (London: G. G. and J. Robinson, 1791).
2 See Conal Condren, Stephen Gaukroger and Ian Hunter (eds.), *The Philosopher in Early Modern Europe: The Nature of a Contested Identity* (Cambridge University Press, 2006).
3 Laurence W. Brockliss, *French Higher Education in the Seventeenth and Eighteenth Centuries: A Cultural History* (Oxford University Press, 1987).
4 Ferdinand Brunot, *Histoire de la langue française* (1930) (Paris: Armand Colin, 1966), chap. 2, 'Extension du concept de philosophie', p. 3.
5 'Prospectus', in Diderot and d'Alembert (eds.), *Encyclopédie*.
6 Michel Foucault, *Society Must Be Defended: Lectures at the Collège de France, 1975–76*, trans. David Macey (New York: Picador, 2003), p. 182.
7 Michel Foucault, *The Archaeology of Knowledge*, trans. A. M. Sheridan Smith (New York: Random House, 1972), p. 192.
8 Daniel Brewer, 'Constructing Philosophers', in Daniel Brewer and Julie Candler Hayes (eds.), *Using the 'Encyclopédie': Ways of Knowing, Ways of Reading* (Oxford: Voltaire Foundation, 2002), p. 26.

9 In forming a corpus I have used Joseph de La Porte, *Les Spectacles de Paris ou suite du calendrier historique et chronologique des théâtres* (Paris: Duchesne, 1751–78); C. D. Brenner, *A Bibliographical List of Plays in the French Language, 1700–1789* (Berkeley, Calif., 1947).

10 Steven Shapin, '"The Mind is its Own Place": Science and Solitude in Seventeenth-Century England', *Science in Context*, 4 (1) (1991): 191–218; Roger Chartier, 'L'Homme de lettres', in *L'Homme des lumières*, ed. Michel Vovelle (Paris: Le Seuil, 1997), pp. 159–209.

11 Philippe Néricault Destouches, *Le Philosophe marié ou le mari honteux de l'être: comédie en vers, en cinq actes* (Vienna: Jean-Pierre van Ghelen, 1744).

12 C. B. Paul, *Science and Immortality: The Éloges of the Paris Academy of Sciences (1699–1791)* (Berkeley, Calif.: University of California Press, 1980).

13 Pierre Hadot, *Qu'est-ce que la philosophie antique?* (Paris: Gallimard, 1995), pp. 17–18.

14 Cited by Paulette Charbonnel, 'Le Réquisitoire de Séguier', *Corpus, revue de philosophie*, 22–3 (1993), pp. 15–37, at p. 21. See also Jean-Claude Bourdin (ed.), *Les Matérialistes au XVIIIe siècle* (Paris: Payot, 1996).

15 Michel Delon, *Le Savoir-vivre libertin* (Paris: Hachette littératures, 2000); Antoine Lilti, *Le Monde des salons: sociabilité et mondanité à Paris au XVIIIe siècle* (Paris: Fayard, 2005).

16 Christian Liccoppe, 'The Crystallization of a New Narrative Form in Experimental Reports (1660–1690): The Experimental Evidence as a Transaction between Philosophical Knowledge and Aristocratic Power', *Science in Context*, 7 (2) (1994): 205–44.

17 Giana Pomata and Nancy G. Sirinaisi (eds.), *Historia: Empiricism and Erudition in Early Modern Europe* (Cambridge, Mass.: MIT Press, 2005).

18 Joanna Stalnaker, *The Unfinished Enlightenment: Description in the Age of the Encyclopedia* (Ithaca, NY: Cornell University Press, 2010), p. 7. John Bender and Michael Marrinan (eds.), *Regimes of Description: In the Archive of the Eighteenth Century* (Palo Alto, Calif.: Stanford University Press, 2005).

19 Daniel Brewer, 'Lights in Space', *Eighteenth-Century Studies*, 37 (2) (2004): 171–86.

20 Jakob Soll, *Publishing the Prince: History, Reading, and the Birth of Political Criticism* (Ann Arbor, Mich.: University of Michigan Press, 2005), p. 3.

21 Steven Shapin, *A Social History of Truth: Civility and Science in Seventeenth-Century England* (University of Chicago Press, 1994).

22 Elisabeth Bourguinat, *Le Siècle du persiflage, 1734–1789* (Paris: Presses Universitaires de France, 1998); Charles Walton, *Policing Public Opinion in the French Revolution: The Culture of Calumny and the Problem of Free Speech* (Oxford University Press, 2009); Robert Darnton, *The Devil in the Holy Water: The Art of Slander from Louis XIV to Napoleon* (Philadelphia, Pa.: University of Pennsylvania Press, 2009).

23 Louisa Shea, *The Cynical Enlightenment: Diogenes in the Salon* (Baltimore, Md.: Johns Hopkins University Press, 2010), pp. 47–8.

24 John Bender, *Ends of Enlightenment* (Palo Alto, Calif.: Stanford University Press, 2012).

25 Pierre Bayle, *Pour une histoire critique de la philosophie; choix d'articles philosophiques du Dictionnaire historique et critique*, ed. Jean-Michel Gros (Paris: Honoré Champion, 2001), p. 511.

26 Ibid. pp. 26–7.
27 Pierre Saint-Amand, 'Les Progrès de la civilité dans l'*Encyclopédie*', in Daniel Brewer and Julie Candler Hayes (eds.), *Using the Encyclopédie*, Studies on Voltaire and the Eighteenth Century, 2002:05 (Oxford: Voltaire Foundation, 2002), pp. 163–71, at p. 170.
28 Brian Stock, *The Implications of Literacy* (Princeton University Press, 1987).
29 Roger Chartier, *The Order of Books: Readers, Authors, and Libraries in Europe between the Fourteenth and Eighteenth Centuries* (Palo Alto, Calif.: Stanford University Press, 1994).
30 Stéphane Van Damme, *Paris, capitale philosophique, de la Fronde à la Révolution* (Paris: Odile Jacob, 2005), pp. 116–24.
31 Charlotte Guichard, 'Taste Communities: The Rise of the Amateur in Eighteenth-Century Paris', *Eighteenth-Century Studies*, 45 (4) (2012): 519–47, and *Les Amateurs d'art à Paris au XVIIIe siècle* (Paris: Champ-Vallon, 2007).
32 Catherine Volpilhac-Auger, *L'Atelier de Montesquieu: manuscrits inédits de La Brède* (Naples/Oxford: Liguori Editore/Voltaire Foundation, 2001), p. 14.
33 Marie Jean Antoine Nicolas de Caritat, marquis de Condorcet, *Vie de Voltaire* (Paris: Quai Voltaire, 1994), pp. 179–80.
34 Stephen Bird, *Reinventing Voltaire: The Politics of Commemoration in Nineteenth-Century France*, Studies on Voltaire and the Eighteenth Century 2000:09 (Oxford: Voltaire Foundation, 2000); Jean-Claude Bonnet, *Naissance du Panthéon: essai sur le culte des grands hommes* (Paris: Fayard, 1998).

12

DOWNING A. THOMAS

Music

Music takes on extremely elastic qualities through the varied forms and meanings it adopted in social, intellectual and political life in eighteenth-century France. Some of these forms and meanings will be very familiar to us today while others may seem quite foreign. This chapter provides a brief account of the meanings attributed to music in eighteenth-century France, the uses to which music was put and the reflections commentators have left us regarding the beauty (or monstrosity) of the music they heard and of the effects it had, or was believed to have, on individuals and groups. In this overview of the role of music at a very different time in history, I hope to convey indirectly some of the strangeness of the ways we live with music today. The approach I take is not an ontological one – claiming to understand what music *is* – but rather an anthropological one – focusing on what music *does*, how music is *engaged* as a means to other ends and how it has generated meanings in specific cultural contexts. Thus I focus less on music understood as a collection of works and composers, or an abstract range of genres and stylistic tendencies, and more on a selection of contexts that provide a non-exhaustive overview of the circulation of music, the meanings with which music was associated or which it helped to transmit and the stories that were told about music. While we can certainly affirm that music took on new forms and meanings during *l'âge des lumières*, the exact nature of the connection between music and Enlightenment remains an open question, one to which the present chapter will return.

Eighteenth-century audiences were diverted, exhilarated, exasperated, fascinated and moved by music. Royalty and the rich and powerful were patrons to composers and musicians, held lavish concerts, staged operas and mounted celebrations of various kinds that featured musical performances. The poor heard music in churches, dances, fairs and in the streets. It is an obvious fact (and for that very reason often overlooked) that because the eighteenth century did not possess our recording technology, any music one heard was being created by a human being at that moment, with the very limited exceptions of musical automata, music boxes and similar machines. We are so surrounded by music today that it is difficult for us to imagine, for example, what the experience of hearing a church organ might have been for earlier listeners. Consider the myriad ways in which we experience music through radio, audio and video recordings, movies, television, internet-based media and even mobile ringtones. Consider, too, the astounding range of public spaces (shops and malls, restaurants and bars, fitness centres, lobbies, elevators, holding music on the telephone) where music is present, functioning mostly as background music. Very little of the music we hear today is produced by a human being in the moment, yet music also seems to accompany almost every waking activity. Film music has become a model for the way we use music in daily life, as a soundtrack to comment on or provide mood for the activities in which we are engaged, a phenomenon that became widespread only after the first decades of the twentieth century when music recording technology extended beyond a few minutes.[1] In the eighteenth century, in contrast, all music was 'live', always an integral part of the moment. Musical sounds were mostly in the foreground (rather than in the background), sounds to which those present could turn their full attention or to which one would listen while engaged in another activity such as eating a meal or dancing. Instead of functioning as a soundtrack, music *marked* occasions such as public festivals, royal celebrations, worship and performances of various sorts. Even when spectators were engaged in other activities during a musical performance, as was the case at the opera, music remained a core element of the spectators' experience.[2]

Yet music changed significantly during the eighteenth century. The century ushered in a time when the music heard by the nobility or in public concerts was no longer exclusively new music. While performed music before the eighteenth century had always been the creation of the present or very recent past, during the eighteenth century audiences and performers began to explore older music. Orchestral instruments were also different from the ones we know today. The string sections were all strung with sheep's intestine, not the nylon and metal strings of today's violins. The horns in the eighteenth-century orchestra were essentially hunting horns and had no valves, offering a very different palate of sounds from those we hear in today's brass. The pitches and temperaments used were also distinct from those that later came into use. In short, musical instruments produced sounds that were noticeably distinct from those with which we are most familiar.

Music had a variety of social, political and religious functions in the eighteenth century. Singing was part of daily church-going and consisted of plainchant (the unison singing of liturgy) and harmonized versions, and was a key feature in religious experience. In the streets, singers sang, hurdy-gurdies blared, charlatans attracted customers with violins and performances, and even the cries of vendors had a music to them: 'there were special verses, intonations, and chanting tunes for every item of food, wine, and merchandise'.[3] Formal music performances could be heard in a number of venues in eighteenth-century Paris. The Concert Spirituel was founded in 1725 by Anne Danican Philidor as a concert series for instrumental music and sacred works set in Latin, though works sung in French came to be included in the repertory. Held at the Palais des Tuileries, a palace destroyed by fire in 1871, the Concert Spirituel was a major institution in Parisian musical life until 1790, one where composers such as Louis-Antoine Dornel and Jean-Joseph Cassanéa de Mondonville, and later in the century Johann Christian Bach and Wolfgang Amadeus Mozart, had motets, oratorios and instrumental works performed.

At the other end of the spectrum were two of the more fascinating venues where music could be found among many other forms of entertainment and commerce. The Foire St Germain, located near the church of St Germain-des-Prés, opened every winter on 3 February and closed on Palm Sunday; and the Foire St Laurent, situated where the Gare de l'Est stands today, ran roughly through the months of August and September. The fairs offered spectacles of all sorts: marionette theatre, acrobatic shows, animal acts, ambulant musicians and farces with spoken dialogue. The official theatres – the Comédie-Française and the Opéra – were in competition with the fair theatres and constantly attempted to enforce the monopolies they held in their respective areas of the theatrical repertory. In 1714, the fair theatre negotiated with the Opéra to be allowed to present plays with music and dance, licensed under the name of Opéra-Comique. But from 1718 to 1724, the Comédie-Française successfully limited the fair theatre spectacles to marionette shows and acrobatics.[4] Other restrictions imposed on the fair theatres limited the number and type of instrumentalists, singers and dancers they could employ and specified how they could and could not mix song and text. But the fair theatres demonstrated exceptional agility in skirting these restrictions. When they were prevented from using spoken dialogue, they developed plays based on monologues and mime. Many works were performed *en vaudevilles*, meaning that spoken dialogue was interspersed with popular tunes sung to new words. These works might be parodies of serious operas – *tragédies en musique* – or other comic works of various kinds. To take one example, the revival of the *tragédie en musique, Atys* (1675), by Jean-Baptiste Lully and Philippe Quinault, during the 1725–6 Opéra season was one of many opportunities the fair theatres seized to mount a parody. At the Foire St Germain in the spring of 1726, *La Grandmère amoureuse, parodie d'Atys* (*The Grandmother in Love, a Parody of*

Atys) was performed by marionettes, one of the many techniques the fairs used to get around restrictions on performance imposed by the official theatres. Towards the end of the story, drawn from Ovid's *Fasti*, the jealous goddess Cybele causes Attis to go mad, castrating himself, at which point she takes pity on him and transforms him into a pine tree. While Lully's and Quinault's opera delicately passes over the castration episode, *La Grand-mère amoureuse* comically restores Ovid's original by having Arlequin (as Cybele) transform Pierrot (as Attis) into a capon instead of a pine tree.[5]

The fair theatres invited audience participation using popular refrains, known as *timbres*, to which new words were sung. This technique allowed the performers to create zany and raucous contrasts between the situations and meanings of the serious works being parodied and the new plots and words to which the tunes were set. It also allowed for music to continue at the fair theatres even when the performers were reduced to silence by the official theatres, because the *timbres* served as cues for audience members to begin singing as displayed placards provided the new words. *Arlequin sultane favorite* (*Arlequin the Sultan's Favourite*), by the librettist Jean-François Letellier, offers an example of the uses of *timbres* in the fair theatres. The play was one of many published by Alain-René Lesage in his anthology of fair theatre repertory, *Théâtre de la Foire ou l'Opéra-Comique*, issued between 1721 and 1737. As the play opens, Arlequin laments his and his master's unfortunate capture in foreign lands. Arlequin sings the following words to the popular tune referred to as 'Joconde': 'We are here as slaves under the power of a tyrant, in a land where the Koran forbids wine cellars, and one sees nary a Cabaret. O unimaginable misery! I am forever separated from wine and brandy!'[6] The *timbre* ('Joconde'), used so that audiences could identify the tune, refers to an episode of marital infidelity from Ariosto's *Orlando furioso*. Previous theatrical uses of the *timbre* would have helped to introduce *Arlequin sultane favorite*, providing audiences with a context for the play they were about to enjoy.[7]

Well-known tunes were used as a vehicle for new words in a variety of social contexts, where words could be sung and very readily passed on to others because the tunes were so familiar. Music was a particularly important cog in the communication network of eighteenth-century Paris, allowing news, seditious political commentary and gossip to circulate and reach a large audience. An example of this network is the Affair of the Fourteen, which began with the arrest of a medical student for having recited a poem attacking Louis XV. The mechanism of *vaudevilles* contributed to the development and success of this network. Everyone sang; and memorization, a practice that played a much more significant role in earlier centuries than it does today, was a key element in the ability of this communication network to function, whether it was to comment on a recent execution, to gossip about the love lives of the rich and famous, to have some fun with burlesque Christmas carols or to develop a line of political satire attacking governmental officials, mistresses and, by extension, the King himself. The mutable and participatory quality of song allowed participants to shape the verses, adding ones as they elaborated on the original words or perhaps objecting to those added by previous recipients of the messages, thus adding layers to the social commentary. In his study of music's role in these communication networks, Robert Darnton has described this phenomenon as 'a sung newspaper', a particularly useful form for a semi-literate society such as that of eighteenth-century France.[8] But, for a variety of reasons – its participatory dimension, the ability to inflect or even change content – it functioned less like a newspaper and more like a vocal version of today's social media. The role of song within this critical, discursive network provides a piece of the answer to the question of music's connection to the Enlightenment.

Opera was the most rarefied and privileged of musical events in eighteenth-century France, sanctioned by the Crown through the exclusive institution of the Académie Royale de Musique (the Opéra), established by Louis XIV and lasting through the Ancien Régime. While forms of French instrumental music functioned as models that were widely adopted abroad, French opera was oddly *l'exception française*, taking root almost nowhere outside the country. It is something of a paradox that French controversies about opera were arguably the most widely known and discussed Enlightenment debates on music in all of Europe, occupying a significant place in the cultural landscape of *l'âge des lumières*, whereas it was not French but Italian opera that was embraced as the universal musical and dramatic art form, with works based on libretti by Pietro Metastasio performed from Naples to Vienna to London. While the provinces saw their first permanent opera houses built during the course of the eighteenth century – in Lyon, Besançon and Bordeaux – the Paris Académie was unquestionably the hub of French operatic activity. The Académie's *privilège* granted it a monopoly over the performance of operatic works, and the institution frequently battled or negotiated lucrative contracts with competing companies, standing firm on the royal monopoly it held. A fraught, though symbiotic, relationship existed between the Académie and the various theatres, for without serious opera the fair theatres would lose the repertory on which their parodies depended. Likewise, the debt-ridden Opéra depended on the contracts the fair theatres negotiated with them to survive financially.

By mid-century, still losing money, the Opéra decided to infuse its repertory with something new by inviting three Italian singers from the Bambini troupe to lead performances of comic *intermezzi* offered alongside larger French works. While three *intermezzi* were performed from August to November 1752, the one that attracted the most attention then as now was Giovanni Battista Pergolesi's *La Serva padrona* (*The Servant Turned Mistress*) (1733). In the aftermath of these performances, from 1752 to 1754, the Querelle des Bouffons erupted in a flurry of pamphlets and other writings of the moment, drawing a stark opposition between partisans of French music and those who championed Italian music. The contrast between Lully's *Acis et Galathée* (*Acis and Galatea*) (1686) and Pergolesi's *intermezzo*, both performed on 1 August 1752, could not have been more striking. The audience that day first saw Lully's myth-based *pastorale héroïque* in which the boorish giant Polyphemus flies into a jealous rage, killing the shepherd Acis, whose lover, the marine nymph Galatea, flees into her element, the sea. This performance was followed by the story, sung in Italian, of a 'hapless couch-potato of an elderly *signore* and his beguilingly clever maid', who manipulates him into marrying her.[9] This extreme contrast at the very heart of the French theatrical establishment – the Opéra – set the stage for the Querelle. As the season progressed, Friedrich Melchior, baron von Grimm, published *Le Petit Prophète de Boemischbroda* (*The Little Prophet of Boemischbroda*), attacking French opera for the monotony of its music and the ridiculous situations of its plots. The anti-French stance of the pamphlet and its mock-biblical style did much to ignite the Querelle, which drew far more attention among the general public than the parliamentary crisis that had erupted the same year, fuelled by hostility between Jansenist and Jesuit sympathizers. Towards the end of the Querelle, Jean-Jacques Rousseau contributed his *Lettre sur la musique française* (*Letter on French Music*), concluding with the resolute claim that, because French music had 'neither rhythm nor melody', and because 'French singing is nothing but non-stop barking … the French have no music and never will'.[10] Because the Opéra amounted to 'the monarch's personal property', albeit licensed to a director who was responsible for its operation, an attack on its repertory was no small affront.[11] The musicians of the Opéra responded by burning Rousseau in effigy.

Dictionaries of music, some of the first histories of music, journalistic writing on music, practical and theoretical treatises on music – all proliferated during the Enlightenment. Music played a privileged role in the intellectual life of the eighteenth century across many fields of discourse and thought. The most influential *philosophes* whom we continue to read today – Voltaire, Rousseau, Diderot – and many other key Enlightenment figures wrote texts about music, integrated music into their philosophical speculations and fictions, wrote opera libretti and even composed music. Diderot's partner in the venture to publish the innovative *Encyclopédie ou dictionnaire raisonné des sciences, des arts et des métiers*, Jean le Rond d'Alembert, published a synopsis of music theory in 1752, the *Éléments de musique*, written to reorganize, clarify and simplify Rameau's elaborate and difficult musical treatises. In 1733, Voltaire collaborated with Rameau on an opera, *Samson*, which was eventually abandoned due to pressure from the Church. Voltaire continued to follow musical developments, as in 1774, when he remarked in a letter to the marquise du Deffand on the reforms that the composer Christoph Willibald Ritter von Gluck had attempted with his 1774 tragedy, *Iphigénie en Aulide* (*Iphigenia in Aulis*): 'it seems to me that you Parisians are going to see a great and peaceful transformation in your government and in your music. Louis XVI and Gluck are going to make new Frenchmen.'[12]

Rousseau's own operatic *intermezzo*, *Le Devin du village* (*The Village Soothsayer*), premiered in 1753 in the midst of the Querelle des Bouffons; and Rousseau was responsible for the articles on music in the *Encyclopédie* which were later incorporated in his 1768 *Dictionnaire de musique*. In the speculative and philosophical works of the eighteenth century, music was an object of fascination and of vigorous debate, a vehicle for speculation on everything from the origins of language and human societies to the nature of scientific methods. For some, it approached the dimensions of the philosopher's stone. Despite its status as an official publication, the *Mercure de France* contributed actively to the debates surrounding music and to the reforms that were beginning to take hold. The types of writing in the *Mercure* expanded during the 1750s beyond traditional reviews of works and performances to include essays, letters and other contributions; and the stances the journal took were hardly supportive of the Opéra and its leadership. Reflecting on the important position music held in current debates, d'Alembert wrote that 'in every nation, there are two things that one must respect: the Religion and the Government. In France, there is a third: *the Music of the country*.'[13] If the Enlightenment is characterized by the development of public debate to contest established authority, then certainly the musical debates of the 1750s are an important part of the story of the Enlightenment.

Of the *philosophes*, Rousseau was unquestionably the one most involved in music theory, criticism and composition. He even attempted an ambitious and youthful reform of nothing less than the entire system of music notation as it was used throughout Europe, presenting his proposal to the Académie des Sciences in 1742. Instead of the system of staves and notes then in place and which we continue to use, he proposed a moveable *do* system made up of the numerals 1 through 7, with various figures placed above or below these numerals to express octave shifts, sharps and flats, ornaments and other modifications. He argued that, with only seven basic numerals, this system would take less time to learn, make transposition easier, take up less space and thus make it appreciably cheaper to print music. Despite these advantages, his system was never adopted, in part because of the tremendous practical usefulness of being able to see the music spatially through the use of staves.

Staging *intermezzi* was a short-term money-maker for François Francœur and François Rebel, the directors of the Opéra, since it cost so much less to stage a brief *intermezzo* than a full-scale French ballet or, even worse for the purse, a *tragédie en musique*. Later in the century, in 1762, Denis-Pierre-Jean Papillon de la Ferté, the administrator of the Comédie-Italienne, ordered the merger of the Opéra-Comique (the fair theatres) with the Comédie-Italienne, the Italian troupe that had been based at the Hôtel de Bourgogne since 1716. In the arrangement, the Comédie-Italienne was forbidden to present sung plays on Tuesdays and Fridays, when the Opéra took precedence. By paying 30,000 *livres* annually to the Académie (roughly fifteen per cent of its gross income) though, the Comédie-Italienne could stage operas on other days.[14] In hindsight, given the success of newer theatrical forms developed at the Opéra-Comique such as the *comédies mêlées d'ariettes* (a mixture of spoken dialogue, newly composed arias and ensembles) and the sentimental culture they helped to foster and in which they took root, the decision by Francœur and Rebel may appear to have been penny-wise and pound-foolish for the Opéra. By the time Jean-Philippe Rameau's 'tragédie en musique', Les Boréades (*The Descendants of Boreas*) was in rehearsal in 1763, audiences were drawn less to the magnificent tragedies of composers such as Rameau (arguably the finest French composer of the eighteenth century) than to the new creations of the Opéra-Comique, such as *Tom Jones* (1765), a work by Antoine Alexandre Henri Poinsinet and François-André Danican Philidor which played on the themes of feeling and sympathy that were increasingly attractive to Parisian audiences.[15] Gluck's arrival in Paris introduced reforms based on his re-evaluation of Italian opera designed to bring the orchestral accompaniment in line with the text, eliminate bravura and reduce the repetitiousness of *da capo* arias. His *Alceste* (1769), written in collaboration with the playwright Raniero Calzabigi, and his *Iphigénie en Aulide* are indicative of this aesthetic shift in tragedy. With the Revolution came the Théâtre de Monsieur (named after the comte de Provence, the King's brother), with its royal pedigree effectively superseding the *privilège* of the Académie de Musique and a 1790 law allowing anyone to start a theatre, opening the field to increased competition.

Unlike the rapt attention that is demanded of today's audiences, whose slightest coughs and shifts can elicit glaring looks or angry shushes from severe *mélomanes*, eighteenth-century audiences often gossiped, murmured and ate during performances, pausing to listen to a particular passage or, at the opera, to a particular singer about whom everyone was talking. As James Johnson has noted, 'circulating, conversing, arriving late, and leaving early were an accepted part of eighteenth-century musical experience, grudgingly tolerated by some and positively encouraged by others.'[16] The parterre – the area of standing room only directly in front of the stage – was a space that encouraged the most direct engagement with the performance and the performers. While audiences at the Comédie-Française and the Comédie-Italienne could disrupt performances and were sometimes arrested for rowdy behaviour, at the opera, despite murmuring and even occasional trouble, audiences were better behaved.[17] Less conducive to a reverential mood as theatres today, the auditorium at the Opéra was still not the noisy venue that it was in Italy.[18] Despite its seat at the apex of the artistic hierarchy, the Paris Opéra auditorium itself left something to be desired, even in the eyes of contemporaries who had different expectations of comfort than that of modern audiences. The dancer and theorist Jean-Georges Noverre described the Académie theatre as 'a pigeon coop, a rat's nest, a cramped, squalid, smoky hovel, revoltingly dirty, a squashed hangar, entirely unworthy of our Academy'.[19] The opera house could also be dangerous. Primarily because of the need for significant amounts of lighting, the Paris Opéra burned to the ground first in 1763 and again in 1781. Contemporaries referred to the theatre boxes with which the auditorium was equipped as *volières* in part because that they looked like stacked chicken coops but also because the 'hens' looking out were locked into their *loges* by an attendant from the beginning of the performance. Social practices and expectations related to luxury, jealousy and the need to distinguish social ranks slowed the reform of theatrical design.[20] One's own visibility as a spectator and proximity to royalty or high nobility trumped comfort and lines of sight in relation to the stage.

In contrast to the nineteenth-century elevation of instrumental music as 'pure' music, in the eighteenth century instrumental music was secondary, and opera was at the summit of the theatrical hierarchy. However, it was not considered first and foremost to be a musical form, even though in most cases its libretto was set to music throughout. Instead, it was classified as a poetic form and treated as such by commentators. Having been imported from Italy in the mid seventeenth century, opera emerged as a French form later in the century, taking on the form of *tragédie en musique* (tragedy set to music). Tragedy was dramatic poetry, whose moral justification came from the corrective effects the experience of terror and pity was considered to have on spectators. In the early years of opera, commentators such as Saint-Evremond and André Dacier attacked it as a false form of tragedy, construing the addition of music and dance to be mere sensual distraction or, worse, a corrupting influence. While some, such as Antoine Arnauld, wrote of the dangers of opera's 'lascivious songs' that were spreading immorality 'throughout France', these concerns mostly faded during the eighteenth century, when more emphasis was given to the aesthetic and moral receptivity prompted by musical feeling.[21] Yet opera's identity as a poetic form persisted.

Indeed, music was understood to function as a kind of language that at times adhered so closely to specific cultural practices and traditions that its meanings were closed to outsiders. In his *Dictionnaire de musique*, Jean-Jacques Rousseau mentions that it was 'forbidden under penalty of death' to sing or play the Swiss herdsman's melody, the 'Ranz-des-vaches' (better known today from the overture to Gioachino Rossini's *Guillaume Tell* [*William Tell*]), 'because it caused those who heard it to burst into tears, to desert or to die, so much it aroused in them the ardent desire to see their homeland again'. Only the Swiss react to the melody in this way, Rousseau explains, because of the tight connection between the tune, 'habit, memories and a thousand circumstances which, brought back by this Air for those who hear it, and recalling their country, their former pleasures, their youth and all their ways of living, awaken in them a bitter grief for having lost all that'.[22] But even music that had no words was understood to be, or to aspire to being, a universal language. As Saint Lambert wrote in his 1702 *Les Principes du clavecin*, a method for playing the harpsichord, musical phrases were to be composed and understood through basic rhetorical principles:

> just as a piece of rhetoric is a whole unit which is most often made up of several parts, each of which is composed of sentences, each having a complete meaning, these sentences being composed of phrases, the phrases of words, and the words of letters, so the melody of a piece of music is a whole unit which is always composed of several sections. Each section is composed of cadences which have a complete meaning and are the sentence of the melody. The cadences are often composed of phrases, the phrases of measures, and the measures of notes.[23]

The primary duty of the musician was to articulate and convey the meaning that the composer had created.

If the poetic model was the dominant one for understanding the creation and structure of music, imitation was the dominant framework for understanding the function and effects of musical art on listeners and spectators. The abbé Jean-Baptiste du Bos explained how the arts affect us in his *Réflexions critiques sur la poésie et sur la peinture* (*Critical Reflections on Poetry and Painting*) of 1719, which, despite the title's focus on poetry and painting, also contains extensive sections on music. Creators of works of art, du Bos explained, 'excite in us artificial passions by offering imitations of the objects capable of exciting real passions in us ... [art] must excite in our soul a passion that resembles the one that the imitated object would have excited'.[24] Because emotions could be considered dangerous, seen as encouraging reckless behaviour or threatening one's health, the standard justification for the emotions generated by artistic works, which was derived from passages of the Augustan poet Horace's *Ars poetica*, was that the arts provided moral instruction through pleasure.[25] Du Bos's treatise, however, did not dwell on what men could learn from art but focused instead on how it afforded pleasure. Symptomatic of the emphasis the eighteenth century placed on delectation, du Bos's objective was to dissect pleasure, to display 'the human heart in the instant it is moved by a poem or touched by a painting'.[26] Du Bos's focus on the passions led him to reflect, first, on the many things to which men turn for distraction. Artistic representations are the basis for 'that conversation with oneself' that affords us a form of studied or meditative distraction (3). These pleasures are pure, du Bos argued, because their enjoyment does not have the deleterious effects of women, wine, gaming or the many other distractions to which men turn to free themselves from boredom and ennui. While the actions and objects represented by artworks are fictions that have only 'a borrowed life', as du Bos put it, they nonetheless affect us in significant ways (10). We are not tricked by paintings or plays into believing that we are truly witnessing the objects and actions depicted. So, although fictional works provoke real joy and sadness, surprise and horror, it is not the case that 'illusion is the source of the pleasure that poetic or pictorial imitations have on us' (146). Often the act of imitation itself is an object of interest and attention on the part of the spectator, du Bos notes, which is particularly noticeable in cases where the objects depicted would not elicit the degree of interest in real life. In these cases, it is the imitator's skill that is on display more than the objects imitated.

If poetry functions in an analogous way to painting by depicting actions through the medium of words, music likewise depicts the sonorous world of action and human passion. This is du Bos's primary claim about music: 'just as the painter imitates the lines and colours of nature, so the composer imitates the tones, accents, sighs, inflections of voice, in short all those sounds through which nature itself expresses feelings and passions' (150). Du Bos likens the resources music has at its disposal to generate imitations (melody, harmony and rhythm) to those painting draws upon (line, colour and shadow). In opera, music adds 'the inarticulate language of man' to 'the energy of the words'. Sounds have always been used to 'move the heart of men', and even the instrumental passages provide imitations of storms, earthquakes, birds and other natural sounds (151, 152). In this way, music imitates sounds found in nature; but, just as poetry can depict situations no one has experienced, such as the pleasures of Heaven and the horrors of Hell, likewise music can represent sounds no one has heard, 'such as the rumbling of the earth when Pluto leaves the underworld, the hiss of the air when Apollo inspires Pythia, the noise that a ghost makes emerging from its tomb' (155). These are instances of what du Bos calls 'truth of convention', conforming to what we might expect or imagine these sounds to resemble (155). Music plays the greatest role when it is connected to theatrical action and meaning. It is for this reason that sonatas and other pieces of instrumental music were considered inferior to theatrical music. Moreover, using music to generate elaborate representations of words (referred to as 'word painting' today) was thought inferior to the use of music to elevate the mind to consider a broader meaning: 'the [musical] expression of a word cannot touch as much as the [musical] expression of a feeling' (156). In a discussion of instrumental portions from Act V of Lully's *Roland*, du Bos remarks that the music seems perfectly matched to ease 'the tumultuous ideas that the activities of the day leave in the imagination' (154). The idea of music as a kind of language that had rhetorical effects at its disposal persisted through the end of the eighteenth century. As the rhetorical understanding of music waned, interest in the demonstrable effects of music on the bodies and minds of listeners gained in importance.

Music was an intriguing focus of speculation in part because it could be seen as speaking in the language of mathematics while at the same time functioning as a cultural object that lay at the heart of so many ritual acts (religious, royal) and social activities. Music was also studied because of the effects, both physical and 'moral' (psychological), that it had or was presumed to have on listeners. Music had been studied since Antiquity with an eye to the effects it had on human health and behaviour. Stories of the power of music start with the Bible: 'and whenever the spirit from God troubled Saul, David took the harp and played; then Saul grew calm, and recovered, and the evil spirit left him'.[27] This particular passage is often quoted in early modern accounts of music's effects. Du Bos devotes several sections of his *Réflexions critiques* to the musical writings of the ancients. He cites the fifth-century writer Macrobius Ambrosius Theodosius on the powerful effects music can have: 'the power that song has on us is so significant', Macrobius writes, 'that military instruments play airs that inspire courage when one must go into battle, whereas they play an air of an opposite nature when it is time to retreat. Instrumental music moves us, it makes us happy or anxious; it even puts us to sleep. It calms us, it offers relief even in bodily illness' (374). The eighteenth century was fascinated by the accounts the Ancient Greeks and Romans gave of their music, of its effects and of the larger cultural and artistic framework in which it flourished. Du Bos approaches the miraculous cures attributed to music by the Ancients cautiously, noting that they are now very rare and unusual occurrences. While he remarks that 'it would be ridiculous to prescribe airs and songs, as one prescribes purging and bloodletting', he notes that the curative powers of music are nonetheless attested in the memoirs of the respected Académie des Sciences (374). He compares the effects of various types of music on morals described by the Ancients to the influence the variety of religious practices has on the inhabitants of various parts of the world. As with the use of music to convey news and information through song, the understanding of music as relative to cultural practices, seen in the proto-anthropological approach of du Bos, offers a connection between music and Enlightenment thought.

The *Encyclopédie* contains a number of references to music's medicinal qualities, from d'Alembert's sceptical account of the use of music to remedy the effects of tarantula bite to the fairly detailed account of music as a form of therapy written by the most important contributor of medical articles to the *Encyclopédie*, Ménuret de Chambaud. Jean-Baptiste-Joseph Lallemant's *Essai sur le mécanisme des passions en général* (*Essay on the Mechanisms of the Passions*), published the same year as the first two volumes of the *Encyclopédie* (1751), focuses on how the body manages sensation. For Lallemant, there is constant activity in the body because the fibres that transmit sensation are continually responding to stimuli, and the entire organism is likewise continually adjusting to the changes within it as a result of these stimuli. His *Essai* explains two ways in which musical sounds can affect human beings: 'Melody acts on the Passions in two ways: either by expressing the movement that it inspires, or by the simple impression that rhythm makes on the ear'.[28] In other words, the human organism either finds in music a likeness to its passions (a mimetic response) or it reacts mechanically to the sounds that penetrate the ear. The former, Lallemant argues, occurs through the effects of vocal music, as a sympathetic response to the voice of another human being, whereas the latter is a physical reaction to pleasant (or unpleasant) sounds as they reach the body.

In 1777, the comte de Mirabeau published a pamphlet with playful and roving discussions of the arts, the passions and criticism, in which he defines music, following Rousseau, as 'the art of combining sounds so that they are pleasing to the ear', though he notes that this simple definition becomes more complicated when one considers the 'infinite number' of its combinations and effects, and the 'vast and limitless knowledge' that music entails.[29] Mirabeau remarks that music and medicine have been allied since remotest Antiquity; yet not everyone is in agreement on the degree of confidence we should have in the accounts of music's effects handed down to us by the

Greek and Roman historians and philosophers. Nonetheless, Mirabeau is convinced that

> music can be of real use in the art of healing. The knowledge of the animal economy, of the action of the fibres, of nerve fluids, of the influence of changes in the air and above all that of the passions on the human mechanism, makes this opinion very probable.
>
> (23)

Although he indicates that he has neither the time nor the fortitude to undertake such research, he adds that 'by examining how music affects men in general, and certain men in particular, one could ascertain to what extent it can function [in this way]; and the results of this research would indicate its potential as a medical remedy' (24). Mirabeau continues, citing authors who have discussed the use of music to encourage soldiers in their marches or to ease the burden of workers in particularly arduous tasks. Giving the example of the 'young beauty' who would rather die than walk thirty minutes but who can dance all night when accompanied by music (the implication, of course, being that she is not only accompanied by music but also by a male companion), Mirabeau notes that 'music can raise the energy level of the human body considerably' (31). He oscillates between considering the physical effects of music and the moral influence it has. Mirabeau concludes this section of his wandering essay with a Borgesian proposal for a theory connecting the full variety of musical expressions to a map of the human passions, taking into account the varied experiences of individuals and the diverse circumstances in which they live: 'I believe that a philosopher-composer could designate the relationship of all modulations, all tempi, all sounds, in other words of melody, with all the passions of the soul, while taking into account the influence that differences in climate, character, of mind and of national prejudices must have' (35). It is clear from Mirabeau's expansive ideas that there were many aspects of music that eighteenth-century thinkers considered to be relatively unexplored and promising for the future of the art.

Joseph-Louis Roger, a doctor associated with the Montpellier school, published his *Tentamen de vi soni et musices in corpore humano* (*Treatise on the Effects of Music on the Human Body*) in 1758. Commenting on the particular effectiveness of music on nervous disorders, his translator, Dr Étienne Sainte-Marie, notes that Roger documented effective treatment of 'catalepsies, hysterical or hypochondriac ailments, malignant fevers, nervous or humoral melancholies, epilepsies, cured by music. Frequent concert-going has also dissipated certain rheumatisms, migraines, nostalgia, etc.'[30] While Roger subscribes to a theory of nerves as strings to which some doctors adhered, and to which others objected because of its overly simplistic assumptions, he makes a point of distinguishing imaginary magical cures from verified medical uses of music; and he chides some of his predecessors for their gullibility, notably Athanasius Kircher and Marin Mersenne, the latter having claimed that hens will flee from the sound of a guitar strung with fox gut (29, 125). He also proposes a more complex version of the string theory than many of his contemporaries: 'Those who have attempted to explain all the effects of music through the movement and the vibrations in the nerves have proposed a vague and far too general theory' (184). Music has a direct impact on the nerves, affecting the flow of nerve fluid, Roger argues. It can also act indirectly by helping the soul move the fluid in salutary ways or redistributing it when it is out of balance. Given that music affects the soul and the body in multiple ways, both directly and indirectly, Roger notes the difficulty of his subject, remarking that it is not yet possible to understand fully the effects of music (251–2). However, his early attempts to understand the physical and psychological ('moral') effects of music and those of his contemporaries are some of the first modern attempts to understand and harness the medical use of sounds. Today's music therapy as an allied health profession clearly owes its existence to the initial and tentative exploration undertaken by doctors from the Montpellier school.

Connections between music and the Enlightenment are discernible at various points during the eighteenth century, with sung news networks, the debates surrounding music in the 1750s and in the connections between music and the body that were explored during the second half of the century. More elusive meanings came to be associated with musical and literary works at the close of the century, and this perceived commonality provided music and literature with a shared mission. The improvisations of Germaine de Staël's eponymous heroine in *Corinne, ou l'Italie* (*Corinne; or, Italy*) (1807) are shot through with music and defined by their musicality. Corinne's character and her music provide a contrast with Lord Oswald Nelvil, the melancholic Scottish aristocrat whom she loves. Tili Boon Cuillé has argued that Staël's use of music through the literary embodiment of Corinne points to a critique of contemporary society and its treatment of women: 'Creating a heroine who incarnates the musical ideal Rousseau evoked in his writings, Staël immolates this ideal to the society whose prejudices his statements tended to reinforce'.[31] Moving into nineteenth-century frameworks, Staël's Corinne and her relation to music point to new directions in musical meaning, ones that diverge significantly from Mirabeau's vision of musical means that could one day be mapped transparently onto the meanings and effects that it has for us as listeners.

NOTES

1 I want to thank my colleague at the University of Iowa, Rick Altman, for engaging me in a conversation on his area of expertise – film and sound theory.

2 This is not to say that noise didn't exist in the eighteenth century or that music was not sometimes associated with or likened to noise. See Charles Dill, 'Ideological Noises: Opera Criticism in Early Eighteenth-Century France', in Roberta Montemorra Marvin and Downing A. Thomas (eds.), *Operatic Migrations: Transforming Works and Crossing Boundaries* (Aldershot: Ashgate, 2006), pp. 65–83.

3 R. M. Isherwood, *Farce and Fantasy: Popular Entertainment in Eighteenth-Century Paris* (Oxford University Press, 1986), p. 4.

4 Pierre Louis d'Aquin de Chateaulyon, *Siècle littéraire de Louis XV, ou lettres sur les hommes célèbres*, 2 vols. (Amsterdam and Paris: Duschesne, 1752), vol. I, p. 17.

5 See Louis Fuzelier and Jacques-Philippe Dorneval, *La Grand-mère amoureuse, parodie d'Atys*, ed. Susan Harvey (Middleton, Wisc.: A-R Editions, 2008).

6 I rely on the translation provided by Jama Liane Stilwell, 'A New View of the Eighteenth-Century "Abduction" Opera: Edification and Escape at the Parisian "Théâtres de la Foire"', *Music and Letters*, 91 (1) (2010): 51–82, at p. 57.

7 Ibid. p. 59.

8 Robert Darnton, *Poetry and the Police* (Cambridge, Mass.: Harvard University Press, 2010), p. 78.

9 Michael Fend, 'An Instinct for Parody and a Spirit for Revolution: Parisian Opera, 1752–1800', in Simon P. Keefe (ed.), *The Cambridge History of Eighteenth-Century Music* (Cambridge University Press, 2009), pp. 295–330, at p. 297.

10 Jean-Jacques Rousseau, *Œuvres complètes*, ed. Bernard Gagnebin and Marcel Raymond, 5 vols. (Paris: Gallimard, 1995), vol. V, p. 328.

11 David Charlton, *Opera in the Age of Rousseau: Music, Confrontation, Realism* (Cambridge University Press, 2013), p. 3.

12 Voltaire, 'Voltaire to Marie de Vichy de Chamrond, marquise du Deffand', *Les Œuvres complètes (The Complete Works)*, ed. Giles Barber (Oxford: The Voltaire Foundation, 1975), vol. CXXV, p. 74.

13 Jean le Rond D'Alembert, *Mélanges de littérature, d'histoire, et de philosophie*, 5 vols. (Amsterdam: Zacharie Chatelain et Fils, 1763), vol. IV, p. 383.

14 Fend, 'An Instinct for Parody', pp. 308–9.

15 On the changes in the operatic repertory and cultural expectations of this period, see Downing A. Thomas, *Aesthetics of Opera in the Ancien Régime, 1647–1785* (Cambridge University Press, 2002), pp. 201–64.

16 James H. Johnson, *Listening in Paris: A Cultural History* (Berkeley, Calif.: University of California Press, 1995), p. 31.

17 David Charlton has recently challenged the 'carnivalesque view of audience inattention', noise and drunken singing at the opera conveyed by James Johnson (Charlton, *Opera in the Age of Rousseau*, p. 187). See also Jeffrey S. Ravel, *The Contested Parterre: Public Theater and French Political Culture, 1680–1791* (Ithaca, NY: Cornell University Press, 1999).

18 Charlton, *Opera in the Age of Rousseau*, p. 188.

19 Jean-Georges Noverre, *Lettres sur la danse*, cited in Claude Jamain, *L'Imaginaire de la musique au siècle des lumières* (Paris: Champion, 2003), pp. 52–3.

20 William D. Howarth (ed.), *French Theatre in the Neo-Classical Era, 1550–1789* (Cambridge University Press, 1997), p. 535.

21 Antoine Arnauld, 'À M. Perrault, de l'Académie Françoise, au sujet de la satire sur les femmes par M. Despreaux', in *Lettres*, 9 vols. (Nancy: Joseph Nicolai, 1727), vol. VII, p. 26.

22 Rousseau, *Œuvres complètes*, vol. V, p. 924.

23 Michel de Saint Lambert, *Principles of the Harpsichord*, trans. and ed. Rebecca Harris-Warwick (Cambridge University Press, 1984), p. 32.

24 Jean-Baptiste du Bos, *Réflexions critiques sur la poésie et sur la peinture* (Paris: École Nationale Supérieure des Beaux-Arts, 1993), pp. 9–10.

25 'Omne tulit punctum qui miscuit utile dulci / lectorem delectando pariterque monendo' (He has won every vote who has blended profit and pleasure, at once delighting and instructing the reader) (Horace, *Satires, Epistles and Ars Poetica*, trans. H. Rushton Fairclough [1926] [Cambridge, Mass.: Harvard University Press, 1978], lines 343–4, pp. 478–9).

26 Du Bos, *Réflexions*, p. 2. Further references to du Bos are given by page in the text.

27 *The Jerusalem Bible* (Garden City, NY: Doubleday & Company, 1968), 1 Samuel 16:23.

28 Jean-Baptiste-Joseph Lallemant, *Essai sur le mécanisme des passions en général* (Paris: Le Prieur, 1751), p. 14.

29 Honoré Gabriel Riqueti, comte de Mirabeau, *Le Lecteur y mettra le titre* (London: n.p., 1777), p. 18. Further references to Mirabeau are given by page in the text.

30 Roger, *Traité*, p. xxiv. Further references to Roger are given by page in the text.

31 Tili Boon Cuillé, *Narrative Interludes: Musical Tableaux in Eighteenth-Century French Texts* (University of Toronto Press, 2006), p. 199.

13

ANTHONY VIDLER

Architecture and the Enlightenment

The titles of the numerous histories of French eighteenth-century architecture, from Emil Kaufmann's *Architecture in the Age of Reason* to Alan Braham's *The Architecture of the French Enlightenment*, certainly suggest that architecture and the Enlightenment had much to do with each other.[1] Emil Kaufmann, the first scholar to examine the works of what he called the French 'neo-classical' (*Klassizismus*) architects following the neo-Kantian research of the Marburg School and Ernst Cassirer's publications on the Enlightenment, was convinced that architecture after 1750 had undergone its own internal revolution, stimulated by the writings of the *philosophes*.[2] Kaufmann in his enthusiasm for modernism even went so far as to entitle his first monograph *Von Ledoux bis Le Corbusier: Ursprung und Entwicklung der autonomen Architektur* (*From Ledoux to Le Corbusier: Origin and Development of Autonomous Architecture*), suggesting emphatically that modernity and 'autonomy' were synonymous and that Ledoux's contribution to this Kantian notion was a proto-bourgeois architecture of geometric abstraction heralding that of Le Corbusier a century later.[3] For him, the writings and designs of Étienne-Louis Boullée (1728–99) and Claude-Nicolas Ledoux (1736–1806) exemplified for architecture what Montesquieu, Rousseau and Kant represented for philosophy. His *Architecture in the Age of Reason* remained canonical until the 1970s. Subsequently, however, with the more detailed study of the archival record by French and British historians, Kaufmann's 'heroes' were somewhat dethroned and contextualized within the general development of eighteenth-century institutional and urban reform, and attention turned away from their 'utopian' writings to the study of the building campaigns of the 1750s and 1760s.[4] Nevertheless, interest in utopianism of all kinds was revived in the 1960s, and Ledoux and Boullée were once more resurrected, this time as anticipators of the 'visionary' architecture and communitarian ideals of nineteenth-century utopian socialists – Charles Fourier, Henri de Saint-Simon and Étienne Cabet.[5]

But, beginning in the early 1970s, Michel Foucault's study of institutional discourses stressing the relations of enlightened reform to spatial power attracted the attention of architects and historians. Now a 'darker' side of an enlightened architecture was revealed by historians in the Centre d'Études et Recherches en Architecture (CERA), a research group led by the architect Bruno Fortier, who had participated in Foucault's seminars and published reports on the architecture of hospitals and shipyards, among other institutional discourses.[6] At the same time, in Britain, Robin Evans was developing his research into the origins of prison design with attention to Bentham's paradigmatic Panopticon, a diagram of architectural power later adopted by Foucault himself.[7]

In the context of the Annales School, however, historians such as Mona Ozouf and Bronislaw Bazcko re-examined the supposedly 'unreadable' texts of Boullée and Ledoux, finding common themes with the philosophical and socio-critical discourse of the age.[8] Social and urban historians further investigated architects' patronage circles, often assembled in Masonic lodges and eating and reading societies; the growing influence on architecture of the École des Ponts et Chaussées, with its emphasis on communication infrastructure (bridges, roads, canals); the development of new publics for the theatre, new economic institutions, and the complex regulations that under the heading of the police were concerned with constructional standards, street lighting, provision of fresh water and drainage.[9] Nevertheless, despite this long historiographical trajectory, there exists no complete treatment of architectural thought in relation to the general intellectual currents of the Enlightenment in France, which is a result not only of the tendency in historical studies to shy away from the traditional history of ideas but more especially of the largely empirical and monographical approaches that still dominate architectural history.

The general argument for the Enlightenment connection can certainly be posed on the stylistic and historicist front: that of the apparently sudden shift in style from the curvaceous *rocaille* of the Pompadour court to the strict 'neo-classicism' of the 1760s – first seen in Servandoni's façade for Saint-Sulpice and developing as the favoured manner of Mme du Barry and later of Quatremère de Quincy and his companion in Rome, Jacques-Louis David. This shift in style can be explained as the result of an increasing interest in archaeology and history, stimulated by the opening up of sites in Italy and Greece. Most notable in its effect on the new style were the visits to the excavations at Herculaneum, by the future marquis de Marigny, with Jacques-Germain Soufflot, who later would build the church of Sainte Geneviève, Jérôme-Charles Bellicard, who engraved and published the results of the expedition, and Charles-Nicolas Cochin, who later would engrave the frontispiece to the *Encyclopédie*.[10] More dramatic was archi-tect-historian Julien-David Leroy's publication of the first measured draw-ings of the Acropolis and other Greek sites in 1758, with a second expanded edition in 1770, which not only stimulated a return to Greek 'origins' but also elaborated a theory of architecture based on the principles of vision and a historical account of Greek architecture derived from his archaeological findings.[11] Such interest in the expansion of classical precedent from purely Roman examples obviously paralleled that evinced by the new encyclope-dists and was certainly supported, as we shall see, by Marc-Antoine Laugier, one of the foremost architectural *philosophes* of the period.

This stylistic shift was accompanied by what historians have seen as the 'proto-modern' aspect of the Enlightenment, demonstrated by the many projects, and some realized buildings, which were dedicated to the new institutions of the emerging bourgeois public order: hospitals, clinics, the-atres, museums, schools and, of course, after Beccaria and Bentham, prisons. Certainly the designers of these projects, whether or not architects them-selves, were following the spirit of philosophic ideals, and the corresponding momentum to improve the hygiene of cities generated by planner-architects such as Pierre Patte and urban reformers such as Jean-Baptiste Robinet (1735–1820) – whose calls for reform echoed those of Voltaire and Diderot – could also be seen in the context of a general urge for social reform.[12]

In the realm of aesthetics, the fascination with discovering a general 'origin' for architecture that would guide its principles as surely as Newton via Voltaire had supposedly guided physics, was a common theme in the writings of Marc-Antoine Laugier, Charles Batteux and even the academic Quatremère de Quincy. These figures would be followed in architecture by Étienne-Louis Boullée, who took Burke's theory of the terrifying sublime literally in the awe-inspiring physical dimensions and scale of his ideal proj-ects, and by Claude-Nicolas Ledoux, who developed the theory of sensa-tions pioneered by Condillac and Helvétius to didactic extremes. Indeed, Boullée and Ledoux were convinced that architecture was the key to the design of a possible new social order, one that, while not politically 'revo-lutionary', was revolutionary enough in architectural terms – as Kaufmann had claimed – and firmly situated within the discourse that could be inferred from a reading of Montesquieu, Rousseau, Diderot and Turgot, and that propelled real projects.

Countering these often contested correspondences, others have remarked with some truth that architects were not the most learned of professionals, that they were more inclined to work with and for any client regardless of their intellectual or progressive stance and that only a very few turned to writing of any kind to justify their designs in ways that could be aligned with Enlightenment thought. Alan Braham, despite the allure of his title, confessed early in his account that he was 'especially struck and not a little relieved to find confirmation of how relatively unlearned was the approach to their art of most architects of the time' and that 'the majority were not essentially philosophers or trained in abstract thought', their 'commitment to theory seeming by and large to have been instinctively practical and emotional, and at times surprisingly casual'.[13]

Here it might be useful to ask not whether there was an architecture *of* Enlightenment, or even whether an 'Enlightenment architecture' ever existed, but rather how might we find intellectual connections between the *philosophes* as they themselves thought about architecture and urbanism and the textual evidence of architects who were concerned to construe their design practice within the general terms set by the encyclopedists and their circle. Admittedly these terms were exceedingly diverse, disputed and often contradictory, as were the usually deliberately misinterpreted versions of the architects, but a certain level of creative misreading is always to be expected in the translation of philosophical thought into physical or imaginary design. In what follows, therefore, I shall concentrate on two kinds of *texts*: those written by *philosophes* and critics reflecting on an enlightened architecture and those written and designed by architects themselves in response.

Perhaps the encyclopedists' most far-reaching influence on architecture came through their support for reforming architectural education, and in the most direct fashion possible. Indeed, it was not by accident that the editors of the *Encyclopédie* selected the architect-theorist Jacques-François Blondel as the first author of articles on architecture. For Blondel, who had already published a long essay on the theory of design prefacing a multi-volume survey of French architecture, had opened what became the most celebrated school of architecture in the late eighteenth century, which offered instruction to the public at large (potential clients), contractors, future engineers, as well as the majority of architects practising between 1760 and the Revolution. Blondel's École des Arts was authorized in 1743 by the Académie d'Architecture itself in the recognition that its own school had become moribund; the École was confirmed in 1750 by the Intendant des Finances (Finance Commissioner) Daniel Trudaine, who was concerned to provide education in civil architecture to the members of his newly established Corps des Ponts et Chaussées [Bridge and Highway Corps] under Jacques Perronet.[14]

Opening the six-volume publication of his lectures, Blondel, in true philosophic fashion, declared, in opposition to the Académie's rule-bound theory, 'We have above all sought to analyse what one could call the reasoning of architecture.'[15] While the bulk of Blondel's articles for the *Encyclopédie* were fairly moderate in tone and ceased with the article 'Goût' ('Taste') on his death in 1774, the scope of his public lectures was much wider and had a fundamental influence on the following generation. Concentrating on what was called '*distribution*' or what now might be understood as the proper arrangement of spaces to fit programmatic requirements, he joined this to a radical reformulation of the idea of '*décoration*', the *art* of architecture. Recognizing the confluence of a range of new institutional programmes with the growth of a new discerning bourgeois public that sought legibility even as the philosophes sought communicability, he emphasized the architect's need to determine the suitable (*convenance*) 'character appropriate to each building': 'un edifice doit, au premier regard, s'annoncer ce qu'il est' (a building, when first seen, must express what it is).[16]

Traditionally, the expression of 'character' had been largely confined to the appropriate decorative motifs and the selection of the Doric, Ionic or Composite order according to propriety, which normally referred to the status of the monument and patron in the social hierarchy. Thus, the simple Doric was reserved for utilitarian structures (barracks, prisons, toll-gates); the Ionic for buildings for pleasure (theatres, palaces for princesses); and the Composite for royal palaces, important churches and the like. With Blondel, the field of expression was opened up to meet the requirements of the new range of building types – character now became the central leitmotif of the architect to be denoted by massing, detailing and, above all, the marking of the interior distribution on the exterior. When the young Quatremère took over writing the 'Architecture' volumes for the *Encyclopédie méthodique* (*Methodical Encyclopedia*) in three volumes between 1788 and 1825, his article on the subject stretched to over forty pages.[17]

Blondel's call for appropriate characterization was demonstrated in practice by many of his students. At least two major public institutions had, by 1770, been completed according to these new precepts: Le Camus de Mézière's Corn Exchange was designed in the form of a Roman amphitheatre or coliseum, while Jacques Gondouin's Surgery School was planned as a replica of an antique school, its *salle* developed according to the descriptions of Vitruvius or, more directly, following the impressions of recent visitors to the newly discovered theatre of Herculaneum.

The *philosophes* themselves, unhindered by traditional professional protocols, were more radical in their treatment of architecture. Perhaps the most critical of the architectural definitions advanced in the *Encyclopédie* was that offered by d'Alembert himself: 'This art, born of necessity and perfected by luxury, Architecture, which being raised by degrees from huts to palaces, is, in the eyes of a Philosophe, if one can speak thus, only the embellished mask of one of our greatest needs'.[18]

In this compact definition, d'Alembert packed most of the problems that accrued to architecture as a supposedly 'rational' art. Indeed, the definition followed the critical separation between rhetoric and grammar established by Port-Royal, but with a difference. Here d'Alembert was concisely cutting the function (distribution) from the form, or, in other terms, the grammar or structure from its rhetoric or 'embellishment'. In this sense, he was articulating what Blondel only intimated, but that would be confirmed by his students and much of nineteenth-century architecture, the difficult separation between *decoration* and *distribution*.

D'Alembert's philosophical argument was confirmed even more bluntly by Marc-Antoine Laugier in his *Essai sur l'architecture* (*Essay on Architecture*) in 1753 with a second edition two years later.[19] Laugier, a lapsed Jesuit writer who had already made a stir in Parisian circles by proposing new criteria of judgement for the new public salons, took his cue from Condillac and Rousseau in attempting to discover the single principle that might govern architecture, and perhaps also from the abbé Batteux, whose *Les Beaux-Arts réduits à un même principe* (*The Fine Arts Reduced to One Principle*) had refused architecture a place among the fine arts.[20]

Laugier, stimulated by Rousseau's efforts to determine the 'origin' of social happiness, developed his theory in a narrative that clearly paralleled Rousseau's, tracing the development of shelter from the partially sheltering tree, to the uncomfortable cave and thence to his 'model' of architectural origins, the primitive hut. 'It is the same architecture as in all the other arts,' Laugier writes, 'its principles are founded in simple nature, and in the procedures of the former are clearly marked the rules of the latter.'[21] 'Man in his first origin' has by instinct and reason constructed a shelter that is 'the model according to which all the magnificences of architecture have been imagined'.[22]

In the frontispiece to the second edition, engraved interestingly enough by Charles Eisen, the same artist who provided Rousseau with the frontispiece to the *Discours sur les sciences et les arts* (*Discourse on the Sciences and the Arts*) illustrating a South African tribesman proudly refusing the agreements of civilization in favour of his tribal encampment, Laugier's 'primitive' hut has been transformed into a geometrically regulated natural principle. Four trees, spaced in a square, miraculously growing vertically to form a double cube, support four horizontal branches as beams, which, in turn, form the bases of an equilateral triangle as a roof – a rustic temple in miniature. Before this structure the winged muse of architecture, seated on the ruins of classical decoration, demonstrates this natural principle to an eager cupid armed with wings of fiery passion – no doubt the perfect Enlightenment architecture student. In this evidently didactic reworking of Dürer's celebrated

1514 engraving *Melencolia*, where the Saturnine angel is passively meditating in front of the abandoned tools and geometrically shaped materials of construction, while her cupid draws impotently on a tablet, Eisen/Laugier produced one of the most significant icons of Enlightenment architecture, one that set the scene for the final reduction of the art to pure geometrical abstraction in the last decades of the century.

Laugier went on to write a second collection of *Observations sur l'architecture* (*Observations on Architecture*), under the pretext that 'all was not yet said on architecture'. But it was left to Blondel's students to carry through the task of theorizing a discipline that, as Blondel's colleague Pierre Patte noted, had been treated previously as an aspect of masonry, but that in fact, 'when considered as a whole', was 'almost entirely susceptible to reasoning' and should be seen in philosophical terms, 'en Philosophe'.[23]

Thus, Patte himself went on to develop important *mémoires* on the subject of planning under the title 'Considérations sur la distribution vicieuse des villes' ('Considerations on the Infelicitous Planning of Towns'), where he extended Blondel's notion of distribution from the single building to the city and its region. Patte treated the proper siting of cities, their infrastructure and communications routes (he advocated a planned canal system), the healthy design of their streets (including the regulation of building heights for light and ventilation as well as water supply and drainage, with separation for pedestrians and vehicles), regional water supply, drainage, sewage systems, burial sites (removed from the centre of the city), zoning of noxious industries (brickworks and tanneries), fire protection (building codes to prevent the spread of fires), the construction of river banks and quays, concluding with advice to young architects and a lesson in the history of construction, including Gothic buildings, and the history of the building of Sainte Geneviève, the Louvre and the church of Saint-Sulpice as a lesson in structural and aesthetic mistakes.[24]

While in these later chapters Patte showed his conservative colours, his resentment of the supporters of Soufflot who had determined that the structure of Sainte Geneviève was sound, together with his campaign to reveal the plagiarism of the *Encyclopédie* for 'stealing' plates from the Académie des Sciences' own survey of industry. His general message was that of a planner in true Enlightenment mode, which used science, technology and rational calculation to counter the aesthetic drives of the younger generation.

If the results of all Patte's proposed improvements had been displayed on a map, the image would no doubt have resembled the 'Paris' he had depicted in a composite plan published in 1765 that showed the various projects submitted by architects in the mid-century competition for a square in which to site the statue of Louis XV.[25] Capitalizing on the fact that each of the projects, instead of concentrating solely on the royal statue, was centred on a public facility and was sited according to requirements considered essential for the health and social welfare of the city, Patte was able to construe Paris as a polynuclear entity, with its quarters served by public squares, water fountains, shops, markets, institutional and cultural monuments. The major *places* in each quarter were in turn to be linked by a network of boulevards, which served to triangulate the city and open it up to light and air, speedy circulation and ordered police.

The direct influence of Enlightenment thought on architectural theory and practice, however, was confined initially to the imaginary environments proposed by idealist and utopian thinkers, often following the tradition established by More and continued by Fénelon; the ideal building campaign for Salentum as described by Mentor to Telemachus in *Les Aventures de Télémaque* (*The Adventures of Telemachus*) was reprised and expanded in Morelly's *Code de la nature* (*Code of Nature*) and continued to influence the anti-city visions of Babeuf. But the most powerful evocation of a new architecture for a new society was to be found in Louis-Sébastien Mercier's *L'An 2440* (*The Year 2440*), in which the city of Paris has been transformed into a philosophic paradise (with all young students carrying the *Encyclopédie* under their arm), including an architecture to match. Mercier demonstrated an easy familiarity with the proposals from architects and administrators as to the correct programmes and architectural forms for new and architecturally unprecedented building types, and he drew liberally from the *mémoires* offered by amateurs and professionals in the continuing public debates over the insalubrity of the city, from the replacement of the old Hôtel-Dieu, later to be damaged seriously by fire in 1772, to the re-siting of the city cemeteries, notably that of the Innocents.[26] Taken together, Patte's plans for Paris and Mercier's descriptions seemed to summarize every enlightened scheme for the embellishment of the capital since Voltaire's barely disguised proposals for the 'ville de Cachemire'.[27]

Thus, in Mercier's imagination, by 2440 the Louvre has been finally completed; the Hôtel-Dieu removed from the centre of the city and replaced by decentralized hospitals; the *hôpital général* Bicêtre and all prisons have been torn down; the cemetery of the Innocents closed; and the houses and shops removed from the bridges across the Seine. Street lighting, fire regulations and police, based on measures developed by Sartine after 1759, have been cleansed of authoritarian taint. Fresh water fountains play on every corner, following the recommendations of the mathematician Antoine Déparcieux in 1763.[28] The street lanterns operate perfectly, according to the proposals developed in a competition by the Académie des Sciences in 1766, a competition for which Lavoisier himself had submitted a *mémoire*.[29] Even the form of the new squares and boulevards is guided by the pattern of the recently completed Place Louis XV with its radiating fan of streets. A combination of physiocratic and Rousseauesque ideals govern a city where circulation – of people, vehicles, air and light – reigns supreme. Traffic flows evenly, and nature re-enters the new Paris, not only through spacious boulevards, parks and squares but also, in an emulation of the terraces of Babylon, on the new horizontal level formed by the flat roofs of the houses.

Similarly, the new institutions of 2440, including the Palais de Justice, the Hôtel de Ville and the 'Temple de Dieu' erected on the site of the old Bastille, are all described according to the new principles of architectural characterization, based on the model of those already erected before 1770 and in line with later projects such as the Bourse, the Caisse d'Escompte, the Théâtre Français, and the Colisée on the Champs-Elysées. Mercier's Temple, standing at the centre of its own square, comprised a huge single rotunda of columns, entered from four equal porticoes, with a simple altar, 'completely bare', at the centre of the plan. A memory of Renaissance ideal 'temples' from Bramante to Raphael, revived under the guise of a combination of the 'temple' of truth depicted by François Cochin in his frontispiece to the *Encyclopédie*, and the open colonnade then under construction by Soufflot for Sainte Geneviève, this temple seemed to anticipate the simple and sombre projects of Boullée after the Revolution.[30]

Mercier's Paris seems to have inspired the immense monumental projects, depicted in monochrome wash, that characterize the works of Étienne-Louis Boullée. Spanning the years 1781 to 1799, that is, through the last years of the Ancien Régime, the Revolution, the Terror, the Convention, to the rise of Napoleon and his expedition to Egypt, they display no direct political affiliations with any of the reigning doctrines or parties; rather, they espouse a belief in scientific progress symbolized in monumental forms, a generalized Rousseauism derived from the *Social Contract*, a dedication to celebrate the grandeur of a 'nation' and, more often than not, a meditation on the sublime sobriety of death. Yet, taken as a collection, as an almost encyclopedic representation of the necessary institutions for an ideal state, and joined to the preface he wrote at the end of his life, Boullée's late works may be interpreted as contributing to his underlying vision of an 'ideal city'.

Upon leaving Blondel's École des Arts in 1746, Boullée was immediately appointed a professor of architecture at the newly established École des Ponts et Chaussées under its director, the civil engineer Jean-Rodolphe Perronet. This position gave him, like Ledoux, access to public commissions, but, more important, to a new vision of the role of building in the social and economic progress of a state and its territories. While his private commissions included religious buildings and grand *hôtels* for the princes of the realm, his public works ranged from the construction of the Prison de la Grande Force and, beginning in 1781, projects for a new opera house, as well as a series of designs linked to real projects but set as exercises for his students in the school of the Académie Royale d'Architecture to which he had been elected in 1762. In quick succession he produced elaborate schemes for a métropole or 'basilica' (1781–2), a coliseum (1782), a museum (1783), a 'cenotaph' in honour of Newton (1784), a royal palace (1785), projects for a new reading room for the Royal Library (1784–5) and a project for a new bridge over the Seine (1787). In the late 1780s, forced by severe illness to retire to his country house outside Paris, his last designs were accomplished after the Revolution: projects for a monument in celebration of one of the most popular of Revolutionary festivals, that of the 'Fête-Dieu' or Supreme Being, a monument to 'public recognition', a palace of justice, a national palace (1792) and a municipal palace (1792).

During the excesses of the Terror, Boullée devoted himself to expanding his œuvre with numerous designs for domestic architecture, 'private architecture', as opposed to the 'grand genre' of public architecture. He was open in his hatred of Robespierre's Committee of Public Safety, calling the agents of the Terror 'perverse beings, tigers lusting for blood' who wanted nothing but to destroy the 'arts, sciences and everything that honours the human spirit'.[31] Finally, undated, but no doubt implicitly condemning the excesses of the Revolutionary governments, were a series of extraordinary designs for funerary monuments, cenotaphs and cemeteries, in the form of pyramids, cones and temples, experiments in what he named as new genres of architecture: 'buried' architecture and the 'architecture of shadows'.

Of his generation of architects, Boullée was perhaps the most deeply learned. His large library contained, beside a full roster of architectural treatises (including Blondel and Laugier), classical and modern literature, classical and modern history, the works of Montaigne, Rousseau, Montesquieu, Voltaire, Nicolas-Antoine Boulanger, Helvetius's *De l'esprit* (*Essays on the Mind*), Mably, Buffon, together with Fénelon's *Les Aventures de Télémaque*, Condillac's *Traité des sensations* (*Treatise on the Sensations*) and *Traité des systèmes* (*Treatise on Systems*), Bailly's *Histoire de l'astronomie ancienne* (*History of Ancient Astronomy*), *Histoire de l'astronomie modern* (*History of Modern Astronomy*), *Lettres sur l'origine des sciences* (*Letters on the Origin of the Sciences*) and *Lettres sur l'Atlantide de Platon* (*Letter on Plato's Story of the Atlanteans*), Raynal's *Histoire philosophique et politique … des deux Indes* (*Philosophical and Political History … of the Two Indies*), a wide selection of geographical and travel accounts and the art criticism of Winckelman, du Bos and many others. He seems also to have had a predilection for English writers – Pope, Fielding and Richardson among others.[32]

Equally important, each of his projects was designed not simply to illustrate the primary Enlightenment concepts of sublimity, character and monu-
mentality but to extend and embody them in three dimensions. His principles
of vision were founded on Condillac, 'un philosophe modern'. 'All our ideas,
all our perceptions come to us from external objects. External object make
different impressions on us through the greater or lesser analogy they have
with our organisation', he wrote in order to establish the relationship of
the sensations provoked by architectural objects with those stimulated by
nature.[33] And it was this new relationship with the idea of nature, itself
transformed in Enlightenment philosophy, that formed the basis of both his
and Ledoux's imaginary architectures of reason. Starting with Lucretius'
De natura rerum, continuing with Plato's *Timaeus* and *Critias*, and with
the newly translated editions of Burke's *A Philosophical Enquiry into the
Origin of Our Ideas of the Sublime and Beautiful* (1761, French trans.
1765) and Kant's *Observations on the Feeling of the Beautiful and Sublime*
(1771, French trans. 1796), Boullée forged a unique theory of architectural
sublimity that introduced not only the Burkean requirements of infinite vis-
tas, repetition and sheer size into the art but also all the conditions of viewing, which included storms, lightning, brilliant sunlight and dark moonlight,
and that finally developed into a mediation on the nature of what might be
an architecture constructed purely out of shadow: 'It seemed to me impossible to conceive of nothing more sad than a monument composed of a
flat surface, naked and stripped, made of a material absorbent of all light,
absolutely devoid of details, and whose decoration was formed of a picture
of shadows delineated by even deeper shadows.'[34] This preoccupation with
the sublime was taken to another extreme by another pupil of Blondel, eight
years younger than Boullée and equally well read, Claude-Nicolas Ledoux
(1736–1806), who was supported through his career until the Revolution
by the reform administrations of Trudaine, Turgot, Necker and Calonne.
His first major commission, the Saline Royale of Arc-et-Semans (Saline de
Chaux) was a product of his working with Trudaine de Montigny's *mémoire*
for the Académie des Sciences, proposing improved methods for salt production as illustrated in the *Encyclopédie*. Not only was his elaboration of
this project into an imaginary city, the Ville de Chaux, in line with other new
settlements such as that of Versoix, that 'philosophical' town supported by
Voltaire, it also provided the fiction for what he considered the architectural
equivalent of the *Encyclopédie*.

In what Ledoux projected in six grand folio volumes, of which only the
first was published before his death in 1806, he displayed what he described
as a collection that brings together all the kinds of buildings used by the
social order, all depicted in the manner of Diderot's plates, with perspective

vignettes above the 'analytical' elaboration of the projects in section, plan and elevation. His use of primary forms – the cube, pyramid and sphere – gave an abstract appearance to programmes that were in many cases lifted from the *Encyclopédie* – from forges, cooperies and charcoal burners' pyres to deist temples, stock exchanges and symbolic constructions dedicated to union, law-giving and virtue. His title, still unique among architectural treatises today, was explicit in its reference to Enlightenment principles: 'Architecture considered in relation to art, manners, and laws.'[35]

The accompanying text, dedicated to Montesquieu's *De l'esprit des lois* (*Spirit of the Laws*), presented architecture as installing Rousseau's 'social pact' in a countryside governed by physiocratic and agronomic economy and a community dedicated to working and playing in an environment where architecture literally figured the occupations of its inhabitants. Thus, a monumental shelter for shepherds was enclosed in a perfect sphere, emulating the sun's own pastoral role; the workshop and habitation of the coopers was given the form of two intersecting barrels.

In an important registration of a new attitude towards nature, the river engineers charged with maintaining the regular flow of water to the pumps and water-wheels of the city lived in a giant drainpipe that overlooked the current. In the text accompanying this last design, Ledoux was evidently evoking the flood portrayed by Nicolas Boulanger ('Déluge', *Encyclopédie*), and it is here that the transformation of nature into a force for destruction and chaos as well as beneficent production emerges in this pre-Romantic vision. In this context, Ledoux's design for the cemetery of his city was both a utilitarian solution – using the excavation caused by the stone quarrying for building – and a symbolic version of the city as a whole. A perfect sphere, half submerged in the ground with a single source of light from its summit, is represented for the citizens in death as a communal space parallel to that which the city provided in life. Illustrating this vision, Ledoux provides an extraordinary engraving, no doubt drawn from one of the popular astronomical treatises of the time but highly edited by Ledoux, representing the planets surrounding the earth, which is half submerged in clouds and lit from the sun. He titles this engraving in lapidary fashion 'Elevation of the Cemetery of Chaux'.

In these and many other imaginary designs, Ledoux took from his poet friend the abbé Delille the idea of a universal pictogrammatical language of communication, with reference to Leibniz's *Nouveaux essais sur l'entendement* (*New Essays on Human Understanding*) (French trans. 1765), that would speak to society transparently even as instrumentally it reformed its spatial organization. The most dramatic of these examples of what a later critic termed '*architecture parlante*' (expressive architecture) was an organized brothel (no doubt inspired by Rétif de la Bretonne's *Le Pornographe*) which was temple-like from the outside but was revealed in plan as a processional sequence along a phallic-shaped gallery.

Ledoux's was to be the last attempt, before the Revolution, to join architecture to society as its structural representation. And if, for Diderot, the construction of an encyclopedia was 'much like the foundation of a city', Ledoux's similar insistence on visual variety in such a construction was a natural outcome of his idea that the foundation of a city would be much like the construction of the *Encyclopédie*.[36] Certainly, his vision of the influence of his ideal city expanding perspectively and productively throughout the globe provided for the next century an architectural *mappemonde* that would inspire Saint-Simon, Fourier, Cabet and their followers in their extensive theoretical and practical attempts at its enlightened colonization.

NOTES

1   Emil Kaufmann, *Architecture in the Age of Reason: Baroque and Post-Baroque in England, Italy, and France* (Cambridge, Mass.: Harvard University Press, 1955); Allan Braham, *The Architecture of the French Enlightenment* (Berkeley, Calif.: University of California Press, 1980). Despite his title, Braham confessed that he was '[e]specially struck and not a little relieved to find confirmation of how relatively unlearned was the approach to their art of most architects of the time. The majority were not essentially philosophers or trained in abstract thought ... Their commitment to theory seems by and large to have been instinctively practical and emotional, and at times surprisingly casual' (p. 8).

2   In a series of studies between 1921 and 1933, Kaufmann developed his thesis that paralleled Ernst Cassirer's writings on the Enlightenment and his attempt to reconcile Rousseau and Kant.

3   Emil Kaufmann, *Von Ledoux bis Le Corbusier: Ursprung und Entwicklung der autonomen Architektur* (Vienna: Rolf Passer, 1933).

4   Meyer Schapiro was the first to challenge what he termed Kaufmann's 'formalist and abstract' method of analysis, too close to that of the Vienna School under the leadership of Hans Sedlmayr ('The New Viennese School', *The Art Bulletin*, 17 [1936]: 258–66). Schapiro called for a more socially aware and nuanced way to connect architectural form with social movements. The battle for ownership of the Enlightenment was joined. Sedlmayr, who had run with the National Socialists during the war, claimed that while Kaufmann was essentially correct in his pathology, he was wrong in his diagnosis: the abstract forms of Ledoux and Boullée were indeed fact *symptoms*, not of an emerging and ultimately triumphant social idealism but of a general decadence characteristic of all modernism. *Verlust der Mitte: die bildende Kunst des 19. und 20. Jahrhunderts als Symptom und Symbol der Zeit* (Salzburg: Otto Müller Verlag, 1948) English trans.: *Art in Crisis: The Lost Centre*, trans. Brian Battershaw (London: Hollis & Carter, 1957). Post-war historians, such as Pérouse de Montclos and Michel Gallet, who meticulously searched the archives for documentation of every Parisian architect in the late eighteenth century, were sceptical of these debates, preferring to stay

with the facts. J.-M. Pérouse de Monclos, *Étienne-Louis Boullée: de l'architecture classique à l'architecture révolutionnaire* (Paris: Flammarion, Arts et Métiers graphiques, 1968); Michel Gallet, *Claude-Nicolas Ledoux, 1736–1806* (Paris: Picard, 1980).

5 Aldo Rossi, 'Emil Kaufmann e l'architettura dell-Illuminismo', *Casabella continuità* 222 (1958), and 'Introduzione a Boullée' (1970), in Rossi, *Scritti scelti sull'architettura e la città 1956–1972* (Milan: CLUP, 1975), pp. 62–71, 346–64, 454–73.

6 Following the publication of Foucault's *Surveiller et punir: naissance de la prison* (Paris: Gallimard, 1975), a group of architectural historians led by Bruno Fortier, Blandine Barret-Kriegel, Anne Thalamy, François Béguin and Michel Foucault published a report on *Les Machines à guérir (aux origines de l'hôpital moderne)* (Brussels: Pierre Mardaga, 1979), and, with Alain Demangeon, *Les Vaisseaux et les villes* (Brussels: Pierre Mardaga, 1978). See also Michel Foucault, 'Space, Knowledge and Power', interview with Paul Rabinow, *Skyline* (March 1982), pp. 16–20.

7 Robin Evans, 'Bentham's Panopticon: An Incident in the Social History of Architecture', *Architectural Association Quarterly*, 3 (1971): 21–37.

8 Mona Ozouf, 'Architecture et urbanisme: l'image de la ville chez Claude-Nicolas Ledoux', *Annales: économies, sociétés, civilisations*, 21 (6) (1966: 1273–304; Bronislaw Baczko, *Lumières de l'utopie* (Paris: Payot, 1978). See also Anthony Vidler, *Claude-Nicolas Ledoux: Architecture and Social Reform at the End of the Ancien Régime* (Cambridge, Mass.: MIT Press, 1989).

9 See Anthony Vidler, *The Writing of the Walls: Architectural Theory in the Late Enlightenment* (Princeton Architectural Press, 1987).

10 See Christian Michel (ed.), *Le Voyage d'Italie de Charles-Nicolas Cochin* (Rome: École Française de Rome, 1991).

11 Julien-David Leroy, *Les Ruines des plus beaux monuments de la Grèce considérées du côté de l'histoire et du côté de l'architecture*, 2nd edn, 2 vols. (Paris: Louis-François Delatour, 1770). See the translation with an introduction by Robin Middleton, *The Ruins of the Most Beautiful Monuments of Greece, Historically and Architecturally Considered* (Los Angeles, Calif.: The Getty Research Institute, 2004).

12 See Vidler, *The Writing of the Walls*.

13 Braham, *The Architecture of the French Enlightenment*, p. 8. It is somewhat paradoxical that he cited four of the most theoretical architects of the time, notably Jacques-Germain Soufflot, François Belanger, Jacques-François Blondel and Julian-David Leroy.

14 See Robin Middleton, 'Jacques-François Blondel and the *Cours d'architecture*', *Journal of the Society of Architectural Historians*, 18 (4) (1959): 140–8.

15 Jacques-François Blondel, *Cours d'architecture, ou, Traité de la décoration, distribution et construction des bâtiments, contenant les leçons données en 1750 et les années suivantes*, 6 vols. plus 3 vols. of plates (Paris: Desaint, 1771), vol. I, p. xvi. The sixth volume of text and the third volume of plates were continued by Pierre Patte.

16 Blondel, *Cours*, vol. I, pp. 390, 132.

17 Quatremère de Quincy, 'Caractère', *Encyclopédie méthodique. Architecture*, 3 vols. (Paris: Panckoucke, 1788), vol. I, pp. 477–521.

ANTHONY VIDLER

18 Jean le Rond D'Alembert, 'Discours préliminaire', in Diderot and d'Alembert (eds.), *Encyclopédie*, vol. I, p. xii.

19 Marc-Antoine Laugier, *Essai sur l'architecture* (Paris: Duchêne 1753).

20 Charles Batteux, *Les Beaux-Arts réduits à un même principe* (Paris: Durand, 1746). For Batteux, who distinguished between three kinds of art (the mechanical arts solely concerned with furnishing mankind's needs; the arts that had as their object the provision of pure pleasure such as music, poetry, painting, sculpture and dance; and those arts concerned with use and pleasure at the same time), architecture fell into this last category, and, therefore, with the mechanical arts, was excluded from the search for the norms of pleasurable beauty (pp. 6–7).

21 Laugier, *Essai sur l'architecture*, p. 10.

22 Ibid. p. 13.

23 'Si l'on considère l'Architecture dans le grand, on s'aperçoit que presque tout y est également à raisonner, et que l'on a vu sans cesse les objets en Maçon, tandis qu'il a fallu les envisager en Philosophe.' Pierre Patte, 'Dédication à M. Marigny', *Mémoires sur les objets les plus importants de l'architecture* (Paris: Rozet, 1769), p. iii.

24 Patte, *Mémoires*, p. iii.

25 Pierre Patte, *Monumens érigés en France à la gloire de Louis XV* (Paris, 1765).

26 Louis-Sébastien Mercier, *L'An deux mille quatre cent quarante* (London, 1772). For the debates over the Hôtel Dieu, see Rondonneau de la Motte, *Essai historique sur l'Hôtel-Dieu de Paris* (Paris, 1787); Jacques Tenon, *Mémoires sur les hôpitaux de Paris* (Paris, 1788).

27 Voltaire, in his two essays on Parisian urbanism, 'Des embellissements de la ville de Cachmire' (1750) and 'Des embellissements de Paris' (1749), *Œuvres complètes* (Paris: Garnier, 1879), vol. XXII, pp. 473, 297, called for the opening up of the city to air, light and circulation.

28 See Antoine Déparcieux, *Trois mémoires sur la possibilité et le facilité d'amener auprès de l'Estrapade de Paris les eaux de la rivière d'Yvette* (Paris, 1763).

29 See Jean-Baptiste Robinet, *Dictionnaire universel des sciences morale, économique, politique et diplomatique ou Bibliothèque de l'homme d'état et du citoyen*, 30 vols. (London: Chez les libraires associés, 1777–83), vol. XXVI, pp. 470–1.

30 Mercier, *L'An deux mille*, p. 108.

31 Étienne-Louis Boullée, 'Architecture', *Essai sur l'art*, ed. Jean-Marie Pérouse de Montclos (Paris: Haemann, 1968), p. 28.

32 See Jean-Marie Pérouse de Montclos, *Étienne-Louis Boullée, 1728–1799: de l'architecture classique à l'architecture révolutionnaire* (Paris: Arts et Métiers Graphiques, 1969), pp. 253–7.

33 Boullée, 'Architecture', p. 61.

34 Ibid. p. 147.

35 Claude-Nicolas Ledoux, *L'Architecture considérée sous le rapport de l'art, des mœurs, et de la législation* (Paris: chez l'auteur, 1804). The published *Prospectus* to this work, projected in six volumes, described the collection as 'an Encyclopedia or Architectural Museum'.

36 'Encyclopédie', in Diderot and d'Alembert (eds.), *Encyclopédie*, vol. V, p. 642.

198

14

ANNE VILA

Medicine and the body in the French Enlightenment

'I defy you to explain anything without the body': so declared Denis Diderot, while refuting the stark mind–body dualism endorsed by some of his contemporaries.[1] Diderot's challenge still resonates today, when explaining things with the body is part of the standard toolkit for approaching the French Enlightenment. The corporeal side of human life was vital to this period, for reasons that go beyond the philosophical materialism that found supporters in certain quarters (including Diderot). The body was also present in other key areas of this era's thought and culture: its sense-based epistemology; the emphasis on somatic expression in theories of painting, acting, music and language; the expanded market for consumer goods, which also expanded the possibilities for physical pleasure and contentment; the value given to factors such as climate and temperament in anthropological accounts of human diversity; and the moral ideology of sentimentalism, which made the body literally instrumental to the transparent communication of personal emotion and edifying fellow feeling.

Body-centred approaches to any historical period do, of course, vary significantly depending on the theoretical preoccupations that drive them. Like the Enlightenment, corporeality has inspired quite a bit of theorizing over the past fifty-odd years. Some of that theorizing was inspired by Michel Foucault, who coined the terms 'bio-power' and 'biopolitics' to describe the structures (institutional and discursive) established by states and other authorities to discipline the body.[2] Other critical trends have also played a part, including feminism, gender studies, postmodernism, psychoanalysis, queer studies, material culture and 'thing' theory, animal/human studies, human/machine studies and the enduring interest in *libertinage*.[3] The body has come to be seen not only as an organism or phenomenal object but as a text, a sign system, a symbolic and constructed object.

Constructivist approaches to the body unquestionably open up new ways of thinking about embodiment – and resistance to embodiment – as modes of selfhood; they also shed light on the creative powers of language, literature and art to create substance that transcends the physical.[4] Such approaches can, however, be difficult to reconcile with more biologically grounded perspectives on the body understood as a living, feeling, labouring, sometimes suffering entity – like those that tend to dominate the history of the life sciences. Medical history has itself been paradoxically disembodied at times: this was often the case in the 1960s, when the field's reigning interpretive model was a triumphalist sort of retrospective that emphasized ideas emanating from 'great men' more than their practical repercussions for flesh-and-blood patients; and this disembodiment can be said to characterize some Foucauldian analyses of medicine as a form of power.[5]

These days, work in the history of medicine is just as often done 'from below' – that is, from the perspective of patients in all of their varieties, and of non-elite health practitioners – as from the top-down view that focuses on the field's dominant figures, doctrines and institutional structures. This shift reflects the influence of new historiographical perspectives shaped by sociology, cultural anthropology and phenomenologist philosophy: scholars interested in eighteenth-century medicine are now attuned to questions such as the cultural framing of bodily perceptions, including those connected to pain and illness, and to the complex, dynamic relations between learned and popular medical culture. The critical subfields of narrative studies and medicine and literature have also shaped work in this field: recent studies of medicine's narrative modes and of sources such as patient letters and personal testimonies have uncovered aspects of the illness experience and patient–practitioner interactions that are not always available in official, authoritative medical discourse.

These developments have helped to elucidate the role that medicine played in multiple threads of eighteenth-century life, such as the burgeoning of commerce and print culture, the rise of privacy and sympathy as social values and the fascination with spectacle – an area to which biomedical investigators made some dramatic contributions, such as the abbé Bertholon's demonstrations of human electricity.[6] Attention to these developments has also shed light on some of the darker sides of medicine in this period, such as the administration of such profitable slave colonies as Saint-Domingue.[7]

In short, the stories now being told about medicine during the French Enlightenment have changed considerably since the days when historian Peter Gay used medicine metaphorically to argue that the *philosophes* saw themselves as 'physicians' embarked on the 'recovery of nerve' for their era and determined to rid the social order of such plagues as religious fanaticism, political injustice and a superstitious populace.[8] Some eighteenth-century medical writers did call themselves *médecins philosophes* and defined their work in direct relation to the period's various meliorist and/or humanitarian missions. However, many prominent physicians had an ambivalent or even disapproving attitude towards the aristocratic Parisian salon culture that was ground zero for the Enlightenment in its best-known French incarnation. These included the vitalists of the Montpellier medical faculty, who were 'suspicious of materialism, sympathetic to religiosity' and dubious about the prospects for individual or collective human progress.[9] Another example is the French-speaking Swiss doctor Samuel-Auguste Tissot, who illustrates both a Calvinist cautiousness towards the high culture of the day and the extra-metropolitan geographic reach of the French Enlightenment. The ideas that such doctors published about the habits and mores of contemporary French society were often highly critical. That attitude, in fact, was central to their writings: doctors who took up the pen to lament some aspect of Enlightenment-era culture viewed their field as uniquely qualified to define what 'being enlightened' truly meant.

Medicine and culture in the eighteenth century

There are no books that I read more readily than medical books, no men whose conversation I find more interesting than physicians; but that is when I am feeling well.[10]

Among the major figures of the French Enlightenment, few were more keenly interested in medicine than Diderot. Not only did he spend decades reading medical books on everything from embryology to catalepsy, he enlisted numerous doctors to write for the *Encyclopédie* and gave a starring role in *Le Rêve de d'Alembert (D'Alembert's Dream)* to one of the most famous physicians of the day, Théophile de Bordeu. However, even this great admirer of medicine had an ambivalent attitude towards medical knowledge. For Diderot, as for many others, doctors and their books were a source of both fascination and fear: although they offered new ways of understanding the body, the mind and human life in general, they could also terrify laypeople through the truths they claimed to uncover – not to mention the harsh remedies they sometimes prescribed.[11]

Compared with the centuries that preceded it, the eighteenth century was relatively healthy. Mortality rates declined and longevity rose, due to factors that included the decline of famine, better crop yields, a reduction in wars on French soil and the declining frequency of the waves of epidemics that had been a regular fact of life in previous centuries (the last major plague epidemic occurred in Marseille in 1720).[12] However, people still lived in fear of falling victim to regionally epidemic contagions such as smallpox and dysentery or to other diseases recognized as transmissible, such as syphilis. They also faced such potentially grave conditions as consumption, known as '*phtisie*' (or '*mal de poitrine*' in French); excretory 'obstruction', the term sometimes applied to cancer; apoplexy, gout and gastric disorders (more prevalent at the high end of the social spectrum); fevers and other sorts of pathological heat; the dangers of pregnancy, childbirth and breastfeeding; and onanism, the century's most famous invented disease.[13] The existence of these various health threats helped to persuade many that the population was in decline, even though modern-day demographic studies prove the contrary.[14] The general sense of alarm was heightened by the epidemic of nervous disorders that was supposedly afflicting contemporary Europe, particularly its cities. Little wonder, then, that people sought the advice and aid of medical practitioners, a category that included physicians, barber-surgeons, apothecaries, midwives, nursing sisters and – moving down the professional pecking order – unlicensed local healers and charlatans.[15]

Medical doctrine underwent major changes during the Enlightenment. Building on innovations of the seventeenth-century scientific revolution such as Harvey's discovery of the circulation of the blood, Cartesian body/machine analogies, advances in anatomy and microscopy, and the natural-philosophical emphasis on empirical observation and experimentation, the dominant medical ideology shifted away from the old Galenic system of humours towards new conceptions of the body and of disease.[16] During the first half of the eighteenth century, faculty-taught medicine revolved around iatromechanism, or the notion popularized by the Leiden professor Herman Boerhaave that the living body could be interpreted according to the laws of hydrostatics, hydraulics and general mechanics. From the 1750s onward, however, the theory that dominated French medical discourse was vitalism, which, as articulated by the Montpellier physicians Bordeu and Paul-Joseph Barthez, envisioned the body as a dynamic network of interrelated activities driven by an underlying force that was unique to living matter. Most of these shifts were pronounced 'revolutionary' by their advocates, which echoed the period's general conviction that the right method of reasoning would usher in quick and dramatic improvements in any field of science or praxis.

Medicine's institutional structures also evolved in important ways. The eighteenth century saw the rise of greater medical professionalization; the reinvention of clinical medicine and consequent refinement of diagnostic techniques; the reform of hospitals, medical education and obstetrics/gynaecology; the emergence of pneumatic medicine to address concerns over atmospheric effects upon the body, which had both commercial ramifications like the production of artificial mineral waters, and political implications for Europe's colonies; and state-sponsored campaigns of medical topography to track the incidence of epidemics and centralize the management of diseases. Health services were expanded to people outside the social elite, increased attention was paid to the ailments of rural people and other manual labourers, and civil medicine and psychiatry developed as distinct branches of the field. Medical treatises and health manuals became more widely available in the vernacular, a phenomenon driven by a mixture of high-minded humanitarianism and medical entrepreneurialism. Finally, both faculty-taught and popularized medical discourse reflected a new insistence on hygiene and 'expectant' medicine, a set of notions derived from Hippocratic theory that emphasized nature's inherent healing powers and the predictable 'critical' patterns followed by diseases – and which helped to steer practitioners away from the copious bleedings, trephinations and other aggressive treatments that were common when iatromechanism was the field's dominant doctrine.

Actual advances in treating illness and providing health care were not, however, the only source of medicine's prominence in the intellectual and cultural climate of the French Enlightenment. Whereas the previous century tended to take a satirical view of doctors (famously evident in Molière's *Le Malade imaginaire* [*The Imaginary Invalid*, 1673]), eighteenth-century literary depictions were generally respectful. This may have been due to the heroic aura that surrounded physicians who took up controversial causes such as smallpox inoculation. However, a more likely explanation is the active presence of physicians in the institutions and networks that structured polite society and the Republic of Letters, including courtly life, salons, academies and epistolary correspondence.[17]

Physicians were particularly present in the lives of the affluent, some of whom were preoccupied with health for reasons that had less to do with disease than with 'unwellness', a state that, as Vladimir Janković notes, was popular precisely because it was indeterminate: 'Feeling out of sorts was an excuse to avoid social contact, refrain from exercise, elicit pity, or obtain professional help.'[18] For those who dwelled in the Enlightenment's cultural climate of delicacy, sensitivity taken to the point of infirmity was not just prevalent but chic, a marker of rank and refinement. The nervous body was a 'type of corporeality attuned to the new cultural values of the social elite'.[19]

In this secular-tending, pre-Freudian era, plumbing the depths of one's interiority often meant pondering one's nervous palpitations, visceral murmurings, odd rashes or worrisome secretions.[20] Popular health manuals fed those anxieties by dispensing detailed advice on all sorts of topics, including domestic medicine, profession-specific dietary regimens, mineral-water cures and bold new therapeutic methods such as Pierre Pomme's ice-bath remedy for the vapours – not to mention Mesmer's suggestive descriptions of the group *baquet* sessions he held to channel magnetic fluids in therapeutic directions. Such books also offered readers the chance to sympathize with the suffering patients whose case histories they related, thanks to the 'humanitarian narrative' style their authors commonly adopted.[21]

Sensibility and vitalist medicine

Chief among the eighteenth century's theoretical inventions was this working assumption: before assessing an individual's physical or moral disposition, one first had to determine how that person reacted and interacted with the world as a sensitive being. Various threads were woven into the rise of sensibility as a concept that bridged body, mind and milieu.[22] One factor was the revalorization of sentiment and the passions that took place in European moral philosophy and literature during the preceding century; another was the emphasis that French sensationalist philosophers such as Étienne Bonnot de Condillac (working in the wake of John Locke's *Essay Concerning Human Understanding* [1690]) placed on the role of bodily sensations in the formation of subjectivity and the development of knowledge (*Traité des sensations* [*Treatise on Sensations*], 1754). The biomedical sciences also played a key role: in the 1740s, the Swiss physician Albrecht von Haller published ground-breaking experimental investigations on the reactive properties of muscles and nerves – or irritability and sensibility, as he named them – that highlighted the inadequacies of mechanistic explanations of the body's physiological processes.[23] The speedy exploitation of Haller's work by the radical materialist and physician Julien Offray de La Mettrie in *L'Homme machine* (*Man a Machine*) (1747) helped place the life sciences at the centre of debates on human nature and the mind–body relation from mid-century on.

Within French medicine, the most important response to Haller came from physicians trained or based in Montpellier, starting with Bordeu's *Recherches anatomiques sur la position des glandes* (*Anatomical Investigations on the Position of the Glands*) (1752). Like Haller and contemporary English physicians such as Robert Whytt, Bordeu believed that sensibility was conveyed via a system of natural, interorganic coordination. He did not, however, perceive that system as limited exclusively to the nervous apparatus. Rather, using a metaphor that would soon reappear in other contexts (like Diderot's writings), he compared the living body to a bee swarm: that is, a holistic federation of semi-autonomous parts, each of which followed rhythms determined by its particular dose of local sensibility, held together by a triumvirate of major vital centres – the brain, chest and lower abdomen. Later Montpellier vitalists such as Barthez (*Nouveaux éléments de la science de l'homme* [*New Elements of the Science of Man*], first edn, 1778) also drew on the notion of sympathy to explain how the body was 'united in reciprocities', in an ongoing process of action and reaction that insured the cohesive functioning of the whole.[24]

Although the notion of sensibility as a vital property was built in part upon a pre-existing moralist rhetoric of *finesse* and *délicatesse*, its implications were not unilaterally positive. That double-edged quality is evident in the two articles devoted to the topic in the fifteenth volume of the *Encyclopédie* (1751–65). In his short entry 'Sensualité (morale)', Louis de Jaucourt declared that the sensitive were, by nature, more humane, more empathetic and more intelligent; yet he also remarked that, along with heightened pleasures, they experienced magnified woes.[25] Similarly, in the much longer medical entry 'Sensibilité, sentiment', the Montpellier physician Henri Fouquet began by proclaiming sensibility 'the faculty of feeling, the sentient principle, or the feeling of all the parts, the basis and preserver of life, animality par excellence, the most beautiful and the most singular phenomenon of nature'.[26] However, he devoted much of the article to the pathological disruptions caused when inner sensations became too acute: sensibility's overall physiological scheme entailed an intricate interplay between the particular organs or vital centres within the body, each of which had its own 'tastes', felt its own passions and expanded or compressed in reaction to them. Vital departments were more or less lively depending on how much stimulation they got – that is, on how much sensibility was 'transported' to them – as a result of habit, age, sex, climate and other factors.

The medical philosophy surrounding sensibility also fostered new methods of reading the body in the state of illness. One was an expanded system of pulse-taking that was heavily promoted in the last ten volumes of the *Encyclopédie*, which another Montpellier-trained doctor, Ménuret de Chambaud, systematically deployed to publicize the 'revolutionary' semiotic system put forth in Bordeu's *Recherches sur le pouls par rapport aux crises (Investigations on the Pulse in Relation to Crises)* (1757). Bordeu's basic premise was that the body was abuzz with all sorts of pulses: for every organ or centre of sensibility, there was a corresponding pulse – a stomachal pulse, a pectoral pulse, a nasal pulse and so on. Each organ-specific pulse could, he argued, be differentiated into a pulse of irritation, a developed pulse and a critical pulse, the last of which revealed how the disease would be resolved through a crisis somewhere in the patient's body.

Another important component of effective diagnosis, in the view of these theorists, was to approach the patient holistically: the clinician had to take into consideration not just the body before him in its present state but all of the factors that could be involved in its ailments, like diet, climate, living and working circumstances, sex, temperament and habits. As Elizabeth A.

Williams explains, 'the Montpellier doctors defined aims for medicine that went beyond mere therapeutics and made of medicine a science that investigated the full range of circumstances determining or impinging on states of health and sickness'.[27]

Perfectibility, degeneration and physical/moral hygiene

Investigating the full range of patients' living and working circumstances was also central to hygiene, a branch of medicine that expanded significantly during the eighteenth century.[28] Medical writers sometimes promoted hygiene as a means of attaining greater enlightenment, for oneself or one's children. In *La Médecine de l'esprit* (*Medicine of the Mind*) (1753–69), for instance, Antoine Le Camus proposed a regimen of sensation management that he felt confident would transform middling minds into great intellectuals; and Charles Augustin Vandermonde's *Essai sur la manière de perfectionner l'espèce humaine* (*Essay on the Means of Perfecting Humanity*) (1756) offered advice on how to counteract debility in one's offspring through breeding techniques and fortifying physical educational methods.[29] The underlying idea of these works was that human beings were perfectible in mind and body, and they could therefore be transformed into healthier, more virtuous and more intelligent beings under the guidance of qualified experts.

There were, of course, sceptics – Diderot, for one – who dismissed the claims of doctors or moralists who held themselves up as experts on perfectibility.[30] There were also some who endorsed Jean-Jacques Rousseau's pessimistic counterview that 'perfection' of the mind and manners led to degeneration rather than greater health or happiness.[31] Vitalist doctors were often staunch advocates of limited perfectibility: Barthez, for example, insisted on the determining power of regional particularities;[32] and other Montpellier medical figures such as Dr Pierre Roussel (*Système physique et moral de la femme* [*The Woman's Moral and Physical System*], 1775) played a key role in the emergence of sexual dimorphism, which divided the attributes of sensibility into complementary but incommensurate sets – feminine versus masculine, yielding versus resistant, womb-based versus cerebral. The tension between optimistic meliorism and pessimistic alarmism was, precisely, one of the factors that gave medical discourse its 'philosophical' dimension. It also provided physicians with multiple points of entry into the book trade.

Print culture and the medicalization of the overcultured

Medicine thrived in eighteenth-century print culture. Portable self-help manuals such as Vandermonde's *Dictionnaire portatif de santé* (*A Portable*

Dictionary of Health) (1759) were widely available, and doctors wrote novels and fictional dialogues to promote therapies for the conservation of beauty (Le Camus, *Abdeker, ou l'art de conserver la beauté* [*Abdeker; or, The Art of Preserving Beauty*] 1754) or the prevention of vapours (Pierre Hunauld, *Dissertation sur les vapeurs et les pertes de sang* [*Dissertation on the Vapours and Blood Loss*] 1756). Samuel-Auguste Tissot had a particularly long string of medical best-sellers, starting with his earliest publications, *L'Inoculation justifiée* (*The Justification for Inoculation*) (1754), *De l'onanisme* (*Onanism*) (1760) and *Avis au peuple sur sa santé* (*Advice to the People in General, with Regard to their Health*) (1761).

Tissot was, in fact, the most successful medical popularizer writing in the French vernacular during the eighteenth century. Trained in Montpellier, he was a highly sought practitioner who attracted patients from all over Europe to his home city of Lausanne (a phenomenon noted by Isabelle de Charrière in her 1788 novel *Lettres écrites de Lausanne* [*Letters Written from Lausanne*]). However, what has kept him in the spotlight as an historical figure was his fame as a medical writer, one whose name was attached to some of the most curious culture-bound disease syndromes of the period. In addition to lending his voice to the medicalization of anti-masturbation discourse, Tissot helped to medicalize two other conditions: the vapours and the so-called 'diseases of scholars' – the latter an umbrella term that referred to the ailments attributed to overstudy, which ran the gamut from indigestion to hair loss to dementia. By describing both conditions as disorders primarily (if not exclusively) of the nerves, Tissot solidified the bodily basis of the ideal of sensibility, even as he critiqued that ideal and the civilization that glorified it.

When Tissot and other contemporary physicians spoke of the vapours, they referred to a catch-all category of nervous affections that included hypochondria or hysteria.[33] Symptoms involved a mixture of bodily and emotional complaints: lethargy, spasms and convulsions, humoral plethora, excessive nervousness, overactive imagination, nausea, headaches, colic, flatulence and ennui. Among the causes commonly held responsible for the vapours were 'unnatural urbane practices' such as fine dining and theatre-going. Tissot typified contemporary medical thinking when he used the trope of the sturdy peasant as the healthful counter-model to vaporous aristocrats in his *Essai sur les maladies des gens du monde* (*Essay on the Disorders of People of Fashion*) (1770). According to the dominant medical conception of the relationship between health, nerves and living circumstances, the higher a person's place in the socio-cultural hierarchy, the more delicate and reactive his or her constitution would be. After a point, increased sensibility yielded not greater refinement of mind and heart but the serious and blameworthy prospect of 'falling ill from feeling too much'.[34]

One of Tissot's most influential efforts to reform an ailing segment of the population was *De la santé des gens de lettres* (*Treatise on the Health of Men of Letters*), first published in French in 1768, re-edited by Tissot several times over the next three decades and translated into several languages before the end of the century.[35] The insalubrious side of learning was already a well-entrenched theme in European culture, as was the myth of the suffering scholar. Starting in the 1750s and 1760s, Tissot and other physicians undertook to medicalize the theme and the myth. They built on two widespread notions: first, the idea that learned people were susceptible to illness because their bodies were strained by cerebral overstimulation and neglect of the non-naturals (especially exercise, sleep and proper diet);[36] and second, the belief that absorption in cerebration made them unfit to participate in the unscholarly social realm.

Tissot described scholars as personally complicit in the ailments they contracted: he compared them to 'lovers who fly off the handle when one dares to say that the object of their passion has defects'.[37] He also decried the broader social damage that had been wrought by 'this love of knowledge, which for a century has been the reigning mania', a comment that echoed the 'mania' rhetoric common in the verbal battles of the pro- versus counter-Enlightenment camps.[38] However, despite his irritation with the faddish pursuit of learning, the tone Tissot took in portraying scholars who had destroyed their health through overstudy was sympathetic, at times even mournful – as when he was describing the loss of his friend M. de Brenles, whom Tissot believed to have succumbed to overstudy. Over the course of its various re-editions, he strove to make the book a collaboration between himself, his fellow physicians and his scholarly readers. He offered easy-to-follow advice for reversing ill-health in scholars; in fact, his remedies were decidedly gentle in comparison with the harsh methods that some endorsed to fortify the 'weak stomach' that supposedly accompanied an active brain.

Not everyone took seriously medical warnings about the effects of strenuous mental application. Charrière, for example, was diagnosed as vaporous at the age of sixteen but refused to accept her friends' opinion that her poor health stemmed from her incessant intellectual activities: she argued just the opposite, insisting that keeping her mind intensely occupied was the only way to combat her low moods.[39] Her correspondence illustrates the positive values that were associated with vapours and melancholy: her correspondents saw them as proof of her refinement and exceptional mind. Moreover, Charrière's regular health bulletins to her friends and acquaintances illustrate the social advantages of suffering from 'nerves': it was, in the words of Michael Stolberg, 'a flexible means of self-fashioning, self-stylisation, and self-dramatisation', and it supplied some sufferers with ample attention from physicians, that is, from men 'who cultivated their ability to listen for professional reasons'.[40]

Listening from afar: medical consultation by letter

Numerous patients wrote letters to famous medical practitioners such as Tissot, Barthez and Théodore Tronchin, which suggests that the desire to recount one's ailments to a sympathetic professional ear was widespread (not least among self-described onanists).[41] Patients both illustrious and obscure had their ailments diagnosed and treated by letter; patient letters were incorporated into medical works; and established surgeons as well as physicians published their consultation letters (real as well as fictional) as a means of instruction for colleagues or students.[42]

Epistolary consultation was a common practice in the eighteenth century for various reasons, including the cost of house calls, the geographic distance that separated patients from consulting physicians, the increased efficiency of the postal system and the spread of popularized medical discourse among laypeople.[43] Most intriguing, perhaps, is the fact that 'doctors did not always feel it was necessary to see patients, or to touch their bodies, diagnosis primarily being based on a narrative or a written account of symptoms'.[44] That is not to say that doctors regarded direct, physical examination as unimportant: rather, when doing a consultation by letter, they relied on either sufferers themselves or a third party – an ordinary physician or a family member – to lay out the symptoms and summarize the pulse and other physical signs in a simple, accurate manner.

The narrative descriptions of illness could involve a network of family and community members who surrounded the ailing patient, making both the experience of illness and its treatment collective affairs that unfolded over time through the exchange of clinical information and therapeutic advice. Epistolary consultation attests to the importance that physicians placed on hearing the voice of sufferers through their letters. It also illustrates that playing doctor on oneself or on others was a popular pastime among laypeople, including the famously ailing Voltaire.[45]

Conclusion

As E. C. Spary has underscored, many people living in the eighteenth century were 'fascinated with new knowledge', and those who catered to that fascination actively drew on print, commerce and their connections within polite society to establish credibility. Spary's point is useful for thinking about Enlightenment-era health claims: new biomedical ideas and therapies were publicly constituted, promoted and contested in a very particular entanglement of science and society.[46] This was clearly true of the craze surrounding Mesmerism, whose practitioners offered the promise of producing an entirely new set of healing sensations through magnetization.[47] It was also true of smallpox inoculation, an even more controversial procedure whose debates were staged just as much in fiction and other sorts of literary works as they were in medical reports. Of course, bodies themselves were pressed into service: inoculists developed and refined their technique on bodies ranging from the well born, such as the children of Lady Mary Wortley Montagu (heralded in Voltaire's *Lettres philosophiques* [*Philosophical Letters*] 1734) to the humble, such as the captive slave population of Saint-Domingue.[48] Biomedical investigators sometimes employed their own bodies to settle disputes over therapeutic claims. Jean-Antoine Nollet, for example, deployed self-experimentation to refute the claims made by Gianfrancesco Pivati that electrically charged 'medicated' tubes could produce physiological responses.[49]

The therapeutic methods promoted by Enlightenment-era doctors can be deeply unsettling for modern readers: take, for example, the use of Leyden jars and other electrical devices to treat diseases attributed to the obstruction of vital fluids, which included paralysis and 'women's ailments'. However, the strange-making effect of encountering views of corporeality so different from our own is useful in that it forces us to move beyond casual identification with this era's ideas and ideals.[50] Bodies mattered in multiple ways in the thought and culture of the French Enlightenment – and medicine's role in making bodies matter in the name of 'enlightenment' is still opening up a host of intriguing avenues of historical inquiry.

NOTES

1 Denis Diderot, *Éléments de physiologie*, in *Œuvres complètes*, 25 vols., ed. Herbert Dieckmann et al. (Paris: Hermann, 1975–), vol. XVII, p. 334.

2 Michel Foucault, *The Birth of Biopolitics: Lectures at the Collège de France, 1978–79*, ed. Michel Senellart, trans. Graham Burchell (Basingstoke: Palgrave Macmillan, 2008).

3 This list updates Caroline Bynum's incisive survey in 'Why All the Fuss about the Body? A Medievalist's Perspective', *Critical Inquiry*, 22 (1) (1995): 1–6.

4 See Anne Deneys-Tunney, *Écritures du corps: de Descartes à Laclos* (Paris: Presses Universitaires de France, 1992); and Natania Meeker, *Voluptuous Philosophy: Literary Materialism in the French Enlightenment* (New York: Fordham University Press, 2006).

5   See the more extensive methodological reflections of Emma C. Spary, 'Health and
    Medicine in the Enlightenment', in Mark Jackson (ed.), *The Oxford Handbook
    of the History of Medicine* (Oxford University Press, 2011), pp. 81–99; Laurence
    Brockliss and Colin Jones, *The Medical World of Early Modern France* (Oxford:
    Clarendon Press, 1997), pp. 1–33; and Michael Stolberg, *Experiencing Illness
    and the Sick Body in Early Modern Europe*, trans. Leonhard Unglaub and Logan
    Kennedy (New York: Palgrave MacMillan, 2011), pp. 1–9.
6   François Zanetti, 'L'Électricité du corps humain chez l'abbé Bertholon et
    quelques contemporains', *Annales historiques de l'électricité*, 8 (2010): 9–20.
7   Karol K. Weaver, 'The Enslaved Healers of Eighteenth-Century Saint Domingue',
    Bulletin of the History of Medicine, 76 (3) (2002): 429–60.
8   Peter Gay, *The Enlightenment: An Interpretation*, 2 vols. (New York: W. W.
    Norton & Co., 1977), vol. II: *The Science of Freedom*, pp. 5–23.
9   Elizabeth A. Williams, *A Cultural History of Medical Vitalism in Enlightenment
    Montpellier* (Aldershot: Ashgate, 2003), p. 6.
10 Diderot, *Éléments de physiologie*, vol. XVII, p. 510.
11 On the perceived dangers of reading, see Alexandre Wenger, *La Fibre littéraire:
    le discours médical sur la lecture au XVIIIe siècle* (Geneva: Droz, 2007).
12 An epidemiological transition occurred in eighteenth-century western Europe
    'from a society whose disease pattern was dominated by infectious diseases to
    a more modern situation where chronic diseases are prevalent' (Brockliss and
    Jones, *Medical World*, pp. 356–70).
13 Stolberg, *Experiencing Illness*, pp. 89–156.
14 See Carol Blum, *Strength in Numbers: Population, Reproduction, and Power in
    Eighteenth-Century France* (Baltimore, Md.: Johns Hopkins University Press,
    2002).
15 See Nina Gelbart, 'Midwife to a Nation: Madame du Coudray Serves France',
    in Hilary Marland (ed.), *The Art of Midwifery: Early Modern Midwives in
    Europe* (London: Routledge, 1993), pp. 78–96; and Colin Jones, 'Pulling Teeth
    in Eighteenth-Century Paris', *Past and Present*, 166 (2) (2000): 100–45.
16 See Brockliss and Jones, *Medical World*, pp. 138–69, 411–33.
17 Daniel Roche, *Les Républicains des lettres: gens de culture et Lumières au
    XVIIIe siècle* (Paris: Fayard, 1988), pp. 308–30.
18 Vladimir Janković, *Confronting the Climate: British Airs and the Making of
    Environmental Medicine* (New York: Palgrave Macmillan, 2010), p. 36.
19 Séverine Pilloud and Micheline Louis-Courvoisier, 'The Intimate Experience
    of the Body in the Eighteenth Century: Between Interiority and Exteriority',
    Medical History, 47 (4) (2003): 451–72, at p. 455.
20 Alain Corbin points out the value of diaries for historians interested in hearing
    the 'murmuring of the viscera to which the elite ... were so attentive before the
    emergence of psychoanalysis' (*Time, Desire and Horror: Toward a History of
    the Senses*, trans. Jean Birrell [Cambridge: Polity Press, 1995], p. 185).
21 Thomas W. Laqueur, 'Bodies, Details, and the Humanitarian Narrative', in Lynn
    Hunt (ed.), *The New Cultural History* (Berkeley, Calif.: University of California
    Press, 1989), pp. 176–204.
22 Some of the following discussion is adapted from Anne Vila, *Enlightenment
    and Pathology: Sensibility in the Literature and Medicine of Eighteenth-Century
    France* (Baltimore, Md.: The Johns Hopkins University Press, 1998).

23 See Hubert Steinke, *Irritating Experiments: Haller's Concept and the European Controversy on Irritability and Sensibility, 1750–90* (Amsterdam: Rodopi, 2005).

24 Elizabeth A. Williams, 'Jean-Charles-Marguerite-Guillaume Grimaud and the Question of Holism in Vitalist Medicine', *Science in Context*, 21 (4) (2008): 593–613, at p. 599.

25 Louis de Jaucourt, 'Sensibilité (morale)', in Diderot and d'Alembert (eds.), *Encyclopédie*, vol. XV, p. 52.

26 Henri Fouquet, 'Sensibilité, sentiment (Médecine)', in Diderot and d'Alembert (eds.), *Encyclopédie*, vol. XV, p. 38.

27 Elizabeth A. Williams, *The Physical and the Moral: Anthropology, Physiology and Philosophical Medicine in France, 1750–1850* (Cambridge University Press, 1994), p. 25.

28 Brockliss and Jones, *Medical World*, pp. 459–79.

29 See Mary Terrall, 'Material Impressions: Conception, Sensibility and Inheritance', in Helen Deutsch and Mary Terrall (eds.), *Vital Matters: Eighteenth-Century Views of Conception, Life, and Death* (University of Toronto Press, 2012), pp. 109–29; and Kathleen Wellman, 'Physicians and Philosophes: Physiology and Sexual Morality in the French Enlightenment', *Eighteenth-Century Studies*, 35 (2) (2001): 267–77.

30 See Denis Diderot, *Réfutation suivie de l'ouvrage d'Helvétius intitulé 'de l'Homme'* (1778).

31 Rudy Le Menthéour emphasizes the 'triangular', polemical relationship that tied together Rousseau, the philosophes and contemporary medicine in *La Manufacture de maladies: la dissidence hygiénique de Jean-Jacques Rousseau* (Paris: Classiques Garnier, 2012).

32 Williams, *Cultural History*, pp. 271–5.

33 Hysteria was not strictly gendered as female in French medicine until the early nineteenth century. See Sabine Arnaud, *L'Invention de l'hystérie au temps des lumières (1670–1820)* (Paris: Éditions de l'EHESS, 2014).

34 Michel Foucault, *Histoire de la folie* (Paris: Gallimard, 1972), p. 314.

35 Antoinette Emch-Dériaz, *Tissot, Physician of the Enlightenment* (New York: Peter Lang, 1992), pp. 331–2.

36 Antoinette Emch-Dériaz, 'The Non-naturals Made Easy', in Roy Porter (ed.), *The Popularization of Medicine, 1650–1850* (London and New York: Routledge, 1992), pp. 134–59.

37 Samuel-Auguste Tissot, *De la santé des gens de lettres*, 3rd edn (Lausanne, 1775), p. 132.

38 Tissot, *Gens de lettres*, p. 185.

39 Philip Rieder, *La Figure du patient au XVIIIe siècle* (Geneva: Droz, 2010), pp. 90–111.

40 Stolberg, *Experiencing Illness*, pp. 182–3.

41 On the letters Tissot received from self-described onanists, see Daniel Teyssière, 'Le Désir de connaître ses maux et leurs remèdes', in Nicole Jacques-Chaquin and Sophie Houdard (eds.), *Curiosité et libido sciendi de la Renaissance aux lumières* (Paris: ENS Éditions, 1998), vol. I, pp. 207–24; and Stolberg, *Experiencing Illness*, pp. 195–212.

42 Patrick Singy, 'Medicine and the Senses: The Perception of Essences', in *The Cultural History of the Senses in the Enlightenment* (London: Bloomsbury Publishing, 2014).

43 Brockliss and Jones, *Medical World*, p. 536.

44 Pilloud and Louis-Courvoisier, 'Intimate Experience', p. 453.

45 On Voltaire, see Anne Vila, 'The Philosophe's Stomach: Hedonism, Hypochondria, and the "New" Intellectual in Enlightenment France', in Christopher Forth and Ana Carden-Coyne (eds.), *Cultures of the Abdomen: Dietetics, Digestion and Obesity in the Modern World* (New York: Palgrave, 2005), pp. 89–104.

46 E. C. Spary, *Eating the Enlightenment: Food and the Sciences in Paris, 1670–1760* (University of Chicago Press, 2012), pp. 1, 6.

47 Robert Darnton, *Mesmer and the End of the Enlightenment* (Cambridge, Mass.: Harvard University Press, 1968); François Azouvi, 'Le Magnétisme animal: la sensation infinie', *Dix-Huitième siècle*, 23 (1991): 107–18; and Jessica Riskin, *Science in the Age of Sensibility: The Sentimental Empiricists of the French Enlightenment* (University of Chicago Press, 2002), pp. 189–225.

48 Weaver, 'Enslaved Healers', pp. 543–4.

49 Nollet attributed the diarrhoea he contracted while trying out Pivati's tubes to something he had eaten, not to electric purgation. Paola Bertucci, 'The Electrical Body of Knowledge: Medical Electricity and Experimental Philosophy in the Mid-Eighteenth Century', in Paola Bertucci and Giuliano Pancaldi (eds.), *Electric Bodies: Episodes in the History of Medical Electricity* (Bologna: CIS-Dipartimeto di Filosofia, Università di Bologna, 2001), pp. 59–60.

50 François Zanetti, 'Quand l'électricité soignait les maladies des femmes: corps et médecine au XVIIIe siècle', in Anna Bellavitis and Nicole Edelman (eds.), *Genre, femme, histoire en Europe: France, Italie, Espagne, Autriche* (Paris: Presses Universitaires de Paris Ouest, 2011), pp. 177–96.

15

CHARLES W. J. WITHERS

Space, geography and the global French Enlightenment

This chapter explores the terms 'France', 'Enlightenment' and 'Geography' and the relationships between them. Rather than see geography either simply as a subject or a set of intellectual practices among the many making up the Enlightenment in France, I want to advance an argument about the importance of thinking geographically, of reading and interpreting the Enlightenment and France – France and its many enlightenments – through a spatial lens. By 'thinking geographically', I mean to enquire into the geographical dimensions of the Enlightenment in France, to explore questions to do with how the ideas and practices that made up the Enlightenment there were at work in different places and to consider how notions of Enlightenment varied over space as well as over time and in their cognitive character.

Why should this matter? Our answers must recognize the wider interpretive context in which the question and this chapter sit. To date and in general, historiographical interpretations of the Enlightenment have focused on its temporal dimensions (its 'when'), its individual personnel and institutional make-up (its 'who'), and upon the cognitive content, social reach and intellectual and practical consequences of its ideas (its 'what' and its 'so what?'). Thinking geographically addresses the importance of 'where' questions. Where were they located, these people who wrote, read and debated works that contemporaries took to be enlightening? How did the Enlightenment's ideas move over space: as print, in review, in debates in academies and salons, as lecture classes, through the presence in person of the author? What were the Enlightenment's variations over place within the space that was, and would become, France? How do geography's analytic languages of place, space and scale aid in understanding the different forms of knowledge that made up the Enlightenment in France?

In considering these and other questions on the Enlightenment and France geographically, a useful but not strict distinction may be made between geography *in*, and the geography *of*, the Enlightenment in France. In the first sense, geography may be seen as one species of Enlightenment knowledge with its particular sites of production, audiences and material expression. Taking the Enlightenment and France as a whole, however, any such individual 'map' of geography's making and reception would be but one feature in an altogether more complex cartography of intellectual endeavour – that second and broader sense signalled above in the geography *of*. Taken together, the many different networks of knowledge-exchange disclosed would begin to show where the Enlightenment was made and received and the strength of the connections between places for the ideas and knowledge in question. Intellectual movements always have a geography as well as a history, material form and their biographical interlocutors. Thinking geographically illustrates that ideas do not 'float free' but are 'grounded' in particular sites and social settings, the study of which can help explain the nature, mobility and reach of the ideas themselves.[1]

This approach is lent weight by the fact that recent research upon these terms has revealed considerable geographical complexity behind these seemingly simple descriptors. In the eighteenth century, France was not one nation, if, by that term, we mean a country of certain territorial bounds, a population sharing, even articulating, a geographical or political consciousness among and between the ranks of the clergy, the nobility and gentry and the populace as a whole, and with everywhere equally developed networks of civic, fiscal and ecclesiastical administration.[2] Even as its shape, territorial unity and national consciousness emerged but slowly, day-to-day and commercial life varied from place to place: eighteenth-century France was a confusion of weights and measures, for example, something that the Revolutionary metrological project that was the metre sought (and failed) to overcome by the adoption of that 'uniform' earth-commensurable unit.[3]

The idea of the Enlightenment as a predominantly European, philosophically oriented and urban phenomenon of principally intellectual critique has been replaced by historiographical interpretations attentive to differences over space: *the* Enlightenment by Enlightenment or even Enlightenments; Eurocentric 'core-periphery' models with, often, France at their heart by accounts that question Europe's dominance and displace the nation – including France – as the necessary unit of analysis. The primacy of moral and philosophical enquiries has been challenged by studies of the emergent sciences and of material improvement; focus has shifted from the Enlightenment as a shared project to the uneven production and mixed reception of variant 'species' of Enlightenment in different institutional and social settings.[4]

Geography, too, took various forms to various ends in Enlightenment France. Mapping was a means to know one's national bounds and a form of territorial representation. Cartography and geography understood as the mathematical expression of topographical survey differed in their aims and means, however, from books of geography whose authors sought to order geographical knowledge in novel ways, to educate the literate citizen and to instil in readers' minds hierarchical conceptions of place and space that embraced the immediate locality, provincial identity, the nation of France and the world as a whole. At global scales, ocean-going exploration undertaken by French *voyageurs naturalistes* such as Louis Antoine de Bougainville, Jean-François de Galaup, the comte de Lapérouse and Nicolas-Thomas Baudin helped enlarge France's geopolitical reach, in North America and the Pacific especially. In these conjoint forms, geography was the subject of debate in academies and salons, critical discourse in learned journals, practical expression in books, atlases and *encyclopédies* and a matter of everyday employment for military engineers and of instruction for the nation's youth.[5]

What follows offers several illustrations – on textual geographies, mapping and geography and stadial theory – of 'thinking geographically' to show how France in the Enlightenment was geographically imagined and practically made as a national space through the agency of geography. The Enlightenment in France, I argue, should always be seen as a spatial phenomenon as well as a temporal and a biographical one.

The Enlightenment geographically: scale, space, place and maps of knowledge

The view from the Enlightenment historian John Robertson that 'the sense of place is as necessary to historical understanding – even to the understanding of ideas – as the sense of time' is now broadly accepted.[6] Numerous examples of geographically attuned interpretations of the Enlightenment may be cited. Robertson's comparative study of Scotland and Naples, for example, examines discourses of political economy in these local settings and 'above national context'. Others have looked not to Scotland, Naples and political economy but to networks of religious radicalism diffusing from Amsterdam.[7] A further setting in which rethought geographical questions of the Enlightenment have come to the fore is in Spanish America. Where Enlightenment in Peru and in Brazil was once a form of intellectual colonialism within countries seen only as 'margins' to the 'core' nations of Enlightenment Europe, recent work has identified the exchange of Enlightenment ideas and the reception and self-fashioning of Enlightenment ideals within Spanish (and Portuguese) America.[8] Simply, there were different species of Enlightenment in different nations and even multiple versions of Enlightenment coexisting and interacting in the same place.[9] We may now, one authority argues, even talk of 'geo-historiography', of geography as the eye of Enlightenment historiography.[10]

Explanation of this interest in thinking geographically rests in part in the 'spatial turn' within the humanities and the social sciences more generally and in the analytic and interpretive power of geography's language of scale, place and space in particular.[11] For cultural historian Daniel Brewer, 'A glance out across fields of knowledge quickly reveals that "space" became the master metaphor of late twentieth-century epistemology.'[12] Brewer's concerns focused on the exigencies and materiality of physical space, on mapping, the development of road networks and postal systems. He addressed the idea of social space, notably courtly space and the spaces of salon culture, 'the sites that made up an expanding public sphere, the sites of urban spectatorship, pleasures, and life'. He also considered colonized space, the relationships between narratives of home and far away, the pervasive discourses of exoticism, of tropicality, of foreignness and the 'other', both real and imaginary. Brewer further identified what he termed epistemic space, in which he considered the classificatory spaces and taxonomic map of knowledge that was Diderot and d'Alembert's *Encyclopédie* and, lastly, the aesthetic space of novels and depictive art, which was both 'real in producing particular ways of looking at human-nature relationships' and 'an imaginary space that the reader-viewer is invited to wish for, to inhabit and occupy, a space where new forms of subjectivity and intersubjective relations are played out'.[13]

Brewer's concern in thinking about the nature of space was not that historical perspectives should be displaced – nor to suppose that they *had* been. As he put it, 'To suggest, though, that contemporary epistemology represents a profoundly spatial way of knowing things does not imply that we need somehow to regain a sense of time, to recover temporal knowledge by returning to history or by turning to the discipline of history.' He is suggesting that a geographical perspective brings new objects into view and provides a way to understand the production of knowledge in general: 'Ultimately, this spatializing perspective provides a powerfully self-reflexive way to investigate not only new objects of study, but also the production of knowledge itself.'[14]

In combination with others' 'geo-historiographical' work on space, place and the decentring of Europe and the nation within Enlightenment studies, Brewer's remarks are useful in thinking geographically about the social dimensions and intellectual content of the Enlightenment in France. Like mine, Brewer's concerns with the epistemology of this 'spatializing perspective' are more than metaphorical, more sophisticated than any limited nominative sense of geography in which events and people are simply located as well as dated.

Commentators upon France and Enlightenment have tended to privilege historical interpretation. Over thirty years ago, Norman Hampson, who observed that 'the Enlightenment is usually regarded as something that happened rather more in France than anywhere else', certainly did so, citing differences between the early eighteenth-century philosophical critiques offered by Charles-Louis de Secondat de Montesquieu and Jean-Jacques Rousseau, for example, and the emphasis upon material and social reform later in the century in the works of Anne-Robert-Jacques Turgot, Jacques Necker, Antoine-Laurent de Lavoisier and Marie Jean Antoine Nicolas de Caritat, Marquis de Condorcet.[15] A more recent overview, albeit one attentive to the Enlightenment's different physical, social and epistemic spaces, likewise adopts a broadly chronological approach:

> The history of the Enlightenment might best be understood within the context of this evolving, pluralistic public sphere with 1750 as a watershed. Before this date, the Enlightenment attack on religious dogma and social distinction based on birth and money, rather than merit, gave the movement an underground character. After 1750, however, and coinciding with the publication of Diderot and d'Alembert's *Encyclopédie*, enlightened thought went mainstream.[16]

Others have called for a much reduced conception of the Enlightenment, in France and more generally, as an intellectual movement which was philosophical, led by and about men, and 'elitist, Voltairean, and incorrigibly Parisian'.[17]

My argument does not deny the validity of historical or other interpretations, nor does it seek to privilege one Enlightenment or setting or personality over another. Instead, it is propositional: that thinking geographically offers a new and rewarding way of considering the Enlightenment, and its many forms and actors in France, as an intellectual and embodied phenomenon that took place and varied over space and between places, rather than over time, something that occurred and moved beyond Paris and that involved subjects other than philosophy.

Geographies of textual knowledge in Enlightenment France: the case of the *Encyclopédie*

In France, as elsewhere, Enlightenment was significant as a textual enterprise.[18] Because books were written and published somewhere, and bought, read and argued about in other places as they and their ideas moved over space, the geographical dimensions intrinsic to book history can illuminate the Enlightenment's nature, authors and audiences, as has been shown of Britain, Ireland and America.[19]

The *Encyclopédie, ou dictionnaire raisonné des sciences, des arts et des métiers*, published in Paris between 1751 and 1772 (as seventeen volumes of articles [1751–65] and eleven of plates [1762–72]) under the editorship of Denis Diderot and Jean-Baptiste le Rond d'Alembert, was perhaps *the* crucial textual expression of the Enlightenment in France. It has been described as one of 'the great works of the Enlightenment', the 'epitome of the French Enlightenment' and, between 1751 and 1772, 'the Western world's most celebrated (and notorious) fountain of knowledge'. The *Encyclopédie* aimed 'to undermine established religion and divine right monarchy, to change the educational, agricultural, commercial, industrial, legal, and tax policies of the French government and to lower the status of the clergy and the high nobility whilst raising that of the merchants and artisans'.[20] Study of the *Encyclopédie* can illustrate the Enlightenment's geographical dimensions in France in several ways: in its publishing history and the sales of the work, in its editors' intentions that the work should provide an ordered map (an epistemic space) for knowledge as a whole and in its content. Let me take the first to highlight my argument here.[21]

Paris was the *Encyclopédie*'s productive locus in terms of publication and authorship: about fifty-nine per cent of all contributors lived in the capital. Beyond Paris, there were four significant 'regional clusters' of contributing authors, in Lorraine, Languedoc and Versailles, and in Switzerland (in Berne, Geneva and Lausanne). In Languedoc, contributing authors gravitated around local academic institutions such as the Société Royale des Sciences and the University in Montpellier. In terms of subscription sales, however – and, in that general sense, to sketch in outline a geography of the *Encyclopédie*'s reception and readership – different spatial patterns of Enlightenment encounter may be traced. The city of Lyon dominated sales, with twice as many subscribers as Paris and for a population about one-fifth the size. Sales were high across provincial capitals such as Besançon, Bordeaux, Dijon and Toulouse. Across France, subscription sales were on the whole higher in cities and towns with administrative and cultural functions, lower in places with a more commercial and industrial function: the *Encyclopédie* was taken up more by a 'heterogeneous public of noblemen, clerics, and a group sometimes identified as the *bourgeoisie d'ancien régime* – notables, clerics, officials, and professional persons, as distinct from the modern industrial bourgeoisie'.[22]

Looked at historically, the *Encyclopédie*'s publication may well embody that key moment between an 'underground' and a 'mainstream' Enlightenment in France. Considered geographically, a different picture emerges. What was largely Parisian in production was not so in uptake. The textual world of the *Encyclopédie* embraced different geographies of intellectual affiliation in its authorship and yet different geographies and social spaces in its reception. In disclosing differences in the geographies of the text's production and reception, Kafker's and Darnton's pioneering work on the *Encyclopédie* points to a variable cartography of textual enquiry and intellectual critique in the Enlightenment in France (admitting, of course, that we may never capture precisely the exact circumstances of readership, of conversation, polite or otherwise, about its nature and content).[23]

Their work also suggests directions for further research. Might it be possible, for example, to know the take-up of George-Louis le Clerc, the comte de Buffon's thirty-seven volume *Histoire naturelle, générale et particulière* (*Natural History: General and Particular*) (1749–89) and so chart the reception of French Enlightenment natural history? One later commentator claimed that this book was read 'by every educated person in Europe'.[24] Was this so of other enlightened Frenchmen and their published words? Published in March 1789, the two-volume *Traité élémentaire de chimie* (*Elementary Treatise of Chemistry*) by Lavoisier, France's leading Enlightenment chemist, arrived in London's Royal Society in November that year: British engagement with the work of Lavoisier's contemporaries such as Pierre-Simon Laplace was delayed by war and his emphasis on analytical mathematics in contrast to Newtonian natural philosophy.[25] In short, Enlightenment knowledge did not move evenly across space. To consider how, when and where books and other forms of print travelled and what were their different social contours of reception is to think geographically about the Enlightenment.

Regulating and representing France: maps, meridians and metrication

Enlightenment France changed shape constantly. Throughout the eighteenth century, the nation was redrawn, reimagined even, by military *ingénieur-géographes* and civilian map-makers whose purpose lay not just in establishing the territorial extent of the nation but also in determining its contents and in mathematically fixing their location and dimensions. At the start of the century, France was shown to be considerably smaller than previously thought (Fig. 15.1). Under the guidance of Jean-Baptiste Colbert, minister-in-chief to King Louis XIV, and the mathematician map-maker Jacques-Dominique Cassini, members of the Académie Royale des Sciences initially led by Jean-Félix Picard and Philippe de La Hire undertook triangulation and trigonometrical measurements with a view to the nation's delimitation – and 'shrank' France noticeably, especially on its western margins and Mediterranean coast.[26] At century's end, concerns to establish the metre as the standard linear basis to French mensuration (and global measurement) foundered in the face of official incompetence, the persistence of local

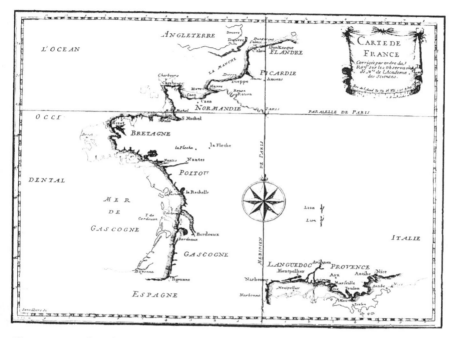

Figure 15.1 Early Enlightenment France reduced. The bold lines show the outlines of France after the work of Picard and La Hire, the faint lines the earlier national outlines from Nicolas Sanson. Jean Picard and Philippe de La Hire, *Carte de France corrigée* (1693). Reproduced with the permission of the Trustees of the National Library of Scotland.

customary measures and the problems of accurately defining a 'standard' metre.[27]

Rather than think, then, of Enlightenment France as territorially fixed and politically self-aware, from which context maps emerged as expressions of a united political will, easily achieved mathematical expertise and a sense of national certainty, it is more accurate to consider this relationship reversed. In Enlightenment France, mapping was undertaken in order to shape and to know the nation. Mapping, military cartography in particular, provided a distinctive language of national self-representation of importance 'to commerce, industry, and the advancement of general statistical knowledge, science and the larger civil society'.[28] Yet such knowledge was not easily achieved. The geographical 'emergence' of Enlightenment France through mapping depended upon heightened standards of accuracy by which to show the nation and lend credibility to the map-makers and to the language and science of geography. Again, particular examples must serve to make these more general claims.

As a child, King Louis XV's interest in geography as a form of natural knowledge was apparent in his short 1718 treatise *Cours des principaux*

Figure 15.2 Enlightenment France regulated and ordered. Note the limited depiction of the physical features and the central place of the (corrected) Paris meridian as the nation's baseline. César-François Cassini de Thury, *Nouvelle Carte ... de la France* (1744). Reproduced with the permission of the Trustees of the National Library of Scotland.

fleuves et rivières de l'Europe (*The Principal Rivers of Europe*), of which, according to Voltaire, only fifty copies were ever produced.[29] As an adult, Louis XV was concerned more with national knowledge, specifically with extending in range and detail the mapping begun in his father's reign under Colbert, Picard, de La Hire and Jacques-Dominique Cassini (Cassini I). Jacques Cassini (Cassini II) was commissioned by Louis in 1733 to undertake the mapping of France to new levels of standardized accuracy in order to fix the nation's boundaries once and for all and for the overall public good. He was later joined by his son, César-François Cassini de Thury (Cassini III, known also as Cassini de Thury). Using triangulation and trigonometry and beginning with Picard's measurements from the Paris meridian, geometers and map-makers worked out from the capital. In places, France's physical geography got in the way: mountainous regions could provide clear lines of sight but were hazardous to work in and slowed progress. In other places, France's human inhabitants proved the hindrance: one surveyor at work near Mézenc in the Ardèche was killed by local villagers who considered his instruments to have bewitched their crops.[30]

The survey was finally completed by 1744, and the map was published in eighteen sheets, with the 800 principal triangles and nineteen base lines providing a lattice-like view of France as a whole, its towns and other key locations marked, the country's physical terrain largely absent: 'It was not in modern terms a national survey based on comprehensive topographical detail, but a geodetic survey which produced a positional illustration of places significant to the requirements of state planning.'[31] Quite apart from the scale of the project, one of the reasons why the survey took over a decade to complete was the fact that Picard's astronomical measurements for the meridian of Paris were found to be in error and so had to be recalculated: small though the error was (about five *toises* or ten metres), it would have had major implications had it been compounded for the nation as a whole. Measurement of the meridian at Paris – from which point Enlightenment France both surveyed itself and fixed its position relative to other nations – was a constant problem for the nation's astronomers and geodesists. Attempts in the early 1720s had been made to fix Paris as the site of the nation's prime meridian and not Cap Ferro in the Canaries as had long been the case, and Cassini III's lengthy analysis in 1744 of the replotted Paris meridian needs to be read as part of a longer-running story about determining the start point for France's terrestrial measurement as well as a vindication of his own capacities as astronomer, geographer and diplomat.[32] Even by the end of the century, leading figures in what was to become Britain's Ordnance Survey were at work fixing through trigonometry the positions of the observatories at Greenwich and at Paris in order to give shape to the respective nations and accurate locations from which to advance astronomy and national mapping.[33] If Paris was the capital of Enlightenment France, it too was constantly on the move.

Cassini de Thury's 'Nouvelle Carte … de la France' ('New Map of France'; see Fig. 15.2) of 1744 may well reflect the 'triumph of the immutable laws of geometry and mathematics over the vast, messy chaos of the terrestrial world' that was Enlightenment France, but it did not satisfy Louis XV.[34] The King requested a yet grander map project, the topographic portrayal of his nation including settlements and human features, and so Cassini III began anew. With the King's approval, Cassini III established the Société de la Carte de France to fund the project, and, from 1756, the maps began to appear, 'unparalleled in their precision, detail, accuracy, and standardisation'.[35] From the 1780s, Cassini III was joined by his son, Jean-Dominique, comte de Cassini (Cassini IV). By then, however, increased opposition to the King's political authority was evident. During the Revolution, the Cassinis' map project was nationalized in 1793. Technically, it was never finished, although the activities of the Dépôt de la Guerre between 1804 and 1815 under the management of Napoleon Bonaparte completed coverage of the nation. By then, however, plans were under way to update the Cassinis' work; Bonaparte commissioned a new national map of France from 1808.[36]

It is easy to get lost in considering France's Enlightenment mapping in detail. What matters is what it stood for then and how we should understand it now. The work of the Cassini cartographic dynasty in delimiting France between 1733 and 1793 must be seen as one leading expression – perhaps *the* leading expression in Enlightenment Europe – of the power of maps to make nations, of the State's view of maps as documents of territorial and political surveillance and of the authority of geographers, map-makers and astronomers. Thinking geographically – about how maps shape nations, about the language of maps and the discursive power of mapping and map-makers – has no better exemplification than the case of Enlightenment France.

Ancient geography/modern geography: geographical method and Enlightenment theory

In the Enlightenment, the *philosophes* and others thought geographically for the good reason that their world was always getting bigger, especially from the later eighteenth century. Voyages of exploration dramatically enlarged the contemporary geographical consciousness, requiring continental margins to be charted, maps and atlases to be redrawn and new explanations to be proposed for the non-European human cultures revealed. Numerous commentators proposed models of 'conjectural history' or 'stadial theory',

in which human cultures and society were judged by their stage of development, from 'savage', 'barbarian', 'commercial', 'polite' or 'advanced', even
'industrial' and so on. Because different parts of the world were more important than others in this respect – the Pacific realm in particular – these new
historical conceptions may also be understood as 'conjectural geographies':
the world beyond Europe was also a world before Europe. Stadial thinking – that is, analysing the relative state of nations and cultures geographically and historically ('geo-historically', to adopt Mayhew's analytic term
above) – was a means by which cosmopolitan thinkers tried to make sense
of the geographical present revealed in the Enlightenment and to understand
the historical past in comparative terms.[37]

Economist and political thinker Anne-Marie-Jacques Turgot used stadial
thinking in several ways in his *Plan d'un ouvrage sur la géographie politique*
(*On Political Geography*) (1751). He used political geography to describe
the human world in a series of what he termed '*mappemondes politiques*'.
Turgot took political geography to encompass four elements: historical study
of the relationships between the physical world, human population and the
formation and continuation of nations; the study of resources, industries
and the development of commercial capacities within nations; transport systems; and differences in the form of political organization around the world.
In the first of his *mappemondes politiques*, Turgot outlined the racial geography of peoples across the globe; in others, he charted changes in 'the most
ancient nations' (China and Egypt) and in classical Europe (the Greek and
Roman empires), and reflected upon the historical development of forms of
political government.[38]

Turgot's use of political geography was consistent with it as a form of
modern geography in Enlightenment France – it was one of geography's
several epistemic distinctions in Diderot and d'Alembert's *Encyclopédie*.
Modern geography also encompassed ancient geography as an established
and widely employed form of historical enquiry and contemporary geographical methodology. Ancient geography involved study of the geographical extent of Roman and Greek culture and of ancient Egyptian and Near
Eastern civilizations and, importantly, the study of what remained of these
past geographies in the modern historical present. Ancient geography, in
short, was a form of stadial reasoning: did the European present represent
a decline, rather than progress from, the classical world? How had ancient
civilizations organized themselves over space? What was left of the historical past in the geographical present?

Historian and orientalist Constantin-François de Chassebœuf, comte
de Volney posed just such questions in his *Les Ruines, ou méditations sur
les révolutions des empires* (*Ruins; or, Meditations on the Revolutions of*

Empires) (1791) wherein he speculated not just upon the common features underlying revealed religion but also upon the role of different systems of governance, notably oriental despotism, and environmental constraints upon agrarian systems, in explaining the decline of Near Eastern civilizations.[39] In the work of geographers such as Edme Mentelle, Jean-Denis Barbié du Bocage, Pascal-François-Joseph Gosselin and Edme-François Jomard, who was influential in the *Description de l'Égypte* from 1802, ancient geography was a form of modern geographical method. In its ancient and modern variants, reasoning geographically was central to historical and political explanation in Enlightenment France.[40]

Conclusions and implications: geography, Enlightenment, France

Things happen in place and events occur across space as well as over time: everything has to be some*where*. Truism though this is, the significance of thinking geographically and not just temporally and biographically about the Enlightenment has been accepted more widely only relatively recently and, excepting Roche's insights into space and mapping, has not before been applied to France. As part of this wider context of geo-historiographical critique in Enlightenment studies, this chapter has proposed a case, necessarily suggestive rather than definitive, about the importance of thinking geographically, specifically with respect to geography *in* and the geography *of* the Enlightenment in France. Thinking about the placed and spaced nature of the Enlightenment, and of the ways in which France came to see itself as a national space during the Enlightenment, is vital to comprehending the different meanings Enlightenment had for its actors, agents and audiences: 'Geography matters, not for the simplistic and overly used reason that everything happens in space, but because *where* things happen, is crucial to knowing *how* and *why* they happen.'[41]

As a form of knowledge, geography was active in a variety of ways in eighteenth-century France. But thinking geographically offers more than this subject-based perspective. Because things happen in place and move over space, we must also think of the Enlightenment in terms of the movement of its ideas and personnel over space as well as over time and consider how ideas and their material expression in the form of books and maps, for instance, overcame the 'gradient' or 'friction' of geographical distance (the geography *of* Enlightenment phenomena).

While this distinction is useful, it is not discrete. It might be possible, for example, to construct a map of the geography of Enlightenment geography: a conceptual and geographical 'baseline' of Paris with its nation-defining meridian, academies, publishing houses, map-makers and

Cassinis at work. But things were done differently in Montpellier and in Paris, where there were certain *quartiers* in the city where geographers, map-makers and their associated trades concentrated.[42] Scale matters, in explanation as well as in geography. And the nation could only be 'made' geographically because *ingénieurs-géographes* criss-crossed French space working, slowly but surely, to standardize what the nation should look like. So, too, might we construct maps of other subjects – of botany or natural history, for example, where the centralizing role of the Jardin du Roi in Paris depended upon long-distance networks of correspondence and plant exchange, specimens from the 'exotic space' that was Indian (specimens then 'misplaced' within French and other European classificatory schema and epistemic spaces) and upon new enlightened ways of thinking about the connections between plants and their geographical distribution.[43]

Thinking geographically calls attention to the importance of place and space, to the networks (of correspondence, friendship, economic ties, political affiliation and so on) that connected places and people over space and, of course, over time, and it requires that we consider the material forms by which knowledge in the Enlightenment moved from place to place (as books, in map form, via conversation, as specimens, experimental results and so on). Geography was a subject of intellectual enquiry and a means to national self-knowledge in Enlightenment France. Geography provides a way of interpreting France and the Enlightenment – not as something fixed but as something shaped by the social settings and the sites and spaces (political, physical and epistemic) in which it took place.

NOTES

1 On ideas having a geography, see David N. Livingstone, *Putting Science in Its Place: Geographies of Scientific Knowledge* (University of Chicago Press, 2003). For a fuller argument on 'thinking geographically' about the Enlightenment, see Charles W. J. Withers, *Placing the Enlightenment: Thinking Geographically about the Age of Reason* (University of Chicago Press, 2007).
2 The best review of this remains Daniel Roche, *France in the Enlightenment*, trans. Arthur Goldhammer (Cambridge, Mass.: Harvard University Press, 1998), especially chap. 2, 'Mastery of Space', pp. 41–74. See also Jacques Revel, 'Knowledge of the Territory', *Science in Context*, 4 (1) (1991): 133–61.
3 On the metre and attempts to measure France to this 'standard' measure, see Ken Alder, *The Measure of All Things: The Seven-Year Odyssey that Transformed the World* (London: Little, Brown, 2002). The variation in linear weights and measures across eighteenth-century France (and Europe) is discussed by Witold Kula, *Measures and Men* (Princeton University Press, 1986).
4 Withers, *Placing the Enlightenment*; David N. Livingstone and Charles W. J. Withers (eds.), *Geography and the Enlightenment* (University of Chicago

Press, 1999); Richard Butterwick, Simon Davies and Gabriel Sanchez-Espinosa (eds.), *Peripheries of the Enlightenment*, Studies on Voltaire and the Eighteenth Century 2008:01 (Oxford: Voltaire Foundation, 2008); Charles W. J. Withers and Robert J. Mayhew, 'Geography: Space, Place and Intellectual History in the Eighteenth Century', *Journal for Eighteenth-Century Studies*, 34 (4) (2011): 445–52; William Clark, Jan Golinski and Simon Schaffer (eds.), *The Sciences in Enlightened Europe* (University of Chicago Press, 1999); Karen O'Brien, 'The Return of the Enlightenment', *American Historical Review*, 115 (5) (2010): 1426–35.

5   A full account of geography in Enlightenment France remains to be written, but see Anne M. C. Godlewska, *Geography Unbound: French Geographic Science from Cassini to Humboldt* (University of Chicago Press, 1999); Numa Broc, *La Géographie des philosophes: géographes et voyageurs français au XVIIIe siècle* (Paris: Éditions Ophrys, 1974); S. Moravia, 'Philosophie et géographie à la fin du XVIIIe siècle', *Studies in Voltaire and the Eighteenth Century*, 57 (1967): 937–1011; Hélène Blais and Isabelle Laboulais (eds.), *Géographies plurielles: les sciences géographiques au moment de l'émergence des sciences humaines (1750–1850)* (Paris: L'Harmattan, 2006); Martin Staum, 'Human Geography in the French Institute: New Discipline or Missed Opportunity?', *Journal of the History of the Behavioral Sciences*, 23 (4) (1987): 332–40; Michael Heffernan, 'Edme Mentelle's Geographies and the French Revolution', in David N. Livingstone and Charles W. J. Withers (eds.), *Geography and Revolution* (University of Chicago Press, 2005), pp. 273–303.

6   John A. Robertson, *The Case for the Enlightenment: Scotland and Naples, 1680–1760* (Cambridge University Press, 2005), p. 53.

7   Jonathan Israel, *Radical Enlightenment: Philosophy and the Making of Modernity, 1650–1750* (Oxford University Press, 2001); Jonathan Israel, *Enlightenment Contested: Philosophy, Modernity and the Emancipation of Man, 1670–1752* (Oxford University Press, 2006); Jonathan Israel, *Democratic Enlightenment: Philosophy, Revolution and Human Rights, 1750–1790* (Oxford University Press, 2011).

8   Neil Safier, *Measuring the New World: Enlightenment Science and South America* (University of Chicago Press, 2008); Jorge Canizares-Esguerra, *How to Write the History of the New World: Histories, Epistemologies, and Identities in the Eighteenth-Century Atlantic World* (Palo Alto, Calif.: Stanford University Press, 2001).

9   This is the thrust of Pocock's survey of Enlightenment: John G. A. Pocock, *Barbarism and Religion*, 4 vols.: vol. I: *The Enlightenments of Edward Gibbon, 1737–1764* (Cambridge University Press, 1999); vol. II: *Narratives of Civil Government* (Cambridge University Press, 2000); vol. III: *The First Decline and Fall* (Cambridge University Press, 2003); vol. IV: *Barbarians, Savages and Emperors* (Cambridge University Press, 2005). See also John G. A. Pocock, 'The Re-description of the Enlightenment', *Proceedings of the British Academy*, 125 (2004): 101–17.

10 Robert Mayhew, 'Geography as the Eye of Enlightenment Historiography', *Modern Intellectual History*, 7 (3) (2010): 611–27.

11 Barbara Warf and Santa Arias, 'Introduction: The Reinsertion of Space in the Humanities and Social Sciences', in Barbara Warf and Santa Arias (eds.), *The Spatial Turn: Interdisciplinary Perspectives* (London and New York: Routledge,

2009), pp. 1–10; Charles W. J. Withers, 'Place and the "Spatial Turn" in Geography and in History', *Journal for the History of Ideas*, 70 (4) (2009): 637–58.

12 Daniel Brewer, 'Lights in Space', *Eighteenth-Century Studies*, 37 (2) (2004): 171–86, at p. 171.

13 Brewer, 'Lights in Space', p. 183.

14 Ibid. pp. 171, 172 and 173, respectively.

15 Norman Hampson, 'The Enlightenment in France', in Roy Porter and Mikulas Teich (eds.), *The Enlightenment in National Context* (Cambridge University Press, 1981), pp. 41–53, at p. 41.

16 Jeffrey Ravel, 'France', in Alan Kors (ed.), *Encyclopedia of the Enlightenment*, 4 vols. (Oxford University Press, 2003), vol. II, pp. 60–5.

17 Robert Darnton, *George Washington's False Teeth: An Unconventional Guide to the Eighteenth Century* (New York: Norton, 2003), p. 6.

18 Robert Darnton, *The Literary Underground of the Old Regime* (Cambridge, Mass.: Harvard University Press, 1982); Robert Darnton, *The Business of Enlightenment: A Publishing History of the Encyclopédie, 1775–1800* (Cambridge, Mass.: Harvard University Press, 1979); Dena Goodman, *Republic of Letters: A Cultural History of the French Enlightenment* (Ithaca, NY: Cornell University Press, 1994).

19 Richard Sher, *The Enlightenment and the Book: Scottish Authors and their Publishers in Eighteenth-Century Britain, Ireland and America* (University of Chicago Press, 2006).

20 Frank A. Kafker, 'Encyclopedias' and Raymond Birn, 'Encyclopédie', in *Encyclopedia of the Enlightenment*, vol. I, pp. 398–403 and pp. 403–9, at pp. 398, 401, 403 and 401.

21 For a fuller discussion, see Withers, *Placing the Enlightenment*, pp. 169–78.

22 These points on the geography of reception are taken from Darnton, *Business of Enlightenment*, pp. 278–323, appendices B and C, pp. 586–93, 594–6; the quote is from p. 287.

23 Robert Darnton, *Business of Enlightenment*; Frank A. Kafker and Serena L. Kafker, *The Encyclopedists as Individuals: Biographical Dictionary of the Authors of the 'Encyclopédie'* (Oxford: Voltaire Foundation, 1988); Frank A. Kafker, *The Encyclopedists as a Group: A Collective Biography of the Authors of the 'Encyclopédie'* (Oxford: Voltaire Foundation, 1996).

24 Ernst Mayr, *The Growth of Biological Thought* (Cambridge, Mass.: Harvard University Press, 1981), p. 330.

25 Jonathan R. Topham, 'Science, Print, and Crossing Borders: Importing French Science Books into Britain, 1789–1815', in David N. Livingstone and Charles W. J. Withers (eds.), *Geographies of Nineteenth-Century Science* (University of Chicago Press, 2011), pp. 311–44.

26 In an extensive literature of mapping France in the Enlightenment, see J. W. Konvitz, *Cartography in France, 1660–1848: Science, Engineering and Statecraft* (University of Chicago Press, 1997); Godlewska, *Geography Unbound*; Valeria Pansini, 'La Géographie appliquée à la guerre: le travail des topographes militaires (1760–1820)', in Blais and Laboulais, *Géographies plurielles*, pp. 167–84.

27 Alder, *The Measure of All Things*.

28 Godlewska, *Geography Unbound*, pp. 158–9.

29 Michael Heffernan, 'Courtly Geography: Nature, Authority and Civility in Early Eighteenth-Century France', in Stephen Daniels, Dydia DeLyser, J. Nicholas Entrikin and Doug Richardson (eds.), *Envisioning Landscapes, Making Worlds: Geography and the Humanities* (London and New York: Routledge, 2011), pp. 94–105.

30 Konvitz, *Cartography in France*, p. 14.

31 Jerry Brotton, *A History of the World in Twelve Maps* (London: Allen Lane, 2012), p. 315. My paragraphs here on the Cassini maps are based on Brotton's chap. 9, 'Nation: The Cassini Family Map of France, 1793', pp. 294–336.

32 Abbé de la Caille, 'Extrait de la relation du voyage fait en 1724, aux Isles Canaries, par le P. Feuillée Minime, pour déterminer la vraie position du premier meridian', *Histoire de l'Académie Royale des Sciences* (Paris: Imprimerie Royale, 1751), pp. 129–51; Cassini de Thury, *La Meridienne de l'Observatoire Royal de Paris, vérifiée dans toute l'étendue du royaume par de nouvelles observations* (Paris: Guerin and Guerin, 1744). For a modern reflection upon these issues of comparative metrology in the French Enlightenment, see Christian Licoppe, 'The Project for a Map of Languedoc in Eighteenth-Century France at the Contested Intersection between Astronomy and Geography', in Marie-Noëlle Bourguet, Christian Licoppe and H. Otto Sibum (eds.), *Instruments, Travel and Science: Itineraries of Precision from the Seventeenth to the Twentieth Century* (London and New York: Routledge, 2002), pp. 51–74.

33 William Roy and Isaac Dalby, 'An Account of the Trigonometrical Operation, Whereby the Distance between the Meridians of the Royal Observatories of Greenwich and Paris has been Determined. By Major-General William Roy, F. R. S. and A. S.', *Philosophical Transactions of the Royal Society of London*, 80 (1790): 111–614.

34 Brotton, *History of the World*, p. 314.

35 Ibid. p. 322.

36 Ibid. pp. 330–1.

37 Withers, *Placing the Enlightenment*, pp. 148–62; Charles W. J. Withers, 'The Enlightenment and Geographies of Cosmopolitanism', *Scottish Geographical Journal*, 129 (1) (2013): 1–18.

38 Michael Heffernan, 'On Geography and Progress: Turgot's *Plan d'un ouvrage sur la géographie politique* (1751) and the Origins of Modern Progressive Thought', *Political Geography*, 13 (1994): 328–43.

39 Michael Heffernan, 'Historical Geographies of the Future: Three Perspectives from France, 1750–1825', in Livingstone and Withers (eds.), *Geography and the Enlightenment*, pp. 125–64.

40 Pascal-François-Joseph Gosselin, *Géographie des Grecs analysée, ou les systèmes d'Erastothènes, de Strabon, et de Ptolémée comparés entre eux et avec nos connoissances modernes* (Paris: Debure l'aîné, 1790); Anne M. C. Godlewska, *The Napoleonic Survey of Egypt: A Masterpiece of Cartographic Communication and Early Nineteenth-Century Fieldwork*, *Cartographica* 25 (University of Toronto Press, 1988); Godlewska, *Geography Unbound*, pp. 268–73.

41 Warf and Arias, 'Introduction: The Reinsertion of Space', p. 1.

42 Licoppe, 'The Project for a Map'. On the local, social and economic spaces of cartographic production within Enlightenment Paris, see Mary Pedley, *The*

Commerce of Cartography: Making and Marketing Maps in Eighteenth-Century France and England (University of Chicago Press, 2005).

43 Emma Spary, *Utopia's Garden: French Natural History from Old Regime to Revolution* (University of Chicago Press, 2000); Kapil Raj, *Relocating Modern Science: Circulation and the Construction of Knowledge in South Asia and Europe, 1650–1900* (London: Palgrave Macmillan, 2007); Roger L. Williams, *Botanophilia in Eighteenth-Century France: The Spirit of the Enlightenment* (Dordrecht: Kluwer Academic Publishers, 2001); Marie-Noëlle Bourguet, 'Landscape with Numbers: Natural History, Travel and Instruments in the Late Eighteenth and Early Nineteenth Centuries', in Bourguet, Licoppe and Sibum (eds.), *Instruments, Travel and Science*, pp. 96–125.

GUIDE TO FURTHER READING

Research on all the aspects of the French Enlightenment represented in this volume constitutes an impossibly huge field. To remain useful, the 'critical works and general studies' represent the most important research published primarily during the past two decades. Items in the 'resources' section provide entry points to work focused on individual Enlightenment figures, on the larger early modern period and on the broader cross-national Enlightenment. The section 'Further readings in the disciplines' contains readings relating to the subject of each chapter.

Critical works and general studies

Adorno, Theodor and Max Horkheimer, *Dialectic of Enlightenment*, trans. Edmund Jephcott. Palo Alto, Calif.: Stanford University Press, 1947.

Aravamudan, Srinivas, *Tropicopolitans: Colonialism and Agency, 1688–1804*. Durham, NC: Duke University Press, 1999.

Ariès, Philippe and Georges Duby (eds.), *A History of Private Life*, ed. Roger Chartier, vol. III, *Passions of the Renaissance*, trans. Arthur Goldhammer. Cambridge, Mass.: Harvard University Press, 1993.

Arnaud, Sabine, *On Hysteria: The Invention of a Medical Category between 1670 and 1820*. University of Chicago Press, 2015.

Baker, Keith Michael, 'Enlightenment and the Institution of Society: Notes for a Conceptual History', in Willem Melching and Wygar Velema (eds.), *Main Trends in Cultural History: Ten Essays*. Amsterdam: Rodopi, 1994, pp. 95–120.

Becker, Carl, *The Heavenly City of the Eighteenth-Century Philosophers*. New Haven, Conn.: Yale University Press, 1932.

Blum, Carol, *Strength in Numbers: Population, Reproduction, and Power in Eighteenth-Century France*. Baltimore, Md.: Johns Hopkins University Press, 2002.

Bonnet, Jean-Claude, *Naissance du Panthéon: essai sur le culte des grands hommes*. Paris: Fayard, 1998.

Brewer, Daniel, *The Discourse of Enlightenment in Eighteenth-Century France: Diderot and the Art of Philosophizing*. Cambridge University Press, 1993.

The Enlightenment Past: Reconstructing Eighteenth-Century French Thought. Cambridge University Press, 2008.

Brewer, Daniel and Julie Candler Hayes (eds.), *Using the 'Encyclopédie': Ways of Knowing, Ways of Reading*. Oxford: Voltaire Foundation, 2002.

Butterwick, Richard, Simon Davies and Gabriel Sanchez-Espinosa (eds.), *Peripheries of the Enlightenment*, Studies on Voltaire and the Eighteenth Century 2008:01. Oxford: Voltaire Foundation, 2008.

Cassirer, Ernst, *The Philosophy of the Enlightenment*, trans. Fritz C. A. Koelln and James P. Pettegrove. Princeton University Press, 1951.

Chartier, Roger, *Lectures et lecteurs dans la France d'Ancien Régime*. Paris: Seuil, 1987.

The Cultural Origins of the French Revolution, trans. Lydia G. Cochrane. Durham, NC: Duke University Press, 1991.

Cohen, Sarah, *Art, Dance and the Body in French Culture of the Ancien Regime*. Cambridge University Press, 2000.

Darnton, Robert, *The Business of Enlightenment: A Publishing History of the Encyclopédie, 1775–1800*. Cambridge, Mass.: Harvard University Press, 1979.

The Literary Underground of the Old Regime. Cambridge, Mass.: Harvard University Press, 1982.

The Great Cat Massacre and Other Episodes in French Cultural History, rev. edn. New York: Basic Books, 2009.

Dobie, Madeleine, *Trading Places: Colonization and Slavery in Eighteenth-Century French Culture*. Ithaca, NY: Cornell University Press, 2010.

Edelstein, Dan, *The Enlightenment, a Genealogy*. University of Chicago Press, 2010.

(ed.), *The Super-Enlightenment: Daring to Know Too Much*. Oxford: Voltaire Foundation, 2010.

Farge, Arlette, *Dire et mal dire: l'opinion publique au XVIIIe siècle*. Paris: Seuil, 1992.

Festa, Lynn, *Sentimental Figures of Empire in Eighteenth-Century Britain and France*. Baltimore, Md.: Johns Hopkins University Press, 2006.

Foucault, Michel, *The Order of Things*. New York: Pantheon, 1970.

Discipline and Punish: The Birth of the Prison, trans. Alan Sheridan. New York: Vintage, 1979.

'What is Enlightenment?', in Paul Rabinow (ed.), *The Foucault Reader*. New York: Pantheon Books, 1984, pp. 32–50.

The Birth of Biopolitics: Lectures at the Collège de France, 1978–79, ed. Michel Senellart, trans. Graham Burchell. Basingstoke: Palgrave Macmillan, 2008.

Gay, Peter, *The Enlightenment: An Interpretation*, 2 vols., *The Rise of Modern Paganism* and *The Science of Freedom*. New York: W. W. Norton, 1995.

Geison, Gerald L. (ed.), *Professions and the French State, 1700–1900*. Philadelphia, Pa.: University of Pennsylvania Press, 1984.

Goodman, Dena, *The Republic of Letters: A Cultural History of the French Enlightenment*. Ithaca, NY: Cornell University Press, 1994.

Gordon, Daniel, *Citizens without Sovereignty: Equality and Sociability in French Thought, 1670–1789*. Princeton University Press, 1994.

(ed.), *Postmodernism and the Enlightenment*. New York: Routledge, 2001.

Goulemot, Jean M., *Adieu les philosophes: que reste-t-il des lumières?* Paris: Seuil, 2001.

Grell, Chantal, *Le Dix-huitième siècle et l'antiquité en France, 1680–1789*. Oxford: Voltaire Foundation, 1995.

Groult, Martine, *L'Encyclopédie, ou la création des disciplines*. Paris: CNRS, 2001.

Habermas, Jürgen, *The Structural Transformation of the Public Sphere*, trans. Thomas Burger. Cambridge, Mass.: MIT Press, 1989.

Hayes, Julie Candler, *Reading the French Enlightenment: System and Subversion*. Cambridge University Press, 1999.

Translation, Subjectivity, and Culture in France and England, 1600–1800. Palo Alto, Calif.: Stanford University Press, 2009.

Hazard, Paul, *The Crisis of the European Mind, 1680–1715*, trans. J. Lewis May. London: Hollis & Carter, 1953.

Israel, Jonathan, *Radical Enlightenment: Philosophy and the Making of Modernity, 1650–1750*. Oxford University Press, 2001.

Enlightenment Contested: Philosophy, Modernity, and the Emancipation of Man, 1670–1752. Oxford University Press, 2006.

Johnson, James H., *Listening in Paris: A Cultural History*. Berkeley, Calif.: University of California Press, 1995.

Jones, Colin, *Charity and Bienfaisance: The Treatment of the Poor in the Montpellier Region, 1740–1815*. Cambridge University Press, 1982.

Jordanova, Ludmilla, *Sexual Visions: Images of Gender in Science and Medicine between the Eighteenth and Twentieth Centuries*. Madison, Wisc.: University of Wisconsin Press, 1989.

Kavanagh, Thomas M., *Enlightened Pleasures: Eighteenth-Century France and the New Epicureanism*. New Haven, Conn.: Yale University Press, 2010.

Lilti, Antoine, *Le Monde des salons: sociabilité et mondanité à Paris au XVIIIe siècle*. Paris: Fayard, 2005.

Livingstone, David N. and Charles W. J. Withers (eds.), *Geography and the Enlightenment*. University of Chicago Press, 1999.

McMahon, Darrin M., *Enemies of the Enlightenment: The French Counter-Enlightenment and the Making of Modernity*. Oxford University Press, 2001.

McManners, John, *Church and Society in Eighteenth-Century France*, 2 vols. Oxford University Press, 1998.

May, Georges, *Dilemme du roman au XVIIIe siècle: étude sur les rapports du roman et de la critique*. New Haven, Conn.: Yale University Press, 1963.

Maza, Sara, *Private Lives and Public Affairs: The Causes Célèbres of Prerevolutionary France*. Berkeley, Calif.: University of California Press, 1993.

Meeker, Natania, *Voluptuous Philosophy: Literary Materialism in the French Enlightenment*. New York: Fordham University Press, 2006.

Porter, Roy and Mikulas Teich (eds.), *The Enlightenment in National Context*. Cambridge University Press, 1981.

Quinlan, Sean, *The Great Nation in Decline: Sex, Modernity, and Health Crises in Revolutionary France, ca. 1750–1850*. Aldershot: Ashgate, 2007.

Racevskis, Karlis. *Postmodernism and the Search for Enlightenment*. Charlottesville, Va.: University Press of Virginia, 1992.

Ravel, Jeffrey, *The Contested Parterre: Public Theater and French Political Culture, 1680–1791*. Ithaca, NY: Cornell University Press, 1999.

Roche, Daniel, *France in the Enlightenment*, trans. Arthur Goldhammer. Cambridge, Mass.: Harvard University Press, 1998.

Rothkrug, Lionel, *Opposition to Louis XIV: The Political and Social Origins of the French Enlightenment*. Princeton University Press, 1965.

Rousseau, G. S., *The Languages of Psyche: Mind and Body in Enlightenment Thought*. Berkeley, Calif.: University of California Press, 1990.

Russo, Elena, *Styles of Enlightenment: Taste, Politics and Authorship in Eighteenth-Century France*. Baltimore, Md.: Johns Hopkins University Press, 2007.

Shea, Louisa, *The Cynical Enlightenment: Diogenes in the Salon*. Baltimore, Md.: Johns Hopkins University Press, 2010.

Smith, Jay M., *Nobility Reimagined: The Patriotic Nation in Eighteenth-Century France*. Ithaca, NY: Cornell University Press, 2005.

Spary, Emma C., *Utopia's Garden: French Natural History from Old Regime to Revolution*. University of Chicago Press, 2000.

  Eating the Eighteenth Century: Food and Science in Paris, 1670–1760. University of Chicago Press, 2012.

Stalnaker, Joanna, *The Unfinished Enlightenment: Description in the Age of the Encyclopedia*. Ithaca, NY: Cornell University Press, 2010.

Turnovsky, Geoffrey, *The Literary Market: Authorship and Modernity in the Old Regime*. Philadelphia, Pa.: University of Pennsylvania Press, 2010.

Van Damme, Stéphane, *Paris, capitale philosophique, de la Fronde à la Révolution*. Paris: Odile Jacob, 2005.

Vasset, Sophie (ed.), *Medicine and Narration in the Eighteenth Century*, Studies on Voltaire and the Eighteenth Century 2013:04. Oxford: Voltaire Foundation, 2013.

Vovelle, Michel (ed.), *Enlightenment Portraits*, trans. Lydia G. Cochrane. University of Chicago Press, 1997.

Wilson, Lindsay, *Women and Medicine in the French Enlightenment: The Debate over Maladies des Femmes*. Baltimore, Md.: Johns Hopkins University Press, 1993.

Withers, Charles W. J., *Placing the Enlightenment: Thinking Geographically about the Age of Reason*. University of Chicago Press, 2007.

Print and on-line resources

ARTFL (The Project for American and French Research on the Treasury of the French Language) provides access to North America's largest collection of digitized French resources. http://artfl-project.uchicago.edu (accessed 19 May 2014).

Delon, Michel (ed.), *Dictionnaire européen des lumières*. Paris: Presses Universitaires de France, 2007. English translation, *Encyclopedia of the Enlightenment*. London: Fitzroy Dearborn, 2001.

Kors, Alan (ed.), *Encyclopedia of the Enlightenment*, 4 vols. Oxford University Press, 2003.

Kramnick, Isaac (ed.), *The Portable Enlightenment Reader*. Harmondsworth: Penguin, 1995.

Wilson, Ellen Judy and Peter Hanns Reill, *Encyclopedia of the Enlightenment*. New York: Facts on File, 2004.

Further readings in the disciplines

Anthropology

Curran, Andrew, *The Anatomy of Blackness: Science and Slavery in an Age of Enlightenment*. Baltimore, Md.: Johns Hopkins, 2011.

Duchet, Michèle, *Anthropologie et histoire au siècle des lumières: Buffon, Voltaire, Rousseau, Helvetius, Diderot*. Paris: Flammarion, 1978.
Sloan, Philip, 'The Gaze of Natural History', in Christopher Fox, Roy Porter and Robert Wokler (eds.), *Inventing Human Science*. Berkeley, Calif.: University of California Press, 1995, pp. 112–51.
Thomson, Ann, 'Diderot, le matérialisme et la division de l'espèce humaine', *Recherches sur Diderot et l'Encyclopédie*, 26 (1999), 197–211.

Architecture

Braham, Allan, *The Architecture of the French Enlightenment*. Berkeley, Calif.: University of California Press, 1980.
Vidler, Anthony, *The Writing of the Walls: Architectural Theory in the Late Enlightenment*. Princeton Architectural Press, 1987.
Claude-Nicolas Ledoux: Architecture and Social Reform at the End of the Ancien Régime. Cambridge, Mass.: MIT Press, 1989.

Art and aesthetic theory

Bryson, Norman, *Word and Image: French Painting of the Ancien Régime*. Cambridge University Press, 1981.
Crow, Thomas E., *Painters and Public Life in Eighteenth-Century Paris*. New Haven, Conn.: Yale University Press, 1985.
Milam, Jennifer, *Fragonard's Playful Paintings: Visual Games in Rococo Art*. Manchester University Press, 2007.
Historical Dictionary of Rococo Art. Plymouth: Scarecrow Press, 2011.
Scott, Katie, *The Rococo Interior: Decoration and Social Space in Early Eighteenth-Century Paris*. New Haven, Conn.: Yale University Press, 1995.
Vidal, Mary, *Watteau's Painted Conversations: Art, Literature and Talk in Seventeenth- and Eighteenth-Century France*. New Haven, Conn.: Yale University Press, 1992.

Commerce

Cheney, Paul, *Revolutionary Commerce: Globalization and the French Monarchy*. Cambridge, Mass.: Harvard University Press, 2010.
Dobie, Madeleine, *Trading Places: Colonization and Slavery in Eighteenth-Century French Culture*. Ithaca, NY: Cornell University Press, 2010.
Roche, Daniel, *A History of Everyday Things: The Birth of Consumption in France, 1600–1800*, trans. Brian Pearce. Cambridge University Press, 2000.
Vardi, Liana, *The Physiocrats and the World of the Enlightenment*. Cambridge University Press, 2012.

Geography

Godlewska, Anne M. C., *Geography Unbound: French Geographic Science from Cassini to Humboldt*. University of Chicago Press, 1999.
Withers, Charles W. J., *Placing the Enlightenment: Thinking Geographically about the Age of Reason*. University of Chicago Press, 2007.

Literature

Aravamudan, Srinivas, *Enlightenment Orientalism: Resisting the Rise of the Novel*. University of Chicago Press, 2012.

DeJean, Joan, *Tender Geographies: Women and the Origins of the Novel in France.* New York: Columbia University Press, 1991.

Delon, Michel, *Le Savoir-vivre libertin.* Paris: Hachette, 2000.

Douthwaite, Julia V., *Exotic Women: Literary Heroines and Cultural Strategies in Ancien Régime France.* Philadelphia, Pa.: University of Pennsylvania Press, 1992.

Marshall, David, *The Surprising Effects of Sympathy.* University of Chicago Press, 1988.

May, Georges, *Le Dilemme du roman au XVIIIe siècle: étude sur les rapports du roman et de la critique.* New Haven, Conn.: Yale University Press, 1963.

Medicine

Gelfand, Toby, *Professionalizing Modern Medicine: Paris Surgeons and Medical Science and Institutions in the Eighteenth Century.* Westport, Conn.: Greenwood Press, 1980.

Ramsey, Matthew, *Professional and Popular Medicine in France, 1770–1830: The Social World of Medical Practice.* Cambridge University Press, 1988.

Rey, Roselyne, *The History of Pain.* Cambridge, Mass.: Harvard University Press, 1998.

Seth, Catriona, 'Textually Transmitted Diseases: Smallpox Inoculation in French Literary and Medical Works', Studies on Voltaire and the Eighteenth Century 2013:04. Oxford: Voltaire Foundation, 2013, pp. 125–38.

Vila, Anne, *Between Enlightenment and Pathology: Sensibility in the Literature and Medicine of Eighteenth-Century France.* Baltimore, Md.: Johns Hopkins University Press, 1998.

Music

Charlton, David, *Opera in the Age of Rousseau: Music, Confrontation, Realism.* Cambridge University Press, 2013.

Cuillé, Tili Boon, *Narrative Interludes: Musical Tableaux in Eighteenth-Century French Texts.* University of Toronto Press, 2006.

Political theory

Baker, Keith Michael, *Inventing the French Revolution: Essays on French Political Culture in the Eighteenth Century.* Cambridge University Press, 1990.

Bell, David, *The Cult of the Nation in France: Inventing Nationalism, 1680–1800.* Cambridge, Mass.: Harvard University Press, 2001.

Gay, Peter, *Voltaire's Politics: The Poet as Realist.* New Haven, Conn.: Yale University Press, 1988.

Hunt, Lynn, *Inventing Human Rights: A History.* New York: Norton, 2007.

Religion

Burson, Jeffrey D., *The Rise and Fall of Theological Enlightenment: Jean-Martin de Prades and Ideological Polarization in Eighteenth-Century France.* Notre Dame, Ind.: University of Notre Dame Press, 2010.

Palmer, R. R., *Catholics and Unbelievers in Eighteenth-Century France.* Princeton University Press, 1939.

Rosenblatt, Helena, 'The Christian Enlightenment', in Stewart J. Brown and Timothy Tackett (eds.), *The Cambridge History of Christianity*, vol. VII, *Enlightenment, Reawakening, and Revolution, 1660–1815*. Cambridge University Press, 2006, pp. 283–301.

Van Kley, Dale, *The Religious Origins of the French Revolution: From Calvin to the Civil Constitution of the Clergy, 1560–1791*. New Haven, Conn.: Yale University Press, 1996.

Science

Daston, Lorraine J. and Peter Galison, *Objectivity*. Brooklyn: Zone Books, 2010.

Riskin, Jessica, *Science in the Age of Sensibility: The Sentimental Empiricists of the French Enlightenment*. University of Chicago Press, 2002.

Shank, J. B., *The Newton Wars and the Beginning of the French Enlightenment*. University of Chicago Press, 2008.

Shapin, Steven, *The Scientific Revolution*. University of Chicago Press, 1996.

Sex and gender

Goodman, Dena, *Becoming a Woman in the Age of Letters*. Ithaca, NY: Cornell University Press, 2009.

Harth, Erica, *Cartesian Women: Versions and Subversions of Rational Discourse in the Old Regime (Reading Women Writing)*. Ithaca, NY: Cornell University Press, 1992.

Schiebinger, Londa, *The Mind Has No Sex? Women in the Origins of Modern Science*. Cambridge, Mass.: Harvard University Press, 1991.

Timmermans, Linda, *L'Accès des femmes à la culture sous l'ancien régime (1995)*. Paris: Champion, 2005.

INDEX

Académie d'Architecture, 187
Académie Française, 126, 139
Académie Royale de Peinture et de Sculpture, 47, 123, 128
Académie Royale des Beaux-Arts, 6
Académie Royale des Sciences, 6, 66
Adorno, Theodor, 10, 62
Agulhon, Maurice, 17
Alletz, Pons-Augustin, 94
Ampère, André-Marie, 74
anthologies of women writers, 95
anthropology, 29
architecture, 184
Argens, Jean-Baptiste de Boyer, marquis d'
    Thérèse philosophe, 115
Ariès, Philippe, 15, 17, 21
art and aesthetic theory, 122
Augustine, 109

Baker, Keith Michael, 45, 112
Barbié du Bocage, Jean-Denis, 227
Barruel, Augustin, 20
Barthez, Paul-Joseph, 202, 204
Batteux, Charles, 186, 189
Baudin, Nicolas-Thomas, 216
Baudoin, Pierre-Antoine, 135
Bayle, Pierre, 158, 161, 162
Bazcko, Bronislaw, 185
Beasley, Faith, 95
Beaumarchais, Pierre-Augustin
    Caron de, 144
Beaurepaire, Pierre-Yves, 20
Bell, David, 112
Bentham, Jeremy, 185
Bergier, Nicholas-Sylvestre, 116
Bernier, François, 38, 39
Bertholon, Pierre, 200
Blondel, Jean-François, 187

Blumenbach, Johann Friedrich, 38
Boerhaave, Herman, 202
books and reading practices, 16
Bordeu, Théophile de, 201, 204, 205
Bossuet, Jacques Bénigne, 107, 108, 112, 114
Boucher, François, 17, 47, 124
Bougainville, Louis Antoine de, 216
Boulainvilliers, Henri de, 80
Boullée, Étienne-Louis, 184, 186, 194
Bourdon, Sébastien, 126
Braham, Alan, 184, 187
Brewer, Daniel, 155, 217
Briquet, Marguerite Ursule Fortunée
    Bernie, 95
Brunot, Ferdinand, 154
Buffon, Georges-Louis Leclerc, comte de, 37, 40, 69, 220
Burke, Edmund, 194

cafés, 49–50
Cagliostro, Alessandro (Giuseppe Balsamo), 26
Carmontelle, Louis Carrogis, 122, 131
Cassini family, 220, 225
Cassirer, Ernst, 9, 62, 184
Catherine the Great, 7, 163
Chardin, Jean-Baptiste Siméon, 48, 130
Charrière, Isabelle de, 207, 208
Chartier, Roger, 8, 161
Clairaut, Alexis Claude, 66
Cochin, Charles-Nicolas, 185
Cochin, François, 192
commerce, 44
Comte, Auguste, 62
Condillac, Étienne Bonnot de, 36, 189, 194, 204
Condorcet, Marie Jean Antoine Nicolas de Caritat, marquis de, 26, 72, 218
Coulomb, Charles-Augustin de, 74

Coypel, Antoine, 125
Crébillon, Claude Prosper Jolyot de, 141, 148
Crozat, Pierre, 124

d'Alembert, Jean-Baptiste le Rond, 5, 19, 70, 110, 115, 130, 188
  "Discours préliminaire de l'Encyclopédie", 60
Dacier, Anne, 95, 101
Darnton, Robert, 7, 50, 63, 145
Daston, Lorraine, 76, 94
David, Jacques-Louis, 134, 185
de la Tour, Maurice Quentin, 78
de Meulan, Pauline, 102
de Pauw, Cornelius, 39
de Toqueville, Alexis, 21
DeJean, Joan, 95
Delon, Michel, 10
Déparcieux, Antoine, 191
Descartes, René, 71, 118, 157, 164
  Discours de la méthode, 3, 109
  Méditations, 109
désenclavement, 11
Desfontaines (François-Georges), 155
Destouches, Philippe Néricault, 156
Dictionnaire de Trévoux, 29
Diderot, Denis, 7, 85, 115, 118, 129, 150, 154, 163, 194, 196, 199, 206
  "*Beau*", 130
  Éléments de physiologie, 201
  Encyclopédie, 6, 154
  La Religieuse, 150
  Le Rêve de d'Alembert, 116, 118, 201
  Les Bijoux indiscrets, 32
  Salon art criticism, 131
  Supplément au voyage de Bougainville, 83
du Bos, Jean-Baptiste, 80, 125, 130, 143
du Châtelet, Émilie Gabrielle Le Tonnelier du Breteuil, marquise, 100
Dumarsais, César Chesneau, 7, 70
Dupont de Nemours, Pierre-Samuel, 112

Edict of Nantes, revocation, 107
Ehrard, Jean, 64
Eisen, Charles, 189
Encyclopédie, 69, 161, 217, 219
  "*Autorité politique*", 83
  "*Beau*", 130
  "*Délicieux*", 115
  "*Économie*", 53
  "*Goût*", 130
  "*Lettres*", 139
  "*Parterre*", 143
  "*Philosophe*", 7, 70
  ordering of knowledge, 5
  relation to *Encyclopédie méthodique*, 75
  religion, 107
  science, 60
Encyclopédie méthodique, 117
Enlightenment
  contemporary interpretations, 1
  critique of, 2–3
  definition, 1–2
  English political theory, 79
  German Romanticism, 10
  intimacy, 8, 25–6
  philosophes' relation to power, 153
  religious culture, 106–13
  social history, 14
  theory of race, 39–40

family, representation of, 16
Félibien, André, 126
Fénelon, François de, 114, 191
  Les Aventures de Télémaque, 83
Filangieri, Gaetano, 153
Fortier, Bruno, 185
Foucault, Michel, 2, 8, 37, 65, 154, 185, 199
Fouquet, Henri, 205
Fragonard, Jean-Honoré, 17, 47, 124, 135
Franklin, Benjamin, 71, 74
Frederick the Great, 7
Freemasonry, 19
French colonies, 41, 46
French Revolution, 8
Fréron, Élie-Catherine, 155
Furet, François, 20

Galaup, Jean-François de, 216
Galison, Peter, 76
Gay, Peter, 64, 200
Genlis, Stéphanie-Félicité du Crest de Saint Aubin, comtesse de, 93, 95, 102
genre painting, 17
Geoffrin, Marie-Thérèse Rodet, 6
geography, 214
Godzich, Wlad, 146
Gosselin, Pascal-François-Joseph, 227
Grégoire, Henri, 41
Greuze, Jean-Baptiste, 17, 48, 130, 132
Grimm, Friedrich Melchior, baron von, 163
  Correspondance littéraire, 7, 130
Gumbrecht, Hans Ulrich, 143
Guyon, Jeanne-Marie, 114

Habermas, Jürgen, 21, 23, 44, 65
  public sphere, 7, 22, 160
Haller, Albrecht von, 204
Hampson, Norman, 218
Hazard, Paul, 64
Hegel, Georg Wilhelm Friedrich, 61
Helvétius, Claude-Adrien
  De l'homme, 81
Hobbes, Thomas, 111
Holbach, Paul-Henri, baron d', 6
Horace, 2
Horkheimer, Max, 10, 62
Hunt, Lynn, 82

intimacy, 25–6

Janković, Vladimir, 203
Jansen, Cornelius, 106
Jansenist theology, 109
Jaucourt, Louis de, 205
Jomard, Edme-François, 227
Journal de physique, 75
Journal des Sçavans, 38

Kant, Immanuel, 2, 21, 26, 61, 194
Kaufmann, Emil, 184
Keralio, Louise-Félicité Guinement de
  Keralio, 95
Kittay, Jeffrey, 146
Koselleck, Reinhardt, 20

La Bruyère, Jean de, 96
La Font de Saint-Yenne, Étienne, 128
La Hire, Philippe de, 220
La Mettrie, Julien Offray de, 204
Lapérouse, Jean-François de, 216
La Porte, Joseph de, 91
La Rochefoucauld, François-Armand-
  Frédéric de, 96
Labat, Jean-Baptiste, 35
Laclos, Pierre Choderlos de
  Les Liaisons Dangerous, 23
Lafitau, Jean-François, 34
Lambert, Anne-Thérèse de Marguenat de
  Courcelles, marquise de, 93, 97–9
Laugier, Marc-Antoine, 186, 189
Lavoisier, Antoine-Laurent de, 66, 220
Le Blanc, Jean-Bernard, 129
Le Brun, Charles, 126
Le Camus, Antoine, 206
Ledoux, Claude-Nicolas, 186, 196
Leibniz, Gottfried Wilhelm von, 31, 149, 195
Lenglet Du Fresnoy, Nicholas, 147

Leroy, Julien-David, 186
Lesage, Alain-René, 148
Lespinasse, Jeanne Julie Éléonore de, 19, 70
Lilti, Antoine, 50
Linnaeus, Carl von, 38
literature, 137
Locke, John, 31, 36, 82, 204
Loménie de Brienne, Étienne-Charles
  de, 156
Louis XV, 26, 221
Loyseau, Charles, 108
Lucretius, 194

Mably, Gabriel Bonnot de, 54, 81
McAlpin, Mary, 150
Machiavelli, Niccolò
  Discourses on Livy, 85
Maleville, Guillaume, 112
Mandeville, Bernard, 53
Marat, Jean-Paul, 26
Marie Antoinette, 49
Marigny, Abel-François Poisson de
  Vandières, marquis de, 133
Marivaux, Pierre Carlet de Chamblain
  de, 142
Marmontel, Jean-François, 144, 147, 155
Maupeou, René Nicolas Charles Augustin
  de, 86
Maupertuis, Pierre-Louis Moreau de, 7, 72, 73
  Vénus physique, 36
Maza, Sarah, 25
medicine, 199
Meeker, Natania, 151
Mentelle, Edme, 227
Ménuret de Chambaud, Jean-Joseph, 205
Mercier, Louis-Sébastien, 71, 191
Merleau-Ponty, Maurice, 64
Meslier, Jean, 86
Mesmer, Franz Anton, 63, 203
Mirabeau, Victor de Riqueti, marquis de, 26, 35
  The Friend of Men, 83
Molière, 156, 203
Montagu, Lady Mary Wortley, 210
Montaigne, Michel de, 96
Montesquieu, Charles Louis de Secondat, 31, 56–8, 82, 111, 113, 218
  De l'esprit des lois, 31, 35, 80, 85, 86, 110, 162, 195
  Lettres persanes, 23, 115, 148
moralist literature, 16
Morelly, Étienne-Gabriel, 191

Mornet, Daniel, 64
music, 167

natural rights theory, 81–4
Necker, Jacques, 218
Newton, Isaac, 68, 161, 164, 220
Nicole, Pierre, 109, 118
Nollet, Jean-Antoine, 74, 210
novel, 8, 145

Ozouf, Mona, 185

Pascal, Blaise, 109
Patte, Pierre, 190
Philosophes, 153
Physiocrats, 35, 54–6, 69, 83, 112
Picard, Jean-Félix, 220
Piles, Roger de, 125, 127, 130
Plato, 194
Pluche, Noël-Antoine, 162
Pomme, Pierre, 203
Pompadour, Jeanne Antoinette Poisson,
    marquise de, 78
Pope, Alexander
    Essay on Man, 30
Poullain de la Barre, François, 94
Poussin, Nicolas, 126
Prévost, Antoine-François, 34, 150
Pringy, Jeanne-Michelle, 96
public sphere, 7, 23, 160

Quarrel of the Ancients and the
    Moderns, 126
Quatremère de Quincy, Antoine-
    Chrysostome, 185
Quesnay, François, 83, 112
quietism, 113

Raynal, Guillaume Thomas François
    Histoire des deux Indes, 7, 32,
        44, 87
Reddy, William, 96
régime d'historicité, 9
religion, 105
Republic of Letters, 7, 18, 22, 75, 203
republicanism, 85
Rétif de la Bretonne, Nicolas Edme, 196
Riskin, Jessica, 63
Robertson, John, 216
Robespierre, Maximilien, 8, 74
Roche, Daniel, 11, 18, 65
rococo art and architecture, 124
Roger, Jacques, 64

Rousseau, Jean-Jacques, 18, 31, 45, 53, 81,
    82, 83, 164, 189, 195, 206, 218
    "*Économie*", 53
    Confessions, 25
    Discourse on Inequality, 82
    Du contrat social, 83, 87
    Julie, ou la nouvelle Héloïse, 150
    political theory, 84
Roussel, Pierre, 92, 206
Royal Academy of Painting and,
    see Académie Royale de Peinture et de
    Sculpture
Royal Academy of Sciences (Prussia), 7

Sade, Donatien Alphonse François, marquis de,
    149, 155
Saige, Guillaume-Joseph, 81
Saint-Amand, Pierre, 161
salon exhibitions, 123
salons, 18–19, 50
Savary, Jacques, 35, 49
Schurman, Anna Maria van, 95
secularism (*laïcité*), 5
sensationalism (*sensibilité*), 73, 123
sex and gender, 91
Shank, J. B., 106, 161
Shelley, Mary, 74
Snow, C. P., 4
sociability, 17–19
Soll, Jacob, 158
Soufflot, Jacques-Germain, 185
Spary, E. C., 209
spatial turn, 11
Spinoza, Baruch, 111
Staël-Holstein, Anne Louise Germaine de,
    93, 102, 137, 151
Stock, Brian, 161
Stolberg, Michael, 209

theatre, 140
Thiroux d'Arconville, Marie-Geneviève-
    Charlotte, 99–101
Thompson, Helen, 151
Timmermans, Linda, 94
Tissot, Samuel-Auguste, 201, 208
Tocqueville, Alexis de, 19
travel writing, 31–4
Tronchin, Théodore, 209
Turgot, Anne-Robert-Jacques, 88, 112,
    218, 226

Valmont de Bomare, Jacques-Christophe, 40
Vandermonde, Charles Augustin, 206

Vernet, Claude-Joseph, 130
Verzure, Mme de, 102
Virgil
  Aeneid, 92
Volney, Constantin-François de Chasseboeuf,
  comte de, 226
Volpihac-Auger, Catherine, 162
Voltaire, 7, 19, 34, 71, 72, 73, 82, 105, 110,
  113, 117, 130, 163, 209, 224
  Candide, 4
  Essai sur les moeurs, 158
  Le mondain, 21, 56
  Le Siècle de Louis XIV, 115

L'Ingenu, 31
Mahomet, 141
OEdipe, 141
Poème sur la loi naturelle, 82
Zadig, 149
Zaïre, 141

Wars of Religion, 107
Watelet, Claude-Henri, 19
Watteau, Jean-Antoine, 47,
  123
Weber, Max, 4
Williams, Elizabeth A., 206

Cambridge Companions to ...

AUTHORS

Edward Albee edited by Stephen J. Bottoms

Margaret Atwood edited by Coral Ann Howells

W. H. Auden edited by Stan Smith

Jane Austen edited by Edward Copeland and Juliet McMaster (second edition)

Beckett edited by John Pilling

Bede edited by Scott DeGregorio

Aphra Behn edited by Derek Hughes and Janet Todd

Walter Benjamin edited by David S. Ferris

William Blake edited by Morris Eaves

Jorge Luis Borges edited by Edwin Williamson

Brecht edited by Peter Thomson and Glendyr Sacks (second edition)

The Brontës edited by Heather Glen

Bunyan edited by Anne Dunan-Page

Frances Burney edited by Peter Sabor

Byron edited by Drummond Bone

Albert Camus edited by Edward J. Hughes

Willa Cather edited by Marilee Lindemann

Cervantes edited by Anthony J. Cascardi

Chaucer edited by Piero Boitani and Jill Mann (second edition)

Chekhov edited by Vera Gottlieb and Paul Allain

Kate Chopin edited by Janet Beer

Caryl Churchill edited by Elaine Aston and Elin Diamond

Cicero edited by Catherine Steel

Coleridge edited by Lucy Newlyn

Wilkie Collins edited by Jenny Bourne Taylor

Joseph Conrad edited by J. H. Stape

H. D. edited by Nephie J. Christodoulides and Polina Mackay

Dante edited by Rachel Jacoff (second edition)

Daniel Defoe edited by John Richetti

Don DeLillo edited by John N. Duvall

Charles Dickens edited by John O. Jordan

Emily Dickinson edited by Wendy Martin

John Donne edited by Achsah Guibbory

Dostoevskii edited by W. J. Leatherbarrow

Theodore Dreiser edited by Leonard Cassuto and Claire Virginia Eby

John Dryden edited by Steven N. Zwicker

W. E. B. Du Bois edited by Shamoon Zamir

George Eliot edited by George Levine

T. S. Eliot edited by A. David Moody

Ralph Ellison edited by Ross Posnock

Ralph Waldo Emerson edited by Joel Porte and Saundra Morris

William Faulkner edited by Philip M. Weinstein

Henry Fielding edited by Claude Rawson

F. Scott Fitzgerald edited by Ruth Prigozy

Flaubert edited by Timothy Unwin

E. M. Forster edited by David Bradshaw

Benjamin Franklin edited by Carla Mulford

Brian Friel edited by Anthony Roche

Robert Frost edited by Robert Faggen

Gabriel García Márquez edited by Philip Swanson

Elizabeth Gaskell edited by Jill L. Matus

Goethe edited by Lesley Sharpe

Günter Grass edited by Stuart Taberner

Thomas Hardy edited by Dale Kramer

David Hare edited by Richard Boon

Nathaniel Hawthorne edited by Richard Millington

Seamus Heaney edited by Bernard O'Donoghue

Ernest Hemingway edited by Scott Donaldson

Homer edited by Robert Fowler

Horace edited by Stephen Harrison

Ted Hughes edited by Terry Gifford

Ibsen edited by James McFarlane

Henry James edited by Jonathan Freedman

Samuel Johnson edited by Greg Clingham

Ben Jonson edited by Richard Harp and Stanley Stewart

James Joyce edited by Derek Attridge (second edition)

Kafka edited by Julian Preece

Keats edited by Susan J. Wolfson

Rudyard Kipling edited by Howard J. Booth

Lacan edited by Jean-Michel Rabaté

D. H. Lawrence edited by Anne Fernihough

Primo Levi edited by Robert Gordon

Lucretius edited by Stuart Gillespie and Philip Hardie

Machiavelli edited by John M. Najemy

David Mamet edited by Christopher Bigsby

Thomas Mann edited by Ritchie Robertson

Christopher Marlowe edited by Patrick Cheney

Andrew Marvell edited by Derek Hirst and Steven N. Zwicker

Herman Melville edited by Robert S. Levine

Arthur Miller edited by Christopher Bigsby (second edition)

Milton edited by Dennis Danielson (second edition)

Molière edited by David Bradby and Andrew Calder

Toni Morrison edited by Justine Tally

Nabokov edited by Julian W. Connolly

Eugene O'Neill edited by Michael Manheim

George Orwell edited by John Rodden

Ovid edited by Philip Hardie

Harold Pinter edited by Peter Raby (second edition)

Sylvia Plath edited by Jo Gill

Edgar Allan Poe edited by Kevin J. Hayes

Alexander Pope edited by Pat Rogers

Ezra Pound edited by Ira B. Nadel

Proust edited by Richard Bales

Pushkin edited by Andrew Kahn

Rabelais edited by John O'Brien

Rilke edited by Karen Leeder and Robert Vilain

Philip Roth edited by Timothy Parrish

Salman Rushdie edited by Abdulrazak Gurnah

Shakespeare edited by Margareta de Grazia and Stanley Wells (second edition)

Shakespearean Comedy edited by Alexander Leggatt

Shakespeare and Contemporary Dramatists edited by Ton Hoenselaars

Shakespeare and Popular Culture edited by Robert Shaughnessy

Shakespearean Tragedy edited by Claire McEachern (second edition)

Shakespeare on Film edited by Russell Jackson (second edition)

Shakespeare on Stage edited by Stanley Wells and Sarah Stanton

Shakespeare's History Plays edited by Michael Hattaway

Shakespeare's Last Plays edited by Catherine M. S. Alexander

Shakespeare's Poetry edited by Patrick Cheney

George Bernard Shaw edited by Christopher Innes

Shelley edited by Timothy Morton

Mary Shelley edited by Esther Schor

Sam Shepard edited by Matthew C. Roudané

Spenser edited by Andrew Hadfield

Laurence Sterne edited by Thomas Keymer

Wallace Stevens edited by John N. Serio

Tom Stoppard edited by Katherine E. Kelly

Harriet Beecher Stowe edited by Cindy Weinstein

August Strindberg edited by Michael Robinson

Jonathan Swift edited by Christopher Fox

J. M. Synge edited by P. J. Mathews

Tacitus edited by A. J. Woodman

Henry David Thoreau edited by Joel Myerson

Tolstoy edited by Donna Tussing Orwin

Anthony Trollope edited by Carolyn Dever and Lisa Niles

Mark Twain edited by Forrest G. Robinson

John Updike edited by Stacey Olster

Mario Vargas Llosa edited by Efrain Kristal and John King

Virgil edited by Charles Martindale

Voltaire edited by Nicholas Cronk

Edith Wharton edited by Millicent Bell

Walt Whitman edited by Ezra Greenspan

Oscar Wilde edited by Peter Raby

Tennessee Williams edited by Matthew C. Roudané

August Wilson edited by Christopher Bigsby

Mary Wollstonecraft edited by Claudia L. Johnson

Virginia Woolf edited by Susan Sellers (second edition)

Wordsworth edited by Stephen Gill

W. B. Yeats edited by Marjorie Howes and John Kelly

Zola edited by Brian Nelson

TOPICS

The Actress edited by Maggie B. Gale and John Stokes

The African American Novel edited by Maryemma Graham

The African American Slave Narrative edited by Audrey A. Fisch

African American Theatre edited by Harvey Young

Allegory edited by Rita Copeland and Peter Struck

American Crime Fiction edited by Catherine Ross Nickerson

American Modernism edited by Walter Kalaidjian

American Poetry Since 1945 edited by Jennifer Ashton

American Realism and Naturalism edited by Donald Pizer

American Travel Writing edited by Alfred Bendixen and Judith Hamera

American Women Playwrights edited by Brenda Murphy

Ancient Rhetoric edited by Erik Gunderson

Arthurian Legend edited by Elizabeth Archibald and Ad Putter

Australian Literature edited by Elizabeth Webby

British Literature of the French Revolution edited by Pamela Clemit

British Romanticism edited by Stuart Curran (second edition)

British Romantic Poetry edited by James Chandler and Maureen N. McLane

British Theatre, 1730–1830 edited by Jane Moody and Daniel O'Quinn

Canadian Literature edited by Eva-Marie Kröller

Children's Literature edited by M. O. Grenby and Andrea Immel

The Classic Russian Novel edited by Malcolm V. Jones and Robin Feuer Miller

Contemporary Irish Poetry edited by Matthew Campbell

Creative Writing edited by David Morley and Philip Neilsen

Crime Fiction edited by Martin Priestman

Early Modern Women's Writing edited by Laura Lunger Knoppers

The Eighteenth-Century Novel edited by John Richetti

Eighteenth-Century Poetry edited by John Sitter

English Literature, 1500–1600 edited by Arthur F. Kinney

English Literature, 1650–1740 edited by Steven N. Zwicker

English Literature, 1740–1830 edited by Thomas Keymer and Jon Mee

English Literature, 1830–1914 edited by Joanne Shattock

English Novelists edited by Adrian Poole

English Poetry, Donne to Marvell edited by Thomas N. Corns

English Poets edited by Claude Rawson

English Renaissance Drama edited by A. R. Braunmuller and Michael Hattaway (second edition)

English Renaissance Tragedy edited by Emma Smith and Garrett A. Sullivan Jr.

English Restoration Theatre edited by Deborah C. Payne Fisk

The Epic edited by Catherine Bates

European Modernism edited by Pericles Lewis

European Novelists edited by Michael Bell

Fantasy Literature edited by Edward James and Farah Mendlesohn

Feminist Literary Theory edited by Ellen Rooney

Fiction in the Romantic Period edited by Richard Maxwell and Katie Trumpener

The Fin de Siècle edited by Gail Marshall

The French Enlightenment edited by Daniel Brewer

The French Novel: from 1800 to the present edited by Timothy Unwin

Gay and Lesbian Writing edited by Hugh Stevens

German Romanticism edited by Nicholas Saul

Gothic Fiction edited by Jerrold E. Hogle

The Greek and Roman Novel edited by Tim Whitmarsh

Greek and Roman Theatre edited by Marianne McDonald and J. Michael Walton

Greek Comedy edited by Martin Revermann

Greek Lyric edited by Felix Budelmann

Greek Mythology edited by Roger D. Woodard

Greek Tragedy edited by P. E. Easterling

The Harlem Renaissance edited by George Hutchinson

The Irish Novel edited by John Wilson Foster

The Italian Novel edited by Peter Bondanella and Andrea Ciccarelli

The Italian Renaissance edited by Michael Wyatt

Jewish American Literature edited by Hana Wirth-Nesher and Michael P. Kramer

The Latin American Novel edited by Efraín Kristal

The Literature of the First World War edited by Vincent Sherry

The Literature of London edited by Lawrence Manley

The Literature of Los Angeles edited by Kevin R. McNamara

The Literature of New York edited by Cyrus Patell and Bryan Waterman

The Literature of Paris edited by Anna-Louise Milne

The Literature of World War II edited by Marina MacKay

Literature on Screen edited by Deborah Cartmell and Imelda Whelehan

Medieval English Culture edited by Andrew Galloway

Medieval English Literature edited by Larry Scanlon

Medieval English Mysticism edited by Samuel Fanous and Vincent Gillespie

Medieval English Theatre edited by Richard Beadle and Alan J. Fletcher (second edition)

Medieval French Literature edited by Simon Gaunt and Sarah Kay

Medieval Romance edited by Roberta L. Krueger

Medieval Women's Writing edited by Carolyn Dinshaw and David Wallace

Modern American Culture edited by Christopher Bigsby

Modern British Women Playwrights edited by Elaine Aston and Janelle Reinelt

Modern French Culture edited by Nicholas Hewitt

Modern German Culture edited by Eva Kolinsky and Wilfried van der Will

The Modern German Novel edited by Graham Bartram

Modern Irish Culture edited by Joe Cleary and Claire Connolly

Modern Italian Culture edited by Zygmunt G. Baranski and Rebecca J. West

Modern Latin American Culture edited by John King

Modern Russian Culture edited by Nicholas Rzhevsky

Modern Spanish Culture edited by David T. Gies

Modernism edited by Michael Levenson (second edition)

The Modernist Novel edited by Morag Shiach

Modernist Poetry edited by Alex Davis and Lee M. Jenkins

Modernist Women Writers edited by Maren Tova Linett

Narrative edited by David Herman

Native American Literature edited by Joy Porter and Kenneth M. Roemer

Nineteenth-Century American Women's Writing edited by Dale M. Bauer and Philip Gould

Old English Literature edited by Malcolm Godden and Michael Lapidge (second edition)

Performance Studies edited by Tracy C. Davis

Piers Plowman by Andrew Cole and Andrew Galloway

Popular Fiction edited by David Glover and Scott McCracken

Postcolonial Literary Studies edited by Neil Lazarus

Postmodernism edited by Steven Connor

The Pre-Raphaelites edited by Elizabeth Prettejohn

Pride and Prejudice edited by Janet Todd

Renaissance Humanism edited by Jill Kraye

The Roman Historians edited by Andrew Feldherr

Roman Satire edited by Kirk Freudenburg

Science Fiction edited by Edward James and Farah Mendlesohn

Scottish Literature edited by Gerald Carruthers and Liam McIlvanney

Sensation Fiction edited by Andrew Mangham

The Sonnet edited by A. D. Cousins and Peter Howarth

The Spanish Novel: from 1600 to the Present edited by Harriet Turner and Adelaida López de Martínez

Textual Scholarship edited by Neil Fraistat and Julia Flanders

Theatre History edited by David Wiles and Christine Dymkowski

Travel Writing edited by Peter Hulme and Tim Youngs

Twentieth-Century British and Irish Women's Poetry edited by Jane Dowson

The Twentieth-Century English Novel edited by Robert L. Caserio

Twentieth-Century English Poetry edited by Neil Corcoran

Twentieth-Century Irish Drama edited by Shaun Richards

Twentieth-Century Russian Literature edited by Marina Balina and Evgeny Dobrenko

Utopian Literature edited by Gregory Claeys

Victorian and Edwardian Theatre edited by Kerry Powell

The Victorian Novel edited by Deirdre David (second edition)

Victorian Poetry edited by Joseph Bristow

War Writing edited by Kate McLoughlin

Writing of the English Revolution edited by N. H. Keeble